Bentham and the Arts

Edited by Anthony Julius, Malcolm Quinn and
Philip Schofield

UCLPRESS

First published in 2020 by
UCL Press
University College London
Gower Street
London WC1E 6BT

Available to download free: www.ucl.ac.uk/ucl-press

A CIP catalogue record for this book is available from The British Library.

ISBN: 978-1-78735-738-9 (Hbk.)
ISBN: 978-1-78735-737-2 (Pbk.)
ISBN: 978-1-78735-736-5 (PDF)
ISBN: 978-1-78735-739-6 (epub)
ISBN: 978-1-78735-740-2 (mobi)
DOI: https://doi.org/10.14324/111.9781787357365

Bentham and the Arts

Contents

Part III. Aesthetics, taste and art

List of contributors

Benjamin Bourcier is associate professor of moral and political philosophy at the European School of Political and Social Sciences (ESPOL) at the Catholic University of Lille. He holds a PhD on Jeremy Bentham's cosmopolitan thought. His main interests are in history of international political thought and cosmopolitanism.

Fran Cottell is an artist and senior lecturer in fine art at Camberwell College of Arts, University of the Arts London. She has been producing performance and installations since the 1970s and for the last 18 years she has been staging live installations displaying the contents, visitors and occupants of her house. Her work questions how to present life, or rather the breath of aliveness, within the fixed frame of the art institution.

Emmanuelle de Champs is professor of British history and civilization at Université Cergy-Pontoise and dean of the Faculty of Languages and International Studies. She was a COFUND research fellow at the Max-Weber-Kolleg, Universität Erfurt in 2017–18 and holds an honorary research fellowship at the Bentham Project, University College London. She has published several books and articles on the intellectual history of Benthamite utilitarianism, including *Enlightenment and Utility: Bentham in French, Bentham in France* ('*Ideas in Context*' series, Cambridge University Press, 2015). She has co-edited, with Jean-Pierre Cléro, *Bentham et la France: fortunes et infortunes de l'utilitarisme* (SVEC, 2009). Her recent work focuses on the late-Enlightenment context in which English utilitarianism emerged.

Frances Ferguson is the author of *Pornography, the Theory: What Utilitarianism did to Action* and other writing on eighteenth- and nineteenth-century topics. She teaches at the University of Chicago.

Anthony Julius is professor of law and the arts, University College London, and deputy chairman of law firm Mishcon de Reya. His book on arts censorship in liberal democracy will be published by Oxford University Press in 2021.

Tim Milnes is senior lecturer in English literature at the University of Edinburgh. Before moving to Edinburgh he was junior research fellow at University College, Oxford. He is the author of *The Testimony of Sense: Empiricism and the Essay from Hume to Hazlitt* (Oxford University Press, 2019), *The Truth about Romanticism: Pragmatism and Idealism in Keats, Shelley, Coleridge* (Cambridge University Press, 2010), *Knowledge and Indifference in English Romantic Prose* (Cambridge University Press, 2003) and *William Wordsworth: The Prelude* (Palgrave, 2009). He is also the co-editor (with Kerry Sinanan) of *Romanticism, Sincerity and Authenticity* (Palgrave, 2010).

Marianne Mueller is a practising architect and professor of architectural design and building typology at the State Academy of Art and Design in Stuttgart. She studied and taught at the Architectural Association in London. Her practice Casper Mueller Kneer Architects is based in London and Berlin.

Malcolm Quinn is professor of cultural and political history, associate dean of research for Camberwell, Chelsea and Wimbledon Colleges of Arts, University of the Arts London and honorary senior research associate, Bentham Project, Faculty of Laws, University College London. He is the author of *Utilitarianism and the Art School in Nineteenth-century Britain* (Pickering and Chatto, 2013) and is general editor of *The Persistence of Taste: Art, Museums and Everyday Life after Bourdieu* (Routledge, 2018). He has published articles on utilitarianism, taste and art in *History of European Ideas* and *Revue d'études benthamiennes.*

Stella Sandford is professor in the Centre for Research in Modern European Philosophy at Kingston University, London. Her main research interests include sex and gender in the history of philosophy, the philosophy of natural history and philosophy and psychoanalytical theory.

Philip Schofield is director of the Bentham Project, Faculty of Laws, University College London and general editor of the new authoritative edition of *The Collected Works of Jeremy Bentham*.

Jan-Melissa Schramm worked as a lawyer before undertaking doctoral work on the changing idea of evidence in the long nineteenth century. She is now reader in literature and law and deputy director of the Centre for Research in the Arts, Social Sciences and Humanities (CRASSH), at the University of Cambridge. She is the author of *Testimony and Advocacy in Victorian Law, Literature and Theology* (Cambridge University Press, 2000), *Atonement and Self-sacrifice in Nineteenth-century Narrative* (Cambridge University Press, 2012), and *Censorship and the Representation of the Sacred in Nineteenth-century England* (Oxford University Press, 2019). She has also co-edited two volumes of essays: *Fictions of Knowledge: Fact, Evidence, Doubt* (Macmillan, 2011), and *Sacrifice and the Modern Literature of War* (Oxford University Press, 2018).

Carolyn Shapiro is senior lecturer at Falmouth University, Cornwall, where she has been teaching critical theory across disciplines since 2002. She was previously a lecturer in the English department at Baruch College, City University of New York. She holds a PhD in Performance Studies from New York University.

List of figures

Acknowledgements

The editors gratefully acknowledge the financial support received from the Faculty of Laws, University College London and the International Society for Utilitarian Studies in hosting the lecture series on Bentham and the Arts at UCL in the first half of 2018 and to the University of the Arts London in preparing the present volume for the press. We are grateful to Dr Tim Causer and Dr Louise Seaward at the Bentham Project, UCL, for help in organizing the lectures, to those who attended and joined in the discussions and again to Dr Causer for making the lectures available online. Especial thanks are extended to Dr Chris Riley, Bentham Project, for formatting the contents of the whole volume before it was submitted to the Press, for identifying and acquiring the images, for tracking down various citations and for dealing with a whole host of queries. It is hard to imagine how this volume would have ever got to the Press but for Chris.

We are grateful to the anonymous referees who reviewed the volume for UCL Press and gave feedback that was both positive and helpful. We were particularly struck by a comment of one of the referees, who pointed out that one of the seventeenth-century entries for the term 'push-pin' in the Oxford English Dictionary appears to be a euphemism for sexual intercourse. Readers might bear this in mind when considering Bentham's statement comparing the relevant merits of push-pin and poetry.

A final word of thanks is extended to our contributors, who entered into this project so willingly, kept pretty much to the various deadlines that the editors set and have collectively produced a truly inter-disciplinary work that will not only have a massive influence on Bentham studies but will resonate across a number of disciplines and hopefully shatter some preconceptions.

Introduction

Philip Schofield

The inspiration for the present volume came from Anthony Julius upon his appointment as University College London's first professor of law and the arts at the beginning of 2017. Given UCL's close association with Jeremy Bentham, and his own misgivings concerning the way in which Bentham, utilitarianism and political economy is standardly – and unsympathetically – contrasted with Coleridge, Romanticism and literature, Julius believed that the time was ripe for a reassessment. With a view to considering the question of 'Bentham and the arts', which, to those who had absorbed the standard account, would appear to be an oxymoron, he approached Philip Schofield, his colleague in UCL's Faculty of Laws and director of the Bentham Project and general editor of the new authoritative edition of *The Collected Works of Jeremy Bentham*. They invited Malcolm Quinn at the University of the Arts London to join the enterprise. Quinn formed the perfect link between Bentham and the arts, having recently published, under the title of *Utilitarianism and the Art School in Nineteenth-century Britain*, a study of the influence of utilitarian thought, and of Bentham in particular, on the introduction of publicly funded art education in Britain at the beginning of the Victorian era.[1] It was decided to invite scholars from a variety of backgrounds – including history, philosophy, psychology, literary studies and the arts – to contribute to a seminar series, which duly took place at UCL in the first half of 2018. It was hoped that the presentations would be of sufficient interest and importance to form the basis for a collection of essays – hopes that were not simply realized but far surpassed. In order to bring coherence and focus to the putative volume, the contributors were all asked to take Bentham's recently published writings on sexual morality as their core material. These writings consisted of three essays entitled 'Of sexual irregularities – or, irregularities of the sexual appetite', 'Sextus', and 'General idea of a work, having for one of its objects the defence of the principle of *utility*, so far as concerns the liberty of taste ... Not Paul, but Jesus', which had been published in *Of Sexual Irregularities, and Other Writings on Sexual Morality* (*Collected Works of Jeremy Bentham*),[2] and in *Not Paul, but Jesus*, Volume III (the work announced in 'General idea'), which had been made available online,[3] pending its appearance in the *Collected Works* as part of the authoritative three-volume edition of *Not Paul, but Jesus*.[4] All these writings date from the mid-1810s. As was to be expected, the contributors ranged much more widely across Bentham's corpus, but these essays, together with John Stuart Mill's critique of Bentham and in particular of his views on poetry, form a common thread through the present volume.

The orthodoxy to which Anthony Julius was exposed during his undergraduate studies at Cambridge, and which forms the impetus for the present volume, had been propagated by F.R. Leavis, arguably the most influential literary scholar of the twentieth century, who had used John Stuart Mill's complementary essays on Bentham and Coleridge – in Mill's view, the two major representative thinkers of the age – in order to draw the distinction between utilitarianism and Romanticism, and thereby had pitted political economy against literature. This theme is the starting-point for Julius's own chapter below, but for present purposes it is worth drawing attention to the fact that, while his essays contained both praise and criticism of Bentham and Coleridge, Mill was particularly disdainful of Bentham's attitude towards notions of taste. In drawing attention to taste, Mill anticipated the issue that looms large in the present volume because of its centrality to the debate on the relationship between utilitarianism and literature and between Bentham and the arts.

Mill argued that every human action could be considered from three 'aspects'. The moral aspect concerned its rightness or wrongness, addressed itself to reason and conscience and led to approval or disapproval; the aesthetic aspect concerned its beauty, addressed itself to the imagination and led to admiration or despising; and the sympathetic aspect concerned its loveableness, addressed itself to human fellow-feeling and led to love, pity or dislike. Bentham's 'error' had been to treat 'the *moral* view of actions and characters, which,' Mill admitted, 'is unquestionably the first and most important mode of looking at them, as if it were the sole one', and had thereby ignored the aesthetic and sympathetic aspects. Mill claimed that it was 'not possible for any sophistry to confound these three modes of viewing an action', although it was 'very possible to adhere to one of them exclusively, and lose sight of the rest', which was precisely what Bentham had done. Mill continued:

> He carried this so far, that there were certain phrases which, being expressive of what he considered to be this groundless liking or aversion, he could not bear to hear pronounced in his presence. Among these phrases were those of *good* and *bad taste*. He thought it an insolent piece of dogmatism in one person to praise or condemn another in a matter of taste: as if men's likings and dislikings, on things in themselves indifferent, were not full of the most important inferences as to every point in their character; as if a person's tastes did not show him to be wise or a fool, cultivated or ignorant, gentle or rough, sensitive or callous, generous or sordid, benevolent or selfish, conscientious or depraved.

Mill claimed that nothing had done more than Bentham's 'error' in this respect 'to place him in opposition to the common feelings of mankind, and to give to his philosophy that cold, mechanical, and ungenial air which characterizes the popular idea of a Benthamite'.[5]

Mill went on to draw attention to 'Bentham's peculiar opinions on poetry'. While denying that Bentham held the fine arts in contempt, Mill explained that he 'entertained no favour towards poetry':

> Words, he thought, were perverted from their proper office when they were employed in uttering anything but precise logical truth. He says, somewhere in his works, that, 'quantity of pleasure being equal, push-pin is as good as poetry:' but this is only a paradoxical way of stating what he would equally have said of the things which he most valued and admired.

Mill explained that Bentham's basic view was that poetry 'consisted essentially in exaggeration for effect: in proclaiming some one view of a thing very emphatically, and suppressing all the limitations and qualifications'. Such a criticism was too extensive, since it could be applied to each and every form of writing 'which undertakes to make men feel truths as well as to see them', and that justifiably did so 'if the portion of truth which it thus enforces be that which is called for by the occasion'.[6]

The passage on push-pin and poetry to which Mill famously refers appears in Bentham's *Rationale of Reward*, a text that had first appeared as the second volume of Étienne Dumont's French recension *Théorie des peines et des récompenses* in 1811, but based on manuscripts written in the 1770s, and translated into English by Richard Smith and published in 1825. In the context of a discussion of the arts and sciences of amusement and curiosity, as distinguished from the arts and sciences of utility, Bentham remarked:

> Prejudice apart, the game of push-pin is of equal value with the arts and sciences of music and poetry. If the game of push-pin furnish more pleasure, it is more valuable than either. Everybody can play at push-pin: poetry and music are relished only by a few.[7]

The above passage is one of the most often quoted passages from Bentham's vast corpus, and constitutes the *locus classicus* for those who deem him to be a philistine. Mill was quite correct that Bentham regarded exaggeration as essential to poetry as Bentham noted in a passage written for *Not Paul, but Jesus*, Vol. III: 'The connection in the way of causality between things in themselves so disparate as music and virtue has been announced by Poetry, and Reason proves it. In Poetry, the force of the connection had indeed been exaggerated: for without exaggeration, that is falsification in a certain form, there can scarce be Poetry.' In the case in question, however, the exaggeration had 'at least a platform of truth to stand upon'. Bentham went on to point out that Shakespeare's sentiment that,

> The man who has not music in his soul
> Is fit for treasons, stratagems and spoils[8]

was not universally true: 'But what *is* true is, that the more occupied a man's mind is with music, and with the sentiments with which music is most accustomed to be accompanied … is so much the less exposed to the temptation of engaging in any such destructive enterprizes.'[9] This was a point that Bentham also made in *Rationale of Reward*: namely that taking delight in the fine arts, apart from the pleasure it gave to the practitioner, also had a societal benefit in keeping the practitioner out of mischief.[10] Returning to *Not Paul, but Jesus*, Bentham went on to say that, in this respect, 'by filling up with innocent recreation that time which might otherwise have been occupied by vice', trap-ball and chess might be said to be 'equally favourable to virtue'.

> But in favour of music, I am inclined to think, we may go farther, and pronounce it to have a connection with virtue peculiar to itself.

> The artificial notes, which music is occupied in the production of, bear for the most part a natural resemblance to the notes expressive of the social affections, of those affections which are so many modifications of benevolence: complaint, entreaty, soothing, condolence, congratulation, co-exultation and the like. There is Music for War, it may be said, as well as for Love. True: but happily the War-music is comparatively but little in vogue: and even in War-Music, it is rather what there is of sociality in war, rather than what there is of malice and cruelty, that is expressed by it.[11]

Again, Mill was quite correct to argue that Bentham did not recognize any separate spheres for aesthetics and sympathy – all was reducible to morality, or, in other words, to feelings of pleasure and pain. For Bentham, if taste referred to the sensations derived from the palate, then the notion made sense;[12] if taste referred to the propensity to derive pleasure from an object, then the notion made sense;[13] but if taste referred to some sort of mental faculty, whether inherited or acquired, then the notion made no sense. The point was that when a person said that they had a taste for something, it made sense insofar as it indicated that the speaker derived pleasure from experiencing it, while to say that something was in 'good taste' could not mean anything more than that, since there was no other standard than the expected pleasure against which to measure the goodness of the taste. The phrase 'good taste', therefore, if it meant anything, meant 'I like it', but it was nonetheless typically used by members of the ruling classes as a claim of superiority over those members of the subject population who, it was pretended, did not have access to this (non-existent) standard. In contrast, the commitment to pleasure as the standard of taste implied social (and political) equality.

Bentham's approach to the relationship between pleasure and taste was the key to his attitude towards sexual morality in the writings from the mid-1810s that, as noted above, form a common thread through the present volume. Bentham had condemned the punishment of homosexuality in his first major published work *A Fragment on Government*, which had appeared in 1776, defended sexual liberty in the 'Pederasty' essay written for his penal code in the mid-1780s and continued to espouse the views he had developed under the influence of the radical Enlightenment and transmit them into the Romantic period.[14] As late as the mid-1820s, when working on another draft of his proposed penal code, and around the time that Mill was beginning to work on Bentham's writings on evidence, Bentham returned, albeit briefly, to some of the themes that he had developed in his writings on sexual morality in the mid-1780s and reiterated in his writings on sexual morality in the mid-1810s. In a short sequence of manuscripts entitled 'Innoxious eccentricities of the sexual appetite, why not included in the scheme of punishment', he pointed out:

> Nature has given to man two cups of physical sweets: the one, containing those which are the produce of the operations by which the individual is preserved; another, containing those which are the produce of the operations by which the species is preserved. Into both, seconded by blind antipathy and pride, what is called Religion has now for about 18 centuries exerted itself in the endeavour either to dash the cup from the hand, or, by the infusion of its gall, to convert the cup of sweets into a cup of bitterness.

The 'pretence' given for denying pleasure in relation to food and drink, whether through the interdiction of certain foodstuffs or fasting in general, was 'the acquisition of the sympathy and the appeasing the antipathy of an Almighty being, who, by a self-contradictory proposition, is at the same [time] stiled benevolent: and not simply benevolent, but supremely benevolent'. All this was despite the fact that to Jesus, 'asceticism in all its forms was an object of undissembled scorn and ridicule. Asceticism is not *Christianity*, but *Paulism*.'[15] In relation to both food and drink and sexual gratification, 'the law of appetite' was '*Maximize enjoyment*', subject to the limits imposed by prudence and benevolence, whereby pleasure should not be experienced at the cost of greater pain either to oneself or to others.[16]

In relation to sexual gratification, Bentham pointed to five categories of 'error' that deviated from the 'standard' that the 'tyrant' had identified, namely sexual intercourse between one man and one woman for the procreation of children. The *error tempore* related to women's menstrual periods, the *error loci* to the use of parts of the body that would not lead to procreation, the *error sexus* to activities with members of the same-sex, the *error species* to activities with non-humans, and the *error numeri*, where (presumably) any other number of persons than two were involved.[17] Bentham wondered whether a casuist would reckon that the sin was greater, the further 'the aberration from the seat and standard of rectitude'. On this basis, the *error sexus* would be worse than the *error loci* where a man's partner was a woman, the *error species* would be worse than the *error sexus*, but worst of all would be sex with an inanimate object. Recollecting an incident from his childhood, Bentham continued:

> Never shall I forget the horror with which a reverend divine once communicated a discovery which, in the field of sin, he had just made. Once upon a time among the antients, wise as they were, Statues – statues soft and flexible made on purpose – had been but too successful rivals to the originals: such was the pride of learning, so delectable to it the discovery, the presence of a schoolboy, son of him to whom it was communicated, was no bar to the communication of it.
>
> The acme of heinousness in this line is not yet reached. If an elastic statue of a faultless biped is in some respects less unlike the original than an original quadruped is, in other respects it is more far removed. But between a woman and a french roll, how immeasurable the distance! A° 1789 at [... ?], while Turks and Russians were in arms,[18] a hapless wigh[t] became the town-talk on account of the extraordinary use he had found for so ordinary an article. But it was to beauty in its proper seat that this passion had been excited: and to the one woman so far inferior were all others, the oven presented to him a less unworthy representative than any he could have found in the appropriate bed chamber. A substitute had he found for her (the lady was told) at a baker's? At what baker's? answer – at any baker's. Unhappy man! it was by the lady's inexorable cruelty he had been driven to this distance.
>
> As in this rather singular instance woman beheld her successful rival and substitute at the baker's, man is in the habit of beholding his at the wax and tallow chandler's.[19]

Mill, who welcomed the prospect of men's 'natural passions' becoming 'as it already is with a large number of women, completely under the control of the reason',[20] would, no doubt, not have regarded Bentham's recounting of this anecdote, and indeed the whole passage, to be in good taste, but it also suggests that Bentham may have rather more to say to us, on these matters at least, than his successor in the utilitarian tradition.

The contributions to the present volume are distributed among three parts dealing broadly with first, philosophy and sexuality; second, intellectual history and literature; and third aesthetics, taste and art. Part I on 'Philosophy and sexuality' opens with Philip Schofield's chapter on 'The epicurean universe of Jeremy Bentham: Taste, beauty and reality', which provides an account of Bentham's utilitarianism within the context of his deeper commitment to a materialist ontology, and is intended to provide some historical context for the ensuing chapters. According to Schofield, Bentham appears to have adopted a materialist ontology and a sceptical attitude towards religion by the time when, aged 16, he was required to subscribe to the Thirty-nine Articles of the Church of England in order to take his degree at the University of Oxford. He later confessed himself to be 'an Epicurean', and this, Schofield suggests, is the key to appreciating why Bentham continues to divide opinion so strongly. What is at stake is illustrated by reference to the respective attitudes of French philosopher Michel Onfray and American political theorist Cathy Gere. Onfray approves of Bentham's positioning himself in opposition to the dominant intellectual tradition represented by Plato, Christianity and Kant, whereas Gere sees his rejection of Kantian autonomy as opening the way for the abuse of marginalized individuals in order to benefit society in general. For Bentham, Schofield explains, there was the physical world and nothing more, at least nothing more that could be known, and all notions (ideals, concepts, angels, gods) that purported to refer to the non-physical world were so much nonsense. The same was true for statements about beauty and taste, insofar as they were made with reference to some metaphysical standard, while those making these statements were claiming not only aesthetic but political superiority over the bulk of the population who failed to appreciate the pretended non-existent standard. In his typology of ethical theories, Bentham had distinguished adherents of the principle of utility from adherents of the principle of sympathy and antipathy. The latter attempted to exercise power and influence by elevating their own opinions into standards that were binding on others. Hence proponents of 'taste' were adherents of the principle of sympathy and antipathy.

In the second chapter entitled 'Not Kant, but Bentham: On taste', echoing Bentham's *Not Paul, but Jesus*, Frances Ferguson points to the comparison that is standardly drawn in aesthetics between the 'commanding figure' of Immanuel Kant and the 'philistine' Bentham, but comes to the non-standard conclusion, through tracing their respective attitudes towards sexuality, that the latter's approach has more to commend it. Both thinkers were operating in a wider cultural environment in which individuals were increasingly claiming a right to be 'acknowledged', as manifested, for instance, in demands for a democratic franchise. Kant's approach, Ferguson explains, was grounded in the notion of individual autonomy, with aesthetic judgment consisting in disinterested first-personal experience. To make an aesthetic judgment was to go beyond the mere perception of an object and any use it might have and to recognize its inherent beauty and sublimity. It was also a judgment that was independent of any social convention. For Bentham, aesthetics in general and taste in particular was reducible to pleasure and pain. He turned to history – represented in both purportedly factual and fictional literature – in order to show what activities had been regarded as pleasurable and desirable. This gave him the opportunity to criticize the law of his own time that punished male-male sex and which, he claimed, originated in a particular reading of certain passages in the Bible. In what she sees as his most striking argument, Bentham points to Jesus's non-condemnation of irregular sexual activities and his rejection of asceticism, not as a means of stating his own views, but as a means of impressing upon persons confessing themselves to be Christians the views that, given this commitment, they ought to hold. Hence, in contrast to Kant's first-person, present judgment, Bentham presents 'a significant expansive account of aesthetic judgment' that draws on the historical record, avoids relativism and yet leaves individual judgment liable to criticism and reformulation.

In the third chapter entitled '"Envy accompanied with antipathy": Bentham on the psychology of sexual *ressentiment*', Stella Sandford draws attention to important parallels between Bentham's and Sigmund Freud's writings on sexuality, particularly the latter's *Three Essays on the Theory of Sexuality* (1905). Understanding sexuality primarily in terms of pleasure (rather than reproductive teleology) and presupposing sexual orientation to be a matter of taste, Bentham, like Freud, defends sexual freedom and denies that same-sex desire is either pathological or unnatural. In some respects, Bentham presents a more radical account of sexual freedom than Freud in that he sees consensual sexual activity as not merely morally neutral but as a positive good. This is linked, Sandford suggests, to Bentham's more straightforward account of pleasure. She points out that, for Bentham, it was not homosexuality, but its virulent condemnation, that required explanation, given that there was no utilitarian justification for condemning it. Bentham identifies the principles of asceticism and antipathy as the grounds for this condemnation. He traces the origin of the ascetic principle, insofar as it condemns sexual pleasure in its 'irregular' shapes, to the Mosaic law and sees it given further and decisive support in the teachings of St Paul. This gives rise, however, to a puzzle. Given Bentham's general theory of motivation – that all actions are motivated by a desire for pleasure and an aversion to pain – how can the principle of asceticism, which seeks to suppress pleasure, be a motive for anything? It turns out that asceticism does in fact give rise to motives, and in the case of the condemnation of homosexuality, the motive is envy. The condemner is envious of the pleasure enjoyed by the partaker in male-male sex and in 'irregular' sexual gratification more generally, the punishment of which leads to the gratification of ill-will or vengeance, and thereby satisfies the pleasure of antipathy. Bentham's psychological explanation for the social antipathy towards same-sex sexuality, Sandford notes, not only anticipates Friedrich Nietzsche's psychology of '*ressentiment*' and the unconscious of Freud, but reveals, in this area at least, a more complicated picture of Bentham's psychological theory than has hitherto generally been recognized.

In the fourth chapter entitled 'Literature, morals and utility: Bentham, Dumont and de Staël', which commences Part II on 'Intellectual history and literature', Emmanuelle de Champs places Bentham's views on taste in the context of Enlightenment and post-Enlightenment debates in the Francophone literature on the relationship between aesthetics, morals and politics. In the eighteenth century it was a commonplace to associate improvement in morals with refinement in aesthetic judgment and to view the diffusion of artistic taste as a means of promoting a cohesive and stable society. Good taste in morals was linked to good taste in the arts, with education providing the means to improve both morals and the appreciation of the arts. This association, De Champs explains, was rejected by Bentham, whose radically individualist account of pleasure led him to deny the existence of any collective standard of taste. Bentham claimed that literary critics robbed the people of innocent pleasures while poetry promoted falsehood. To a writer such as Turgot, the utilitarian emphasis on individual pleasure threatened the consensus on which society rested. De Champs then illustrates how Bentham's ideas on taste were received by two representative figures, namely Étienne Dumont, Bentham's friend and translator, and Germaine de Staël, the writer and literary critic. Dumont attempted to take elements from both Rousseau and Bentham – adhering to the former's views on morals and aesthetics but rejecting his politics, and adhering to the latter's social science but rejecting his views on taste. Dumont defended literary criticism on the grounds that it promoted interest in artistic endeavour and helped to form public opinion, accepting that there was good and bad taste, as opposed to Bentham who denied that the notions of good and bad could be applied to taste. Influenced by her reading of Kant, de Staël argued that idealism bridged the gap between morals and politics through a universal aesthetic sensitivity. She therefore rejected Bentham's approach as part of her rejection of Enlightenment rationalism and materialism more generally.

In the fifth chapter entitled 'Jeremy Bentham's imagination and the ethics of prose style: Paraphrase, substitution, translation', Jan-Melissa Schramm explores Bentham's techniques of phraseoplerosis and paraphrasis, whereby abstract terms were placed in propositions that were then translated into equivalent propositions that contained terms representing real (physical) objects, in the context of eighteenth- and nineteenth-century debates on translation. At the end of the seventeenth century, the parameters of the debate were set by John Dryden, who had identified three categories of translation: the first was metaphrase or literal translation; the second was paraphrase, where the translator followed the sense, though not the exact words, of the author; and the third was imitation, where the translator merely took inspiration from the original. The question arose as to whether the form and style of a passage could ever be separated from its content. At one end of the spectrum was the view that word-for-word translation was possible, while at the other end was the view that each author had an inimitable style that expressed an untranslateable individuality.

Bentham believed that his techniques of phraseoplerosis and paraphrasis provided an accurate method of connecting linguistic representation with physical reality, but this translation of ideas put him at odds with those literary critics who rejected the possibility of such a reductive exposition, and saw instead an unbreakable synthesis between form and content. Bentham's own writings, moreover, proved challenging for his contemporaries to assess. Critics, notably but not only William Hazlitt in *The Spirit of the Age* (1825), commented on his prolixity and inaccessibility while appreciating the value of his ideas. At the same time it was recognized that Bentham's translator Étienne Dumont, while not providing literal translations of Bentham's prose, a task that Dumont himself regarded as impossible, had translated his ideas and hence made them accessible. Schramm then draws a connection between the techniques of substitution in language and that of representation and substitution in ethics and politics. Critics of Bentham's approach, and of utilitarianism more generally, deplored the treatment of individuals as interchangeable units in a calculation of utility undertaken for the benefit of the community as a whole. John Stuart Mill, for instance, criticized Bentham for his lack of imaginative sympathy – he could not change places with, or 'enter into the mind and circumstances of', another – while Charles Dickens in *Hard Times* was concerned with the implications of treating individuals as elements in a utility calculation. Schramm concludes by reminding us that the issue at stake is how to reconcile 'fairness for all' with 'personal fulfilment for each uniquely valuable human being'.

In the sixth chapter entitled '"Is it true? … what is the meaning of it?": Bentham, Romanticism and the fictions of reason', Tim Milnes notes that assessments of the relationship between Benthamite utilitarianism and Romanticism have been heavily influenced by John Stuart Mill's characterization of Bentham and Coleridge as the great counterweights of early nineteenth-century British thought. According to Mill, the fundamental imperative of Bentham's thought is epistemological and empirical and hence concerned with truth, while in Coleridge's work, it is hermeneutic and aesthetic and hence concerned with meaning. Milnes argues that Mill presents a simplistic and misleading picture and that the relationship between Bentham's utilitarianism and Romanticism needs to be rethought. The critical point of reference for both utilitarians and Romantics, as represented by Bentham and William Hazlitt respectively, was David Hume's account of language as a product of social convention, which thereby sustained certain fictions of belief that made civilized life possible. Bentham's response to Hume's theory of fictions was to develop his technique of paraphrasis, which translated figurative language into less figurative language that was ultimately grounded in real entities, including pleasure and pain. What counted as a real entity, notes Milnes, was not correspondence between word and object, but coherence within the linguistic community in question. Hence, Bentham subordinated truth to meaning. Hazlitt, who had famously criticized Bentham and associated him with what he regarded as the objectionable philosophy of empiricism, materialism and egoism, responded to Hume by relocating fictions of belief from the sphere of social convention into that of mental construction, elevating the imagination and subordinating reason, and thus privileging the artist at the expense of the philosopher. Far from abandoning truth, Hazlitt idealized it by placing it at the indeterminate boundary between reason and imagination. Mill's binary opposition between utilitarianism, fact and truth on the one side, and Romanticism, feeling and meaning on the other, appears far less plausible, concludes Milnes, when Bentham is read as a 'proto-pragmatist' and the Romantics as 'thwarted idealists'.

Continuing the theme of the relationship between Bentham and Romanticism, in the seventh chapter entitled 'More Bentham, less Mill', Anthony Julius complains that literature and the visual arts are neglected in the liberal defence of free speech, and he lays much of the blame at the feet of John Stuart Mill, both because of the nature of his writings on the subject and the enormous influence that they have had and continue to have. Despite his reputation among literary critics, Mill, claims Julius, is 'feeble in his aesthetic positions' and in *On Liberty*, which contains his classic defence of free speech, he is 'hostile to literary free speech'. Julius shows how Mill's pronouncements on poetry were superficial and how he deprecated the novel, and goes on to explain how Mill's approach to higher and lower pleasures opened the door to literary and artistic censorship. The point was that Victorian progressivism made a link between sexual continence and human improvement, and hence Mill would not have entertained the idea that sexual material might serve a literary or aesthetic purpose.

Bentham, Julius notes, has been characterized as a philistine, due in part to Mill's criticism of his attitude towards poetry, as expressed in the two aphorisms that he attributed to him, namely that 'pushpin is as good as poetry' and that 'all poetry is misrepresentation'. Mill was worried first, that by refusing to acknowledge the superiority of poetry over a child's game, the utilitarians were vulnerable to the charge that their philosophy was fit only for pigs; and second, 'that a shared understanding of language leaves no space for poetry'. Julius retorts that in relation to the first aphorism, Bentham was opening up debate, while Mill was shutting it down, and in relation to the second, that Bentham was no more culpable than any other philosopher who worked within a positivist account of language, including Mill himself. Julius then proceeds to reconstruct Bentham's aesthetics – confessedly from a charitable point of view – through his 'several engagements with Romanticism'. He argues that Bentham is just as much a creature of Romanticism as he is of the Enlightenment, and sees his attitude to the arts not so much as rejecting the Romantic but giving an alternative conceptualization of it in terms of pleasure. 'Bentham found common ground with his fellow Romantics, but then pushed *beyond* them', notes Julius. Indeed, both Bentham and the Romantics championed pleasure, disparaged the notion of taste, refused 'to separate the corporeal from the spiritual', and were, crucially, committed to free speech. Bentham's defence of the liberty of taste, particularly in sexual matters, combined with his condemnation of censorship, implied freedom of literary speech – 'what may be *practised*', writes Julius, 'may also be *written about*'. If liberalism is to find a defence of free speech that convincingly incorporates aesthetic expression, concludes Julius, it will be necessary to 'work with Bentham'.

In the eighth chapter entitled 'Enlightenment unrefined: Bentham's realism and the analysis of beauty', which commences Part III on 'Aesthetics, taste and art', Malcolm Quinn begins by discussing attacks on Bentham's hedonic utilitarianism as a form of cultural barbarism. He argues that we should not concur with Karl Marx's view that 'the arch-philistine, Jeremy Bentham' was the 'heavy-footed oracle of the "common sense" of the nineteenth-century bourgeoisie', but instead should interpret Bentham as recognizing that a 'common-sense' approach to the analysis of beauty would be self-defeating if it attempted to impose social norms that could separate the beautiful from the ugly. Bentham's praise for William Hogarth's prints *Beer Street* and *Gin Lane* of 1751 exposes the contradictions of the position that Hogarth adopted in his manifesto *The Analysis of Beauty*, published two years later. In this text, Hogarth attempted a rational, impartial analysis of the truth of beauty, to assist the ordinary observer and defeat the artificial rules of art promoted by so-called connoisseurs. In advocating an aesthetics of 'plain truth', Hogarth argues that the body of a living woman is more beautiful than a statue of Venus and that the form of a woman's body surpasses that of a man. In Bentham's terms, however, a definition of beauty based on reproductive sexuality was not tenable, because sexuality was an inclination without a fixed object that ignored the distinction between the beautiful and the ugly.

In the ninth chapter entitled 'Jeremy Bentham's principle of utility and taste: An alternative approach to aesthetics in two stages', Benjamin Bourcier contrasts Bentham's commitment to legislative non-interference in matters of taste with his provision for moral education in the private sphere. It was the duty of government to ensure respect for and equal treatment of each person's taste, that is the disposition to derive pleasure from a particular activity or state of affairs. It was also incumbent on government to avoid imposing one particular conception of happiness on everyone. The point was that the liberty of taste was necessary in order to bring about the greatest happiness. For Bentham, all pleasure was good, and the only legitimate criterion of morality was the quantity of pleasure, and hence prohibiting some enjoyment on the grounds that it was distasteful was morally wrong. Making 'war upon pleasure' in this way, which characterized the adherent of the principle of asceticism, was the trademark of the tyrant and despot. Veiled in the pretence of promoting virtue, it was a means of securing the interests of the ruling few at the expense of the subject many.

In private ethics, Bourcier points out, there is a danger that the radical subjectivism of taste will lead to anarchy. In response, Bentham gave the deontologist the role of educating individuals as to how they might reap the greatest pleasures from the choices that they made. Each individual was the best judge of their own pleasure, and it was senseless to tell a person that something that they enjoyed was in bad taste. Nevertheless, a person's tastes might change, either because they become better informed or because they no longer derive pleasure from the experience in question. The advice of the deontologist was necessary to support the individual in understanding how to join their interest with their duty by pointing out the pains and pleasures that were likely to result from the alternative courses of action open to them. The deontologist also helped to form public opinion, through which the moral sanction operated, and acted as a further constraint on individual choice.

In the tenth chapter entitled 'From pain to pleasure: Panopticon dreams and Pentagon Petal', Fran Cottell and Marianne Mueller explain the background to an artwork consisting of a long bench in the shape of five interconnected pentagons and installed on a site that is now the Rootstein Hopkins Parade Ground adjacent to Tate Britain in Millbank, London, but where Bentham at one time had hoped to construct his panopticon prison. The panopticon scheme was effectively rejected by government in 1803, and in 1813 construction began for a very different design of prison: the Millbank Penitentiary. Cottell and Mueller's work explores the relationship between architectural form and social behaviour, which was the central theme of Bentham's panopticon, but rather than modelling behaviour, as Bentham intended, their aim is to advance the possibilities for social intercourse in an open-ended way. In this chapter, Cottell and Mueller describe the architectural features of the proposed panopticon and its aim of facilitating surveillance. They contrast the openness and airiness of the unrealized prison with the darkness and unhygienic conditions of the prison that was actually built. Moreover, while the panopticon was intended to be circular, Millbank Prison was configured as a series of hexagons, each of them with a central watchtower, but from which very little could in fact be seen. Millbank Prison was closed in 1892, and the site turned over to a military hospital.

Cottell and Mueller point out that, in general, people are resistant to the use of architecture to determine their behaviour. Inspired by the Dutch architect Herman Hertzberger, they attempt to design spaces that 'allow for and stimulate the spontaneous interpretation of users in pursuit of pleasure and empowerment'. In using the Rootstein Hopkins Parade Ground, they wanted to subvert the historical associations of the site with the exercise of power and the imposition of pain (even Bentham's panopticon, despite its humanitarian features, would still have been a place of punishment and hence a space for the infliction of pain) by installing a structure that could be used in multifarious ways and promote pleasurable activities. The pentagon design of Millbank Prison was reinterpreted to form a flower-shaped bench, though its dimensions were such that it could as easily be walked upon or lain upon as sat upon. It might be used for private one-to-one conversations or for social group encounters. Cottell and Mueller describe the various ways in which the space was used by the diverse communities that lived in, worked at, or merely visited the Millbank site. The anti-Benthamism of the architectural concept was translated into the very Benthamic enterprise of converting pain into pleasure.

In the eleventh and final chapter of the volume, dealing appropriately with Bentham's auto-icon, entitled 'Bentham's image: the corporeality check', Carolyn Shapiro argues that Bentham's own auto-icon is 'the corpo-realization of what underlies Bentham's theories of logic, language and legislation'. That Bentham wished to ground everything in the physicality of the human body is shown in the constant references in his writings to real entities, that is to physical bodies and in particular the sensations of pleasure and pain – this is the corporeality that underlies the greatest happiness principle. His interest in etymology involved relating the meaning of words to the physical image that lay at their 'root'. Shapiro points out that Bentham's writing was a physical activity related by pain and pleasure to all other activities, including those involving sexual gratification. She highlights the parallels between Bentham's manuscript corpus and his own body – his corpse – in that they both needed to be crafted by other hands – the editor and the surgeon – following instructions of various sorts left by Bentham himself.

Shapiro points out that Bentham criticized religion for its unjustifiable leap from the notion of physical to that of moral impurity, and its consequent demand for punishment, and hence the infliction of physical pain, for those deemed to be impure, despite the lack of any physical grounding. This was an example of the operation of the principle of antipathy, a passion located in the breasts (physical bodies) of rulers, in order to subdue those subject to them. Moving from the real, physical body to the imaginary paved the way for tyranny. The religiously inspired principle of asceticism, propagated by Paul despite being opposed by Jesus, was characterized by groundless pronouncements of immorality. The solution for Bentham was to remove fiction from language and link language to the physical by means of the techniques of phraseoplerosis and paraphrasis. The body, when language loses its connection to the physical, is claimed for mischievous and malign purposes, as exemplified in the condemnation of homosexuality when the body is co-opted by asceticism. Shapiro posits that the homosexual body, like that of Jesus, stands open to other bodies, while Bentham in turn proposes an intercoursing body with its 'inlets' to pleasure. Bentham proposed to invite William Beckford, novelist and homosexual, to collaborate with him on the *Not Paul, but Jesus* manuscripts and thereby to give form and order to his corpus, just as his surgeon Thomas Southwood Smith would be invited to give form and order to his corpse.

Finally, it is worth remembering that, in the spring and early summer of 2018, Bentham's auto-icon, consisting of his skeleton, clothes and wax head, was transported across the Atlantic ocean in order to appear in a major exhibition entitled 'Like life: Sculpture, color, and the body' at the Metropolitan Museum of Art, New York.[21] Given the received view of Bentham as a philistine, there is some irony in the fact that Bentham's own remains have themselves been transformed into a work of art.

Notes

1 Quinn, 2013.
2 Bentham, ed. Schofield *et al.*, 2014.
3 Bentham, 2013.
4 The preparation of *Of Sexual Irregularities* and *Not Paul, but Jesus*, Vol. III for publication was generously funded by the Leverhulme Trust. Bentham discussed many of the same themes in material headed 'Pederasty', written in about 1785 for a proposed penal code, and published in a non-authoritative but mainly reliable version in Crompton, 1978.
5 Mill, ed. Robson *et al.*,1969, 75–115 at 112–13.
6 Mill, ed. Robson *et al.*, 1969, 113–14.
7 Bentham, ed. Bowring, 1843 [hereafter Bowring], ii. 253.
8 See *The Merchant of Venice*, v. i. 83–5, usually rendered as 'The man that hath no music in himself, / Nor is not mov'd with concord of sweet sounds, / Is fit for treasons, stratagems, and spoils'.
9 University College London Library, Bentham Papers [hereafter UC], box cxlix, fo. 64; Bentham, ed. Quinn, 2001, 131 n.
10 Bowring, ii. 254.
11 UC cxlix. 65.
12 Bentham, ed. Goldworth, 1983, 79.
13 Bentham, ed. Schofield *et al.*, 2014, 4.
14 Henry Sidgwick, usually recognized, along with Bentham and John Stuart Mill, as the third of the triumvirate of great classical utilitarian philosophers, claimed that Bentham was the pre-eminent representative of the Enlightenment and that Benthamism was 'the legacy left to the nineteenth century by the eighteenth', being the force against which the new 'philosophy of Restoration and Reaction has had to struggle continually with varying success'. See Sidgwick, 1904, 136 ff.
15 UC clviii. 10 (20 December 1824).
16 UC clviii. 11 (20 December 1824).
17 UC clviii. 12–13 (20 December 1824), 14–15 (13 January 1825).
18 The name of the place in which the following anecdote is set has so far proved to be illegible, but if Bentham was referring to the time he spent at Krichëv in Russia, he has misremembered the date. The Russo-Turkish war broke out on 5/16 August 1787, and Bentham left Krichëv on 19/30 November 1787, arriving back in England in early February 1788.
19 UC lxviii. 15–16 (13 January 1825).
20 See Mill to Lord Amberley, 2 February 1870, in Mill, ed. Mineka and Lindley, 1972, 1692–3.
21 See Anon, 2018.

References

Anon. 'Like Life: Sculpture, Color, and the Body', Metropolitan Museum of Art, New York (2018) [https://www.metmuseum.org/exhibitions/listings/2018/like-life].

Bentham, J. 'A Table of the Springs of Action', in *Deontology: Together with A Table of the Springs of Action and Article on Utilitarianism* (*CW*), ed. A. Goldworth. Oxford: Clarendon Press, 1983.

Bentham, J. *Not Paul, but Jesus*, Vol. III: *Doctrine*. London: Bentham Project, UCL, 2013 [http://discovery.ucl.ac.uk/1392179/3/npbj.pdf].

Bentham, J. *Of Sexual Irregularities, and Other Writings on Sexual Morality* (*CW*), eds. P. Schofield, C. Pease-Watkin and Michael Quinn. Oxford: Clarendon Press, 2014.

Bentham, J. *The Works of Jeremy Bentham*, ed. John Bowring. 11 vols. Edinburgh: William Tait, 1838–43.

Bentham, J. *Writings on the Poor Laws: I* (*CW*), ed. Michael Quinn. Oxford: Clarendon Press, 2001.

Crompton, L. 'Jeremy Bentham's Essay on Paederasty', *Journal of Homosexuality* 3 (1978): 383–405 and 4 (1978): 91–107.

Mill, J.S. 'Bentham', in *Essays on Ethics, Religion and Society*, eds. J.M. Robson, F.E.L. Priestley, and D.P. Dryer, *The Collected Works of John Stuart Mill: Volume X*. Toronto: University of Toronto Press; London: Routledge, 1969, 75–115.

Mill, J.S. *The Later Letters of John Stuart Mill 1849–1873*, eds. F.E. Mineka and D.N. Lindley, *The Collected Works of John Stuart Mill: Volume XVII*. Toronto: University of Toronto Press; London: Routledge, 1972.

Quinn, Malcolm. *Utilitarianism and the Art School in Nineteenth-Century Britain*. London and New York: Routledge, 2013.

Sidgwick, H. 'Bentham and Benthamism in Politics and Ethics', in *Miscellaneous Essays and Addresses*. London: Macmillan, 1904.

Part I.
PHILOSOPHY AND SEXUALITY

Chapter 1

The Epicurean universe of Jeremy Bentham: Taste, beauty and reality

Philip Schofield

1. *Fountain* and the Thirty-nine Articles of the Church of England

The French artist Marcel Duchamp (1887–1968) is credited with creating the first 'ready-made', that is a manufactured, mass-produced object, with or without some degree of modification, presented as an artwork. An early example was *Fountain*, an upturned, pseudonymously signed urinal that he submitted for exhibition in New York in 1917, and which is one of the best known and most controversial artworks of the twentieth century.[1] According to the French philosopher Michel Onfray, for instance, *Fountain* 'demolished Kant's *Critique of Practical Reason* and thus Platonism in art and elsewhere. More than twenty centuries of classical theory about Beauty went up in smoke in the blink of an eye.'[2] In an interview given in or around 1961, Duchamp distinguished ready-mades from *objets trouvés* or 'found objects', such as pebbles or feathers. He stated that 'the so-called "found object" is completely directed by personal taste' that 'decides that this is a beautiful object and is unique', whereas his own ready-mades could be and often were 'duplicated, thus avoiding the cult of uniqueness, of art with a capital "A."' He continued: 'I consider taste – bad or good – the greatest enemy of art. In the case of the ready-mades, I tried to remain aloof from personal taste and to be fully conscious of the problem.' He had produced his ready-mades in small numbers, since to produce a large number 'would immediately produce a personal taste', while he had added 'as little as possible' to them in order to 'try to keep them pure'. Duchamp, however, was aware that he had not necessarily provided a satisfactory solution to the problem of taste, 'because many people can prove I'm wrong by merely pointing out that I choose one object rather than another and thus impose something of my own personal taste'.[3]

Michel Onfray, as we have seen, argues that Duchamp's *Fountain* represents the point at which the Platonic ideal of beauty was shown to be a sham, though Duchamp himself was less confident that he had delivered the fatal blow against the notion of taste that he had hoped to deliver. It might be argued, however, that Duchamp's aim had been accomplished a century and a half earlier by Jeremy Bentham (1748–1832), whose objection to the notion of taste can be traced back to his reluctance, at the age of 16 in 1764, to subscribe to the Thirty-nine Articles of the Church of England in order to take his Bachelor of Arts degree at the University of Oxford. Fifty years later in *Church-of-Englandism* he admitted that he still felt 'shame' at 'the sin of [his] boyhood', and that confessing his disbelief was an '*expiation;* an atonement for that early sin'.[4] Bentham explained that he had his doubts about the truth of the Articles. He was sent, together with some other students, to a Fellow of his College whose role was to assuage such doubts, and who told them that it was not for 'uninformed youths … to presume to set up [their] private judgments against a public one, formed by some of the holiest, as well as best and wisest men that ever lived'. In the end, Bentham subscribed because he did not want to disappoint his father Jeremiah, who had earmarked him for a career in the law in the hope that he would rise to its very eminence as Lord Chancellor of England.[5] It is remarkable, given his background, that Bentham had any doubts at all. Both of his grandmothers' fathers had been Church-of-England clergymen.[6] His father Jeremiah, himself a staunch Church-of-England man, was a lawyer in the City of London who had acquired an extensive property portfolio and had bought a house in Queen's Square Place, Westminster with an enormous garden, adjacent to St James's Park, which Jeremy eventually inherited in 1792. Aged seven, Jeremy was sent to Westminster School, where he wrote devotional Latin verses on Christ's passion.[7] Aged 12, he was sent to the Tory University of Oxford, where he dutifully attended his classes and translated Cicero's *Tusculan Disputations* at the command of his father.[8] He was, therefore, immersed into the culture of a politically conservative, religiously orthodox, financially privileged, upper-middle class and by all expectations upwardly mobile metropolitan family (his step-brother did eventually become a peer of the realm).[9] How could he, by the age of 16, have become sceptical about religion, and resent for the rest of his life being forced to subscribe to the Thirty-nine Articles? There is a hint in young Jeremy's translation of the *Tusculan Disputations* that not everything was as it should be.[10] To the passage that he had translated as, 'for tho' Plato were to give no reason for his Assertions (see what deference I pay him) he would even bear me down by his Authority', Bentham added a footnote for his father:

> N.B. a very poor reason, truly! That Tully should believe any thing that Plato said, merely because he said it, is, in my Opinion, as absurd as if I were to believe the Soul was mortal, merely because you said it … .[11]

One wonders whether the comment raised concerns in Jeremiah's mind about his son's orthodoxy.

Bentham is, of course, noted for his utilitarianism, but, according to his own account, he did not formulate his version of the principle of utility until 1769[12] – hence his unwillingness to subscribe to the Thirty-nine Articles could not have been based upon any explicitly utilitarian consideration. His unwillingness arose from doubts about the truth of the Articles, and his resentment concerned the compromise, as he saw it, of his intellectual integrity – that is, being forced to lie. Bentham emphasized the point when he explained that, while attending William Blackstone's lectures in 1764, he had been concerned about the fictions – in other words, the lies, the untruths – that he had detected in Blackstone's account of English law.[13] The question, therefore, turns on the young Bentham's understanding of truth. While he gives us no contemporary account, there are plausible grounds for reading back his view of truth from his later writings on ontology and epistemology in order to appreciate the nature of his doubts about the Thirty-nine Articles. Having said that, we need not read back too far. Although his most detailed writings on these subjects date from the mid-1810s,[14] he had formulated his central ideas by the early to mid-1770s. In short, he argued that the only thing that had any real existence was the 'substance' that formed the physical universe, that any proposition that made any claim grounded ultimately on a non-physical entity was nonsensical, and that any claim that misrepresented events or states of affairs in the physical world was untrue. He presumably held this view, or had more than an inkling of it, by the time that he subscribed to the Thirty-nine Articles.

It seems plausible to assume that, at some point during his studies at Oxford, he had discovered Epicurus. He may have been attracted to Epicureanism through the account, albeit not a sympathetic one, that he had found in Cicero's *Tusculan Disputations*. It is worth remembering that he had always been a voracious reader, and so he may have gone on to study more recent and contemporary writers who belonged to the Epicurean tradition.[15] Given what Bentham says later about his formative influences, one of these Epicurean writers, and perhaps the most important, was the French materialist philosopher Claude Adrien Helvétius. There is no evidence, however, that Bentham had read Helvétius's *De l'esprit* before subscribing to the Thirty-nine Articles: according to Bentham's later reminiscences (not always totally reliable), a copy 'fell into [his] hands' when he was aged 20.[16] At some point he read Lucretius's *On the Nature of Things* (*De Rerum Natura*), which contains the most detailed surviving account of Epicurus's philosophy.[17] One might speculate that it was his profound fear of ghosts, instilled into him at a young age by mischievous servants, that made a materialist account of the universe attractive to him – if all that existed was the physical world, there were no spirits and hence no ghosts of which to be afraid.[18]

There is no doubt that Bentham explicitly allied himself with the Epicurean tradition in opposition to the nonsense that he regarded as emanating from Plato and the Stoics. In an early manuscript from the mid-1770s, Bentham noted that he 'had [the principle of utility] from Epicurus, from Carneades, from Horace, from Helvetius, from Beccaria'.[19] In 1818 Bentham gave the title 'The Epicureans the only philosophers deserving of the name' to a proposed section of *Not Paul, but Jesus*, Vol. III. He began the section as follows:

> From the days of their founder to the present, Epicurus and those who have discoursed and acted as he is said to have acted, constitute a standing but[t] to the invectives of hypocrisy and imbecillity, whether cloathed in the mantle of philosophy or that of religion.
>
> They have, in a word, been so many utilitarians, or rather non-ascetics: no where have they looked for happiness but where it was to be found … .[20]

Where they looked for it, of course, was in pleasure. In a similar vein, in a note at the head of a manuscript written for the same essay, he wrote: 'Limitations [to the pursuit of pleasure] are those dictated by 1. prudence. 2. probity. 3. benevolence. *Conceditur* this Epicureanism:

but Stoicism is either folly or hypocrisy.'[21] In *Deontology*, his extensive work on ethics dating from the mid-1810s, at the start of a chapter discussing the *summum bonum* of the ancient philosophers, Bentham noted: '*Summum bonum* consummate nonsense' and 'Anti-Epicureans quarrellers with their bread & butter.' The problem was that neither Socrates, Plato, Aristotle, nor any of their disciples, nor the Stoics, having rejected pleasure, could agree what the *summum bonum* consisted in or even say anything intelligible about it.[22] Going on to condemn Socrates and Plato for 'talking nonsense, on pretence of teaching morality and wisdom', he described how the people in general, 'who were content with reaping pleasures under the guidance of common sense', were for that very reason 'considered [by them] as ignorant and as composing the vulgar herd'.[23] If the Platonists and Stoics were wrong, 'how must it have been', asked Bentham ironically, 'with those sensualists, with those hogs, the Epicureans?' According to the account in *Ethices Compendium in usum juventutis academicae*, the elementary textbook on moral philosophy used by undergraduates at Oxford and which Bentham himself had studied,[24] the Epicureans, he noted, 'Hogs as they were', had looked for the *summum bonum* in bodily pleasure. Bentham doubted, however, whether the Epicureans had looked for a *summum bonum* at all, whether they believed in the existence of such a thing, and whether 'in their account of pleasure, pleasure in every shape that was not bodily should have been omitted'. The Epicureans, he continued, could not have been unaware, since everyone knew it, that some pleasures had their 'seat' in the mind, while others had their 'seat' in the body. The author of *Ethices Compendium* had gone on to criticize the bodily pleasures on the grounds that they were 'ignoble', 'short', and 'unsavoury', and in this latter case gave rise to 'blushes'.[25] Bentham pointed out that the term 'ignoble' meant nothing, and in any case it was the mind that felt pleasure, whatever its 'seat', and not the body. If a pleasure was indeed of short duration, he asked, what did that matter? And finally, if the recollection of a pleasure taken in an 'improper manner' led to an 'unsavoury' recollection, what did that matter for a pleasure taken in a 'proper manner'?[26]

2. Bentham versus Kant

Whether Bentham was inspired by Epicurus or by some other sceptical writer, the moment when his scruples as a 16-year-old boy were brushed aside by the combined might of the University of Oxford and the Church of England, seconded by the considerable weight of paternal authority, was arguably not only a seminal moment in his own life, but also a seminal moment in the history of Western philosophy and in the history of aesthetics. Recent works by Michel Onfray and Cathy Gere illustrate what is at stake. In *A Hedonist Manifesto*, Onfray characterizes the overwhelmingly dominant philosophical tradition in Western civilization as Platonic, Christian and Kantian. This tradition, accepted by the majority of contemporary philosophers, is characterized by the acceptance and celebration of a non-materialist universe that is superior to the physical universe that our bodies inhabit. Onfray points out that Plato has his forms, Christianity has its God and Kant has his ideals. A dualism is posited between the material and the ideal, the body and the spirit, phenomena and noumena, the descriptive and the prescriptive, with the latter elevated over the former. In short, Platonism, Christianity and Kantianism all posit a metaphysics that ascribes superiority to the ideal domain over the physical, to the other-worldly over the this-worldly, to the spirit over the body. Those Epicurean philosophers who have opposed the dominant tradition, including Bentham and John Stuart Mill, are branded as pigs.[27] Yet their concern, states Onfray, was to deconstruct myths, to get rid of gods, to provide solutions for the actual world, and to value pleasure and the common good.[28] In relation to art and aesthetics, Onfray argues, as we have seen, that Marcel Duchamp's *Fountain*, intended for exhibition in New York in 1917, was the point at which the dominant approach was exposed as nonsense.

Having rejected the dominant Kantian world view, Onfray advocates 'The Revolutionary Transformation of Individuals', based to a significant extent on Benthamite utilitarianism. While generally admiring Karl Marx and Michel Foucault, Onfray criticizes them for doing

> much damage to Anglo-Saxon Utilitarianism. First, they harmed it for reasons surrounding the intellectual and political power struggles of their time. Second, they harmed it by promoting excessive specialization: Foucault's sole focus on the panopticon, without concern for the project's totality, inspired him to write foolish things about Bentham. Hedonist utilitarianism is much more than a grocer's philosophy or the invention of modern totalitarianism! … It's a funny kind of grocer who pushes for the decriminalization of homosexuality (*Essay on Pederasty*, 1785!), the rights of minorities (women and children), a dignified status for animals who were cruelly tortured as if by executioners, and a humanization of the conditions of incarceration in *Panopticon*

> (1791). The supposed inventor of totalitarianism also wrote a catalog of the crimes committed by religion (*The Influence of Natural Religion Upon the Temporal Happiness of Mankind*, 1822), and called out the hypocrisy of politicians (*Book of Fallacies*, 1824). In *Deontology*, he subordinated politics to ethics; all hedonist politics is concerned with *the greatest good for the greatest number*. The goal remains valid.[29]

While some of the detail in this passage might be revised, and indeed a great deal added, Onfray has appreciated the radical challenge that Benthamism entails to the dominant Kantian world-view.

While Onfray praises Bentham for his Epicureanism, a far different assessment is offered by Cathy Gere in *Pain, Pleasure, and the Greater Good*. In her history of medical ethics, she allies herself with Onfray's dominant tradition and contrasts Benthamite utilitarianism, with its Epicurean foundations in materialism and the sensations of pain and pleasure, with the notions of autonomy, transcendent human dignity, self-determination and free consent, which she associates with Kant and Christian humanitarianism. According to Gere, in *A Table of the Springs of Action* Bentham 'established the framework that would unite medicine, utilitarianism and politics' for 150 years,[30] until 'the decisive victory' of patient autonomy over 'medical utility' at Robert Kennedy's American Senate hearings into health care and human experimentation in 1973.[31] 'In place of tradition, sentiment and rights,' notes Gere, 'Bentham insisted on the brute physicality of pain and pleasure' and thereby invented, without noticing it, a whole new discipline of 'moral physiology'.[32] The manipulation of human subjects by the application of pain and pleasure formed the basis of his proposed system of pauper panopticons. Taking particular exception to Bentham's use of the treadmill (or the walking wheel, as she terms it), Gere contends that 'the poor were to be manipulated in the spirit of training non-human animals' – a project that was eventually realized in the laboratories of the twentieth-century behavioural psychologists, where oppressed classes, who were 'deemed to have least to lose', were sacrificed for the sake of the greater good.[33] Hence, she draws a lineage from the utilitarianism of Bentham, through the deterministic and associationist psychological theories of James Mill and Edward Bain, to the twentieth-century behaviourists Edward Thorndike and B.F. Skinner. Echoing those who have linked utilitarianism with totalitarianism, she sees no essential moral distinction between fascist human experimentation in Hitler's Germany and American utilitarian medicine as practised in the years after the Second World War.[34]

Gere's contempt for utilitarianism appears to be all the more bitter since, as she confesses, she had once been 'a zealot of utility', but had eventually abandoned it, describing it as a 'delinquent … path', after finding an 'alternative, based on respect for others and self-respect'.[35] She tells us that 'utilitarianism can send scientists down the proverbial well-paved road to hell', that utilitarianism constitutes 'flagrant moral elitism', that Bentham had 'exposed the vein of moral nihilism in utilitarianism', that Skinner was '[e]very bit as bumptious' as Bentham, speaks of the 'totalitarian/utilitarian error', and refers to utilitarianism as being 'like a greased pig',[36] thus invoking the traditional characterization of Epicureanism by its opponents. 'The "concept of man" that stepped into the breach' was 'the vision of autonomy, dignity and freedom' found in Kant's moral philosophy. 'The activists and reformers of the 1960s found that their disgust with the utilitarian calculus of human experimentation resonated precisely with [Kant's] injunction that no rational being should be used as a means to an end.' Kantianism encapsulated 'the spirit of informed consent and the sanctity of autonomous decision making'.[37] But the victory over medical utilitarianism in the 1970s did not prove to be the end of the problem, according to Gere. In the 1980s two new disciplines emerged – neuroeconomics and behavioural economics – both explicitly indebted to Bentham: 'Unchained from the walking wheel of Bentham's Panopticon, Epicurus has been set to work greasing the machinery of global capitalism.'[38] There is, therefore, more work to be done, in Gere's view, to oppose the re-emergence and resurgence of utilitarianism.

Gere relies on emotive language and on literary fiction (Mr Gradgrind *et al.*)[39] as the basis for her condemnation of utilitarianism. A difficulty with her account is that she conflates the moral injunctions of the principle of utility with the psychological claim that sentient creatures are motivated by a desire for pleasure and an aversion to pain. Her assumption is that where there is experimentation that involves the investigation of pain and pleasure as stimuli to action, there also is utilitarianism. She states, for instance, that David Ferrier 'turned … psychology into an experimental science, driving utilitarianism deep into the emergent discipline of neurology', and that 'Skinner's mechanistic psychology more or less entailed extreme utilitarian ethics'.[40] She admits, moreover, that most of the scientists who gave evidence at the Kennedy hearing in 1973 did not defend their practices on the grounds of utilitarianism,[41] and even states that the physicians and researchers who she condemns considered themselves as having 'inalienable rights' to promote the greater good, which is a Kantian and not a utilitarian justification, and which she might have acknowledged given that she is aware that Bentham branded notions of inalienable rights as nonsense.[42]

Gere does at least appreciate that animal experimentation would have 'troubled' Bentham,[43] but points out that the logic of treating humans as animals was that, once animal experimentation had become acceptable, it was a short step to make human experimentation acceptable.[44] One such experiment that Gere finds particularly obnoxious was Robert Heath's anti-homosexual therapies, which were eventually discredited and replaced by an 'ethic of choice and self-determination'.[45] It need scarcely be said that Gere seems to be unaware of Bentham's writings on sexual morality, containing his arguments in favour of sexual liberty and in particular the decriminalization of male same-sex relationships.[46] There is, moreover, no antithesis between Bentham's utilitarianism and the notion of consent.[47] Bentham would, however, have objected to Kantian notions of 'inalienable dignity' and 'autonomy', and that every person had to be treated as an end in themselves and not as a means to an end,[48] as being either nonsensical or trivial. In *The Book of Fallacies*, for instance, Bentham referred to the claim that 'the end justifies the means' as the 'Atrocity-justifier's argument'. His criticism had been sparked by a report in a newspaper that the Peterloo Massacre of 16 August 1819 (the means) had been justified by the need to rescue the country from seditious meetings (the end). The danger and absurdity lay in treating some objective as an end and thereby justifying the obtainment of that end at any cost. The end might, for instance, be the acquisition of a penny loaf. The goodness of the end was 'indisputable', but that did not mean that one was justified either in giving a pound for it or in getting it for nothing by cutting the baker's throat. For Bentham, the good and evil associated with both the means and the end needed to be weighed against each other in order to decide whether an action was justified.[49] Finally it seems to be without irony that Gere, in her 'Afterword', places some hope for the future of humanity in her own delight at encouraging a threatened species of butterfly to thrive in her Californian garden[50] – Epicurus would have approved! Bentham, for his part, was not content merely to tend his own garden – though he did do that assiduously at Queen's Square Place – but had a much broader ambition of tending everyone's garden – of being, as his Guatemalan admirer José del Valle put it, the 'legislator of the world'.[51]

3. Bentham's critique of metaphysics

I have suggested above that Bentham found Epicureanism attractive because of its materialism and the associated rejection of any form of metaphysics. It is important, then, to explore how Bentham presented his own views in order to appreciate why he would have rejected any claim concerning the existence of a metaphysics of beauty, whatever form that metaphysics took, whether as a mathematical proportion and symmetry, a set of ideal forms or an inherent sense of the sublime and the beautiful akin to the notion of the moral sense. This brings us back to Bentham's ontology and epistemology. A difficulty in addressing this topic is that, since the revival of Bentham scholarship in the 1960s, it has suffered from two related problems. The first is that insufficient attention has been given to Bentham's ontology as the basis for his utilitarianism, and the second is that, where attention has been paid to it, fictions have often been confounded with fictitious entities. The confusion stems from Charles Kay Ogden's edition of *Bentham's Theory of Fictions*, published in 1932.[52] The title seems to have been Ogden's invention, while the content is arranged under main headings that Ogden also devised. Ogden's text is not one that Bentham himself organized, but consists in a compilation containing the whole of 'A Fragment on Ontology' and extracts from 'Rationale of Judicial Evidence', 'Essay on Language', 'Essay on Logic', 'Chrestomathia', and 'A Fragment on Government'. All this material is taken from the Bowring edition of Bentham's *Works*, and, with the exception of the extracts from 'Rationale of Judicial Evidence' and 'Fragment on Government', was edited by Bentham's physician Thomas Southwood Smith. The Bowring/Smith versions of 'Ontology', 'Language' and 'Logic' are themselves a mish-mash taken from Bentham's unpublished manuscripts.[53] Ogden, therefore, created his own mish-mash out of the Bowring/Smith mish-mash and called it Bentham's 'Theory of Fictions'.[54] Ogden did not recognize any important distinction between a fiction and a fictitious entity – to the text of *Theory of Fictions* he appended both a discussion of legal fictions from Bentham's *Rationale of Judicial Evidence* and an extract from Bentham's nephew George's *An Outline of a New System of Logic*, under the heading 'The Classification of Fictions', in which he provided succinct expositions of the various 'entities', including fictitious entities, that his uncle referred to.[55] Ogden's confounding of fictions and fictitious entities has been unreflectingly followed in much of the succeeding scholarship.[56] It is necessary, therefore, to disambiguate fictions and fictitious entities, and show the relation of the latter to real entities, in order to understand the philosophical basis of Bentham's materialism. The expositions of all these terms involve, in one way or another, the notions of truth and utility.[57]

We have seen above how the youthful Bentham reacted against what he viewed as the falsehood in the Thirty-nine Articles and the fictions relied on by Blackstone in his lectures on English law. In *A Fragment on Government*, published in 1776, his critique of a short passage in Blackstone's 'Introduction' to *Commentaries on the Laws of England*, Bentham remarked that English law was characterized by 'Fiction, tautology, technicality, circuity, irregularity, [and] inconsistency … . But above all the pestilential breath of Fiction poisons the sense of every instrument it comes near.'[58] In 'Constitutional Code Rationale', written in 1822, he noted: 'By fiction, in the sense in which it is used by lawyers, understand a false assertion which, though acknowledged to be false, is at the same time argued from, and acted upon, as if true.' He went on to argue that fiction served the sinister interest of lawyers and other officials on the particular occasions on which it was used, but more generally it served their interest and that of rulers together by producing 'demoralization' in the community as a whole. The 'object and effect' of demoralization was to cause men to regard with indifference, or even with approval, both 'the perpetration of injustice' and the employment of 'falshood – wilful, deliberate and self-conscious falshood – in a word *mendacity*' as a means of producing that injustice.[59] In the passage on fictions reproduced by Ogden, and taken from *Rationale of Judicial Evidence*, Bentham condemned fictions on the grounds that they consisted in falsehood and that their effect was mischievous: 'Fiction of any use to justice? Exactly as swindling is to trade?' Bentham went on to give examples of fictions in English law, including the common recovery whereby entails were 'barred', the addition of an *ac etiam* clause to writs whereby actions could be tried in the central common law courts that were not otherwise entitled to try them, and the action of ejectment for the trial of freehold title.[60] Throughout this passage lies, falsehoods and fictions are equated.[61] A fiction, therefore, was a proposition that was known to be false in fact. A fictitious entity, on the other hand, was not a proposition, but a term. In order to understand Bentham's notion of a fictitious entity, we need first to turn to the notion of a real entity.

In 'Essay on Logic', Bentham explained that the 'source of perception' – and, it might be added, the only source – was 'an individual portion of matter', 'a real, corporeal entity', '*a body*', by which an '*impression*' was made on '*sense*'. Strictly speaking, these impressions were the immediate source of perception, and the body itself but the '*secondary* and *comparatively* remote' source. The existence of the object of perception was, therefore, 'a subject of *inference* [rather] than of perception', and such inference was frequently found to be erroneous – we heard a sound, for instance, and assumed it was raining, but when we looked out of the window we saw that it was the wind rustling the leaves in a tree.[62] Hence, Bentham described a two-stage process by which the mind, or more specifically the perceptive faculty, experienced the physical universe – at the first stage, the physical object gave rise to an impression in the organs of perception, and at the second stage, the impression was recognized by the perceptive faculty in the mind. Knowledge of the physical world was inferential, because what we perceived were impressions and not the objects themselves. There were, therefore, two different, but related notions that Bentham termed perceptible real entities. The first were our own perceptions, whether impressions produced 'by the application of sensible objects to the organs of sense' or ideas 'brought to view by the recollection of these same objects'.[63] The second group were '*bodies* of all sorts'.[64] Again, he explained that these (he presumably meant impressions and ideas) were in fact the sole perceptible entities, while corporeal substances were inferential. He went on, however, to make a second distinction that also involved inference, namely a distinction within real entities between perceptible and inferential entities, the former being those of whose existence we were persuaded directly through perception, and the latter those of whose existence we were persuaded by a process of reasoning or reflection. With reference only to substances, the term perceptible real entities applied to corporeal substances, and inferential to incorporeal ones, that is to such inferential, because imperceptible, entities as the human soul, God, angels and devils. The soundness of the inference from perceptions to the existence of the corporeal body of which it was a perception was far stronger, Bentham noted, than that from the existence of corporeal to that of incorporeal substances:

> Suppose the non-existence of corporeal substances – of any hard corporeal substance that stands opposite to you – make this supposition and as soon as you have made it, act upon it, pain, the perception of pain, will at once bear witness against you, and be your punishment, your condign punishment. Suppose the non-existence of the above-mentioned inferential incorporeal substances, of any of them, or all of them, and the supposition made, act upon it accordingly – be the supposition conformable or not conformable to the truth of the case, at any rate no such

> immediate counter-evidence, no such immediate punishment, will follow.[65]

Inferential real entities, such as the human soul and God had never been perceived, and their reality 'can not, therefore, be considered otherwise than as a matter of *inference*'. If one were not persuaded of the inference, that is that the human soul or God were real entities, it was likely that one would assign the former to the class of fictitious entities, consisting of the aggregate of such 'psychical entities' as were said to compose the mind, and the latter to the class of non-entities.[66] To summarize, there were two inferences: the first, from perceptions to substances; the second, from substances perceived to substances unperceived. For Bentham, to assume the physical non-existence of entities that revealed themselves to us through sense perception would tend to produce evil consequences. Such evil consequences would not follow were we to assume the physical non-existence of entities that had not been perceived and were possibly not perceivable. The individual bodies that we did perceive and could be assumed to have physical existence were real entities.

Bentham did not only refer to real and fictitious entities, but to fabulous entities and also, as we have seen, to non-entities. The basic distinction, to which all others had to be referred, was that between real and fictitious entities: '*Real entities – fictitious entities* – under one or other of these denominations may be comprehended every object that ever was or can be present to any faculty of the human frame – to perception, memory, or imagination.' Bentham recognized that the term 'fictitious entity' seemed to involve a contradiction in that the term 'entity' suggested that the thing represented had existence, while the term 'fictitious' suggested that it did not. Why not, then, use the term 'non-entity'? Bentham answered that the 'root' of the contradiction lay in language, 'that instrument without which, though of itself it is nothing, nothing can be said, and scarce any thing can be done'.[67] Hence, while fictitious entities did not exist, the names of fictitious entities did exist (sounds and written words are, after all, perceptible): 'To language then – to language alone – it is that fictitious entities owe their existence – their impossible, yet indispensable existence.' Every name that existed in a language (Bentham presumably meant every name that would potentially make sense when placed in a proposition) was either the name of a real entity or the name of a fictitious entity.

> What will moreover be seen is, that the fiction – the mode of representation by which the fictitious entities thus created, in so far

as fictitious entities can be created, are dressed up in the garb, and placed upon the level, of real ones – is a contrivance but for which language – or at any rate language in any form superior to that of the language of the brute creation – could not have existence.[68]

It is important to note that Bentham refers to the fiction involved in the creation of fictitious entities, and not that fictitious entities were fictions. The fiction was the apparent predication of real existence to the subject represented by the name of a fictitious entity.[69] In other words, to claim that the subject so represented had physical existence would be a falsehood, but unless we spoke as though it did have existence, our language would not rise above that of animals, and since thought was dependent on language, our thought would not rise above that of animals. Bentham explained that names were first applied to real entities, and thereby an association formed between the name and the reality of the object to which it was assigned. There had then arisen 'a very natural propensity' to ascribe reality to every object given a name, including fictitious entities.[70]

Bentham warned against confusing fictitious entities with fabulous entities, which were 'either fabulous persons or fabulous things'. They were 'supposed material objects of which the separate existence is capable of becoming a subject of belief: and of which accordingly the same sort of picture is capable of being drawn in the mind as of any really existent object'.[71] Fabulous entities were, therefore, created by the imagination, and consisted of a combination of entities that had not been perceived, but if the fabulous entity did exist, it would be perceivable: for instance a golden mountain, a diamond billiard ball, Hamlet, and so forth. Fictitious entities, on the other hand, although represented by noun substantives, did not, unlike fabulous entities, 'raise up in the mind any correspondent image'.[72] Bentham explained the notion of non-existence in terms of the annihilation of physical substance or body:

> Of body … the annihilation is conceivable without difficulty. Why? because in whatsoever place, that is within whatsoever portion of space, within whatsoever receptacle composed of mere space, any body is at any given time conceived to be, it may thenceforward be conceived to be removed from that place, and so successively from any and every other portion of space.[73]

It was through the idea of absence that 'the transcendent and awful idea of non-existence' was 'attained'. Take a body existing in a particular place, and suppose it non-existing in that place, 'you suppose its *absence*, its *relative* non-existence: expell it in like manner from every place, you suppose its *absolute* non-existence'. An entity was either in existence or not in existence: there was no other possible state for an entity to be in.[74] A fabulous entity, then, was, in strictness, a non-entity, which, in turn, was the absence of any real entity.

How, then, did Bentham make sense of fictitious entities with their necessary, but merely linguistic existence? As he pointed out, in law – which was, of course, his main philosophical and practical concern – many of the leading terms, such as right, duty, obligation and power, did not correspond to any physical thing. Similarly, the words 'matter', 'form', 'quantity', 'quality', 'relation', 'place', 'time', 'motion' and 'action', together with their related ideas, all designated fictitious entities.[75] They were like terms in algebra, which were used as shorthand to represent more complex entities. Such terms, the names of fictitious entities, made sense insofar as they could be expounded by showing their connection with real entities, objects that existed in the physical world. One took a proposition that contained the name of a fictitious entity and reformulated it in a proposition that had the same meaning but contained the names only of real entities, or were closer to real entities (one might say, for instance, that a person enjoyed liberty when he had the capacity to move his limbs without impediment, wherein motion or movement was a step closer to the physical world than liberty). Bentham gave the name 'paraphrasis' to this process of demonstrating the relationship of the names of fictitious entities or abstract terms to real entities or objects that had physical existence. Insofar as this operation could be successfully carried out, the proposition containing the abstract term made sense; insofar as there existed no physical 'root' for the abstract term, the proposition in which it was contained made no sense. Hence, it made sense to talk about a legal right, where it was possible to identify the legislator who had commanded its creation and enforcement, whereas it made no sense to talk about a natural right, because there was no such legislator.[76]

In short, the name of a fictitious entity did not represent an object that had physical existence, but it facilitated discourse to speak of it as though it did exist. It made sense to say that a certain person lay under an obligation to another person, or enjoyed a right, but no one had ever seen, heard, touched, tasted, smelled or, assuming a sixth sense,[77] had sex with an obligation or a right. A proposition including the term 'obligation' or the term 'right' would make sense if it could be expounded by paraphrasis, that is if it could be translated into another proposition with the same import but which contained only real entities. According to Bentham, the only source of knowledge was sense-perception. The only source from which sense-perception could be derived was the physical substance of the universe. There were no innate ideas. To the objection, made by Platonists and Kantians, that we must have the innate idea of a perfect circle in order to recognize that a particular geometric shape is a circle, Bentham would have responded that there is no such thing in the physical universe as a perfect circle, that the only place that a perfect circle exists is in the imagination, and that the idea is created by the mind's power of abstraction, based on all the imperfect circles that we have encountered in the physical world. Similarly, the proposition $1 + 1 = 2$ would in itself be meaningless for Bentham – there is no innate mathematics in the mind. The sum $1 + 1 = 2$ is an abstraction, derived, for example, from the experience of taking an apple, and then taking another apple, placing them next to each other, and calling the resulting situation 'two' apples. The proposition makes sense only when it is related to objects in the physical world. When, in his account of paraphrasis, Bentham referred to the 'fictitious proposition' that 'An obligation is incumbent on a man',[78] he did not mean that this proposition was a legal fiction or any other sort of fiction. It might, of course, have been false to state that, in a certain situation, a certain person lay under a legal obligation, but equally it might have been true. A fiction was a lie, but a proposition containing a fictitious entity or several fictitious entities might be true: a true fiction was a contradiction in terms.[79]

4. Aesthetics as sympathy and antipathy

We can now see why, for Bentham, talk about any notion of the sublime or the beautiful that was based on some form of metaphysics, in other words appealed to some non-physical quality, was so much nonsense. If the proposition that some entity was beautiful were to make sense, the notion of 'beautiful' had to be expounded by the process of paraphrasis, and thus be shown to have its root in real entities. In the end, for me to say that something was beautiful was to say nothing more than that I liked that thing, and to say that I liked that thing was to say that it gave me pleasure. Conversely, for me to say that something was ugly made sense only if it meant that the thing in question gave me pain.[80] The point was that, for Bentham, feelings of pleasure and pain were real entities. It was this assumption that underlay his threefold division of moral theories into the principle of utility, the principle of asceticism and the principle of sympathy and antipathy or of caprice. An adherent of the principle of utility, noted Bentham, 'approves or disapproves of every action whatsoever, according to the tendency which it appears to have to augment or diminish the happiness of the party whose interest is in question', where happiness was understood as a balance of pleasure over pain.[81] To talk about the principle of utility made sense because it was founded on the real entities of pleasure and pain. All rival theories, which were necessarily wrong if the principle of utility were right, fell into two groups. The first group, which consisted in variants of the principle of asceticism, was 'constantly opposed' to the principle of utility; while the second, which consisted in variants of the principle of sympathy and antipathy, was 'sometimes opposed to it, and sometimes not'. The adherent of the principle of asceticism 'approves or disapproves of any action, according to the tendency which it appears to have to augment or diminish the happiness of the party whose interest is in question; but in an inverse manner [to the principle of utility]: approving of actions in as far as they tend to diminish his happiness; disapproving of them in as far as they tend to augment it'. An adherent of this principle was 'any one who reprobates any the least particle of pleasure, as such, from whatever source derived'. The principle had been adopted by 'a set of religionists', who had done so in the hope of avoiding punishment in an afterlife, and by 'a set of moralists', namely the Stoics, who had condemned what they had considered to be the 'gross' pleasures of the body in order to pursue whatever was 'refined', which they had called 'the honourable, the glorious, the reputable, the becoming, the *honestum*, the *decorum*', in fact any thing but pleasure. Both branches of ascetics had come together 'upon various occasions against the common enemy, the partisan of the principle of utility, whom they joined in branding with the odious name of Epicurean'.[82]

The adherent of the principle of sympathy and antipathy approved or disapproved of actions, neither on account of their tendency to increase, nor on account of their tendency to decrease, the happiness of the persons affected by them, 'but merely because a man finds himself disposed to approve or disapprove of them: holding up that approbation or disapprobation as a sufficient reason for itself, and disclaiming the necessity of looking out for any extrinsic ground'. The amount of punishment that the adherent of the principle of sympathy and antipathy attached to any action was measured by the degree of his dislike: 'if you hate much, punish much; if you hate little, punish little: punish as you hate. If you hate not at all, punish not at all: the fine feelings of the soul are not to be overborne by the harsh and rugged dictates of political utility.'[83] All so-called standards of right and wrong, apart from the principles of utility and asceticism, were in fact reducible to the principle of sympathy and antipathy. By dressing up his own opinions or sentiments in the garb of some fictional standard, whether termed the moral sense, common sense, the law of nature, right reason, or repugnancy to nature, the adherent of the principle of sympathy and antipathy attempted both to avoid 'the obligation of appealing to any external standard' and to persuade others to take his own sentiments as authoritative.[84] The notion of 'repugnancy to nature' was a particular aspect of the principle of sympathy and antipathy that Bentham criticized in his later writings on sexual morality, but he had made the same point, as he noted, in *An Introduction to the Principles of Morals and Legislation*.[85] Bentham there explained that acts, such as the exposing of children by the Greeks and Romans, were often condemned, 'upon the principle of antipathy', for being '*unnautral*', but all that unnatural meant, if it meant anything, was 'unfrequent'. However, the usual complaint was that the act was all too frequent. The term 'unnatural' expressed nothing but 'the disposition of the person who is talking of it: the disposition he is in to be angry at the thoughts of it'. The person who claimed that an act was unnatural was in fact saying that he did not like to practise it and, therefore, it should not be practised by others.[86] There was no 'difference in taste' and no 'difference in opinion' from which the adherent of the principle of sympathy and antipathy might not 'extract a ground of punishment'.[87]

Hence, to say, I like this, or, I like that, and so ought you (or so must you), was to be an adherent of the principle of sympathy and antipathy. Taste was capricious, and herein lay Bentham's opposition to the notion of taste. Insofar as those who referred to taste were appealing, or pretending to appeal, to some metaphysical standard, they were talking nonsense; but what they were in fact doing was making a claim that their own opinion was to be the standard for others. This was as much as to say that their pleasure was more important than any other person's pleasure, or perhaps that the pleasure of persons of their social class – persons who shared a similar place in 'the conjoint scales of power, opulence and factitious dignity'[88] – were more important than those of another social class. This was the claim made by the highest class, the aristocracy, and they had the advantage that their wealth and power made the claim appear plausible, and even be accepted, by their inferiors in power, wealth and titles. Bentham remarked that, 'The Democratical [section of the community] refers or soon will refer every thing to the standard of Utility … the Aristocratical, to as great an extent and as long as possible, to the standard of taste: itself being the arbiter of taste'.[89]

The adherent of the principle of utility had no basis for claiming that the pleasure of one person was worth more than the equal pleasure of any other person, and hence ruled out all claims based on superiority of taste. It might be objected that the 'person of taste', when thinking of an object or action of which he disapproved, experienced pain as a result, and that such pain should be taken into account by the adherent of the principle of utility. Moreover, if the pain was sufficiently intense, or experienced by a sufficiently large number of people, then the adherent of the principle of utility should condemn the object or action in question. Bentham's response would be that the problem did not lie in the object or action complained about, but in the attitude, often founded in prejudice, of the complainant.

An explanation of this point requires a brief discussion of sanctions. For Bentham, a sanction was a source of pain and pleasure. In *An Introduction to the Principles of Morals and Legislation* he identified four sanctions: the physical sanction arose 'from the ordinary course of nature'; the political sanction from an official acting under the authority of the state; the moral or popular sanction from members of the community in general; and the religious sanction from a supernatural being.[90] In his later writings, Bentham added the sympathetic and antipathetic sanctions, which were imposed by specific or 'assignable' individuals, as opposed to the moral sanction where there were no assignable persons as such. An instance of the operation of the sympathetic sanction occurred when an individual imposed some pain on a person who had harmed his friend, while an instance of the operation of the antipathetic sanction occurred when an individual imposed some pain on a person who had benefited his enemy.[91] The sympathetic and antipathetic sanctions arose, therefore, from pre-existing feelings of sympathy and antipathy, which themselves might be based on prejudices of various kinds. Hence, a person who today we would term 'homophobic' would be so-called because of his inclination to punish two males who he believes or imagines are experiencing pleasure from having sex with each other. The males in question consent and undertake the action because it gives them or they expect it to give them pleasure. The observer condemns it because the thought of it causes him pain. That pain arises from the antipathetic sanction, that is from his own internal beliefs, and not from the action itself. Addressing the adherent of the principle of sympathy and antipathy, Bentham stated: 'it is for you to get the better of your antipathy, not for him [the actor of a non-mischievous action] to truckle to it'.[92] The point is that, if the action is prevented, the pain is not experienced, but neither is the pleasure of the actors. If the prejudice is removed, the pain is not experienced, but the pleasure of the actors remains. Hence, the latter course is that which is approved by the adherent of the principle of utility.

In summary, there was no independent value of beauty to which the 'person of taste' could claim privileged access; all that taste reflected was the pleasure that one gained from a particular object or state of affairs. Once this was recognized, since no one person's pleasure was more important than that of another person's equal pleasure, no one person's 'taste' could be regarded as superior to that of any other person's. It took Bentham many years and many projects to work through the implications of the materialist, Epicurean world-view that he had adopted, and which incorporated a radical scepticism towards the metaphysics that had hitherto been the dominant tradition in the history of ideas, but as he did so, established institutions and practices in law, religion, politics and economics became the subject of ferocious criticism, and the systems of thought on which they rested were attacked. Bentham's utilitarianism brought the radical Epicurean tradition into the mainstream, but only briefly. John Stuart Mill, who was Bentham's most influential successor in the utilitarian tradition, while not rejecting his Epicurean legacy, began the retreat from outright materialism back towards metaphysics through his condemnation of Bentham's critique of taste[93] and with his distinction between higher and lower pleasures and his associated claim that it was 'better to be a human being dissatisfied than a pig satisfied; better to be Socrates dissatisfied than a fool satisfied'.[94] Mill would have disapproved of Duchamp's *Fountain*, but Bentham would have been greatly amused by it.

Notes

1 Hick, 2017, 17–19.
2 Onfray, 2015, 39.
3 Kuh, 1962, 90–2.
4 Bentham, ed. Crimmins and Fuller, 2011, 39–40 n.
5 Bentham, ed. Crimmins and Fuller, 2011, 35–6.
6 Bentham, ed. Crimmins and Fuller, 2011, 31.
7 Stone, 2016.
8 Bentham, ed. Goldworth, 1983, 300; Bentham, ed. Sprigge, 1968, 34–44, 53–5. The surviving parts of Bentham's translation are at British Library, Additional MS 33,537, fos. 85–120, and Add. MS 33,544, fos. 132–7.
9 Charles Abbot (1757–1829), after distinguishing himself as speaker of the House of Commons 1802–17, was created Baron Colchester.
10 The phrase 'Every thing is now as it should be' had been used by William Blackstone in Blackstone, 1765–9, iv. 49. Bentham took it to be characteristic of Blackstone's conservatism. For Bentham on Blackstone see Schofield, 2018, 23–40.

11 BL Add. MS 33,537, fo. 99. (Thanks to Chris Riley for this reference.)
12 Bentham, ed. Bowring, 1843 [hereafter Bowring], x. 54.
13 Bentham, ed. Goldworth, 1983, 293; Bowring, 1843, x. 45.
14 These writings include 'Essay on Logic', 'Essay on Universal Grammar' and 'Essay on Nomenclature and Classification', for the latter of which see Bentham, ed. Smith and Burston, 1983, 139–276.
15 While Epicureanism was often the subject of disdain in the early modern period, there were many influential writers who were attracted to the doctrine: see Wilson, 2009, 266–86.
16 Bowring, 1843, x. 27.
17 There are citations to Lucretius at UC xxvii. 1 (not dated, but probably written in the early to mid-1770s) and xcvi. 220 (not dated, but again probably written in the early to mid-1770s). Four lines from *De rerum natura* (Book v, lines 1011–14) are reproduced in 'Principles of the Civil Code', at Bowring, 1843, i. 349. Bentham mistakenly attributes a quotation to Lucretius at BL Add. MS 29,809, fo. 180 (24 February 1819) that actually occurs in Publius Papinius Statius, *Thebaid*, III. 66.
18 On Bentham's fear of ghosts see Schofield, 2009, 1–2.
19 See UC c. 11. (Thanks to Rex Mixon for this reference and general advice on Bentham's relationship to Epicurus.) See further Hoesch, 2018; Schofield, 2019. Bentham's citation of Horace is briefly discussed in Rosen, 2003, 15–16, a work that explores more generally the link between Epicureanism and utilitarianism with particular reference to the notion of justice.
20 See UC clxi. 501 (1 January 1818), reproduced in *Not Paul, but Jesus*, Vol. III: *Doctrine*.
21 UC clxi. 227 (19 December 1817).
22 See UC xiv. 57 (9 September 1814). The text of this folio is reproduced at Bentham, ed. Goldworth, 1983, 135, but these notes, and several others, at the top of the folio are not recorded.
23 Bentham, ed. Goldworth, 1983, 135–9.
24 See Bentham, ed. Sprigge, 1968, 59–60.
25 Anon, 1745, 9: 'Harum praeterea sensus est brevis, praeteritarumque in suavis saepe recordatio, et erubescenda.'
26 Bentham, ed. Goldworth, 1983, 139–41.
27 For the ancient origins of this insult see Warren, 2002, 129–49.
28 Onfray, 2015, 7–11.
29 Onfray, 2015, 137–8. The points about grocers and totalitarianism reflect the criticisms of utilitarianism made by Marx and Foucault respectively.
30 Gere, 2017, 114. For *Table of the Springs of Action*, first published in 1817, see Goldworth, 1983, 79–115 (where unfortunately, no doubt due to typesetting and production constraints, it does not appear in the form of the table originally conceived by Bentham).
31 Gere, 2017, 20.
32 Gere, 2017, 92.
33 Gere, 2017, 96–7, 129.
34 Gere, 2017, 44.
35 Gere, 2017, 24, 221.
36 Gere, 2017, 26, 45–6, 92, 172–3, 189, 203.
37 Gere, 2017, 189.
38 Gere, 2017, 210.
39 For a reassessment of the relationship between utilitarianism and literature in the nineteenth century see Blake, 2009.
40 Gere, 2017, 143, 172.
41 Gere, 2017, 58.
42 Gere, 2017, 43, 93.
43 Bentham is well known for a statement at Bentham, ed. Burns and Hart, 1970, 282–3 n., that what mattered was not whether animals could reason but whether they could suffer. An important statement of his position in relation to animal welfare appears in a letter dated 4 March 1825 published in the *Morning Chronicle*, 9 March 1825, and reproduced in Bowring, 1843, X. 549–50.
44 Gere, 2017, 160–1.
45 Gere, 2017, 92–4.
46 See Bentham, ed. Schofield *et al.*, 2014.

47 See, for instance, Bentham, ed. Schofield *et al.*, 2014, 3, 59, 138–9.
48 Gere, 2017, 199, 203.
49 Bentham, ed. Schofield, 2015, 327–8. For Bentham's view that dignity presented an 'idea' that was 'not altogether a very determinate one', namely the quality in a person by which respect towards him was produced in others, see Bentham, ed. Schofield, 1989, 48, and his criticism of dignity as a 'pretence' for 'depredation' on the part of rulers see Bentham, ed. Schofield, 2015, 320.
50 Gere, 2017, 236–7.
51 See Bentham, ed. Schofield and Harris, 1998, 370.
52 Ogden, 1932.
53 Bentham envisaged that the material that Smith presented in these three essays – namely 'Ontology', 'Logic', and 'Language' – would appear in a single work under the title of 'Essay on Logic'.
54 Bentham does not refer to this material as 'Theory of Fictions' – moreover, there is (as yet) no evidence that he ever used this phrase. The most suggestive passage that I have found for Ogden's phrase 'theory of fictions' is at BL Add. MS 33,550, fo. 4: 'It was for want of a clear conception of this distinction [i.e. between names of real entities and names of fictitious entities] that many an empty name is considered as representative of a correspondent reality: in a word, that mere fictions are in abundance regarded as realities.' Bentham's point here was that the distinction had led him to see that such terms were not capable of being defined *per genus et differentiam*, but only through paraphrasis.
55 See Ogden, 1932, 151–6, reproducing extracts from George Bentham, 1827. George Bentham had worked intensively on Bentham's writings on logic when living with his uncle at Queen's Square Place.
56 In his essay on Bentham's theory of probability (though it is in large measure concerned with Bentham's ontology), G.J. Postema, for instance, refers indiscriminately to fictions and fictitious entities: see Postema, 1983, 37–64. Following Postema's account of Bentham's ontology, Michael Quinn, 2013, purportedly compares Bentham and Fuller on legal fictions, but, having argued that Bentham viewed any proposition involving a fictitious entity as a fiction, spends much of the article comparing Bentham on fictitious entities with Fuller on legal fictions. Quinn also mistakenly equates fallacies with fictions (474). A further error made by some commentators, and which seems to originate with Mack, 1962, 180–4, is that Bentham's logic of the will is concerned with fictions.
57 Bentham considered these subject-matters under the general heading of 'logic'. 'By Logic taken at large', he explained, 'may be understood the art of applying to best advantage to the purpose of discourse the faculty of discourse', and referred to it as 'this all-comprehensive art and science'. See Bentham, ed. Schofield, 2015, 408 n. The notion of 'best advantage' links Bentham's exposition to the principle of utility. Alternatively, Bentham defined logic as 'the art, which has for its object or end in view, the giving to the best advantage, direction to the human mind and thence to the whole human frame, in its pursuit of any object or purpose, to the attainment of which it is capable of being applied.' UC ci. 92 (3 August 1814). He went on to state that, 'Of the art and science of logic the prime, and that the most immediate, use is the establishment of clear and determinate ideas' and that this objective would be achieved through such operations as methodization, distinction, definition, division and exposition. See UC ci. 103 (5 August 1814). Given that the pursuit of well-being was 'the end of every action', logic had the same end. See UC ci. 107 (25 September 1815).
58 See Bentham, ed. Burns and Hart, 1977, 392–501 at 411 n.
59 Bentham, ed. Schofield, 1989, 267–9.
60 See Baker, 1990, 54–6, 319–21, and 341–3, for explanations of the *ac etiam* clause, the common recovery and the action of ejectment respectively.
61 Bowring, 1843, vii. 283–7.
62 UC ci. 118 (25 July 1814).
63 In distinguishing between impressions and ideas, Bentham was following David Hume: see Hume, ed. Norton and Norton, 2007, i. 7.
64 UC cii. 13–14 (26–7 September 1814).
65 UC cii. 15 (25 September 1814).
66 UC cii. 9–11 (27 September 1814).
67 UC cii. 21 (23 September 1814).
68 UC cii. 23 (23 September 1814).

69 See UC cii. 25 (23 September 1814): 'Of fictitious entities, whatsoever is predicated is not, consistently with strict truth, predicated ... of any thing but their respective names.'

70 UC cii. 24 (23 September 1814). See UC ci. 340 (7 August 1814): 'Words, viz. words employed to serve as names, being the only instruments by which, in the absence of *things*, viz. the *substances*, themselves, the ideas of them can be presented to the mind, hence, wheresoever a word is seen which to appearance is employed in the character of a *name*, a natural and abundantly extensive consequence is – a disposition and propensity to suppose the existence, the real existence, of a correspondent object – of a correspondent thing – of a thing to which it ministers in the character of a name.'

71 UC ci. 342 (7 August 1814).

72 UC ci. 322 (7 August 1814).

73 UC cii. 38 (26 September 1814).

74 UC cii. 74–5 (2–3 October 1814).

75 See UC cii. 35–50 (25–9 September 1814).

76 This was the thrust of Bentham's critique of the French Declaration of the Rights of Man in 'Nonsense upon Stilts': see Bentham, ed. Schofield *et al.*, 2002, 317–401.

77 See Bentham, ed. Schofield *et al.*, 2014, 51–3.

78 UC ci. 222 (23 August 1814).

79 See further Schofield, 2015.

80 For a full account see Schofield, ed. Zhai and Quinn, 2014, 90–118.

81 Bentham, ed. Burns and Hart, 1970, 11–13.

82 Bentham, ed. Burns and Hart, 1970, 17–19.

83 Bentham, ed. Burns and Hart, 1970, 25.

84 Bentham, ed. Burns and Hart, 1970, 25–6 & n.

85 See Bentham, ed. Schofield *et al.*, 2014, 6–8, 132.

86 Bentham, ed. Burns and Hart, 1970, 27–8 n.

87 Bentham, ed. Burns and Hart, 1970, 29.

88 Bentham, ed. Schofield, 1989, 144.

89 Bentham to Dumont, 29 November 1821: Bentham, ed. Conway, 1994, 445.

90 Bentham, ed. Burns and Hart, 1970, 35.

91 Bentham to Étienne Dumont, 29 November 1821, Bentham, ed. Conway, 1994, 444, and Bentham to Dumont, 26 May 1822: Bentham, ed. Fuller, 2000, 86–7; and Bentham, ed. Goldworth, 1983, 201–5, 277–8.

92 Bentham, ed. Burns and Hart, 1970, 29 n. cf. Bentham, ed. Burns and Hart, 1970, 32, where in a discussion of the distinction between the motives for action and the proper grounds of action, Bentham states: 'Antipathy ... can never be a right ground of action.'

93 See 'Bentham', first published in 1838, in Mill, ed. Robson *et al.*, 1969, 75–115 at 113.

94 See 'Utilitarianism', first published in 1861, in Mill, ed. Robson *et al.*, 1969, 203–59 at 212.

References

Anon. *Ethices Compendium in Usum Juventutis Academicae*. Oxford: Edward Broughton, 1745.

Baker, J.H. *An Introduction to English Legal History*. 3rd ed. London: Butterworth, 1990.

Bentham, G. *An Outline of a New System of Logic, with a Critical Examination of Dr. Whately's 'Elements of Logic'*. London: Hunt and Clarke, 1827.

Bentham, J. 'A Fragment on Government', in *A Comment on the Commentaries and A Fragment on Government* (*CW*), eds. J.H. Burns and H.L.A. Hart. London: Athlone Press, 1977.

Bentham, J. *An Introduction to the Principles of Morals and Legislation* (*CW*), eds. J.H. Burns and H.L.A. Hart. London: Athlone Press, 1970.

Bentham, J. *'Legislator of the World': Writings on Codification, Law, and Education* (*CW*), eds. P. Schofield and J. Harris. Oxford: Clarendon Press, 1998.

Bentham, J. *Not Paul, but Jesus*, Vol. III: *Doctrine*. London: Bentham Project, UCL, 2012 [http://discovery.ucl.ac.uk/1392179/3/npbj.pdf].

Bentham, J. *Chrestomathia* (*CW*), eds. M.J. Smith and W.H. Burston. Oxford: Clarendon Press, 1983.

Bentham, J. *Church-of-Englandism and its Catechism Examined* (*CW*), eds. J.E. Crimmins and C. Fuller. Oxford: Clarendon Press, 2011.

Bentham, J. *Deontology: Together with A Table of the Springs of Action and Article on Utilitarianism* (*CW*), ed. A. Goldworth. Oxford: Clarendon Press, 1983.

Bentham, J. *First Principles Preparatory to Constitutional Code* (*CW*), ed. P. Schofield. Oxford: Clarendon Press, 1989.

Bentham, J. *Of Sexual Irregularities, and other Writings on Sexual Morality* (*CW*), eds. P. Schofield, C. Pease-Watkin, and Michael Quinn. Oxford: Clarendon Press, 2014.

Bentham, J. *Rights, Representation, and Reform: Nonsense upon Stilts and other Writings on the French Revolution* (*CW*), eds. P. Schofield, C. Pease-Watkin, and C. Blamires. Oxford: Clarendon Press, 2002.

Bentham, J. *The Book of Fallacies* (*CW*), ed. P. Schofield. Oxford: Clarendon Press, 2015.

Bentham, J. *The Correspondence of Jeremy Bentham: Volume I* (*CW*), ed. T.L.S. Sprigge. London: Athlone Press, 1968.

Bentham, J. *The Correspondence of Jeremy Bentham: Volume X* (*CW*), ed. S. Conway. Oxford: Clarendon Press, 1994.

Bentham, J. *The Correspondence of Jeremy Bentham: Volume XI* (*CW*), ed. C. Fuller. Oxford: Clarendon Press, 2000.

Bentham, J. *The Works of Jeremy Bentham*, ed. John Bowring. 11 vols. Edinburgh: William Tait, 1838–43.

Blackstone, W. *Commentaries on the Laws of England*. 4 vols. Oxford: Clarendon Press, 1765–9.

Blake, K. *Pleasures of Benthamism: Victorian Literature, Utility, Political Economy*. Oxford: Oxford University Press, 2009.

Gere, C. *Pain, Pleasure, and the Greater Good: From the Panopticon to the Skinner Box and Beyond*. Chicago: University of Chicago Press, 2017.

Hick, D.H. *Introducing Aesthetics and the Philosophy of Art*. 2nd ed. London: Bloomsbury, 2017.

Hoesch, M. 'From Theory to Practice: Bentham's Reception of Helvétius', *Utilitas* 30:3 (2018): 294–316.

Hume, D. *A Treatise of Human Nature*, eds. D.F. Norton and M.J. Norton. 2 vols. Oxford: Clarendon Press, 2007.

Kuh, K. *The Artist's Voice: Talks with Seventeen Artists*. New York and Evanston, IL: Harper and Row, 1962.

Mack, M. *Jeremy Bentham: An Odyssey of Ideas 1748–92*. London: Heinemann, 1962.

Mill, J.S. 'Bentham' [1838], in *Essays on Ethics, Religion and Society* (*Collected Works: Volume X*), eds. J.M. Robson, F.E.L. Priestley, and D.P. Dryer, 75–115. Toronto: University of Toronto Press; London: Routledge, 1969.

Mill, John Stuart. 'Utilitarianism' [1861], in *Essays on Ethics, Religion and Society (Collected Works: Volume X)*, eds. J.M. Robson, F.E.L. Priestley, and D.P. Dryer, 203–59. Toronto: University of Toronto Press; London: Routledge, 1969.

Ogden, C.K. *Bentham's Theory of Fictions*. London: Kegan Paul, 1932.

Onfray, M. *A Hedonist Manifesto: The Power to Exist*, trans. J. McClellan. New York: Columbia University Press, 2015.

Postema, G.J. 'Fact, Fictions, and Law: Bentham on the Foundations of Evidence', in *Facts in Law*, ed. W. Twining. Wiesbaden: Franz Steiner, 1983.

Quinn, Michael. 'Fuller on Legal Fictions: A Benthamic Perspective', *International Journal of Law in Context* 9:4 (2013): 466–84.

Rosen, F. *Classical Utilitarianism from Hume to Mill*. London: Routledge, 2003.

Schofield, P. *Utility and Democracy: The Political Thought of Jeremy Bentham*. Oxford: Oxford University Press, 2009.

Schofield, P. 'Jeremy Bentham on Taste, Sex, and Religion', in *Bentham's Theory of Law and Public Opinion*, eds. X. Zhai and Michael Quinn. Cambridge: Cambridge University Press, 2014.

Schofield, P. 'Jeremy Bentham on Utility and Truth', *History of European Ideas* 41:8 (2015): 1125–42.

Schofield, P. 'The "Least Repulsive" Work on a "Repulsive Subject": Jeremy Bentham on William Blackstone's *Commentaries on the Laws of England*', in *Blackstone and His Critics*, eds. A. Page and W. Prest. Oxford: Hart Publishing, 2018.

Schofield, P. '"The First Steps Rightly Directed in the Track of Legislation": Jeremy Bentham on Cesare Beccaria's *Essay on Crimes and Punishments*', *Diciottesimo secolo* 4 (2019): 65–74.

Stone, N. 'Jeremy Bentham's Westminster poems', *Camden: A Liberal Arts Magazine*, Summer 2016, 85–8.

Warren, J. *Epicurus and Democritean Ethics: An Archaeology of Ataraxia*. Cambridge: Cambridge University Press, 2002.

Wilson, C. 'Epicureanism in Early Modern Philosophy', in *The Cambridge Companion to Epicureanism*, ed. J. Warren. Cambridge: Cambridge University Press, 2009.

Chapter 2
Not Kant, but Bentham: On taste

Frances Ferguson

1. Kant avec Bentham

The history of modern aesthetic thought is usually traced to Immanuel Kant and his *Critique of the Power of Judgment,* with an obligatory nod to the German philosopher Alexander Gottlieb Baumgarten, who had first used the term 'aesthetics' in 1735 to identify judgements of taste.[1] Kant's place in modern aesthetic thought is so secure that it commands acknowledgement: even writers who oppose it root and branch feel the need to frame their work as a response to it. Bentham, by contrast, has scarcely figured in discussions of aesthetics, in spite of his avowed interest in measuring actions and objects in terms of their ability to generate pleasure and losses to it.

Kant's account of aesthetics revolved around individual autonomy, and he treated aesthetic judgement as an emblem of the freedom of individuals, their ability to form judgements themselves even when others did not share them. Bentham's first-personal stance, by contrast, was seen to be mired, on one hand, in sensory experience that could not move past its commitment to 'number one' and, on the other, to strategic thinking that was all too oriented to outcomes. Kantian aesthetics aimed to achieve a first-personal experience that was at the same time disinterested – that is, unconcerned with the actual existence of the aesthetic object and detached from immediate satisfactions. Bentham was seen to suggest that judging subjects thought only about improving their situations. To support this view of Bentham's thought, literary critics and aesthetic historians cited John Stuart Mill's remark that Bentham 'says, somewhere in his works, that "quantity of pleasure being equal, push-pin is as good as poetry".'[2] Subsequent readers felt no need to look to Bentham for illumination on anything like aesthetic pleasure, because Mill had painted Bentham as a philistine. Mill conceded that Bentham was an admirer of music and even 'painting, sculpture and the other arts addressed to the eye', but he accused Bentham of disparaging 'All poetry [as] misrepresentation'.[3] Bentham's philosophy could, in Mill's words, 'teach the means of organizing and regulating the merely *business* part of the social arrangement'[4] but it could not speak to emotions such as love or religious feeling. Bentham's intellectual project was thought to be utilitarian in the narrowest sense, both aesthetic and anti-aesthetic.

In the following discussion, I affirm the recurrent consensus that Kant and Bentham lay out opposed positions, but I argue that Bentham should be credited with a significant and expansive account of aesthetic judgement. Although Kant and Bentham did not address one another's views directly, juxtaposing their positions on taste helps to focus their foundational questions and their characteristic answers. Kant's thinking about aesthetics springs from his sense of the inadequacy of explanations of aesthetic feeling if those explanations can be resolved into cognitive statements about what objects are or statements about sensory satisfaction. The reflective judgement of aesthetics is provoked by perceptual experience, in Kant's view, but it quickly shows itself to exceed the sensory experience that occasions it. Sexuality does not figure in any of his discussions of aesthetic judgement, but appears, instead, in *The Metaphysics of Morals,* in an itemization of the duties of spouses to one another. 'In this act a human being makes himself into a thing,' a situation that is only admissible because 'while one person is acquired by the other *as if it were a thing,* the one who is acquired acquires the other in turn; for in this way each reclaims itself and restores its personality'.[5]

In contrast to Kant, Bentham highlighted the importance of sexual appetite in 'Of Sexual Irregularities' and *Not Paul, but Jesus*, expanding the catalogue of senses from five to six to include the sexual sense, which he termed Sextus and abbreviated in his manuscripts as 'Sex'.[6] He thus reserved a central place for sexual experience in his thinking about taste. In addition to installing sensory experience – and sexuality considered as sensory experience in its most intense form – in taste, Bentham gave a public face to sexuality. In other words, he analysed the legal system as a social transcendental, treating it as an entity that needed to be considered as a self-consistent whole (rather than the iteration of laws tested primarily by their longevity, which he took William Blackstone to have laid out in his *Commentaries on the Laws of England*).[7] In *An Introduction to the Principles of Morals and Legislation,* Bentham had argued for rationalizing English law, in particular to assign punishments that were proportional to the crimes they aimed to prevent or redress.[8] In 'Of Sexual Irregularities' and *Not Paul, but Jesus,* he aimed both to argue against the severe punishments that were meted out to persons who practised 'irregular' pleasures and to demonstrate how the penal system created a new layer of derivative pleasures and pains. The English laws governing sexuality privileged some persons' judgement (of disgust) on other persons' pleasure, and allowed the practitioners of 'regular' pleasures to take pleasure in the sufferings visited on practitioners of 'irregular' pleasures.

Bentham held up the English law as an aesthetic regime that became systematic in the moment that it meted out capital punishments for male-male sexuality.[9] Such an analysis of the English law as structured human interaction made it possible for him on the one hand to maintain a resolutely sensual aesthetics, and on the other to depict how social interaction created occasions for aesthetic judgement at a different level. Aesthetic experience did not for him, as it did for Kant, begin in first-personal experience and end in first-personal reflection. It needed to be tracked to its social manifestations. Kant and Bentham both rejected the idea that aesthetic judgements were and should be justified by appeal to the taste of the majority. But Bentham had a more robust answer than did Kant to the time-honoured claim that there is no point in disputing about taste because everyone thinks his own taste best. Bentham's analysis of the laws governing sexual behaviour in what he called its 'irregular' forms amounted to an argument that one should dispute the validity of the taste (the disgust of the many) that English law encourages about taste (the sexual pleasure of the minority).

Kant omitted sexuality from his treatment of aesthetics, because his account of sexual objectification in the *Metaphysics of Morals* made it seem that a literature that evidenced sexual desire would be a contradiction in terms. Sexuality, one might imagine him saying, is so much concerned with the existence of one's sexual object as an object that it allows no latitude for the reflective judgement that operates in taste. Bentham, however, discovered something like evidence of reflection in two opposed directions. He identified an extensive literature eulogizing sexuality that he counted as public reflection. Canvassing an assortment of literary works that included Virgil's *Aeneid* and eclogues, Plutarch's lives, and Plato's dialogues, he treated them as evidence of pleasures that continued to declare themselves even when the immediate physical sensations that occasioned them were past, or only anticipated.[10] Moreover, he treated the legal statutes that enforce the taste of some (who feel disgust) in criminalizing the taste of others (who practise male-male sexuality) as, equally but oppositely, a representation of aesthetic judgement. Kant's exclusion of sexuality from discussions of taste made aesthetic judgement primarily individual and incidentally social. Bentham's inclusion of sexuality in discussions of taste made aesthetic judgement at least as social as individual.

Kant and Bentham thought that aesthetic discussion needed to address two quite different issues. Kant's way of framing his central problematic obliged him to draw a sharp line of distinction between aesthetic experience and what he termed the merely sensuous. A full stomach or the gratifying warmth of a fire might give sensory satisfaction, but Kant thought that reflective aesthetic experience could not be explained in those terms. He aimed to identify what was involved in taking pleasure in imitations or derivatives of actual phenomena. When one could look at a mountain, why did one need a painting of a mountain? When a viewer was hungry, how did one explain his ability to admire a beautiful painting of food that he could not eat? And, further, why would one take pleasure in natural objects that remained what they were whether they pleased or not? For Kant, the treatment of aesthetic judgement needed to explain why the understanding did not exhaust our relation to the world – needed to say why we are drawn to what Niklas Luhmann calls a 'doubling of reality'.[11]

For Kant, sensuous experience triggers aesthetic response: one needs to have a perceptual object rather than merely a non-sensuous and allegorical thought for aesthetic experience. But in his view sensuous experience quickly refers beyond itself to supersensuous faculties that can recognize beauty and sublimity in objects that were not designed for human appreciation. Aesthetic pleasure, because it is outside the realm of any human negotiation or exchange, is enough of an accomplishment for it to seem proximate to morality. Bentham, by contrast, continually imagines sensory experience in terms of the possibilities of pleasure between persons. And while Kant suggests that aesthetic pleasure provides something like training in individual autonomous judgement that is an intimation of morality, Bentham argues that the laws governing sexuality provide a basis for challenging the morality of the law itself.

Kant, in the *Critique of the Power of Judgement*, and Bentham, in 'Of Sexual Irregularities' and *Not Paul, but Jesus*, develop very different pictures of the way in which aesthetic judgement relates to social judgement. Kant sees aesthetic judgements as symptoms of individual freedom because they cannot be compelled, and when he introduces the question of the acknowledgement of other people's aesthetic judgements, his discussion of taste comes close to depicting other people's individual judgements as both imaginable enough for discussion and unavailable to be taken up. The aesthetic judgement dictates agreement with its pronouncements even in the absence of actual social endorsement. Bentham, on the other hand, begins and ends in examples of shared experience – to such an extent that he names masturbation as the only non-violent form of sexual pleasure-taking that he would proscribe.[12] His stated reason is that masturbation, being a form of sexual pleasure that an individual always has available to himself or herself, can become addictive.[13] Masturbation is for him the sensuous version of Kant's projecting that an individual might become monomaniacal and go 'mad with reason'.[14] Many might exculpate masturbation on the grounds that it is, if a crime, at any rate a victimless crime, but Bentham objects to it as an example of antisociality, of allowing oneself to become what twenty-first-century parlance terms a loner. For Bentham continually imagines experience taking place in a world that always includes other people, a world in which one has partners to sexual activity and allies and opponents in games and the various representations of games that he devises in his plans for prisons and schools.

Kant, defending the importance that individuals attach to their own aesthetic judgements, struggles to reconcile individual aesthetic judgements with sociability. Although he suggests that social motivations underwrite aesthetic judgements of both the beautiful and the sublime, his discussions of taste show him searching for a principle of reconciliation that would allow aesthetic judgements to cement social relations rather than disrupt them. Aesthetic judgements for him present themselves as such thoroughly inaugural moments that they raise questions about their possible integration into a social world. While Kant wants to analyse the importance of the faculty of judgement, Bentham looks at pleasure from the outside, citing various love songs and historical accounts and accepting them as a plausible record of a history of pleasure that has been built up over time. The love song that was written to appeal to a particular person and the biographical sketch that was intended to recount a particular person's activities are for him especially important for philosophy precisely because they were not devised as philosophical examples developed to illustrate an account of aesthetic experience. Their evidentiary use is all the more compelling because he takes them merely to have expressed pleasure-seeking desires and not to have participated in a philosophical debate about pleasure and its objects. That is to say: he takes love songs at their word.

2. Kant on taste and other people

Kant offered up an account of aesthetics that conspicuously minimized the importance of sensation, and of immediate advantage and purpose. Moreover, he had no interest in assessments that might claim any degree of confirmation or success of the kind that games of bridge or whist or push-pin do when they identify winners and losers as play unfolds. In subordinating anything like actual purposes to what he termed purposiveness, he made the look of purposiveness the very mark of the self-transcendence that aesthetic experience might afford. He centred his discussion on our appreciation of natural beauty and the difficulty we have explaining it if we do not have the reasons of the landscape gardener or the forester. He thus distinguished purposiveness from purposes – in his famous phrase 'purposiveness without purpose' – and treated the pleasure that we take in representations as a symptom of individual human freedom because we are treating unmotivated beauties as if they were meant for us. When we find this tree or that flower beautiful, our pleasure is disinterested and entirely unforced – by others and even by a distinct purpose. And when we realize that we take pleasure in green even though our friends like blue, Kant would say that we see further evidence that aesthetic judgement is symptomatic of freedom. We like what we like from a first-personal perspective. Aesthetic judgement is insistently first-personal. We as aesthetic individuals like what we like; we do not like it because someone else does. And this first-personal basis allows Kant to frame aesthetic judgement as a distinct counter to the kind of imitativeness that he associates with the unfreedom of childhood.[15] Indeed, autonomy is so central a notion for Kant that children become his example of the difference between a mere imitation of someone else's taste and aesthetic judgement that deserves the name. Aesthetic judgement for Kant involves not just an expression of individual freedom. In the process of freeing an individual from recognizing an object exclusively in terms of its purpose – what it is supposed to be – acts of aesthetic judgement in Kant reveal both the subjective element of the experience of beauty for a perceiver and catch objects up in the allure that results from the 'activity of the subject' in lingering over 'the consideration of the beautiful because this consideration strengthens and reproduces itself'.[16]

Here I am simply rehearsing some of the most basic elements of Kantian aesthetic doctrine as he lays it out in the third and last of his three critiques. Most starkly put, the three different critiques identify three different stages of freedom or subjectivity. In the *Critique of Pure Reason*, Kant describes how our perceptions of physical objects in the world are determined by the existence of those objects. Although he takes human faculties of representation to fall short of capturing the thing-in-itself (the *Ding an sich)*, judgements of the understanding are as minimally subjective as he thinks it is possible to be. In the *Critique of the Power of Judgement,* however, the pleasure in perception operates in advance of and independent of any cognition of the object, so that aesthetic judgement escapes from the trammels of the determining judgements that pure reason makes. And, finally, the *Critique of Practical Reason* establishes moral judgement as the supreme expression of individual autonomy, 'the supersensible attribute of the subject, viz. freedom'.

The three Kantian critiques – in so far as they try to isolate three different ways that humans have for operating in the world – identify the conditions of possibility for cognitive, aesthetic and moral judgements. But because they aim to distinguish the various relations to experience, the examples – particularly for the aesthetic judgement – betray their origin in laboratory conditions. On the one hand, we might imagine that the *Critique of the Power of Judgement* rightly treats all its examples as provisional, mere ways of gesturing towards the basic lines of argument. On the other hand, the observations for living that Kant offered his students in the lectures on anthropology that he delivered between 1772 and 1796 continually take up examples of pleasure and displeasure in social conduct that sit uneasily with the position he lays out in the *Critique of the Power of Judgement*. The anthropological lectures describe and rationalize social roles and modes of behaviour; the *Critique* provides a tortuous path for human sociability. For even though Kant maintains that we only decorate our houses out of a sense of sociability, he also insists that our aesthetic judgements do not arise – or should not arise – from imitating others.

The philosopher Paul Guyer has suggested friendly amendments to Kant's account of the individualized sociality of aesthetic judgements, even as the sociologist Pierre Bourdieu has, in opposition to Kant, insisted that aesthetic judgements are such thoroughly socio-economic and socially imitative acts that they can be used to diagnose class positions.[17] But neither of them addresses the worry I have developed – largely as a result of reading Bentham's 'Of Sexual Irregularities' and *Not Paul, but Jesus*. The examples in the *Critique of the Power of Judgement* are designed to distinguish aesthetic experience from mere recognition of both an object ('that's an oak') and of someone else's aesthetic experience ('she likes oaks'). They thus depict the possibility of individuals acknowledging something new to the world – whether for oneself alone or for presentation to others. This is the aspect of Kant's attack on imitativeness that has convincingly led to the kind of interest in language games and conversations that proceed by someone's saying something, being understood and being replied to not with a repetition of the same words but with statements that are themselves new. We do not need an example from someone else, he thinks, to take pleasure in natural beauty, just as we do not need to have heard a particular statement before to understand it.

But the claim about universal communicability operates in a surprising way. This is the claim that we hold firm to our evaluations of aesthetic objects and insist that they are shareable even if others do not immediately share them. It is a position that Kant lays out as a generalization from experience rather than a mere conjecture. While the inability to ground aesthetic judgements in distinct acts of cognition might make someone look comparatively unwilling to take their stand on aesthetic judgement, Kant represents them, paradoxically, as more assertive than acts of understanding. The rather surprising result of this line of argument is that, as Kant describes them, reports on the physical senses are open to more pluralistic accounts than aesthetic judgments. A sensory statement of taste is definite but not universalizable. Someone tasting cilantro (coriander) can readily pronounce it to be a pleasant herb even while accepting someone else's assertion that it tastes like soap. Someone who is colour-blind may not see red or green where I do, but they do see some colour (something like brown). We may label it a mild disability not to experience the taste of cilantro as pleasant and not to see colour as most other people see it, but we do not require every individual to uphold our most common statements about cilantro or colour. While we do not relinquish our perceptions, we make room for the possibility that others' perceptions might differ from ours.

Aesthetic judgement as Kant presents it is, however, more militant. It has a certain intransigence and intractability. While it can seem accommodative in yielding up claims to rational explanation and suasion, I am suggesting that we can hear in Kant something like the snarl with which Wordsworth says in the preface to *Lyrical Ballads* that he does not imagine that he can reason his readers into an appreciation of the kind of poetry he is offering them.[18] Kant tends to present concessiveness about the first-personal aesthetic judgement as appropriate only in the future – as an acknowledgement of one's future self. In the kind of example that will be repeated in lionizing literary biographies, Kant suggests that the artist is someone heroic enough to maintain his poetic convictions in the face of his friends' disparagements. He may change his mind later, when he is another person who can see his earlier work differently, but Kant suggests that he is right not to accept editorial judgements and amendments at the time he is writing.[19]

What I mean to stress about Kant's account of aesthetic judgement as he lays it out in the *Critique of the Power of Judgement* in 1790 and in the lectures on anthropology is its emphasis on the importance of an individual's trusting himself. The anthropological account stages itself as a discussion of persons who are social persons, and in that sense it values the social exchange of observations about the beautiful between persons. Thus he can affirm that 'Taste is … a faculty of making *social* judgements of external objects within the power of imagination',[20] and that 'taste concerns the communication of our feeling of pleasure and displeasure to others, and includes a susceptibility, which this very communication affects pleasurably, to feel a satisfaction … about it in common with others (sociably)'.[21] In the *Critique* this appeal to the common and communicable appears with the greatest intensity in the discussion of a common sense. He maintains that, even though we are grounding our judgment only on our feeling, we treat that feeling 'not as a private feeling, but as a common one'.[22] In other words, we perform acts of aesthetic judgment as ourselves but also as exemplars. We can thus see ourselves as exemplifying humanity in our own persons (as he says in the discussion of the sublime).

Yet what I mean to stress here is that this line of argument develops something of a one-way street for the communicability of aesthetic judgements. Kant makes it clear that he thinks aesthetic judgements cannot count on being accepted, but at the same time he thinks that the experience of non-confirmation does not undermine the experience of conviction: 'Now this common sense cannot be grounded on experience for this purpose, for it is to justify judgements that contain a "should": it does not say that everyone *will* concur with our judgement but that everyone *should* agree with it.'[23] Through something very much like a grammatical sleight of hand, Kant, by moving from the first-person singular to the first-person plural, makes individual aesthetic judgements look as though they have a claim on other people, even if their assent is not forthcoming. But both the *Critique* and the lectures on anthropology continually warn us against being taken in by pleasures that others put on offer. We rightly cease to take pleasure in the song of a bird, he thinks, when we realize that a young boy made it and not a nightingale. And we should distance ourselves from the fashionable, because it appeals to 'a compulsion to let ourselves be led slavishly by the mere example that many in society give us'.[24]

Kant's emphasis on the centrality of individual judgement in aesthetics and in morality has produced a legacy of important restatements and extensions of his first-personal stance. Onora O'Neill, for instance, offered a powerful, and powerfully Kantian, treatment of the issue of trust in the lectures she presented several years ago on the BBC. There she essentially argued against imagining that external standards, benchmarks and supervision could generate trust: ultimately trust arises from an individual's requiring herself to be trustworthy – and thus inspiring others to be so as well.[25] For Ludwig Wittgenstein and many of his commentators, the problem of pain assumed serious proportions – pain being indubitable from the first-person perspective, but laying one open to scepticism when someone else tells you about it. When I have a headache I know I do. When you have a headache I may wonder how bad it is and, even, whether you are simply producing an excuse that rests only on your testimony and is both unimpeachable and open to other people's doubt. Trusting others becomes, in one line of Kantian thought, a moral obligation to recognize them and their first-personal exemplarity of humanity in the absence of any possible empirical confirmation of the truthfulness of their statements.

But it is in his discussion of emotions that Kant offers a particular challenge to trust in the form of scepticism about one's ability to assess one's own emotions and their entanglement in a mixture of motives. In the *Lectures on Anthropology*, Kant offers numerous observations on pain and pleasure. By making pain internal to human nature, he makes it ineliminable and even fortunate. It is merely a stage on the road to pleasure and productivity: 'As an incentive to activity, nature has put pain in the human being that he cannot escape from.'[26] But he does not merely make statements about the way that nature has arranged us as individuals. He also notices how we notice other people's pain. 'It is', he says, 'not exactly the nicest observation about human beings that their enjoyment increases through comparison with others' pain.'[27] He does not mention *Schadenfreude* alone. He also focuses on cases that involve mixtures of pain and pleasure: an object such as the death of a woman's husband 'can be unpleasant; but the pain [the grieving widow feels] concerning it pleasing'.[28] With such a shift from the widow's pain to her observer's pleasure, Kant expands the range of pleasurable objects.

With remarks like those I have just quoted, Kant seems to be replying without directly confronting the centrality that Bentham accorded to Epicurus as the truest philosopher. Using pleasure and pain as the measure of human conduct, Kant seems almost to be saying, is impractical because pleasure and pain are so intimately interconnected. But at the beginning of his *Lectures on Anthropology*, he also seems to be anticipating a criticism of his first-personal position and attempting to distinguish it from egoism. He relieves himself of an obligation to connect his metaphysics to his remarks, and insists that anthropology concerns thinking 'in which one is not concerned with oneself as the whole world, but rather regards and conducts oneself as a mere citizen of the world'.[29] The human being may, from the day he 'begins to speak by means of the "I" … [bring] his beloved self to light' if egoism is allowed to progress 'unchecked'.[30] And appeals to other people make it possible for him to imagine himself as mistaken. One avoids logical egoism, the egoism of the understanding, whenever one checks with others about the testimony of one's own senses – to ask, say, whether experiencing a room as hot is 'just me'. One avoids aesthetic egoism by recognizing that he 'deprives himself of progress' by '[isolating] himself with his own judgements' and not listening to the appraisals of others.[31] And he objects to what he identifies as an eudaemonism wherein a moral egoist 'limits all ends to himself' and prefers 'utility to duty'.[32]

This tendentious equation between moral egoism and utility may have set the tone for much of the criticism of Benthamite utilitarianism and its characterization as a philosophy that always begins from 'number one'. But precisely because Bentham is infinitely less concerned than Kant to identify an appropriate first-person perspective, Bentham's writings on sexual irregularities provide a stronger statement than Kant does about other people's pleasure. On the one hand, Kant produces a variety of observations on human conduct to show how we judge it – in a fashion that suggests how far he himself is from sorting the aesthetic from the understanding and the reason. On the other, he is driven to wry remarks about why we believe reports from others. 'It is', he says, 'so certain that we cannot dispense with [newspapers as a] means of assuring ourselves of the truth of our judgement that this may be the most important reason why learned people cry out so urgently for *freedom of the press*.'[33] We value reports, particularly – and perhaps almost only – when they confirm us in the judgements we already have.

Such a statement – for all its distancing – tends to collapse the lines of distinction among different kinds of judgement: and it does so even as the *Critique of the Power of Judgement* has isolated them to suggest how aesthetic judgement imposes certain limits on itself. Ralf Meerbote has made an accurate and trenchant statement on Kantian reflective judgement in the *Critique* in saying: 'In the act sense, reflective judgement is mere reflecting.'[34] This is as much as to say aesthetic judgements do not amount to acts because they do not do anything in the world. But confining aesthetics to reflection that never enters the field of action is a limitation that sits uneasily alongside Kant's account of anthropology, which sounds like a series of statements about the social world that individual observers might make. The *Lectures on Anthropology*, that is, resembles a conduct book with various urbane rules of thumb that might be used as a guide to living. Kant's anthropology honours the attention we accord to the objects of our perception and the people we encounter, but it does not offer much in the way of what Luhmann calls second-order observation, a way of observing how individual observations interact with public social and legal systems. Kant's way of avoiding excessive satisfaction with one's own judgements is to change one's understanding of the situation of the observer – to shift from one's attachment to one's own perceptions and evaluations to a consciousness of oneself in the role of 'mere citizen of the world'.

3. On observation

I have said as much as I have about Kant to prepare the way for further explicit and implicit distinctions between his aesthetics and Bentham's. But I also want to underscore one crucial preoccupation that Kant and Bentham shared. What is often seen as a generalized movement toward democracy does not arise specifically in relation to discussions of government in the eighteenth and early nineteenth centuries. Accounts that emphasize the rise of democratic feeling can suggest that the right to express one's opinion (by publishing one's view or by voting) emerged through a series of abstract arguments about rights. What I want to propose instead is that such things as the extension of the franchise ultimately acknowledged the fact that a broader and broader segment of the population was being called upon to notice features of their world and the people in it. Writing in the wake of Locke's appreciation of consciousness and its ability to take hold of sensible ideas and to develop abstract ideas through reflection, Kant and Bentham, in their different ways, recognized that people, by virtue of taking their perceptions seriously, were claiming a right to acknowledgement. This was the fundamentally democratic gesture that they were continually honouring as they insisted that questions of civil society did not – could not – proceed merely as an elaboration of the will of the governors. More and more people were authorized, encouraged and pressured to pay attention – to observe. To some extent I am describing the knock-on effects of the printing press as Bentham, William Godwin and Joseph Priestley all gesture towards it. But I also mean to point to the importance of the rise of intellectual domains such as anthropology (as a science of the observation of persons in society) and aesthetics (as a philosophy concerned with the modes of our observing). And those intellectual products, momentous as they are, are in their way slight by comparison with the importance of the rise of the newspaper and the rise of the novel. For daily newspapers and regular periodical publications do not just deliver information to us. In their variety, they both convince us of the rightness and the freedom of our views (as Kant wryly said) and also constitute a demand that we notice – that we pay attention to – the world and inform ourselves of the ways in which the circumstances it offers are continually being updated. Novels commit their characters so thoroughly to the project of observing others that they can, as in Jane Austen, make their plots out of the observations we rightly call gossip and the occasional observational correction that a novelistic plot can deliver. Catherine Morland of *Northanger Abbey* may be mistaken in thinking that General Tilney must have murdered his wife because her rooms are unvisited and Tilney no longer seems in mourning eight years after her death. But the novel insistently asserts that she may have been wrong in her observations but that she has not been wrong to observe. Everyone observes: 'every man is surrounded by a neighbourhood of voluntary spies, and … roads and news papers lay everything open'.[35]

Austen's novel points a humorously accusatory finger at novels that have worked up Catherine's imagination, but a wider target here is the pleasure people take in having opinions and sharing opinions, most often about other people – and especially in feeling that they know other people better than others do and even better than those other people know themselves. The distinctive fictional device known as free indirect style or free indirect discourse captures the dilemma. Persons in society are continually in the position of talking to one another, having something to say if only by way of rehearsing every news item they have read that day. And both gossip and novelistic free indirect style have a tendency to overwrite the thoughts and motives of the persons whom they ventriloquize. Free indirect style, in which a narrator seems to merge with the inner thoughts of the character, participates in an activity of over-knowing analogous to the way we over-know political figures or anyone else who counts for us as a public personage.

This phenomenon of over-knowing – feeling certainty about things well past any remit provided by what one can plausibly claim to know – is, I think, the issue that Bentham is getting at when he insists, in what H.L.A. Hart describes as 'a dangerously ambiguous phrase', that 'that to which expression is given [in language], that of which communication is made is always the man's opinion nor anything more'. Hart may be right to say that 'it may even be true that human discourse could not function as it does unless there is a generally, though not universally, respected convention that we do not say what we do not believe'.[36] I think, however, that Bentham's point is the one that Luhmann has foregrounded in saying that, 'Whatever we know about our society, or indeed about the world in which we live, we know through the mass media'.[37] We have heard tell. The mass media here stand in for all communications that revolve around reports, the communications that we take as reliable even though we have not proved them for ourselves and the communications we make in our reports to others. These are communications – such as those of novels and of newspapers, law and literary works – that explicitly interpose themselves between persons and effectively disrupt the convention of face-to-face interaction that might lead us to believe that we usually say only what we believe and usually believe what others say to us. Luhmann's analysis helps us see that even face-to-face interaction is not a guarantee of truthfulness but only a communication made as 'always the man's opinion nor anything more'.

Aesthetic judgement as Kant models it is a notably intense version of conviction in a report. When Kant imagines a check on the conviction of individual judgement, he appeals to an individual's capacity to shift roles – to think of himself as a 'mere citizen of the world' who knows that there are other citizens in it. Yet one can easily imagine that the perspective that one takes as a citizen of the world is virtually no check at all and that it opens on suspicions like those that John Stuart Mill expressed about majority rule and its impulse towards tyranny. For one particularly tyrannical aspect of individual egoistic judgement is its tendency to lapse into a conviction of its own minority status, and to intensify itself in the process of imagining itself as a moral stance because of its minority status.

It is at this point that we can begin to see the advantage that Bentham derives from adopting the stance of an observer rather than a self-observer when he includes sexual pleasure, on the one hand, and governmental structures, on the other, in his account of pleasure. The task that Bentham imposes on himself in 'Of Sexual Irregularities' is to argue in favour of the decriminalization of male-male sexuality – and to do so by analysing the legal structure of punishments and submit it to rationalization. In the face of his awareness of social and dissocial judgements that attend anyone's sexual choices, he does not pitch his argument as an appeal to a public audience. It is not an oratorical performance. Nor does 'Of Sexual Irregularities' and the writing associated with it rally men who have sex with men to think of themselves as an identity group. Although Bentham seems to have imagined that William Beckford, who had been banished to the continent for his sexual congress with young men, might have been willing to edit the volume, the work is not a call to action on the part of men who have sex with other men.[38] Nor does it suggest that persons should be allowed their sexual pleasures so long as they keep them out of view of the general public – and closet themselves or take themselves off to a more tolerant continent. Instead, in the face of a daunting consciousness of the opprobrium that his arguments will receive, Bentham argues that it is not male-male sexuality but the law that must justify itself.[39] 'It belongs to [any man in power who marks] out for punishment' anyone who engages in non-normative sex 'to shew cause why he has done so' and to demonstrate 'that the effect and tendency of … the practice is … productive not only of mischief, but of a net balance [on] the side of mischief'.[40] While Kant's citizenly judgement may seem merely like a magnification of his individual judgement, Bentham addresses individual sexual choices not just by rescuing them from opprobrium. He also situates individual choice within a legal structure that functions – or, rather, should function – as a public statement of the moral choices of the society, a comprehensive guide to behaviour that draws its various elements into a systematic whole so as to be able to judge penalties and assess their proportionality.

Bentham's position here effects an astonishing reversal. He recognizes that male-male sexuality is so widely scorned and criminalized in English society that popular judgements on it move with the kind of instantaneity that Kant associated with judgements of natural beauty. For him, 'there is no disputing about taste' does not translate into a statement of every individual's freedom to maintain their aesthetic judgements in the absence of social confirmation. For him judgements of taste are merely evaluations that we happen not to dispute. He recognizes that the senses are legislative within an individual, in that one experience of pleasure recommends further experiences of that kind (in what Hume called habit and what later analysts would describe as sexual identity or sexual orientation). At the same time, however, they never develop the relative imperviousness to social opinion that Kant at least heuristically claims for aesthetic judgements. Judgements of taste are for Bentham cumulative within the individual and socially cumulative as well, not merely communicable but communicated.

In the effort to argue against judgements that seem to go without saying, Bentham describes the supports to the popular opprobrium attached to irregular sexuality. The legal code and the pronouncements of judges and news reports all encourage his contemporaries to calumniate male-male sexuality. Recognition of such cumulative judgements leads Bentham to adopt a striking way of depicting principles in argument. Contemporaries such as Joseph Priestley urged that orators inculcate belief and opinion in others by doing such things as putting their own beliefs on display and recommending them in manifest sincerity of affirmation.[41] Bentham, however, does not lay out his own thinking as a direct address to an audience – either specific individuals such as particular legislators or members of the public at large. Instead, he depicts principles, stipulations and definitions as analogous to theorems in geometry. He invokes theorems instead of representing proofs in their lengthiest forms, as some writers use definitions to limit the scope of a discussion, and opposing parties in court can use stipulations to accept certain facts without fighting them out. Such principles or theorems are the shorthand – the expositional accelerants – that individual judgements derive from a historical survey of legal and religious opinions. In judgements of sex, the Principle of Antipathy, or the Principle of Asceticism, has, Bentham thinks, established itself so firmly that most people never pause to ask why they confidently pronounce anyone else's sexual experience disgusting. What Mill called 'Bentham's method of detail' takes the form of his unpacking the Principle of Antipathy, or the Principle of Asceticism, of his 'elaborate demonstrations' of their underpinnings.[42]

Bentham appeals to his own theorem, the Greatest Happiness (or Least Misery) Principle, or the Principle of Utility,[43] to evaluate the Principle of Antipathy, of Asceticism. His insight is to see that one may not be able to talk anyone out of their tastes in art or sex but that one can treat the written cultural record as evidence of positive pleasures. On any occasion when one pronounces 'the very idea' of someone else's way of taking pleasure 'a cause for disgust', one is underwriting a legal system that incorporates aesthetic judgements by making some tastes punishable. 'The affection of antipathy,' Bentham says, has 'the property to seek its gratification in the pleasure of subjecting to pain the person by whose conduct the dissocial affection has been excited'.[44] And, in alignment with his life-long practice, Bentham's contribution to the discussion of the social behaviour of individuals is to insist that the law as it stands should be put under obligation, should justify itself by something other than the claim to be natural. The repeated use of an inflammatory word such as 'unnatural' should not be allowed to stand for an unalterable cultural and legal edict. Instead, those who propose punishment should show that particular acts are crimes and therefore need to be censured.

'Of Sexual Irregularities', 'Sextus', and *Not Paul, but Jesus* present a particularly striking way of offering criticism of legal and popular sanctions against male-male sexuality. These writings do not attempt to counter prevailing opinion simply by affirming a different opinion or trying to win their way with satire. Occasional brilliant turns of phrase remind us that Bentham as the author of the *Book of Fallacies* could produce accounts as satirical as Flaubert's in his *Dictionary of Received Ideas*, but Bentham in 'Of Sexual Irregularities', 'Sextus', and *Not Paul, but Jesus* offers long-form descriptions that analyse the position of those who hold opposed views, and he does so without satirizing them. He commits himself to understanding taste as judgements of pleasure and pain (or the absence of pleasure), and he similarly commits himself to observing the work that dyslogistic words such as 'unnatural' do in condensing a judgement and picking out sundry occasions for deploying it. Infanticide and rebellion may not have much in common – and indeed might seem opposed to one another – but the dyslogistic work of the epithet 'unnatural' pulls them together.

I will leave to the side Bentham's elucidation of the work of the senses, except to observe the obvious importance of his decision to represent sex as the sixth sense, and to note its intensity by comparison with the five senses that are conventionally named.[45] Bentham's exploration of the testimony of the various senses and comprehensive iteration of the various possible combinations of sex acts, as important as they are, are chiefly important for setting up the question: why does anyone think that sex between men is 'disgusting'? His analysis of the immediate and longer-term effects of male-male sexuality makes it hard to see why pleasure-giving acts should be censured – indeed, punished as capital crimes – when his analysis acquits them of doing damage to individuals. He takes up the possibility that women might be injured by male-male sexuality if it led to women's being neglected and the possibility that society at large might be injured by non-procreative sex. In both cases, he acquits male-male sexuality of deleterious effects. He takes the former objection to male-male sexuality to be so vague as to be virtually meaningless, while also suggesting that it would not diminish women's authority for there to be some men who were 'unsusceptible' to their influence.[46] And he maintains that Thomas Malthus's projections of population – and his own analysis – have established that society has more to fear from redundant, or excessive, population than from a low birth rate.[47]

The centrepiece of Bentham's discussion is what turns out to be a history of the Principle of Asceticism. And it is Bentham's reliance on a historical record that most sharply distinguishes him from Kant. When Kant presents various kinds of aesthetic objects as pleasurable, he focuses on the possibilities that those objects offer for aesthetic judgements in the present. Attention falls so directly on the judgement being passed on the beauty of an object that its content becomes nearly irrelevant. A beautiful object – whether painting or poem – precisely because it is not treated under the terms of the understanding – does little to co-ordinate the judgements of the characters depicted within its precincts. (Hence, the persistent disagreements about what aesthetic objects are and mean.) Bentham, by contrast, consults a historical literary record – materials in writing that fall on both sides of the distinction we now draw between the historical and the literary. He names both actual and legendary characters, not to anatomize their writings and their exploits, but instead to capture evidence of their beliefs. When Kant in the *Anthropology* speaks of writings about sexual love, he notices its deceptiveness: writers use 'obscure representations', he maintains, in writing about 'sexual love, in so far as its actual aim is not benevolence but rather enjoyment of its object' and in the process waste 'wit ... in throwing a delicate veil over' behaviour that announces its own animality.[48] Bentham, however, takes classical poems and histories as evidence that a number of ancient writers believed that sex acts between men were pleasurable and desirable. And he also notes that classical literature did not take a man's desire for sex with another man to disqualify him from admiration and heroic renown. Socrates was 'represented, if not as a model of perfect virtue, as a model of the most perfect virtue that heathenism admitted of'.[49] Virgil's shepherd Corydon singing his love laments for Alexis and the Theban band celebrated for their courage all mark out 'love operating in this irregular shape', and mark it as '*pius*' (a noble emotion). As Bentham observes, 'In a case such as this, fiction in its nature affords more conclusive evidence than any particular realities: it shews the conclusion drawn by opinion from universal and continual experience.'[50]

Bentham's compelling point here is that literature is evidence of judgements of taste that needed no apologies in their own time. It testifies to behaviour that is 'not simply innoxious but positively beneficial', and 'never performed' 'unless attended with pleasure'.[51] The eulogistic aims of love poetry and tales of heroes bespeak a taste that never imagines that it will be judged harshly by posterity. In that global sense, it expresses the convictions of the heart's affections, and does so without self-censorship. In that regard, it provides an amendment to – and improvement on – John Stuart Mill's distinction between oratory that is heard and poetry that is overheard. Literature testifies to feelings that need not seek for any further justification. They carry conviction within them. It was a thought that various writers had as they were trying to free literature from absorption in its own history and conventions, from simply being enmired in one poet's conversation with other, previous poets. And it was a thought that Wordsworth had clearly had a couple of decades earlier when he pronounced that 'Poetry is the history or science of feelings' and that Anna Letitia Barbauld had had when she declared that novels testify to individual and social judgements in their time – and do so more accurately than laws and the opinions of posterity do.[52]

Bentham's aim, then, in extending an account of judgement and taste to include the sexual sense is to draw attention to the issue of conviction. When Bentham observes that it is simply tautologous to say that 'to every man that which is his own taste is the best taste', he is restating Kant's observation that everyone thinks that everyone else should share and second their aesthetic judgements. But he is extending judgements of taste to include the pleasures of the sixth sense, of sex, so as to secure them against derogation by others. 'In the case of the fine arts, when the object is of a complex nature, by being made to observe this or that circumstance which he had not observed before – this or that feature of defect or excellence which till now had passed unobserved – a man may now and then be made to change his taste. But in the field of appetite – of physical appetite – so simple is the object, no place can be found for any such discovery.'[53] People continue to have sex – albeit with greater and lesser frequency at different points in their lives – because sexual experience is so intensely pleasurable that they are willing to risk all manner of trouble and inconvenience in pursuit of it.

Sexual pleasure in its various forms – including the form of sex between men – counts for Bentham as an unambiguous pleasure. He takes sexual taste to be so unsusceptible to fashion and other people's taste that he recounts a story from Lucian in which a young man is so enamoured of a statue of Venus that he has sex with it – not by following prescribed heterosexual practices but by having sex with 'a part which is common to' both sexes.[54] People do not, in Bentham's account, have regular or irregular sexual experiences because they have been educated by other people's examples. The education of the senses – the education out of the senses – begins, however, when the priests of Bentham's conjectural history treat other people's pleasures as a currency which they can traffic in. In a conjectural history of religion that will turn out to have specific bearing on sexuality, the idea of a god or gods creates priests, those who claim to be able to interpret the wishes of a supersensible being. Priests develop political authority and social precedence by claiming special knowledge of the divinity. And the most important strategy that the priesthood develop for maintaining and consolidating their authority is the Asceticism Principle: it confiscates the pleasures of others by offering those pleasures up in sacrifice, a sacrifice meaningful because painful (and painful because it involves forgoing pleasure). Normativity by priestly cabal.

In Bentham's version of a discourse on the origin of inequality, conducted as a discussion of sexuality and pleasure, the ascetic principle exercised by priestly authority has its purchase because it functions as legislation: it recommends a pattern of ascetic behaviour among the faithful and makes conspicuous acknowledgement of the law of asceticism desirable. While Kant has made confidence in one's own (non-sexual) tastes central to aesthetic experience, and Bentham has argued that individuals can trust their own sexual tastes, Bentham asserts that priestly evangelism for asceticism has thrown individuals into self-doubt and, more importantly, suspicion of others. Social, political and religious precedence mystify in so far as they distract individuals into distrusting – and calumniating – other people's judgements. In Bentham's view, the doctrine of original sin itself feeds into this pattern of despotic asceticism. As continually ratified in the service of the Church of England, it traffics in a market of pleasures and pains by allowing individuals to purchase indulgences merely by uttering a few words to disparage others: 'All men are sinners. Yet some are saved. Therefore, without prejudice to salvation, a certain quantity of sin may always be committed', he writes in paraphrase of Anglican doctrine.[55] 'At so cheap a price as that of a few words', one may acquire 'the reputation of the love – the ardent love – of virtue'.[56] This social transaction has its analogue in the supposedly soul-saving act of imagining that any potential sinfulness in one's own pleasures may be washed away by making the pleasures of others look damnable. And Bentham underscores his observation by aptly quoting Samuel Butler's *Hudibras* on the technique of 'Compound[ing] for sins they are inclined to, / By damning those they have no mind to'.[57]

Now as Bentham lays out the various kinds of sexual behaviour that have been made punishable by death, he does not avail himself of the most direct challenge to the legitimacy of the laws. He does not say, 'By whose authority?' or, more simply, 'Who says so?' Nor does he adopt Sade's mockery of the Christian Gospels. Though he indicts the laws governing sexuality of absurdity, his most stunning argument is that Christian scriptural teaching is a plausible grounding for Christian belief, and that it only needs to be recovered from the texts that have grown up around it and obscured it in the process. The writings of the Hebrew Bible, the Christian Gospels and the letters of Saint Paul may all be bound together in the volume called the Bible, and they may thus make up one composite text. Together they make up a form of legislation – prompts to behaviour. But, as he fully recognizes, they enjoin all manner of different behaviours: one could gloss practically any action by saying, 'The Bible tells me so.'

Bentham's approach, in response to such a recognition, is to sift the Scriptures and perform a crucial act of philological criticism, much like that of Spinoza in the *Tractatus Theologico-Politicus*. Bentham argues that the ascetic principle – enunciated, affirmed and reaffirmed by Moses, John the Baptist and Paul – has no legitimacy in the face of the statements that the Gospels attribute to Jesus and to the statements they make about him. Moses and Paul may have legislated minutely to condemn sex between men and varieties of sex between men and women, but, Bentham says, Jesus did not. Although a writer like Sade recounts the Gospel story with a sneer, Bentham treats Jesus's words and deeds as worthy evidence of his 'scheme of instruction'. Further, Bentham recommends that the Christians among whom he lives take that legislation as the basis of their conduct and their judgments on the conduct of others. Jesus framed his teachings as an explicit repudiation of Mosaic law, and the Gospels demonstrate that such repudiation extended to laws governing sexuality. The Gospels, Bentham points out, both show Jesus's tolerance for male-male sexuality and also attest to his personal sexual relations with men and with women.

What seems to me most remarkable about Bentham's line of argument here is how thoroughly he detaches it from his own religious beliefs – or, rather, his beliefs about religion (that there is no God and that the image of an omniscient and omnipotent judge that Christianity holds out is a pernicious one). Instead, he focuses on identifying the best version of other people's beliefs – or, rather, the beliefs that they should lay claim to in identifying themselves as Christians. The legislation of Jesus – the legislation of the Gospels – is what British Christians should keep before them. Any backsliding into what Bentham takes to be the viciousness of Moses or the militant asceticism of Paul should be arrested simply by their recalling to themselves who they are, what their name is: Christians. Jesus may have replaced the law of Moses, but his succession was more than merely chronological. Thus, though Paul wrote after Jesus's death, the persistence of the name Christianity shows how little his teachings have a claim to succeed those of Jesus. (Paul's writings are, as Joseph Priestley continually insisted, among the 'corruptions of Christianity'.)

Bentham may see the congruence between Jesus's teachings and the principle of utility, in so far as both centre on increasing human pleasure and decreasing human pain, but he is not asking his fellow Britons to subscribe to utilitarianism. He is saying, above all else, that the very name of their religion – Christianity – constitutes an ongoing affirmation of Jesus's pre-eminence as a guide to their thought and behaviour. They are not Paulists but Christians. The principle of asceticism may have been honoured in long-standing practice, but the continuing embrace of the name of Christians should count as a principle of principles. Christianity is what Christians say they believe.

The significance of this line of argument is that Bentham never needs to rely on simple relativism: he need not admit every judgement on the grounds that someone has believed it at some point in time or in some place in the world. Nor does he ever need to claim that the ancients held the correct views, or that the moderns have eliminated errors as moral judgements have been transmitted and refined over time. Instead, he establishes a coherent picture of the laws as he knows them and a coherent picture of the laws as others should know them. These are two different routes toward arriving at what one might think of as organic form. In neither case is organic form a sign of immediacy or naturalness. In the case of law, the organic quality of the law derives not from the stories of natural cultural growth that someone like Edmund Burke put forward. In the case of the Scriptures, the organic quality of the law derives from submitting the body of texts to the pressure of the authority of Jesus. Both of these contrast sharply with the Kantian depiction of organic form, which introduces immediacy and perceived satisfaction. Benthamite form holds judgements to account, and produces what biblical scholars might have called a harmony of Christian Scripture so as to capture what he takes to be other people's reasons – public law, Christian Gospels. Not Paul, but Jesus. Not Kant, but Bentham.

Notes

1 Editor's Introduction: Kant, trans. Guyer and Matthews, ed. Guyer, 2000, p. xiv.

2 See Wimsatt and Brooks, 1957, 414–15. Wimsatt and Brooks draw on Mill, ed. Robson, 2006, 113. See Bentham, 'Rationale of Reward', in Bowring, 1843, ii. 198–266, 253.
3 Mill, ed. Robson, 2006, x. 114.
4 Mill, ed. Robson, 2006, x. 99.
5 Kant, ed. Gregor, 2006, 427.
6 Bentham, ed. Schofield *et al.*, 2014; Bentham, 2013. The editorial introduction to *Of Sexual Irregularities* reports that Bentham headed the text sheets for one essay on sexuality 'Sex.' – 'Bentham's abbreviation for "Sextus," referring to the sixth sense or sexual appetite', p. xvii. Louis Crompton published related material: Crompton, 1978. Philip Schofield first published the text of 'Sex' in Bentham, ed. Engelmann, 2011.
7 See Bentham, ed. Burns and Hart, 1977, for the opening salvoes in Bentham's long-running criticism of William Blackstone's *Commentaries on the Laws of England* (1765–9).
8 Bentham, ed. Burns and Hart, 1996.
9 In the balance of this essay, I shall speak of Bentham's discussion of male-male sexuality and leave to the side his discussions of female-female sexuality and infanticide. He speaks briefly of female-female sexuality, but notes that it is not met with capital punishment, for all its apparent analogy with male-male sexuality. He observes in 'Of Sexual Irregularities' that female-female sexuality is 'left altogether exempt from punishment' (57). Bentham, on the other hand, groups male-male sexuality with infanticide to bring out the importance of capital punishment in raising questions about the proportionality of punishment. Although he opposed criminalization of these 'irregular' sex-related charges, he focused his argument for decriminalization on male-male sexuality in the thought that it was the most actively punished sex-related behaviour in his time.
10 Bentham, ed. Schofield *et al.*, 2014, 32–3.
11 Luhmann's analysis initially addresses journalism and the periodical press, but he is interested in a wide range of 'copying technologies', including realist novels and other entertainments. Luhmann, 2000, 4–5, 55–9.
12 Bentham, ed. Schofield *et al.*, 2014, 30.
13 See Engelmann, 2014.
14 Kant, trans. Bernard, 1966, 117. In Guyer's translation, 'to rave with reason', 156.
15 Kant, ed. Zoller and Louden, 2007, 348.
16 Kant, trans. Guyer and Matthews, ed. Guyer, 2000, 107.
17 Guyer, 1979, 22–9, 159–66; and Editor's Introduction: Kant, trans. Guyer and Matthews, ed. Guyer, 2000, pp. xxiii–xxx. Bourdieu, trans. Nice 1984, 4–5, 53–63.
18 Wordsworth explains that he had been reluctant to introduce the poems in *Lyrical Ballads* with a substantial preface, 'since [he] might be suspected of having been principally influenced by the selfish and foolish hope of *reasoning* him into an approbation of these particular poems'. Coleridge and Wordsworth, ed. Gamer and Porter, 2008, 172.
19 Kant, trans. Guyer and Matthews, ed. Guyer, 2000, 163.
20 Kant, ed. Zoller and Louden, 2007, 344.
21 Kant, ed. Zoller and Louden, 2007, 347.
22 Kant, trans. Guyer and Matthews, ed. Guyer, 2000, 123.
23 Kant, trans. Guyer and Matthews, ed. Guyer, 2000, 123.
24 Kant, ed. Zoller and Louden, 2007, 348.
25 O'Neill, 2002, 96.
26 Kant, ed. Zoller and Louden, 2007, 338.
27 Kant, ed. Zoller and Louden, 2007, 341.
28 Kant, ed. Zoller and Louden, 2007, 340.
29 Kant, ed. Zoller and Louden, 2007, 241–2.
30 Kant, ed. Zoller and Louden, 2007, 240.
31 Kant, ed. Zoller and Louden, 2007, 241.
32 Kant, ed. Zoller and Louden, 2007, 241.
33 Kant, ed. Zoller and Louden, 2007, 240.
34 Meerbote, ed. Cohen and Guyer, 1982, 73.
35 Austen, ed. Butler, 1995, 186.
36 Hart, 1982, 13–14.
37 Luhmann, trans. Cross, 2000, 1.
38 Bentham, ed. Schofield *et al.*, 2014, pp. xxiv–xxv. The editors of *Of Sexual Irregularities* quote portions of newspaper reports from 1784 and 1785 about Beckford's sexual activity and his

whereabouts. Beckford left England in 1785, and returned only briefly and occasionally for the next twenty years. 122–3 n.

39 Bentham speaks at various points of his own consciousness of the anger that his writings on sexuality are likely to arouse. In 1823 he published the first volume of *Not Paul, but Jesus* under the pseudonym Gamaliel Smith. Bentham, ed. Schofield *et al.*, 2014, p. xi. For an example of Bentham's explicit concern about countering popular opinion, see Bentham, ed. Schofield *et al.*, 2014, 8.

40 Bentham, ed. Schofield *et al.*, 2014, 5.

41 Priestley, 1777, 108–13. See George, 1998, 81–109, 106.

42 Mill, ed. Robson, 2006 , X: 83.

43 Bentham, ed. Schofield *et al.*, 2014, 4.

44 Bentham, ed. Schofield *et al.*, 2014, 3.

45 The editors of *Of Sexual Irregularities* note that Buffon spoke of sexual sensations as the sixth sense, and their note on William Beckford includes an interesting suggestion that Beckford lays out various chambers in *Vathek* as if they constituted a mapping of the senses. See Bentham, ed. Schofield *et al.*, 2014, 122 n.

46 Bentham, ed. Schofield *et al.*, 2014, 36–7.

47 Malthus, ed. Appleman, 2004, 20–6. See Bentham, ed. Schofield *et al.*, 2014, 78–9.

48 Kant, ed. Zoller and Louden, 2007, 247.

49 Bentham, ed. Schofield *et al.*, 2014, 88.

50 Bentham, ed. Schofield *et al.*, 2014, 33.

51 Bentham, ed. Schofield *et al.*, 2014, 58.

52 Wordsworth, ed. Gamer and Porter, 2008, 288. Barbauld, ed. McCarthy and Kraft, 2001, 416–17.

53 Bentham, ed. Schofield *et al.*, 2014, 77.

54 Bentham, ed. Schofield *et al.*, 2014, 77.

55 Bentham, 2013, 77.

56 Bentham, 2013, 49.

57 Bentham, 2013, 50.

References

Austen, J. *Northanger Abbey*, ed. M. Butler. London: Penguin, 1995.

Barbauld, A.L. '*On the Origin and Progress of Novel-Writing*', in *Anna Letitia Barbauld: Selected Poetry and Prose*, eds. W. McCarthy and E. Kraft. Peterborough, Ontario: Broadview, 2001.

Bentham, J. 'Rationale of Reward', in *The Works of Jeremy Bentham*, ed. John Bowring. 11 vols. Edinburgh: William Tait, 1838–43.

Bentham, J. *A Comment on the Commentaries and A Fragment on Government (CW)*, eds. J.H. Burns and H.L.A. Hart. London, Athlone Press, 1977.

Bentham, J. *An Introduction to the Principles of Morals and Legislation* (*CW*), eds. J.H. Burns and H.L.A. Hart. Oxford: Clarendon Press, 1996.

Bentham, J. *Jeremy Bentham: Selected Writings*, ed. S. Engelmann. New Haven, CT: Yale University Press, 2011.

Bentham, J. *Not Paul, but Jesus*, Vol. III: *Doctrine*. London: Bentham Project, UCL, 2013 [http://discovery.ucl.ac.uk/1392179/3/npbj.pdf].

Bentham, J. *Of Sexual Irregularities, and Other Writings on Sexual Morality* (*CW*), eds. P. Schofield, C. Pease-Watkin, and M. Quinn. Oxford: Clarendon Press, 2014.

Bourdieu, P. *Distinction: A Social Critique of the Judgement of Taste*, trans. R. Nice. Cambridge, MA: Harvard University Press, 1984.

Coleridge, Samuel Taylor and Wordsworth, William. *Lyrical Ballads: 1798 and 1800*, eds. M. Gamer and D. Porter. Peterborough, Ontario: Broadview, 2008.

Crompton, L. 'Paederasty', *Journal of Homosexuality* 3:4 (1978), 389–406 and 4:1 (1978), 91–107.

Engelmann, S. 'Queer Utilitarianism: Bentham and Malthus on the Threshold of Biopolitics', *Theory and Event* 17:4 (2014): 157–64.

George, A.L. 'Grounds of Assent in Joseph Priestley's *A Course of Lectures on Oratory and Criticism*', *Rhetorica* 16:1 (Winter 1998): 81–109.

Guyer, P. *Kant and the Claims of Taste*. Cambridge, MA: Harvard University Press, 1979.

Hart, H.L.A. *Essays on Bentham: Jurisprudence and Political Philosophy*. Oxford: Clarendon Press, 1982.

Kant, I. *Anthropology, History, and Education*, eds. G. Zoller and R.B. Louden. Cambridge: Cambridge University Press, 2007.

Kant, I. *Critique of Judgment*, trans. J.H. Bernard. New York: Hafner Publishing, 1966.

Kant, I. *Critique of the Power of Judgment*, trans. P. Guyer and E. Matthews, ed. P. Guyer. Cambridge: Cambridge University Press, 2000.

Kant, I. *Practical Philosophy*, trans. and ed. M.J. Gregor. Cambridge: Cambridge University Press, 2006.

Luhmann, N. *The Reality of the Mass Media*, trans. K. Cross. Stanford, CA: Stanford University Press, 2000.

Malthus, T.R. *An Essay on the Principle of Population*, ed. P. Appleman. New York: Norton, 2004.

Meerbote, R. 'Reflection on Beauty', in *Essays in Kant's Aesthetics*, eds. T. Cohen and P. Guyer. Chicago: University of Chicago Press, 1982.

Mill, J.S. *Collected Works, Vol. X: Essays on Ethics, Religion, and Society*, ed. J.M. Robson. Indianapolis: Liberty Fund, 2006.

O'Neill, O. *A Question of Trust: The BBC Reith Lectures 2002*. Cambridge: Cambridge University Press, 2002.

Priestley, J. *A Course of Lectures on Oratory and Criticism*. London: J. Johnson, 1777.

Wimsatt, W.K. Jr. and Brooks, C. *Literary Criticism: A Short History*. New York: Vintage, 1957.

Wordsworth, William. 'Note to "The Thorn"', in *Lyrical Ballads*, eds. M. Gamer and D. Porter. Toronto, Ontario: Broadview, 2008.

Chapter 3
'Envy accompanied with antipathy': Bentham on the psychology of sexual *ressentiment*

Stella Sandford

Introduction

Jeremy Bentham's recently published writings on sexuality (written between 1814 and 1818) are an important (and surprising) addition to the history of philosophical sexuality studies. In 'Of Sexual Irregularities', 'Sextus', 'General Idea' and Volume III of *Not Paul, but Jesus*, Bentham argues that homosexual sexual pleasure is in general a good and argues for the 'Proposed ultimate liberty – viz. all-comprehensive liberty for all modes of sexual gratification not predominantly noxious'.[1] At numerous points in these writings, there are striking parallels with Freud's writings on sexuality, particularly the latter's *Three Essays on the Theory of Sexuality* (1905). Like Freud, Bentham finds no moral distinction between same-sex and heterosexual sexuality. Understanding sexuality primarily in terms of pleasure (rather than reproductive teleology) and presupposing sexual orientation to be a matter of taste, Bentham, like Freud, denies that same-sex desire is either pathological or unnatural and argues for a measure of sexual freedom against its deleterious suppression by 'civilization'. This means that, unlike the *psychopathia sexualis* of the late-nineteenth and early-twentieth centuries it is the pathology of the ferocious condemnation of homosexuality, not the seeker of same-sex pleasure, that Bentham's analysis tries to understand.

However, this chapter aims to show that Bentham's conception of sexuality is surprisingly radical, even in relation to Freud. It begins with a brief discussion of the common aspects of Bentham's and Freud's conceptions of sexuality, according to which Bentham can argue that it is not homosexuality, but, on the contrary, the violent persecution of homosexuality, that is an offence to morality and justice. The chapter then examines Bentham's explanation for the unwarranted and vicious condemnation of same-sex sexuality, and the problem of the relationship in this explanation between what Bentham calls the 'principle of antipathy' and the 'principle of asceticism'. Arguing that the role of the principle of asceticism, which ostensibly has the main explanatory force, is in this instance underwritten by the principle of antipathy and the (often hidden) motive of pleasure in it, the chapter concludes that Bentham's writings on sexuality reveal a more complicated picture of his psychology than is usually suggested by its reduction to the categories of 'psychological egoism' or 'psychological hedonism'.

Bentham and Freud: Sexuality and pleasure

In Bentham's writings on sexuality two areas of agreement with Freud's later writings stand out. First, both Bentham and Freud display a clear-eyed, non-moralistic acceptance of the fact of human sexuality in all its diversity and a basic understanding that the pleasures of sexuality are experientially separate from the function of reproduction, and thus that the phenomenon of sexuality itself, as an element of human existence, constitutes a topic of interest independent of discussion of reproductive function. If this is largely presupposed in Bentham's writings on sexuality, Freud's innovation in relation to his philosophical and sexological predecessors is the determination of a non-reproductive, non-teleological concept of sexuality defined in terms of pleasure seeking.[2] In Freud's early theory of sexuality, adult, genitally-organized heterosexuality is one way in which the sexual drive may express itself. But the sexual drive is itself essentially perfectly indifferent to sexual difference; indeed, to all difference. There is no essential relation between the sexual drive and its object – that is, there is no essential or innate heterosexuality, as was usually previously presumed. As the sexual object is merely soldered to the sexual drive, sexual preferences cannot be said to be either 'natural' or unnatural'. Freud uses the terms 'normality' and 'abnormality', but almost always in inverted commas, either literally or metaphorically, and 'normal' and 'abnormal' come to mean something like 'usual' or 'common' or 'expected' and their opposites; that is, they do not have a moral meaning. Bentham is similarly sensitive to the use of this kind of terminology (as will be discussed later) and it is his characterization of sexuality as a sixth sense *on a par with the other senses*, subsuming sexual object-choice under the idea of taste, that, in his view too, severs sexuality from any 'natural' object and from reproduction. At the end of the nineteenth century, when the idea of a sixth sense was raised again by Paul Moreau de Tours – probably without any knowledge of Bentham's work – it had reverted to the idea of a reproductive sense: the '*sens génésique*', the 'generative sense'.[3] In this respect, Bentham was very far ahead of his time.

Armed, as it were, with these conceptions of sexuality, both Bentham and Freud display what we would now call a 'liberal' attitude to homosexuality, and both clearly argue, albeit in different ways and to differing degrees, for sexual liberty. In fact, Bentham is much the more radical here (except where 'solitary pleasures' are concerned). His writings go considerably beyond what would later be found in Freud's writings, asserting non-mischievous homosexual acts to be 'in themselves nothing but good – pure good'[4] and arguing for the benefits of liberalization, for the 'addition expectable from it to the sum of happiness', that is, from the 'Proposed ultimate liberty – viz. all-comprehensive liberty for all modes of sexual gratification not predominantly noxious'.[5] The writings of both Bentham and Freud clearly acknowledge the cost to the individual's happiness of repressive social moralities forbidding sexual expression. Freud was perhaps less concerned with homosexual desire than with the cost of '"civilised" sexual morality'[6] to women, who were subject to more and greater restriction than men, as Bentham of course also realized. But Bentham's emphasis on male homosexuality stems from the legal context of his writings on sexuality and is a response to the fact that homosexuality was still punishable by death under English and Scottish law when he was writing.[7]

Second, both Bentham and Freud locate the principal spring of human action, its greatest motivating force, in what Bentham calls the pursuit of pleasure and Freud calls the pleasure principle.[8] From very early in Freud's writings, from the 1890s, and increasingly through the years, Freud understood pleasure primarily in terms of excitation and satisfaction, even though the idea of both remain undefined and ambiguous in his work. Arguably, all pleasure was, for Freud, ultimately related to sexuality, it being understood that what Freud means by 'sexuality' goes far beyond and encompasses much more than the popular conception.[9] Because of the ambiguous place of excitation in the psychic economy, there is for Freud no straightforward distinction between pleasure and unpleasure. Both are a matter of excitation and tension and to that extent are effectively indistinguishable. If satisfaction means the end of excitation and tension (which is one of Freud's definitions of pleasure), it also means the end of pleasure.

Although Freud argued for increased sexual liberty, locating the origin of many neuroses in sexual repression, he was also clear that some measure of sexual repression was the *sine qua non* of human civilization, and thus that human beings are condemned to a certain discontent or unease (*das Unbehagen*). This is not to pit human nature (represented as the unfettered sexual drive) against human culture (repression), because the human being is, ontologically, a cultural being. Further, Freud's discussions of sexuality do not refer to a contingent, episodic aspect of human experience; they deal with the being-sexual of human being. 'Sexuality' is not a separable quality predicated of human being; it is integral to the specificity of human being or human existence itself. Freud's theory of sexuality is also therefore a philosophical anthropology that identifies our troubled relationship with pleasure, and specifically sexual pleasure, as the irritating grit that determines, both positively and negatively, the specificity of the form of human subjectivity.[10]

Bentham, on the other hand, has a generic conception of pleasure and deals with sexual pleasure as one of its species. In comparison with Freud, pleasure seems to be quite straightforward for Bentham. Indeed, the sense of the uncomplicated, not to say joyous, nature of sexual pleasure conveyed in Bentham's writings is one of their chief attractions and surprises. Although Bentham frequently speaks of pleasure and the avoidance of pain in the same breath, his conception of pleasure is in general more positive than Freud's (it is positively pleasure, not predominantly negatively avoidance of pain). In a brief mention of the 'pleasure of the sexual sense' in *An Introduction to the Principles of Morals and Legislation*, Bentham writes that it 'seems to have no positive pain to correspond to it: it has only a pain of privation, or pain of the mental class, the pain of unsatisfied desire'.[11] Bentham does not ask the philosophical question 'what is pleasure?', perhaps because pleasure is the kind of physical idea upon which other, non-physical ideas might be based; that is, reference to pleasure is for Bentham an *explanans* not an *explanandum*. Unlike Freud, sexuality appears to carry with it no existential charge for Bentham; his conception is more purely physiological than Freud's. In 'Sextus' he offers the following definitions:

> the sexual appetite is, in figurative language, the seat of the desire of that pleasure of which the organs by which the two sexes are distinguished from each other is, in plain language, the seat.
>
> Any act having for its object the administering an immediate gratification to the sexual appetite may be termed an act of sexuality.[12]

In *Not Paul, but Jesus*, Vol. III, in Bentham's division of the acts 'whereby the senses are put to use or affected', sexuality (which he calls the 'sixth sense')[13] falls into the class of those acts in which the sense is 'the seat as well as the inlet' of pleasure or pain, and those 'of which the most prominent effect is the production of positive pleasure'.[14] He also writes that, 'No condemnation can justly be passed on any pleasure on any such ground as to that of its *shape*, *seat*, *source*, or *inlet*'.[15] That sexual pleasure, even in this blunt and predominantly physical conception, is in general a good seems to Bentham rather obvious. As with all other actions, it is necessary to determine the 'general tendency' of sexual acts, to assess the ways in which the individuals most directly concerned *and their community* are affected, in order to calculate whether the scales tip in favour of a yield of pleasure or pain. When we are talking – as Bentham most often is – about sexual acts between consenting adult parties in private, the tendency, as far as Bentham is concerned, is to increase happiness. Of course, not all expression or practice of sexuality is like this. Bentham is clear that rape, for example, is an evil, where any pleasure obtained by the aggressor is far outweighed by the pain caused to the victim. In 'Sextus', remarking on the 'State of the public mind in England in relation to the irregularities of the sexual appetite', he writes of adultery and rape as 'noxious' and notes the oddity of the fact that the anger excited in the 'public mind' by rape is 'very inconsiderable' compared with the anger excited by consensual sex between males.[16] In general, however, the requisite calculations having been made, and all other things being equal, it is Bentham's view that sexual pleasure is in general good. As far as Bentham is concerned, sexual pleasure is, further, like any other pleasure, largely a matter of taste. If one man's taste differs from another's, there is no *a priori* or empirical ground to class his pleasure as unnatural or abnormal. Thus, for Bentham, just as for Freud, same-sex sexual pleasure is no oddity to be explained or condemned and homosexuality is not a pathology.[17] Because of this straightforward conception of sexuality as a sixth sense, Bentham's writings on sexuality contain no analysis of sexuality itself. It is as if, for Bentham, there is nothing about sexuality that needs explaining.

Bearing all this in mind, in the various writings on sexuality Bentham runs through the arguments raised against 'irregular pleasures' and offers reasoned refutations. This turns out to be a relatively easy task, because the objections themselves are hardly reasoned; they are, rather, often fairly flimsy expressions of prejudice.[18] So given the weakness of the counter-position, and given that sexual pleasure is generally an obvious good, what does need to be explained, according to Bentham, is the ferocious condemnation of homosexuality.[19] A great part of Bentham's writings on sexuality are thus concerned with the causes of the severity of the disapprobation and punishment of homosexuality. This shift of focus from homosexuality itself and its acts to the phenomenon of the condemnation of the acts is evident in Bentham's definition of the adjective 'unnatural' applied to homosexuality. In relation to the practice itself, 'the use of the adjunct unnatural … is a very precarious indication of any quality as having place in the practice'; indeed 'the only matter of which it affords any indication that can be depended upon is the existence of a sentiment of disapprobation, accompanied with passion, in the breast of the person by whom it is employed'.[20]

Bentham's writings on sexuality reveal an awareness of the fact that, historically, a whole set of political, juridical, moral, social, cultural, aesthetic and psychological issues converge in the topic of the regulation of sexuality. (This may come as a surprise to some Foucauldians.) If we were to try to layer these issues and seek to determine the order of influence, if not quite of causality, among them, they come to rest, I suggest, on quite specific psychological considerations. This is not to say that this is essentially the case, but that this is Bentham's analysis of the historical situation in and of which he writes.

In general, as Philip Schofield puts it, it is for Bentham the 'sovereign masters' of pleasure and pain that 'constitute … not only the foundation of human psychology, determining what individuals actually did, but also the foundation of ethics, pointing out what they ought to do'.[21] Bentham's psychological theory can then be characterized as egoistic or as 'psychological hedonism', according to which it is 'a fact of human nature that we are motivated solely by a desire for pleasure and aversion to pain'.[22] In *A Table of the Springs of Action* Bentham reduces all '*psychological entities*, mostly *fictitious*' to the appellation 'motive', and the science of motives (or springs of action), which he calls 'psychological dynamics', is based on 'psychological *pathology*', that is, on feelings, or, basically, on pleasures and pains.[23]

This 'motivational psychology', as McReynolds calls it,[24] is, with all due respect to Bentham, ultimately rather simple. John Stuart Mill, in his essay on Bentham, famously criticized, both implicitly and explicitly, Bentham's knowledge of human nature, accusing him of a lack of imagination and, because of this, an inability to enter into the mind of another.[25] But while this may be true of the general basis of Bentham's psychological hedonism, the particular analysis of the psychological determinants of the condemnation of homosexuality are, on the contrary, rather acute and point to a psychology of greater depth and nuance than Bentham's explicit pronouncements on psychology in general tend to indicate.

Antipathy and asceticism

So what does Bentham say about this? It having been shown, as far as Bentham is concerned, and with reference, of course, to the principle of utility, that acts of consensual homosexual sex are not noxious or mischievous, that they rather contribute to the sum of happiness than detract from it, and that there have never been any serious arguments produced against this view, the question is: why are they punished with such ferocity? According to what principles, and with what cause? Do these principles legitimately warrant, and does this cause legitimately ground, the case for punishment?

In the most general terms, and to the extent that the causes of error in moral reasoning here are the same as they are elsewhere, Bentham identifies the principle of antipathy and the principle of asceticism as the *de facto* (but not justified) grounds of the virulent condemnation of homosexuality.[26] These are 'spurious principles with which the field of morals is infected'.[27] But what exactly are they?

In *An Introduction to the Principles of Morals and Legislation* Bentham writes:

> Among principles adverse to that of utility, that which at this day seems to have most influence in matters of government, is what may be called the principle of sympathy and antipathy. By the principle of sympathy and antipathy, I mean that principle which approves or disapproves of certain actions ... merely because a man finds himself disposed to approve or disapprove of them: holding up that approbation or disapprobation as a sufficient reason for itself, and disclaiming the necessity of looking out for any extrinsic ground. ... measuring out the quantum (as well as determining the ground) of punishment, by the degree of the disapprobation.[28]

This, Bentham goes on say, is not really a principle at all, or is a principle only in name, being rather the negation of all principles.[29]

As is well known, the principle of utility, or the greatest happiness principle, is the rational principle according to which a right and proper action is determined and according to which legislation is formed, taking into account the fundamental motivations of the pursuit of pleasure and the avoidance of pain. The principle is separate from, but acknowledges the rule of, the 'two sovereign masters' of pleasure and pain. In contrast, the so-called principle of antipathy has achieved no separation from the feelings of the individual who acts according to it. If the principle of utility is the moral principle according to which the individual's immediate motivation of pleasure seeking is judged in the context of the happiness of the greatest number, the motivations of the individual guided by the psychological, not moral, principle of antipathy seek only spurious justification for their immediate enactment. In *A Table of the Springs of Action*, 'Antipathy' is the eleventh of the types of pleasures and pains. The list of its corresponding dyslogistic motives or 'specially derived and directed affections' and abstract moral qualities is the longest in the table.[30] Antipathy itself is of course a feeling, as the very word suggests, but it is also called 'ill-will' and gives rise to more specific pleasures, such as those of revenge. The specially derived and directed affections include hatred and spite, associated with the quality of 'ill-nature'; abhorrence and execration, associated with the qualities of maliciousness and venomousness; rage and fury, associated with the qualities of cruelty and ferocity; and, in groups of their own, revenge and vengeance; and envy and jealously. All of these things are evoked in Bentham's writings on sexuality in explaining the punishment of homosexuality.

Bentham accepts the fact that persons may feel physical disgust, physical antipathy, for homosexuality – indeed he expresses, or at least feigns to express, his own disgust at several points. But this can never be grounds for moral disapprobation. This may be the feeling behind condemnation, but it is not a warrant for it. There is no sense in asking, as far as Bentham is concerned, what causes physical antipathy; it is simply a fact of individual taste. The principle of asceticism, the explanatory importance of which seems to increase in Bentham's later writings on sexuality, seems to be rather different. It is defined in *Not Paul, but Jesus*, Vol. III:

> By asceticism I understand any system or article of doctrine in and by which endeavours are used to engage men to forego pleasure in any shape for any other cause than the procurement of still greater

> pleasure in the same or some other shape, or the avoidance of pain to an amount more than equivalent: or to subject themselves [to] pain for any other cause than the avoidance of still greater pain, or the procurement of pleasure to an amount more than equivalent.[31]

Whereas antipathy is a feeling that acts as a motive that explains certain actions or determinations of the understanding, it is difficult, within the term of Bentham's philosophy, to understand how the religious (Pauline) principle of asceticism could serve as a motive for action. In a sense, all motives resolve into one for Bentham: the desire for pleasure and for the avoidance of pain. If, as Philip Schofield says, this means that 'actions are motivated by the prospect of obtaining some pleasure or of averting some pain',[32] how can the principle of asceticism – that is, the principled condemnation and avoidance of pleasure – really be a motive? If antipathy is, effectively, one of the springs of action, what kind of a thing is the principle of asceticism? Or, what hidden springs of action lie behind it?

To answer these questions requires a more detailed account of Bentham's analysis of the causes of the condemnation of homosexuality where, in fact, various other causes, too, are identified. 'Of Sexual Irregularities', which approaches its subject from the point of view of the penal code, enumerates four causes: antipathy, envy, 'Opportunity of affording a safe gratification to the passion of antipathy' and 'Desire of the praise of virtue – desire of reputation on the ground of love of virtue'. Religious objections and the principle of asceticism are discussed under the third of these heads, Mosaic religion (but not Jesus's teachings) being taken to have provided a warrant for the unleashing of 'unbridled vengeance'.[33] Here religious prohibition and condemnation has a subsidiary function, sanctioning the gratification of antipathetic passions while satisfying the desire to ingratiate oneself with the 'almighty being'. 'General Idea' and *Not Paul, but Jesus*, Vol. III give seven and six causes respectively. In these texts, the framing of the discussion in terms of a more general critique of religion ostensibly brings religious causes to the fore. 'General Idea' includes as causes in their own right the principle of asceticism (from 'a religious source')[34] and a religious conception of moral purity, while *Not Paul, but Jesus*, Vol. III: *Doctrine* cites Mosaic prohibition and the way in which abhorrence of a very great sin (homosexuality) is played off against indulgence in more pardonable sins.[35] Thus Schofield and Pease-Watkin are right that the later writings 'placed much greater emphasis on religious asceticism as the source of traditional sexual morality, and hence as the target for criticism'.[36]

This is particularly evident in *Not Paul, but Jesus*, Vol. III, a great part of which comprises commentary on passages from scripture in which Bentham argues not only that there is no evidence at all that Jesus ever condemned sexual indulgence, but also that the scriptural evidence does not allow us to rule out the possibility that Jesus himself partook of the 'eccentric pleasures of the bed'.[37]

But granted that the religious principle of asceticism may well be the major quasi-ideological, *socio-cultural explanation* for the condemnation of homosexuality, Bentham's writings on sexuality dig deeper, proposing a psychological explanation that accounts for the otherwise inexplicable (in his own terms) success of the principle of asceticism. At this psychological level the principle of antipathy, and one of its 'specially derived and directed affections' in *A Table of the Springs of Action* – envy – play the main role.

Envy (the second named cause in 'Of Sexual Irregularities') is, more specifically, envy of the enjoyment of the enjoying party, to the extent that the envying party does not share in it,[38] or, as Bentham puts it in 'General Idea', envy 'on the score of source and mode of gratification, in which the Censor does not participate'.[39] In his elaboration of this point in 'Of Sexual Irregularities', Bentham distinguishes between envy in cases of active competition (competition for an enjoyment which both parties seek but which the envying party is less successful in achieving), which he describes as 'emulation accompanied with antipathy', and envy of the procurement of a pleasure which the envying party does not seek and 'enjoyment of a kind in which it is out of his power to participate'. This latter is, Bentham says, connected with a different kind of antipathy; that is, there is here an antipathy towards the very act itself as well as an antipathy towards the enjoying party, and the antipathy is greater in the case of envy of an enjoyment that one does not seek. Bentham ends this short section with what seems to be an unrelated remark to the effect that differences of opinion in politics and religion do not produce envy. The point, presumably, is that differences in taste or opinion do not give rise to envy except where a considerable yield of pleasure is involved, be it sexual pleasure, pleasure in possession, pleasure in power and so on.

The third cause of the severity of the disapprobation and punishment of homosexuality identified in 'Of Sexual Irregularities' is 'Opportunity of affording a safe gratification to the passion of antipathy', that is, revenge or vengeance, more specifically gratification of ill-will without fear of punishment.[40] The fourth cause is 'contemplation of the opportunity of encreasing a man's own reputation … by the same means by which one of his passions, viz. the passion of malevolence, receives its gratification'.[41] These two causes are closely related to the extent that both involve the gratification of malevolent feeling under pretence of virtue.

In discussing revenge Bentham implicitly asks first, how does difference of taste give rise to ill-will? He says, in a contorted way, in a paragraph that is difficult to understand, that in that part of the field of taste that is sexuality, given the right circumstances, one will find many people with a disposition to homosexuality.[42] This was the case in ancient Greece, for example. So how has it come about that homosexuality is condemned? Basically, the origin is in Mosaic religion. As elaborated at much greater length in *Not Paul, but Jesus*, Vol. III, this is no part of the teachings of Jesus, but the Mosaic prohibition found fertile ground in the teachings of Paul, whose asceticism was such that even that mode of sexual intercourse which is necessary for the continued existence of the species is only unwillingly tolerated and endured.[43] Homosexual sexual acts, with no chance of procreation, would of course be all the more condemned. Later, summing up, Bentham says that if we are taught that homosexuals are the enemy of God, then 'The Being infinite, such ought to be our love, such consequently our hatred for his enemies – such consequently, in determination and efficiency, the acts in and by which that hatred is exercised, manifested, gratified, demonstrated.'[44]

Although it is not explicit, we can see that this pious condemnation of homosexuality is the occasion for the gratification of the passion of antipathy, in an act that simultaneously secures one's moral, i.e. Christian, credentials. (According to Bentham, 'it is the property [of antipathy] to seek its gratification in the pleasure of subjecting to pain the person by whose conduct the dissocial affection has been excited.')[45] Virtuous conduct, Bentham says, cannot in general be maintained 'without more or less of self-denial', but here is an occasion 'to put in, without any expence in the shape of self-denial, the appearance of the love of virtue, and, thereby, the appearance of virtue itself'.[46] Bentham's argument is thus that the explanation for the condemnation of homosexuality and its severity really lie in antipathy, or more particularly the opportunity to gratify antipathy in vengeance, and piety is only ever really a cover for this; it is not a real cause. All the emphasis in the argument is on antipathy and gratification of ill-will.

But if there is no self-denial here, how is it that Bentham connects all this up to asceticism? The argument concerning pious condemnation follows immediately upon a discussion of asceticism – but how are these related? What is the relation of asceticism to the pious condemnation?

From one perspective there is a gap in Bentham's argument, because, granted Bentham's claim that asceticism is the result of a misinterpretation of scripture, it still needs to be explained how a principle that does not seek to maximize pleasure or minimize pain could ever become part of human existence. Bentham famously claims that pleasure and pain 'govern us in all we do, in all we say, in all we think: every effort we make to throw off our subjection, will serve but to demonstrate and confirm it. In words a man may pretend to abjure their empire: but in reality he will remain subject to it all the while.'[47] This suggests that the operation of the principle of asceticism needs to be seen in terms of its secret yield of pleasure. To the extent that the operation of the principle of asceticism is of a piece with the virulent condemnation and punishment of homosexuality, the pleasure is considerable: the pleasure in the gratification of ill-will or in vengeance.

In 'Of Sexual Irregularities' and 'Sextus', the analysis suggests that condemnation and punishment of homosexuality is, in Bentham's society, one of the principal means, if not the principal mean, through which asceticism (denial of pleasure) is converted into pleasure (gratification of ill-will or revenge). This is part of the dissocial appetite according to which a person (called malevolent) desires to see others foregoing pleasure or undergoing pain,[48] or even subjecting persons to pain.[49] The pleasures of the indulgence of these dissocial appetites are in general said to be akin to 'the sort of enjoyment which an ill-taught boy gives himself by tail-piping a dog, or an ill-taught man by bull-baiting, or an English judge by consigning a man to the pillory for an offence which affords a hope of his having a jaw broken or an eye beat out by the surrounding populace'.[50] But in the case of antipathy towards homosexuality and the free reign given to the dissocial appetites in its prosecution, the thirst for violence is such that 'nothing less than the heart's blood of the intended victims marked out for slaughter by the dissocial appetite has hitherto been able to satisfy'.[51] Thus there is a social and religious sanction (in the sense of official approval) for a particularly intense gratification of violent and bloodthirsty appetites in the punishment of homosexuality.

This is in fact even more explicit in the later *Not Paul, but Jesus*, Vol. III, where the principle of asceticism seems to play the larger role. Indeed there, the condemnation and punishment of homosexuality under religious sanction is seen as the unique instance in which the law colludes with the desire for the gratification of antipathy. Religious tolerance in England forbids (legally and through customary morality) the gratification of the 'dissocial affection … to that degree of intensity which is afforded by the death of the victim' in cases of antipathies produced by difference of religious opinion. Neither the 'men in power' nor those who would share in the pleasures of power can obtain gratification from persecuting religious dissenters to death. But in the case of homosexuality 'the man in power has stept in and afforded to the wounded mind the relief which in almost every other part it is to be condemned to be ever hoping for without ever attaining it. Behold there, says he, your victim: behold here my arm which, if you can bring him within my reach, is ready for the sacrifice.'[52]

But still, how is it connected to asceticism? It is connected to asceticism, I suggest, to the extent that asceticism is sacrifice and asceticism thus gives rise to antipathy via envy. In 'Sextus', where asceticism is defined as sacrifice,[53] Bentham writes that, whereas not everyone could offer the 'vulgar sacrifices' of wine and meat, 'The pleasures, these were things which every man had to offer: these were things by which every man might be sacrificed. Of all pleasures, the most exquisite were the pleasures of the sexual appetite.'[54] Believing another to be enjoying pleasures that one has oneself sacrificed will give rise to envy. Bentham says that condemnation of, that is, the public announcement of one's antipathy to, homosexuality gives the appearance of virtue 'without any expence in the shape of self-denial', but if asceticism holds sway there has been denial – denial of sexual pleasure, even if not denial of specifically homosexual pleasure. Bentham suggests that any natural antipathy to homosexuality needs to be 'wound up to the highest pitch'[55] by piety, but envy really seems to play the crucial role in his analysis and provides the compelling psychological motive, just because of its complicated relation to pleasure.

Accordingly, it is in fact envy that is the primary motive in Bentham's analysis, to the extent that the piety of religious condemnation is judged to be more or less fake and asceticism produces the conditions in which envy will flourish. Bentham speaks often of the way in which gratification of ill-will is clothed in the appearance of virtue and this is one of the main arguments against the false piety of anti-homosexuality, as it stifles real virtue under the pretence of it. Pretence to virtue is what Bentham calls a 'substituted motive';[56] in his discussion of substituted motives in *A Table of the Springs of Action*, antipathy covered by 'public spirit' or 'love of justice' forms a specific example. The covered '*desires* and *motives*', Bentham says, 'may accordingly be considered as *the unseemly parts of the human mind*'.[57]

Note that Bentham says that it is not just motives but also *desires* that are covered by substituted motives. And as McReynolds remarks, with these ideas 'Bentham entered, however haltingly, into the realm of motivations existing beneath the surface of one's awareness, an area to be conceptualized later by Freud in terms of that fictitious entity called the Unconscious.'[58] Perhaps it is that the more unseemly the desire, the more vehement must be its denial, and the more severe must be the substitutive condemnation. What hidden spring, what unseemly desire, might then lie behind Robert Peel's condemnation of homosexuality as, 'the crime of crimes – the crime against which, when put in the balance all other crimes put together weigh but as a feather'?[59] Bentham says that he saw with his own eyes a judge, fresh from 'consigning two wretches to the gallows' for the offence of homosexuality: 'Delight and exultation glistened on his countenance.'[60] This suggests not just substitutive motives but also substitutive satisfactions and substitutive pleasures. As Bentham says in *Not Paul, but Jesus*, Vol. III: 'In the sufferings of those who presume to disobey his prohibitions [on homosexuality], the malevolent affection in the ascetic beholds a sort of compensation or indemnity for the privations which he suffers himself.'[61]

Conclusion

In sum, the quick answer to the question 'what is the cause of the severity of the condemnation of homosexuality?' is this: it is the principle of antipathy and the principle of asceticism. But the principle of asceticism, being the complete reversal of the egoistic hedonism that apparently governs human life, cannot itself be a spring of action; it must be the cover of other springs. I have suggested that what it covers is, once again, the principle of antipathy, and this in its specific form of envy. At base, so Bentham's psychological analysis suggests, the condemnation of homosexuality is to be explained by the envy that the condemners feel for the pleasure that the homosexual gets and that they themselves do not get but which, we might have to add with Freud, they do desire. Envy is not itself a pleasurable feeling, but in envious condemnation of homosexuality, the pain of envy is converted into the pleasures of the gratification of vengeance and – who knows? – the sadistic, i.e. possibly sexual pleasure, of seeing others suffer; certainly, Bentham's analysis does not rule that out. Thus, I suggest, Bentham's discussion of the phenomenon of the condemnation of homosexuality contains a subtle psychological analysis of possibly unconscious human motivation and substitutive pleasures, which is a little more complex than the popular idea of his psychological hedonism sometimes leads us to believe.

Notes

1 Jeremy Bentham, 'General Idea of a Work, Having for One of its Objects the Defence of The Principle of *Utility*, so Far as Concerns the Liberty of Taste, Against the Conjunct Hostility of the Principle of *Asceticism* and the Principle of *Antipathy*; and For its Proposed Title, proposed on the Grounds of Expected Popularity, Or at Least Protection Against Popular Rage, – Not Paul, but Jesus' (1817), 142. This work, along with 'Of Sexual Irregularities – Or, Irregularities of the Sexual Appetite' (1814) and 'Sextus' (1816) are now published in Bentham, ed. Schofield *et al.*, 2014. As the editors of *Of Sexual Irregularities* explain (p. xi), 'General Idea' was intended as a prospectus for part of the larger work *Not Paul, but Jesus*. Material from 'Sextus' was redrafted to form the third volume of this larger work, which is available online: [https://www.ucl.ac.uk/bentham-project/publications/online-editions, accessed 30 April 2019].

2 To see this clearly one should look more to the first, that is the 1905, edition of his *Three Essays on the Theory of Sexuality* than the last, heavily revised 1924 edition, which is marked by an accommodation with a developmental, normative, conception of natural heterosexuality. See Freud, trans. Kistner, ed. Van Haute and Westerink, 2016; Sandford, ed. Gipps and Lacewing, 2019, 83–105.

3 Moreau de Tours, 1880.

4 Bentham, 'Sextus', 92.

5 Bentham, 'General Idea', 142. In his earliest work on homosexuality, 'Offences Against the Self: Paederasty', which was written in 1785, Bentham does express disgust at and abhorrence for homosexuality, characterizing it as the procurement of sexual pleasure by means of 'the wrong sex' (Bentham, 1785, 389), a 'perverted taste' (390). Nevertheless, he still argued forcefully against prosecution for homosexuality and against any of the alleged grounds for the severity of its condemnation. As L. Crompton says, it may be that, at this early stage 'the use of traditional homophobic language was the price Bentham felt he had to pay for treating the questions from a reformist point of view'. Crompton, ed. Parekh, 1993, 260. The older Bentham felt no such need.

6 See Freud, ed. and trans. Strachey, 1959.

7 Philip Schofield and Catherine Pease-Watkin have pointed out that Bentham was not working on his penal code when he began his writings on sexuality (1814) and that the prominence of the discussion of religious asceticism in these writings suggests that they are more a critique of religion than a contribution to the penal code. Nevertheless, they write, the primary concern is to recommend decriminalization of male homosexuality and other 'irregular' sexual acts. See Bentham, ed. Schofield *et al.*, 2014, p. xii.

8 In Robinson, 1995, 192, Daniel N. Robinson makes this link between Bentham and Freud explicit: 'Bentham's … "pleasure principle" would find new expression in the psychoanalytic theories of Freud'.

9 See, for example, Freud, trans. Kistner, ed. Van Haute and Westerink, 2016.

10 For a more detailed argument see Sandford, ed. Gipps and Lacewing, 2019.

11 Bentham, ed. Burns and Hart, 1996, 47 n.

12 Bentham, 'Sextus', 51.

13 See, for example 'Sextus' (which means 'Sixth'), 51; 'General Idea', 127; *Not Paul, but Jesus*, Vol. III, 54.

14 Bentham, 'General Idea', 127.

15 Bentham, *Not Paul, but Jesus*, Vol. III, 23. Because the emphasis is so squarely on this rather blunt conception of sexual pleasure, Bentham's question is never 'should two men be able to live a life of loving companionship together?' but rather 'should they be allowed to have sex?' It is not that anything in Bentham's writings speaks against same-sex love and companionship, just that the issue does not seem to concern him in the writings on sexuality.

16 Bentham, 'Sextus', 66–7.

17 Just as with Freud, sexual pathology, as far as the individual and the community are concerned, can only be the repeated exercise of forms of sexuality that produce more pain than pleasure. The happy pervert who harms no one is not subject to a pathology. Indeed, for Freud such perversion is one way of fending off neurosis: '[Neurotic] symptoms are formed in part at the expense of abnormal sexuality; *neurosis is so to speak, the negative of perversion*.' (Freud, ed. and trans. Strachey, 1959).

18 Bentham, 'Of Sexual Irregularities', 5. On the 'alleged mischiefs' of same-sex sexual pleasure and Bentham's arguments against this see, for example, 'Of Sexual Irregularities', 25–42 (and *'Beneficial effects resulting from the direction thus given to the sexual appetite'*, 43–5); 'Sextus', Chapter 7, 79–83, Chapter 14, 105–8 (and Chapter 11, 92–6 and Chapters 16–17 on 'Advantages from the proposed liberty', 110–15).
19 See Crompton, ed. Parekh, 1993, 259.
20 Bentham, 'Of Sexual Irregularities', 6.
21 Schofield, 2009, 45, and Bentham, *IPML* (*CW*), 11.
22 Schofield, 2009, 53.
23 Goldworth, 1983, 90.
24 McReynolds, ed. Parekh, 1993.
25 Mill, ed. Robson, 1996, 91. For more of Mill's criticism of Bentham on this point see Capaldi, 2004, 139–43.
26 See, for example, Bentham, 'Of Sexual Irregularities', 4.
27 Bentham, 'General Idea', 132.
28 Bentham, *IPML* (*CW*), 21–2.
29 In a footnote added later (1789) Bentham says that the principle of antipathy should rather be called the principle of caprice: Bentham, ed. Burns and Hart, 1996, 32.
30 Bentham, ed. Goldworth, 1983, 85.
31 Bentham, *Not Paul, but Jesus*, Vol. III, 10–11. Part I of *Not Paul, but Jesus*, Vol. III is titled 'Asceticism' and the definition of the principle of asceticism and its opposition to the principle of utility is the first matter of business: Chapter 1, §1 'Asceticism what – its opposition to Utility – their relation to Happiness, pleasure and pain'.
32 Schofield, 2009, 45.
33 Bentham, 'Of Sexual Irregularities', 18.
34 Bentham, 'General Idea', 135.
35 The full lists of causes in these two later texts are as follows. 'General idea': principle of asceticism, antipathy, notions of purity, envy, desire of praise for virtue, opportunity of gratifying antipathy, and precautionary self-defence against the imputation of homosexuality to oneself. *Not Paul, but Jesus*, Vol. III: Mosaic religion, antipathy, philosophic pride (exalting oneself above those who cannot renounce vulgar pleasure; which amounts to secular and religious forms of pride in adherence to the principle of asceticism), opportunity of purchasing the appearance of virtue at a cheap price, bartering abhorrence of a great sin for indulgence in a lesser, and the gratification of antipathy, including sharing in the power of the punishers.
36 Bentham, ed. Schofield *et al.*, 2014, p. xiii. Elsewhere Philip Schofield again understands the essays on sexuality – 'a systematic defence of sexual liberty' – as being part of a broader critique of religion. See Schofield, ed. Zhai and Quinn, 2014, 90, 118.
37 See *Not Paul, but Jesus*, Vol. III, Chapter 13 'The Eccentric Pleasures of the Bed, Whether Partaken of by Jesus?', 177–96.
38 Bentham, 'Of Sexual irregularities', 9.
39 Bentham, 'General Idea', 135.
40 Bentham, 'Of Sexual Irregularities', 10. See also Bentham, 'General Idea', 136.
41 Bentham, 'Of Sexual Irregularities', 10.
42 Bentham, 'Of Sexual Irregularities', 11: 'Of that part of the field of taste, or in other words, of pleasure – in one part, viz. in that which regards the pleasures of the sexual appetite, under and in consequence of a favourable concurrence of circumstances, the requisite disposition in the mind of the subject many has either been found or produced.'
43 Bentham, 'Of Sexual Irregularities', 16. Bentham locates the origin of Mosaic law in the antipathies peculiar to Moses himself. He writes: 'In the breast of Moses, the sentiment of antipathy found an object and an exciting cause in every sort of irregularity belonging to this class [of sexual act]. Religion was at his command: in Religion, every caprice to which, in his fertile brain, imagination had ever given birth found a ready instrument, and that an irresistible one.' (Bentham, 'Of Sexual Irregularities', 12.)
44 Bentham, 'Of Sexual Irregularities', 19.
45 Bentham, 'Of Sexual Irregularities', 4.
46 Bentham, 'Of Sexual Irregularities', 21, 22.
47 Bentham, *IPML*, 11.
48 Bentham, 'Of Sexual Irregularities', 17.
49 Bentham, 'Of Sexual Irregularities', 20. See also Bentham, 'Sextus', 93.

50 Bentham, 'Of Sexual Irregularities', 22.
51 Bentham, 'Of Sexual Irregularities', 23.
52 Bentham, *Not Paul, but Jesus*, Vol. III, 50–1.
53 Bentham, 'Sextus', 72.
54 Bentham, 'Sextus', 73. The vulgar sacrifices of wine and meat was in effect, Bentham argued, the sacrifice of the pleasure that humans might have had in their consumption.
55 Bentham, 'Of Sexual Irregularities', 19.
56 Bentham, ed. Goldworth, 1983, 113.
57 Bentham, ed. Goldworth, 1983, 114, 115.
58 McReynolds, ed. Parekh, 1993, 204. It is not a criticism of Freud to call 'the Unconscious' a fictitious entity, either in terms of Bentham's understanding of that term, or in terms of Freud's own understanding of the fictional nature of his models.
59 Bentham, 'Sextus', 68 n. This is part of a fragment amid Bentham's manuscript on the subject of homosexuality in Ireland, headed 'Not Paul', with the subhead 'Sexualities'. It is part of a précis of Peel's contribution to a Commons Debate in 1816. See editors' notes, Bentham, ed. Schofield *et al.*, 2014, 67.
60 Bentham, 'Sextus', 96 n.
61 Bentham, *Not Paul, but Jesus*, Vol. III, 29.

References

Bentham, J. 'Offences Against Oneself: Paederasty' [1785], *Journal of Homosexuality* 3:4 (1978): 389–406.

Bentham, J. *An Introduction to the Principles of Morals and Legislation (CW)*, eds. J.H. Burns and H.L.A. Hart. Oxford, Clarendon Press, 1996.

Bentham, J. 'A Table of the Springs of Action', in *Deontology: Together with A Table of the Springs of Action and Article on Utilitarianism (CW)*, ed. A. Goldworth. Oxford: Clarendon Press, 1983.

Bentham, J. *Of Sexual Irregularities, and Other Writings on Sexual Morality (CW)*, eds. P. Schofield, C. Pease-Watkin, and M. Quinn. Oxford: Clarendon Press, 2014.

Capaldi, N. *John Stuart Mill: A Biography*. Cambridge: Cambridge University Press, 2004.

Crompton, L. 'Jeremy Bentham's Essay on "Pederasty": An Introduction', in *Jeremy Bentham: Critical Assessments, Vol. III*, ed. B. Parekh. London and New York: Routledge, 1993.

Freud, S. '"Civilized" Sexual Morality and Nervous Illness' [1908], in *The Standard Edition of the Complete Psychological Works of Sigmund Freud, Vol. IX*, ed. and trans. James Strachey. London: Hogarth Press, 1959.

Freud, S. *Three Essays on the Theory of Sexuality (The 1905 Edition)*, trans. U. Kistner, eds. P. Van Haute and H. Westerink. London and New York: Verso, 2016.

McReynolds, P. 'The Motivational Psychology of Jeremy Bentham', in *Jeremy Bentham: Critical Assessments, Vol. II*, ed. B. Parekh. London and New York: Routledge, 1993.

Mill, J.S. 'Bentham', in *Collected Works of John Stuart Mill, Volume X: Essays on Ethics, Religion and Society*, ed. J.M. Robson. London and New York: Routledge, 1996.

Moreau de Tours, Paul. *Des aberrations du sens génésique*. Paris: Asselin, 1880.

Robinson, D.N. *An Intellectual History of Psychology*. 3rd ed. Madison: University of Wisconsin Press, 1995.

Sandford, S. 'From *Geschlechtstrieb* to *Sexualtrieb*: The Originality of Freud's Conception of Sexuality', in *The Oxford Handbook of Philosophy and Psychoanalysis*, eds. R.G.T. Gipps and M. Lacewing. Oxford: Oxford University Press, 2019.

Schofield, P. *Bentham: A Guide for the Perplexed*. London and New York: Continuum, 2009.

Schofield, P. 'Jeremy Bentham on Taste, Sex and Religion', in *Bentham's Theory of Law and Public Opinion*, eds. X. Zhai and M. Quinn. Cambridge: Cambridge University Press, 2014.

Part II.
INTELLECTUAL HISTORY AND LITERATURE

Chapter 4
Literature, morals and utility: Bentham, Dumont and de Staël

Emmanuelle de Champs

In the 1770s the French minister Turgot discussed the utilitarian doctrines of Helvétius in a series of letters with his friend Nicolas de Condorcet the mathematician and philosopher. After reminding his correspondent that calls to increase pleasure and minimize pains perverted morals, he added that the principle of utility was unable to create emotion or appeal to aesthetic sentiment. 'The proof', he concluded, 'is that men are moved by novels and tragedies, and that a novel would not please if its characters conformed to the principles of Helvétius, or rather put them into practice.'[1] In Turgot's statement, as in most contemporary discussions of taste, moral values were strongly entwined with aesthetic judgment. Like morals, taste was shaped by society and allowed shared values to circulate. Peaceful manners, the rise of polite society, conversation between the sexes and the refinement of taste were, therefore, marks of a high degree of civilization. Like many of his contemporaries on both sides of the Channel – including, as we shall see, Helvétius himself – Turgot believed that these values had reached a high point in Enlightenment sociability. But, according to him, the weight given to individual pleasures in utilitarianism threatened to subvert the consensus on which society rested.

As recent work by Malcolm Quinn and Philip Schofield has shown, the notion of taste as an aesthetic and moral value provides a good entry point into the issues raised by Benthamite utilitarianism. More specifically, it highlights the specific juncture between individual enjoyment and collective utility: against most of his contemporaries, Bentham contended that taste was strictly an individual matter; that it did not depend on any collective standard.[2] He was fond of repeating that 'there [was] no good or bad taste'.[3] For this reason, his view that 'prejudice apart, the game of push-pin is of equal value with the arts and sciences of music and poetry'[4] has long been taken as revealing the shallowness of his aesthetic thought and his refusal to take the arts seriously.

Did the principle of utility as such challenge the conventions of taste, as Turgot believed, and as Bentham's statement seems to confirm? In what sense can utility be substituted for taste as a ruling principle? This article contends that Bentham's position may be better understood by locating it within late Enlightenment debates in France, with which Bentham was directly acquainted.[5] This is by no means the only context in which Bentham's views could or should be read, as Malcolm Quinn's recent article on Bentham's aesthetic views in relation to Hume's makes clear, but the European dimensions of these debates deserve to be taken into account. Indeed, Bentham's works of the 1780s were infused with references drawn from sources written in French as well as in English. They were, moreover, targeted both to anglophone and francophone readers. Revealingly, the manuscripts in which Bentham's ideas on taste were presented were written in two versions, one in French and one in English.[6]

Shortly after completing *An Introduction to the Principles of Morals and Legislation*, Bentham went back to the question of pleasure in the context of a series of bilingual manuscripts on the topic of reward written around 1782. What he planned to do with these sheets is not entirely clear.[7] It is there, however, that the most complete statements about aesthetic pleasures are to be found. None of this material was published before 1811, in French, under the editorship of Étienne Dumont, as part of *Théorie des récompenses*.[8] It was in turn translated into English in 1825 as *The Rationale of Reward*.[9] Though discussions of aesthetic pursuits are relatively short, they cast meaningful light on Bentham's position. The first part of this chapter looks at the place of morals and aesthetics in these manuscripts. It locates it in the complex field of aesthetic reflection in the French Enlightenment, especially among materialist thinkers frequently acknowledged by Bentham as his sources.

The complex connection between utility and beauty not only shaped Bentham's own understanding of the moral value of taste in general and of literature in particular, but also early readers' own reactions to the material. What is more, it also impacted on the reception of Bentham's ideas in the 1810s and 1820s, a time when the foundations of moral and aesthetic judgment were being profoundly reshaped throughout Europe. The second part of this chapter relies on two case studies that trace the early reception of Bentham's views by two francophone Genevans, both active agents of cultural transfers in Europe. It explains first on which terms Étienne Dumont read and edited the material, and then how Bentham's aesthetic ideas came to be known and discussed by Germaine de Staël in the 1810s.

1. Bentham's aesthetic individualism

1.1 The arts in Bentham's morals and legislation

In Chapter V of *An Introduction to the Principles of Morals and Legislation*, written in 1780, Bentham did not single out aesthetic sentiment as a source of pleasures or pains. Music received a mention, but the passage focused on the pleasure of performance rather than on that of the audience.[10] Similarly, the description of the 'pleasures of a country scene', taken as an example of complex pleasures, was centred around the enjoyment afforded by the sights, smells and sounds of the natural world, not those of representation.[11] With the *Introduction* being mostly concerned with laying the foundations for a utilitarian reform of penal law, the omission would not have been significant if Bentham had not himself, in other texts, drawn attention to the place of the arts and taste within a utilitarian system.

In the manuscripts on reward of the 1780s, Bentham examined the various ways in which the legislator could make use of the 'matter or reward' (or, in other words, money and honour) to procure services or encourage actions that were beneficial to general utility. The force of reward alongside that of punishment in influencing human actions, he argued, had been throughout neglected by legislators and moralists. In such statements, Bentham followed Helvétius, whose influence he consistently acknowledged.[12] If human actions were motivated by individual interest, that is, the search for pleasure and the avoidance of pain, then these were also the instruments the legislator and the moralist should use to shape individual behaviour. For Helvétius, 'the purpose of moralists is nothing but to determine the use that these rewards and punishments must be put to, and the help they might afford in uniting personal and general interests. This union', he concluded, was 'the masterpiece which morals should have in view.'[13]

By using reward and punishment together, the legislator and the moralist would be able to shape behaviour and achieve the conciliation of individual and collective interests. In the 1780s Bentham was thus keenly aware of the fact that the 'negative' means in the hands of the legislator (legal sanctions) had to be supplemented by 'positive' incentives to change people's behaviour. Helvétius's close friend, Baron d'Holbach, whose extensive writings were widely acknowledged as a summary of materialist thought in the 1770s, insisted on the power of reward as a way of shaping behaviour. That Bentham might have read his books can be surmised, even if there is no direct reference to them. In his manuscripts on reward, he discussed one of d'Holbach's examples on the power of reward to encourage virtue, borrowing an example quoted in *Système Social* (1773), namely the custom of awarding an honorary title to the most virtuous young woman in the French village of Salency.[14]

In the manuscripts on reward, Bentham used the field of the fine arts as a matrix to understand how official institutions could shape the public sphere in matters that did not fall under penal sanction. First, the arts furnished a means to reinforce the positive impact of actions that benefited both the individual and society without punishment and, conversely, bring out the disastrous consequences of actions that were detrimental to the individual and to society.[15] Hence, Bentham praised Hogarth's series *Gin Lane* as an effective means of illustrating the noxious effects of alcohol consumption – the engravings were praised not for their beauty, but for their expressiveness and didactic clarity.[16]

The state could also act in more indirect ways. As Bentham pointed out, the Royal Society of Arts established in London in 1754 provided a good example of how reward could be used to shape behaviour. On the one hand it bestowed rewards in the shape of prizes and medals to artists and inventors whose works were worthy of being commended, and on the other, through open competitions on specific themes, it invited the best minds to submit works on a given topic. Bentham suggested that his two-pronged approach could be put to different purposes beyond artistic achievement: for instance to invite discoveries and improvements in the sciences – he had in mind the rewards promised by the Board of Longitude – or honours and distinctions rewarding individual achievements in any branch of knowledge.[17] Bentham also laid down rules for the judicious use of subsidies and to avoid prevarication and nepotism, two abuses of reward. This led him to consider whether public money should be devoted to the encouragement of the fine arts in general and, therefore, to address the issue of their utility.

Bentham defined the place of the fine arts within a broader typology of useful pursuits. Within 'Arts and Sciences' four broad categories could be delineated: 'arts and sciences of agreement', 'arts and sciences of curiosity', 'of immediate utility' and of 'remote utility'. As purely agreeable pursuits, the fine arts belonged to the first category:

> By arts and sciences of agreement, I mean those which are ordinarily called the *fine arts*; such as music, poetry – or at least most branches of poetry – painting, sculpture and the other arts which aim to imitate figures, architecture and gardening considered in their ornamental branches, &c. I must here use &c., for this is not the place to embark on metaphysical distinctions. One could also comprise games of all kinds under this head.[18]

In including games in the same category as the fine arts, Bentham followed Montesquieu, whose fragmentary 'Essay on Taste' had been posthumously included by Diderot and D'Alembert in the *Encyclopédie*.[19] Bentham similarly regarded their utility as limited: altogether, the fine arts occupied only one of the four categories of the Arts and Sciences: the other three were reserved for useful inventions and scientific discoveries.

But Bentham made it clear that as sources of pleasure, the fine arts had *some* utility and should be encouraged by the utilitarian legislator.[20] He insisted: '[o]ne must not feel justified in regarding them as devoid of all utility: on the contrary, no [other activities] have more claims to be called useful. For what is useful, if not that which gives pleasure?'[21] He had already expressed similar views in manuscript notes a decade earlier, when he had examined Rousseau's argument against the frivolousness of theatre-going. Rousseau – here paraphrased by Bentham – had argued against D'Alembert that 'every amusement that is useless is an evil to a being to whom life is so short and time so pretious'. Bentham flatly set out to 'deny the truth of [this]' and insisted that no pleasure was to be considered evil.[22] In singling out Rousseau in this instance, Bentham attacked one form of asceticism (the deliberate prohibition of one kind of pleasure).[23]

While allowing the legislator to acknowledge the role of the fine arts in procuring pleasure, Bentham also set strict limits to his intervention. Indeed, in *An Introduction to the Principles of Morals and Legislation,* he had reminded his readers that the faculty to derive pleasure from this or that pursuit depended on 'circumstances influencing sensibility', which varied from one individual to another.[24] The role of the government was, therefore, not directly to provide pleasure to individuals, but to support contributions that had a beneficial impact on the public in general, and not those that procured pleasure to one patron or amateur, or to only one class of people.[25] In including games in the category of 'agreeable arts and sciences' alongside the fine arts, Bentham not only refused to carve a specific space for aesthetic sentiment, but also opened up the social sphere of enjoyments.

1.2 Taste, interest and the people

Like Rousseau's, Bentham's approach to art was marked by a strong anti-aristocratic concern, but, as will become apparent later, on very different grounds and with very different implications. First, the radicalism of Bentham's refusal to admit a hierarchy between pleasures and to set apart aesthetic sentiment deserves to be explored. It is useful to compare his position with that of Helvétius. Starting from similar considerations that the fine arts procured pleasure to the senses, Helvétius believed that the refinement of taste provided evidence of progress in humanity's ability to experience pleasure. Describing the pleasures of the 'philosopher' in a posthumously published poem entitled *Le bonheur*, he wrote that the philosopher 'does not abandon the pleasures of the senses, but he masters them. Poetry, Music, Painting, Sculpture and Architecture are for him new sources of pleasures.'[26] In Helvétius's view, the object of any utilitarian legislator should thus be to increase sensibility to the fine arts in order to maximize pleasure.

In *De l'esprit,* Helvétius explored the political implications of the idea. The junction between the aesthetic sphere and that of politics was effected seamlessly through the concept of 'interest', which, as Reinhard Koselleck points out, operated in both fields: in Helvétius's words, a painting pleases us because it *interests* us.[27] What is more, in a political system organized around the principle of interest, common tastes were a guarantee that the citizens shared similar interests or sources of pleasures. Enlarging the audience of the arts therefore served a political function. On the contrary, fragmented audiences revealed that no common ground existed between citizens:

> In governments [in which] citizens are not united by a common interest, the diversity of personal interests must necessarily go against universal applause. In such countries, one can only reach limited success, because the passions depicted appear more or less interesting to particular audiences.[28]

This argument could support a critique of aristocratic government: for instance, d'Holbach answered the common opinion that the arts had prospered under Louis XIV by insisting that nobody had cared to spread artistic taste among the people, which had ultimately jeopardized the safety of government by dividing the rich and the poor.[29] The implications of Helvétius and d'Holbach's statements were that, to ensure a cohesive and politically stable society, artistic taste should be shared and open to as many people as possible. The role of the legislator was to promote a common interest, that is, a common appreciation of the beautiful.

In eighteenth-century terms, as the polite sphere was believed to be expanding, this translated into a debate on the usefulness of artistic criticism. Critics were important agents in creating a common taste and acted as intermediaries between the artists and the public. They played a central part in the artistic education of the people. But Bentham had only harsh words for those who sought to bestow praise or blame on specific art forms or art works:

> If these principles are correct, we shall know how to estimate those ingenious rather than useful critics who, under pretence of purifying the public taste, endeavour successively to deprive mankind of a larger or smaller part of the sources of their amusement. These modest judges of elegance and taste consider themselves as benefactors to the human race, whilst they are really only the interrupters of their pleasure – a sort of importunate hosts, who place themselves at the table to diminish, by their pretended delicacy, the appetite of their guests.[30]

Criticizing critics was a familiar argument within debates on taste in the period. In his *Philosophical Dictionary*, for instance, Voltaire lambasted such an influential figure as Boileau, who he accused of using the means of criticism to ridicule the work of his rivals.[31] Voltaire did, however, believe that there was such a thing as good taste, whose prescriptions could be said to be universal and which could be spread by '*connaisseurs*'. The taste of the public, even of the vulgar, could and should be improved – it marked the refinement of a society: 'only connoisseurs can reclaim the favour of the public, and this is the only difference between the most enlightened and the most brutish nations'.[32] In the same line, d'Holbach lambasted 'those impudent critics, full of bad faith, armed by low jealousy, who seem to declare war on talent', but he encouraged 'fair, instructive and polite' criticism.[33] For Diderot, attacking critics served to reclaim taste for the people themselves, emphatically not to subvert the idea of a common taste. The public was the sole arbiter of taste; experts and critics only served to distract them from the expression of their preferences. The political implications of such a view became clear when the French Revolution turned against the aristocratic patronage of the arts and closed down the academies in 1793.[34]

Bentham's position ran along different lines: by imposing a given standard of taste, critics robbed everyone of their enjoyment. They ruined the pleasure of many and caused the financial ruin of authors thrown out of fashion by their dictates.[35] His strong focus on individual appreciation and his refusal to admit the existence of one common standard of taste set him apart. Indeed, for him, the arts played no role in the structuring of a political public sphere, but merely illustrated the confiscation of power by an aristocracy, be it that of the nobility or that of self-proclaimed critics.[36] In this specific case, Bentham implied, utility lay in the pursuit of individual pleasures, not of collective ones.

1.3 Poetry, truth and morals

The specificity and radicalism of Bentham's position both stand out in his treatment of poetry. It was the only artistic pursuit he examined in detail in the manuscripts, concluding not only that push-pin was in most cases as good as poetry, but that it was to be *preferred* to poetry: '[p]oetry is useful insofar as it amuses. But the game of push-pin, if it amused as much, would be preferable'.[37] Such remarks were not confined to the section on the fine arts. More than other arts, poetry was presented as intrinsically corrupting, especially because of its closeness to political power. Indeed, through flattery and exaggeration, poets encouraged the lowest instincts in rulers, as Louis XIV's bloody wars testified. Voltaire himself, whom Bentham otherwise admired, was made partly responsible for encouraging Frederick II of Prussia's military conquest in Silesia through elegies and poems. Poetry was dangerous because it inflamed sentiments instead of appealing to reason and led sovereigns away from considerations of utility. What was more, the embellishments required by poetry were structurally contrary to truth:

> The felicity of life and the perfection of happiness and virtue depend upon the accuracy of our information and the rectitude of our judgements with relation to several topics we are interested in. But the tendency which poetry has to promote such accuracy and that rectitude is not very remarkable: on the contrary the tendency it has, at least in most branches, in all perhaps, but the dramatic, seems to be rather on the other side.[38]

On poetry, Bentham's usual references appear to be inverted: he sided with Plato, who famously ejected poets from the Republic and disagreed with Helvétius, who had pointed out that poetry and eloquence were beneficial when they reinforced the impressions made on the public and added moral value and efficiency to discourse.[39] D'Holbach was more cautious and underlined the fact that eloquence was a double-edged sword that could be used to further false principles as well as good ones.[40] Bentham went much further and claimed that poetry was intrinsically synonymous with falsehood and distortion.

Bentham's insistence on the close link between poetry and falsehood can be connected to his epistemology. Indeed, the analysis of poetry, as a mode of discourse, played a pivotal function in eighteenth-century aesthetics. As Hans Aarsleff has recently explained, after the work of Étienne de Condillac it was widely believed that primitive language was the direct product of emotion and sensation, not of reflection. What we perceive we perceive at once. According to Condillac, early languages reflected this simultaneity. Unlike contemporary languages that depend on analysis and reflect logical relations in complex grammatical sentences, the first language of humanity directly mirrored immediate perceptions and conveyed several ideas and sentiments simultaneously. This pseudo-historical hypothesis translated into an epistemological theory which contended that ancient languages like Greek and, to a lesser extent Latin, relied more than contemporary ones on the grammatical 'inversion' of parts of speech and were, therefore, more expressive and closer to poetry.[41]

In contrast, when Bentham wrote on the origins of language, he suggested another narrative. For him the true unit of meaning was not emotion or sensation, but a thought process that associated analysis and synthesis and resulted in the production of a proposition. The basic unit of meaning was, therefore, a logical thought process. Instead of praising Latin and Greek for their direct appeal to emotions, Bentham commended the English language, which fulfilled 'all the purposes of discourse taken together'.[42] Beauty in a language, which he did not exclude altogether, had to do not with conciseness but with the existence of numerous parts of speech expressing accurate logical relations.[43] Poetry was, therefore, remote from the original working of the mind and prone to distort reality. In singling out poetry as the *locus* of lies and exaggeration, Bentham denied it could have any positive moral value.

Bentham's refusal to ascribe more than a minimal moral value to the arts went beyond his indictment of the mendacity of poetry. More generally, he believed that love for the fine arts was harmless and beneficial only to the extent that it drove people away from boredom and, therefore, from violence.[44] This opinion consistently ran against the idea that the fine arts had a civilizing effect on the morals of a nation by shaping common taste between the people. The force of this argument was regularly reasserted in the eighteenth century as narratives about the formation of taste followed those of the formation of morals: in both cases, philosophers needed to account for the way in which individual appreciation gradually came to espouse common standards or common views. This issue was especially pressing for empiricists who started methodologically from individual perception: if everything proceeded from sensation, how could one reach beyond one's own feelings? In morals, Bentham consistently opposed appeals to a 'common sense' or a 'moral sense' and grounded moral appreciation in the estimation of the greatest happiness of the greatest number.[45] In aesthetics – and probably also in sexual morality – he refused to make such a move and only accepted individual pleasure as a standard.

Again, this refusal set him apart from Helvétius and d'Holbach who tried to reconcile calls to utility with artistic appreciation. D'Holbach claimed, for instance, that 'a beautiful action of Antiquity pleases us because we feel its utility, because we put ourselves in the place of the person who did it and of those who witnessed it, and because we wish those we live with would do the same'. His explicit conclusion was that 'good taste in morals does not differ from good taste in the arts'.[46] In saying this he was doing little more than repeating a common eighteenth-century trope which can also be illustrated by Rousseau's statement that 'the good is nothing else than the beautiful put into action'.[47] This was a standard pillar of the debate on the moral role of novels that was prominent in the second half of the eighteenth century both in France and in Britain and provided the background to Turgot's position discussed in the introduction to this chapter.

The vocabulary of 'moral taste' allowed d'Holbach to examine the origins of moral ideas through a comparison with aesthetic ones. Natural sensibility differed from one person to the other: the diversity of original tastes was related to differences in the organs of perception, be they external (good or bad eyesight, or an ear for music) or internal (the configuration of our brain). It followed that 'men disagree as much on their assessment of physical beauty as on that of moral beauty'. However, education and custom trained and shaped individual organs, making it possible gradually to reach agreement in aesthetic and in moral matters with our contemporaries. In other words, we become 'connoisseurs in morals, just as we become connoisseurs in painting, sculpture, architecture and so on'.[48] Bentham consistently rejected such a parallel.

In considering the fine arts Bentham was throughout intent on keeping taste at the level of the individual, refusing to consider it as a social, or collective form of appreciation and, therefore, refusing to establish any hierarchy between them – the criterion of 'the greatest happiness' came here to be applied strictly to one individual. In the field of artistic taste, the principle that everyone was the best judge of his or her interest was rigorously applied. In asserting this, Bentham derived radical implications from a strictly individualistic understanding of pleasure and pain. His theory of taste was, however, subordinate to a theory of social and political organization, which limited the anarchical consequences of such a strictly individualistic perspective. It seems plausible to contend that a complete individualism predominates in Bentham's aesthetic thought and that its materialistic implications deserve to be further studied.

2. The early reception of Bentham's aesthetics: Rousseau, Dumont and Madame de Staël

2.1 Bentham and Rousseau: Étienne Dumont's attempt at synthesis

Dumont received Bentham's manuscripts on reward (probably both in French and in English) in July 1794.[49] These sheets were not included in the first batch of writings he published in 1802 but came out nine years later in *Théorie des peines et des récompenses* (1811). Dumont conducted most of the work on this material in the summer of 1807.[50] He came back again to the manuscripts for the third French edition that appeared in 1826, but without making any substantive change to the sections on the fine arts.[51]

Despite Dumont's usual disclaimer in the preface that he had partly rewritten Bentham's words, a comparison with the manuscripts reveals that he remained faithful to the original for his chapters on the fine arts. He reproduced passages in which Bentham warned against the lure of poetry as an instrument of falsehood. He included the fragments on the civilizing tendency of games as well as Bentham's criticism of literary critics in general and Addison in particular. Dumont's version even expanded Bentham's attack on satirists.[52] In an editorial footnote he hinted, however, at a possible disagreement with Bentham's position. 'I could not', he wrote, 'follow the author's position that as far as literary tastes are concerned there is no right or wrong.' But he did not develop his own views there, and in the rest of the footnote he in fact supported Bentham's views and adapted them to the cultural references of his francophone readers. Was it not true, he wrote, that 'plays by Hardi and Garnier' gave audiences as much pleasure as those by the great Corneille?[53] This contrasts with Dumont's private reaction to the passages, as he recalled in his notebooks:

> In his treatise on *Rewards*, B[entham] severely attacks literary critics, especially Addison's *Spectator*, who under pretence of reforming taste destroyed a variety of harmless muses: under his mace, he crushed the small literary family of doggerel rhymes, acrostics, poems cast into the figures of eggs or wings, of witticisms, &c. What has he done? asks Bentham, what has it led to? He has deprived those who enjoyed these witticisms of innocent pleasures, he has treated them as idiots and men of depraved and bizarre taste, he has ridiculed them and abandoned them to the contempt of society.[54]

After thus acknowledging Bentham's position, Dumont insisted on the *usefulness* of literary criticism as a genre. Indeed, while Bentham believed that critics inflicted pain on the authors they attacked, Dumont argued that bad publicity was better than no publicity: authors 'should not', he wrote, 'fear criticism, but [fear] being forgotten'. Critiques prompted refutations and counter-critiques, while bad reviews 'brought larger audiences to the theatre houses'. Such a view of the literary field, where reputations were being fought over, is interesting because Dumont's argument was not primarily about literary merit in itself, but solely about the excitement and animation brought by literary quarrels that had agitated the literary sphere in the seventeenth and eighteenth centuries.[55] By looking at the effects of controversies on sales, Dumont took Bentham's utilitarian reasoning in a new direction. He also legitimated the idea that the literary field was central to understanding the formation of public opinion, an idea that, as we have seen, Bentham rejected.[56]

But Dumont also explored other avenues. He examined Bentham's view that 'good taste' was synonymous with 'prejudice', and that 'there is no good or bad taste, or rather that they are all good provided they are not contrary to utility'.[57] This rephrasing of Bentham's position was only partially correct, for Bentham refused to connect public utility and taste systematically, as we have seen. To trace the origin of Dumont's ideas, we need to turn to the second most important intellectual influence on his thought: Jean-Jacques Rousseau. In *Letter to D'Alembert*, as we have seen, Rousseau had famously argued against the frivolousness of the theatre that perverted the moral and political character of citizens. In his notebooks, Dumont attacked, like Rousseau, the moral debasement brought about by games and entertainment:

> Imagine two equally talented men, the first having been raised in a society in which these [literary] frivolities were in vogue, and the second in a society in which only serious and philosophical works were valued. Twenty years on, how different from one another will they be! The first will have turned into a Pantalone-Phoebus, a frivolous speaker, the second will be generally useful, or prepared to be useful.

Throughout, Dumont attacked petty literature in terms that would be entirely alien to Bentham and were reminiscent of Rousseau's contempt. Both believed that the pleasure of frivolous amusement was intrinsically corrupting: society needed 'labourers', not 'rope-dancers' and 'conjurers', Dumont argued. Where Bentham praised the harmless pleasures of push-pin, Dumont lambasted games that 'prolong childhood into the mature age'.

Dumont did not, any more than Rousseau, believe that artistic pleasures were intrinsically corrupting. There were good and bad poems, good and bad novels, and taste was the crucial discriminating principle at work. Bad poetry was simply formal; it set out to triumph over self-imposed constraints; it was nothing but a show of cleverness. But true poetry, however, had a strong moral dimension: 'when its object is to bring the harmony of style to perfection, to present ideas with more details, to decorate them with deeper images, to help memory by regularly returning sounds or rhythmical measures, it deserves an honourable place among the works of the human mind'.[58] As we have seen, there was nothing new about those arguments that praised poetry as the perfection of the use of language to persuade, to memorize and, above all, to feel. On this point too, Dumont's manuscripts prove simultaneously how much he imbibed from Bentham and how far he still remained from wholeheartedly accepting the moral implications of utilitarianism.

In another notebook (undated like the first but also evidently written while or shortly after he was working on Bentham's manuscripts on reward), he proposed an original synthesis. On the one hand, he followed Bentham in attacking writers who made use of literary flourishes to present their own feelings and opinions as 'eternal, unshakeable, immortal truths like God and nature' and acted like 'despots'.[59] Such mercenary writers corrupted the morals of the people. Dumont provided several examples of how literature could confirm prejudices and blind reason: Voltaire's antisemitism and anticlericalism, Rousseau's hatred of the rich and Sieyès's attack on the nobility. Like Bentham, Dumont believed that acting according to utility meant renouncing prejudice in order to appeal to reason and facts. At the same time, Dumont held that style could be sublime when it was 'devoid of all allegiance to the two false principles' of asceticism and sympathy/antipathy. Some works, indeed 'can pass as beautiful in very different times'. Style was good when it reinforced good ideas.[60] His own remarks on what constituted good style reinforced this view: it avoided superfluous words and phrases, it did not add gratuitous ornaments, and it did not indulge in unnecessary repetition.

Brought up in Geneva, Dumont had imbibed Rousseau's writings and held them as a standard as far as style was concerned. After his death in 1829, the *Bibliothèque de Genève* published two short articles drawn from his manuscripts on Rousseau.[61] In these pages Dumont drew a sharp distinction between Rousseau as political philosopher and Rousseau as writer and moralist. As Richard Whatmore explains, like many Genevan reformers of his generation, Dumont rejected Rousseau's radical political views.[62] His embrace of Bentham's ideas in the mid-1790s furnished him with new arguments to attack Rousseau's political philosophy. Borrowing Bentham's vocabulary, he argued that Rousseau had been enslaved by the 'sentimental principle, the principle of sympathy and antipathy, a dogmatic and cutting principle demanding blind acceptance, while it itself refuses to bow to the standards of common reason'. Refusing to define his words, Rousseau remained, Dumont argued, 'ill-at-ease in abstract writing', unable to prove his assertions, preferring sentiment to analysis. Following passion and not reason had direct consequences on Rousseau's politics: this led him to 'prefer savagery over civilization' and to claim hastily that 'all governments on earth are based on usurpation'.[63]

Dumont's trajectory has been described as a move 'from Rousseauism to Bentham'.[64] If we follow Richard Whatmore, in politics, Dumont's estrangement from Rousseau's ideas became clear in the aftermath of the Terror in the mid-1790s, though he was frequently 'drawn back'[65] to his works and engaged with them throughout his life, as countless references in his manuscripts testify. What has not been noticed, however, is how long Dumont maintained his admiration for

Rousseau's literary achievements. This, as we have seen, could not be separated from a moral evaluation of his philosophy. In fact, Dumont argued that, in literary and moral matters, Rousseau's weaknesses turned into strengths as his stylistic genius approached perfection. Rousseau knew how to bring situations to life, how to 'rise from ideas to images and from images to feelings'.[66] Dumont pitted the dry and subversive style of the *Social Contract* against the charming scenes of *Julie, or the New Heloise,* which placed its characters in the midst of moral quandaries and described their reactions. In praising the moral examples found in the novel, Dumont embraced Rousseau's view that morals could be acquired by imitating virtuous models (be they fictitious or real) rather than by applying systematic reasoning: '[l]et us take for ourselves great examples to imitate rather than vain systems to follow', Rousseau had written.[67] By 'presenting' his characters 'as if one knew them', Dumont continued, Rousseau struck the right chord. This method, by which scenes were presented to the readers, served to 'imprint moral truths into their memories' because 'a dry maxim will not penetrate the heart, it cannot be received unless it is united to an action in which we feel an interest'.[68] Rousseau himself had described this process through an analogy between the field of morals and that of aesthetics:

> One practices seeing as well as sensing, or rather exquisite vision is but a delicate and refined sentiment. So it is that a painter beholding a beautiful landscape or standing before a beautiful tableau is enraptured by objects that are not even noticed by the common Observer. How many things are there which one perceives only through sentiment and which one cannot account for?[69]

Surprisingly for an admirer of Bentham, Dumont praised Rousseau's morals at length, describing them as an alliance of 'Spartan' inflexibility and of human fallibility. In *The New Heloise,* Rousseau had indeed shown how even the most virtuous soul, that of Julie, could sometimes lapse, which made her virtue all the more admirable. But separating Rousseau's morals from his politics, as Dumont did, went against the avowed intention of the author who believed that fiction was a proper vehicle to illustrate not only morals, but also the origins of political society, or the role of luxury in national economy, to give but a few examples.[70] It is to be noted that Dumont's private papers reveal a similar disjunction in the case of Bentham's morals, which he rejected while continuing to praise his model of social science.

Whether Dumont's understanding of the political and moral implications of Rousseau's and Bentham's works was correct or not is not in question here. His own writings on the subject, however, confirm the difficulty of understanding Bentham's aesthetics, even for one of his closest readers, and fitting it within the shared culture of the late Enlightenment. Dumont's own attempt at synthesis is interesting because it shows how increasingly difficult it became to make sense of Bentham's position after Rousseau and in the early Romantic period. This comes further to light when we examine the evolution of Germaine de Staël's ideas on utilitarianism and the arts. Her views were considerably more influential than Dumont's because they were widely publicized, unlike his, which were kept private. Much more openly than Dumont, she claimed that the moral and aesthetic flaws of utilitarianism directly undermined its political and methodological prescriptions.

2.2 Madame de Staël: Style against utility

Madame de Staël's writings, which spanned the period from 1788 to 1817, represented another step in the changing articulation of aesthetics and politics. The daughter of Jacques Necker (a Genevan banker and twice finance minister to Louis XVI), Germaine de Staël embraced a literary career and soon became one of the most influential French-language writers of her generation. Her first published work, *Letters on the Writings and the Character of Jean-Jacques Rousseau* (1788), provided in more ways than one a model for Dumont's own essays on Rousseau. Like Dumont, she considered Rousseau's politics impracticable, but she abundantly praised his style in close connection with his moral thought.[71] *The New Heloise*, for instance, was admirable because it was 'a great moral idea put into action and made dramatic'.[72] As Dumont did later, she subscribed to the idea that morals came to life in Rousseau's novels and were served by a style that appealed to sentiment rather than to reason. But she went further and argued that, in morals, eloquence and sentiment provided a safeguard against the slow calculations of the mind on the one hand, and from the hasty and dangerous passions of the heart on the other. Rhetoric she therefore saw in a good light, as a necessary social adjunct to virtue.[73] For her, eloquence developed the sentiments that then allowed individuals to 'tap the resources they find in themselves', those of friendship, family love and the intellectual pleasures.[74] Literary fiction, in this respect, played a central role – a theory that Mme de Staël put into practice in her own novels *Delphine*

(1802) and *Corinne* (1807). For her, as for Rousseau, literature was the proper vehicle of morals:

> One may extract from good novels a purer, higher morals than from any didactic work on virtue. The latter genre is dryer, and therefore necessarily more indulgent. Maxims made to be applied generally never reach the delicate heroism which may be held as model [in a novel], but which one cannot reasonably turn into a duty.[75]

In *On Literature*, published in 1800, she insisted on the powers of literary style that triggered moral and aesthetic sentiment and, 'moving the mind and the body together, produced a shudder of admiration which incited us to generous actions'.[76] Reading good literature also developed moral sensibility by fortifying sentiment. This entailed more than a simple parallel between two different spheres of judgment: Madame de Staël insisted that, by placing characters in specific circumstances and illustrating their moral deliberations, novels put the reader in the characters' shoes and thereby acted as a training ground for moral decision-making. Moreover, this was true of words as well as of actions: 'every time they are called to choose between different phrases, writers and orators select the one which calls up the most delicate idea – their minds choose between phrases, just as their souls should decide between different actions in life. And the habit of doing one may lead to the other.'[77] In this way, style regained, in Madame de Staël's work, a central moral function.

Her encounter with Benthamite utilitarianism coincided with her own philosophical and political development. Through Genevan circles, she was acquainted with Dumont with whom she also corresponded. In 1802, when *Traités de législation civile et pénale* was published in Paris, extracts had been read and discussed at Coppet, her house in the vicinity of Geneva.[78] In the summer of 1807, as he was working on Bentham's manuscripts on reward, he received from her a copy of *Corinne, ou l'Italie*, her latest novel.[79] They met again in London in 1813.

Bentham's ideas interested her because they addressed a question that went to the heart of her reflections on contemporary politics after the Revolution, at a time when 'one is led to reflect deeply on the nature of happiness in morals and in politics, on its direction, on its goals, on the hurdles which still separate us from this goal'.[80] In the late 1790s she briefly toyed with the idea that utilitarianism could provide a solution to this problem because it gave legislators a method to reach general happiness. At that stage, she did not altogether reject calculation and political engineering from the sphere of politics. But already she believed that what was true for the people as a whole was inherently incorrect in the case of individuals, a paradox that she formulated in this way:

> The legislator takes men as a whole, the moralist one by one; the legislator must deal with the nature of things, the moralist with the diversity of sensations; finally, the legislator must always examine men from the point of view of their mutual relations and the moralist, considering each individual as a moral entity, a compound of pleasures and pains, of passions and reason, sees man under various angles, but always in relation to himself.[81]

In drawing a clear line between the moral and the political subject, she went against one of the postulates of many of her contemporaries. This was not unconnected with her increasing belief that literature, not legislation, could transcend the opposition of individual and collective interest because it appealed to humanity as such.

Reading Kant in the early 1800s had a profound impact on Madame de Staël, not least because it allowed her to take her views of the connection between aesthetic and moral judgment further. But in those years, as her public position became increasingly precarious because of her growing opposition to Napoleon, she came increasingly to reject utilitarianism as a philosophical system because she associated it with the opportunism of many of her French contemporaries who had adapted to the increasing violations of liberty under the Terror and the Empire. Kant's works allowed her to propose an alternative aesthetic, moral and political theory and went together with her rejection of Enlightenment rationalism.[82] In *On Germany*, published in 1813, she set her recent reading of Kant against both English empiricism and French materialism, whose common roots she found in Hobbes's and Locke's writings. Without closing the door to experience or maintaining an indefensible innatism, she believed that Kant's system achieved 'a synthesis of experimental philosophy with the idealist doctrine'. Tellingly it was Kant's definition of the sublime that provided the key to individual liberty against all forms of political coercion, thus allowing the gap between morals (rooted as it was in aesthetic appreciation) and politics to be bridged. This led her to see 'enthusiasm' as the root of all moral qualities and as evidence of a common humanity: unlike pleasant sensations that remained individual, admiration for the beautiful, in the arts or in morals, was universal.

> The enthusiasm triggered by the beautiful does not have anything to do with either sensations or judgement; it is an innate disposition

> akin to the sentiment of duty and the necessary primitive notions of the mind. We recognise truth when we see it, because it is the external image of an ideal whose type resides in our intelligence. Tastes might be diverse in all things that are agreeable, for such pleasures are rooted in sensation, but admiration for the beautiful in the arts or in nature must be universal, because all men's souls contain sentiments of divine origin which beauty awakens and makes them enjoy.[83]

Tellingly, the praise of enthusiasm was conducted alongside a sustained criticism of Bentham's principle of utility as presented by Dumont.

This confrontation was played out in London in 1813, shortly after the book came out. Banned from France and under threat in Geneva, Madame de Staël reached London after a long journey through Germany and northern Europe. During her stay, she was received in Whig salons, especially at Bowood, now the seat of the third marquess of Lansdowne. Her visit was documented in some detail by Étienne Dumont, a familiar of Bowood and Whig circles since the late 1780s and therefore a perfect host for his Genevan friend.[84] In these conversations, Dumont unambiguously defended Bentham's utilitarianism – on moral and political grounds rather than on aesthetic ones. As he recalled in his letters to Maria Edgeworth (whose attempts to put utilitarian experience into novels also deserves further study), he soon refused to argue with her in public:

> I shall only tell you that she has nothing but utmost contempt for poor utilitarian philosophy, that she reduces it to a miserable calculus of personal interest. I threw a four-or-five-page protest at her and was furiously attacked in return. I do not want to have anything more to do with this – I am too heavy for aerostatic balloons. To define, according to her, is to kill. Moral classifications are nothing but anatomy: one builds a skeleton and when one says 'rise up and walk', it remains still. This is the point she will not be brought to depart from.[85]

By 1813, as Dumont bitterly remarked, two distinct positions were deeply entrenched and Dumont's own attempt at synthesis remained buried in his manuscripts.

Conclusion

The impossible dialogue between Madame de Staël and Dumont was an important step in the radicalization of positions that had been closely intertwined since the second half of the eighteenth century. Madame de Staël's arguments against utilitarianism, both in print and in person, had a deep influence, especially in England. One can, for instance, turn to Carlyle's 1827 essay for the *Edinburgh Review* entitled 'State of German Literature', which explicitly drew on de Staël's *On Germany*. Though he did not mention Bentham directly, he evidently had English utilitarians in mind when he further dramatized the opposition between utility and poetry. In the late eighteenth century, he wrote, '[utility] was set up for the universal measure of mental as well as material value; poetry, except of an economical and preceptorial character, was found to be the product of a rude age; and religious enthusiasm was but derangement in the biliary organs'. '[I]ts partisans', he concluded, 'in subsequent satirical controversies, received the nickname of *Philistern* (Philistines).'[86] This characterization became immensely popular as it was taken up by John Ruskin and Matthew Arnold and continued to be influential throughout the nineteenth century.[87]

In contrast, one purpose of this chapter has been to show that such a radical presentation does not do justice to the challenge utilitarianism posed to eighteenth-century aesthetics and morals. In the half-century that separated Turgot's statement from Madame de Staël's, utilitarian writers such as Helvétius, Bentham and Dumont each explored different ways in which utility and aesthetic sentiment could be articulated. Bentham's position appears to be the most radical – a conclusion that a comparison in the following years with John Stuart Mill's position seemed to confirm.

Notes

1 The author wishes to thank Knud Haakonssen and Michael Quinn for comments and suggestions on this chapter, as well as audiences at the 'Bentham and the Arts' conference series at UCL and at the Max-Weber-Kolleg in Erfurt University. This chapter is part of a project that has received funding from the European Union's Horizon 2020 research and innovation programme under the Marie Skłodowska-Curie grant agreement No. 665958. De Condorcet and Turgot, ed. Henry, 1970, 144.

2 Quinn, 2013; Schofield, ed. Zhai and Quinn, 2014; Malcolm Quinn, 2017.

3 Schofield, ed. Zhai and Quinn, 2014, 92. According to John Stuart Mill, Bentham was heard regularly repeating this view, see Schofield, 2014, 116. Étienne Dumont made a similar remark, see below.

4 Bowring, 1843, II, 253.

5 For a methodological discussion of the issues at stake in displacing Bentham's thought to a French-speaking context see De Champs, 2015, 11–17.
6 The original language of quoted passages is noted.
7 The first allusions to an 'Essay on reward' are to be found in a letter to Lord Ashburton in 1782. Bentham continued to work on the topic until the end of his stay in Russia in 1787. Bentham, ed. Christie, 1971, pp. xxxi, 182, 524.
8 Bentham, ed. Dumont, 1811.
9 Bentham, ed. Smith, 1825; here quoted from the Bowring edition, vol. II.
10 Bentham, ed. Burns and Hart, 1996, 43 n.
11 Bentham, *IMPL* (*CW*), 49–50 n.
12 Rosen, 2003; De Champs, 2015, 42–5.
13 Helvétius, ed. Stenger and Steffen, 2016, 189.
14 'Système Social': Holbach, ed. Jackson, 2004, 286 n. Bentham took up the example at UC cxlii. 119.
15 This aspect of his thought has attracted interest in recent years, due in part to the parallel development of 'nudge theory'. See Engelmann, 2003; Michael Quinn, 2017; Brunon-Ernst, 2012.
16 Malcolm Quinn, 2017, 28 & n.
17 'In the language of the London Society of Arts reward *ex promisso* is termed a *premium*: while a reward given *ex post facto* is distinguished by the name of *bounty*. This nomenclature, however, could not be generally adopted without confusion: put in the language of the legislator the term bounty is applied to rewards given *ex promisso*: The bounties upon exportation and importation for example are all in this predicament.' UC cxlii. 128. Remarks on the Board of Longitude are at UC cxlii. 94 (French).
18 UC cxlii. 248 (French), *Théorie* II, 215–6, *Rationale*, II, 253. Throughout this paper, when multiple versions have been found, references are first to the manuscripts, then to the corresponding passages in *Théorie des Récompenses* and lastly to *Rationale of Reward* (Bowring edition).
19 'Goût'. Voltaire, in *Encyclopédie, ou dictionnaire raisonné des sciences et des arts et des métiers*, ed. Diderot and D'Alembert, 17 vols. (Paris: 1751–65), VII, 761.
20 See also, Schofield, ed. Zhai and Quinn, 2014, 92–3.
21 UC cxlii. 248 (French), *Théorie*, II, 216; Bentham, *Rationale*, II, 253.
22 Bentham, ed. Long and Schofield, 2016, 351; See Rousseau, ed. Bloom *et al.*, 2004, 251–351.
23 Bentham, 1996, 17–21.
24 Bentham, 1996, 51–73.
25 *Théorie*, II, 67; *Rationale*, II, 212–3.
26 Helvétius, 1772, 33.
27 Koselleck and Orth, ed. Brunner *et al.*, 1982.
28 Helvétius, ed. Stenger and Steffen, 2016, 169.
29 Holbach, ed. Jackson, 2004, 256.
30 *Théorie*, II, 219–20; *Rationale*, II, 254.
31 'Criticism'. Voltaire, ed. Cronk, 2011.
32 'Goût'. Voltaire, *Œuvres alphabétiques II*. ed. Cronk and Mervaud, 2016, 511–2.
33 Holbach, ed. Jackson, 2004, 631.
34 Guichard, 2012.
35 *Théorie*, II, 220–1.
36 The democratic implications of this view were explicitly drawn out later in the Constitutional Code: see Schofield, ed. Zhai and Quinn, 2014, 95.
37 UC cxlii. 249, 240; *Théorie*, II, 217; *Rationale*, II, 253.
38 UC cxlii. 241.
39 Helvétius, ed. Stenger and Steffen, 2016, 398–9.
40 Holbach, ed. Jackson, 2004, 622.
41 Aarsleff, 2016, 733–35; see also the remark that, for Diderot, 'the study of inversion becomes the transition to aesthetics', in Chouillet, 1973, 170.
42 Bentham, ed. Smith and Burston, 1983, 395.
43 Bentham, ed. Smith and Burston, 1983, 407. It is worth noting that, alongside this theory of language, Bentham also proposed another one, which attributed an important place to images: meaning could also be conveyed through the method of 'archetypation', that is to say by conjuring up an image and appealing to the imagination as well as to reason.

44 UC cxlii. 248; *Théorie*, II, 219; *Rationale*, II, 254; On this point, see also Schofield, ed. Zhai and Quinn, 2014, 94.
45 Bentham, 1996, 26 n.
46 Holbach, ed. Jackson, 2004, 57–8.
47 Rousseau, ed. Stewart and Vaché, 1997, 47.
48 Holbach, ed. Jackson, 2004, 57–62.
49 Bentham, ed. Milne, 1981, 50.
50 'I have almost finished revising *Rewards*', Dumont wrote to Samuel Romilly on 18 June 1807 (MSS Dumont, 17, f. 206).
51 Dumont claimed he had made numerous small improvements to the style of the volume, see letter to Frédéric Soret, 13 February 1825, MSS Dumont, 34, f. 79.
52 *Théorie*, II, 217–24.
53 *Théorie*, II, 221 n.
54 MS Dumont, 21, ff. 90. The reference is to Joseph Addison, 'True and False Wit', *The Spectator*, no. 62 (11 May 1711). For Bentham and Addison see Malcom Quinn's contribution to this volume.
55 For an overview see Lilti, 2007.
56 On this connection see Spector, 2009.
57 MS Dumont, 21, f. 91v.
58 MS Dumont, 21, ff. 92–3. In eighteenth-century satires, '*Pantalon-Phébus*' was a pompous character with ludicrous literary aspirations.
59 MS Dumont, 22, f. 26.
60 MS Dumont, 22, f. 26–7, and MS Dumont 47, f. 7.
61 Dumont, 1836 a and b, 128–35 (a) and 298–313 (b).
62 Whatmore, ed. Lifschitz, 2016, 4.
63 Dumont, 1836, 130; Against this 'impracticable' philosophy, Dumont found in Bentham the model for 'a science of legislation separate from the discussion of forms of government, the irresolvable issue that had caused dreadful upheaval in civil life across the European mainland'. Whatmore, ed. Lifschitz, 2016, 12.
64 Blamires, 2008, 207.
65 Whatmore, ed. Lifschitz, 2016, 1.
66 Dumont, 1836b, 299.
67 Rousseau, ed. Stewart and Vaché, 47.
68 Dumont, 1836, 303–5.
69 Rousseau, ed. Stewart and Vaché, 48.
70 The connection is, however, sometimes problematic, for instance in the case of the vindication of social and political hierarchies in *The New Heloise*.
71 For de Staël's position regarding Rousseau's politics see Craiutu, ed. Rosenblatt and Schweigert, 2017. De Staël's influence in shaping the romantic connection between poetry and politics has recently received attention in English, see Pearson, 2016.
72 'Lettres sur les écrits et sur le caractère de Jean-Jacques Rousseau', De Staël, 1871, I, 5.
73 'Eloquence has often been called dangerous, but I believe it is necessary when one needs to set virtue against passion. It begets movements in the mind which decide immediately in favour of a course of action … eloquence alone can add impulsive force to reason and give it enough spirit to fight against the passions.' De Staël, 1871, I, 14.
74 'De l'influence des passions sur le bonheur des individus et des nations', De Staël, 1871, I, 160–71.
75 'Essai sur les fictions', De Staël, 1871, I, 70.
76 De Staël, 1991, 68.
77 De Staël, 1991, 69–70.
78 See De Champs, 2015, 188.
79 'I received a very interesting letter from Mme de Staël: she has lately published *Corinne or Italy*, she sent it to me, she wrote, because her friends believe it is her best to date', Dumont wrote in June 1807, see MSS Dumont, 17, f. 205.
80 'De l'influence des passions', De Staël, 1871, I, 107.
81 'De l'influence des passions', De Staël, 1871, I, 171.
82 Monchoux, 1966.
83 *De l'Allemagne*, De Staël, 1871, II, 168, 186, 185. For the attack on utilitarianism, see 206–7.
84 For a description of her visit that draws on Dumont's letters, see King, 1970.

85 Quoted in King, 1970, 15.
86 Carlyle, 1839, 74.
87 Winch, ed. Collini *et al.*, 2000; De Champs, ed. Reynier and Delyfer, 2016.

References

Aarsleff, H. 'An Essay on the Context and Formation of Wilhelm von Humboldt's Linguistic Thought', *History of European Ideas* 42:6 (2016), 729–807.

Bentham, J. *An Introduction to the Principles of Morals and Legislation* (*CW*), eds. J.H. Burns and H.L.A. Hart. Oxford: Clarendon Press, 1996.

Bentham, J. 'Appendix IX. Hints towards the Composition of an Elementary Treatise on Universal Grammar', in *Chrestomathia* (*CW*), eds. M.J. Smith and W.H. Burston, 394–409. Oxford: Clarendon Press, 1983.

Bentham, J. *Preparatory Principles* (*CW*), eds. D.G. Long and P. Schofield. Oxford: Oxford University Press, 2016.

Bentham, J. *The Correspondence of Jeremy Bentham, Vol. 3, 1781–1788* (*CW*), ed. I.R. Christie. London: Athlone Press, 1971.

Bentham, J. *The Correspondence of Jeremy Bentham, Vol. 5, 1794–1797* (*CW*), ed. A.T. Milne. London: Athlone Press, 1981.

Bentham, J. *The Rationale of Reward*, ed. Southwood Smith. London: Robert Heward, 1825.

Bentham, J. *The Works of Jeremy Bentham*, ed. John Bowring. 11 vols. Edinburgh: William Tait, 1838–43.

Bentham, J. *Théorie des peines et des récompenses*, ed. Étienne Dumont. 2 vols. London: B. Dulau, 1811.

Blamires, C. *The French Revolution and the Creation of Benthamism*. Basingstoke: Palgrave Macmillan, 2008.

Brunon-Ernst, A. *Utilitarian Biopolitics. Bentham, Foucault and Modern Power*. London: Pickering and Chatto, 2012.

Carlyle, T. 'State of German Literature', in *Critical and Miscellaneous Essays*, I: 28–94. London: James Fraser, 1839.

Chouillet, J. *La formation des idées esthétiques de Diderot 1745–1763*. Paris: Armand Colin, 1973.

Condorcet, Jean-Antoine-Nicolas de, and Anne-Robert-Jacques Turgot. *Correspondance inédite de Condorcet et de Turgot : 1770–1779*, ed. C. Henry. Geneva: Slatkine Reprints, 1970.

Craiutu, A. 'Rousseau and Madame de Staël: A Surprising Dialogue', in *Thinking with Rousseau: From Machiavelli to Schmitt*, eds. H. Rosenblatt and P. Schweigert, 235–51. Cambridge: Cambridge University Press, 2017.

De Champs, E. *Enlightenment and Utility: Bentham in French, Bentham in France*. Cambridge: Cambridge University Press, 2015.

De Champs, E. 'Aestheticism and Utilitarianism: A Victorian Debate and Its Critical Legacy', in *Reconnecting Aestheticism and Modernism: Continuities, Revisions, Speculations*, eds. C. Reynier and C. Delyfer, 107–19. London: Routledge, 2016.

Dumont, E. 'Observations sur le caractère et les écrits de Rousseau', *Bibliothèque Universelle de Genève. Nouvelle Série* 2 (1836a): 128–35.

Dumont, E. 'Observations sur le style de Rousseau', *Bibliothèque Universelle de Genève. Nouvelle Série* 2 (1836b): 298–313.

Engelmann, S. '"Indirect Legislation", Bentham's Liberal Government', *Polity* 31:3 (2003): 368–88.

Guichard, C. 'Taste Communities: The Rise of the Amateur in Eighteenth-Century Paris', *Eighteenth-Century Studies* 45:4 (2012): 519–47.

Helvétius, C.-A. *Le Bonheur, poème en six chants*. London: s.n., 1772.

Helvétius, C.-A. *De l'esprit*, eds. G. Stenger and J. Steffen. Paris: Champion, 2016.

Holbach, P.-H.T. d'. *Système Social. La morale universelle. Catéchisme de la nature. Œuvres Philosophiques 1773–1790*, ed. J.-P. Jackson. Paris: Coda, 2004.

King, N. '"The Airy Form of Things Forgotten": Madame de Staël, l'utilitarisme et l'impulsion libérale', *Cahiers Staëliens* 11 (1970): 5–26.

Chapter 5

Jeremy Bentham's imagination and the ethics of prose style: Paraphrase, substitution, translation

Jan-Melissa Schramm

In the course of the eighteenth century, English political thought became increasingly transhistorical and transnational in character. To begin with, commentators weighed contemporary experience against the standards of the Greco-Roman classical past: by the 1790s, England's leading exponents of constitutional reform were also regularly comparing their own designs with two very different experiments in social organization – the fledgling democracy of the newly independent America and the republic of revolutionary France.[1] These two laboratories, in which competing ideas of governance were being tested, formed triangular points of reference for Jeremy Bentham and his contemporaries Edmund Burke, William Godwin, Thomas Paine and Mary Wollstonecraft.[2] Burke, for example, had supported American independence, while he critiqued developments in France; Paine, on the other hand, supported both nations in their pursuit of 'liberty' in *The Rights of Man*, the first volume of which he composed while living in Paris between 1787 and 1789 and which he dedicated to George Washington. In Paine's terms, 'the cause of America is in great measure the cause of all mankind': in France, too, the principles at stake – popular government, secularism and the rejection of tradition and the duties owed to the dead – all likewise affected 'the standard of liberty for all nations'.[3] Yet the movement towards the adoption of such universal values came at great cost, particularly in the case of the French Revolution, which descended into the brutal violence of the Reign of Terror between 1792 and 1794, consigning English radicals to despair and persuading many to defend existing social institutions if the only likely alternative was civil war. For while the political rhetoric of the period was that of 'experiment', outcomes were far from abstract and results were registered on the suffering bodies of the living.

As Emmanuelle de Champs has observed, Bentham was a Francophile, visiting the country on five occasions and acquiring considerable proficiency in the language. She writes that 'the principle of "the greatest happiness of the greatest number", the foundation of Benthamite utilitarianism, was the product of an on-going philosophical dialogue between France and Britain, illustrating the wealth and depth of cultural transfers between the two nations',[4] and in particular she reveals Bentham's intellectual indebtedness to Voltaire, Helvétius, and D'Alembert. In turn, Étienne Dumont's magisterial translation of Bentham's writings, published as *Traités de législation civile et pénale* in 1802, enabled Bentham's work to reach a wide European readership at a time when many nations were debating codification and the form of their laws. Bentham's writing – both its achievements and its renowned difficulty – can only be properly understood within the context of this bilingual sphere. In this chapter, I will use the techniques of translation to ask questions about Bentham's own reliance on the art of 'paraphrase' as a foundational tool of his logic, and then to open up broader questions about the relationship between the work of substitution (on which translation depends) and ethics in the period.

On translation

In this arena of cosmopolitan and transatlantic exchange, the cultural work of translation on which comparative studies relied received vigorous and sustained scrutiny. Clearly the work of the Church and of civil courts had long involved sophisticated strategies of interpretation of the Bible and of Roman Law from various Greek and Latin sources – and indeed, according to the Oxford English Dictionary, the term 'paraphrase' (as a form of translation) seems to have been used for the first time in 1548 in the title of Erasmus's *The First Tome … of the Paraphrase upon the New Testament* – but the political developments of the eighteenth century posed new challenges. The writings of the poet and literary critic John Dryden (1631–1700) initially framed the terms of Enlightenment debate. Translation, he observed in 1680, could be broken down into three constituent parts:

First, that of Metaphrase, or turning an Author Word by Word, and Line by Line, from one Language into another: Thus, or near this manner, was *Horace* his *Art of Poetry* translated by *Ben Jonson*. The second way is that of Paraphrase, or Translation with Latitude, where the Author is kept in view by the Translator, so as never to be lost, but his words are not so strictly follow'd as his sense; and that too is admitted to be amplified, but not alter'd. Such is Mr. *Waller's* Translation of *Virgil's* Fourth *Æneid*. The Third way is that of Imitation, where the Translator (if now he has not lost that Name) assumes the liberty, not only to vary from the words and sense, but to forsake them both as he sees occasion; and taking only some general hints from the Original, to run division on the Ground-work, as he pleases. Such is Mr. *Cowley's* practice in turning two Odes of *Pindar*, and one of *Horace*, into English.[5]

In this schema, the 'ideas' of the original author, the substance of the passage, are separated out from, and privileged above, the vehicle or style in which they are communicated. But Dryden continues:

The sense of an Author, generally speaking, is to be Sacred and Inviolable. If the Fancy of *Ovid* be luxuriant, 'tis his character to be so; and if I retrench it, he is no longer *Ovid*. It will be replied, that he receives advantage by this lopping of his superfluous Branches; but I rejoyn, that a Translator has no such Right: when a *Painter* Copies from the life, I suppose he has no priviledge to alter Features, and Lineaments, under pretence that his Picture will look better: perhaps the Face, which he has drawn, would be more Exact, if the Eyes, or Nose were alter'd; but 'tis his business to make it resemble the Original.[6]

Dryden's teasing out of the 'sense of an Author' from the rhetorical 'luxuriance' with which such 'sense' may be expressed gestures towards tensions that gathered force in the years to come as the discipline of literary criticism was increasingly institutionalized and professionalized (and indeed valorized as the replacement for the national religion) – that is, whether translation ranks 'among the most useful branches of literary education', essential for understanding the place of English in the wider community of global literatures, or whether the form and style of a passage can never be separated from the ideas it is seeking to communicate, and thus, if a translator 'retrench[es a work], he is no longer Ovid'. The argument that the style of William Shakespeare or

Charles Dickens or Alfred Tennyson is distinctive and uniquely his own – in Dryden's terms, that no 'advantage' can be attained by the 'lopping of [their] superfluous Branches' – underpinned belletristic assessments of the original works as inevitably superior to any 'paraphrased' or translated versions.

In Annmarie Drury's reading, Dryden's 'codification of the categories of metaphrase, paraphrase, and imitation comprises his most influential … contribution to thought about translation', and his successors did not fundamentally alter this taxonomy.[7] Writing in 1795, in his *Essay on the Principles of Translation,* Lord Alexander Fraser Tytler observed:

> If the genius and character of all languages were the same, it would be an easy task to translate from one into another; nor would anything more be requisite on the part of the translator, than fidelity and attention. But as the genius and character of languages is confessedly very different, it has hence become a common opinion, that it is the duty of a translator to attend only to the sense and spirit of his original, to make himself perfectly master of his author's ideas, and to communicate them in those expressions which he judges to be best suited to convey them. It has, on the other hand, been maintained, that, in order to constitute a perfect translation, it is not only requisite that the ideas and sentiments of the original author should be conveyed, but likewise his style and manner of writing, which, it is supposed, cannot be done without a strict attention to the arrangement of his sentences, and even to their order and construction. According to the former idea of translation, it is allowable to improve and to embellish; according to the latter, it is necessary to preserve even blemishes and defects; and to these must likewise be superadded the harshness that must attend every copy in which the artist scrupulously studies to imitate the minutest lines or traces of his original.[8]

Tytler attempts to articulate rules for effective translation, but his definition of paraphrase remains much the same as Dryden's – while a 'moderate liberty of amplifying and retrenching the ideas of the original has been granted to the translator of prose',[9] too great a licence, which preserves the sense of the original while supplanting its style, is often more accurately described as a 'free commentary' or a loose 'imitation' rather than a translation. At its most mechanical, then, the practice of translation can be 'a mere question of substitution; a = x, b = y',[10] but as Thomas Warren noted, in a review of Tytler's work in 1895:

> The individual man is the feeling and the thinking unit. And no two units feel or think exactly alike … if we looked closely enough into the matter, we should find that there is an intransferable, untranslateable individuality about our thoughts themselves.[11]

This reveals for us the two ends of the translation spectrum – at the one end, literal word-for-word substitution which emphasizes utility and an instrumental approach to communication, and at the other, an inimitable style that is the expression of an untranslatable individuality. It is little wonder that the status and value of art itself seemed to be at stake in such debates.

Revolution and the politics of prose style and form

But by the late eighteenth century, with the declaration of the American War of Independence and the subsequent collapse of the French Revolution into the Reign of Terror, the significance of rhetorical style was far more than a question of aesthetics. Numerous critics have noted the extent to which frank, sincere, first-person narration was implicated in an enthusiasm for Revolutionary ideals: Jean-Jacques Rousseau's *Confessions*, published in two parts in 1782 and 1788, used the direct immediacy of first-person voice to generate a distinctively radical sensibility. Revealing both his intimate personal strengths and his sometimes terrible flaws, Rousseau argued for complete textual transparency – the idea that speech may be a window into a man's soul, which, if it were pure enough, would eradicate the need for social control by the state. As Gregory Dart has observed, as a consequence, 'fully-wrought autobiography was, at least during the early years of the nineteenth century, a dangerously radical form in both England and France, not least because of its continuing potential to challenge existing notions of the relationship between private reflection and public politics, the individual personality and history'.[12] The oratorical style of other radicals was seen as equally direct and confrontational, and in England the great rhetorical exemplars of the 1790s were Burke and Paine, who represented not just contrasting political positions but very different formal practices as well. Burke's conservative *Reflections on the Revolution in France* (1790) was widely critiqued as depending on a virtual rather than an actual representation of the people in a reformed House of Commons but it was attacked as much in terms of its style as its political affiliation. Burke's writings were widely denounced as overwrought, hysterical, sentimental, theatrical – designed to appeal to the passions over and above reason and the faculty of judgment. Paine in response insisted on self-representation as the basis of parliamentary government and, in terms of style, positioned himself within the artless and sincere tradition of unrehearsed Protestant speech much lauded by the Royal Society. Questions of content could not be separated from the style in which they were conveyed: the disclosure that a man read Burke rather than Paine was regarded as an accurate and immediate indicator of his wider political affiliation.

Many radical sympathizers in England greeted the outbreak of the French Revolution with enthusiasm. William Wordsworth, for example, anticipated the long awaited realization of human utopia: 'Bliss was it in that dawn to be alive,/ But to be young was very Heaven!'[13] For a moment the canvas of history seemed a *tabula rasa* on which a sketch of a fairer and more equitable society might be drawn. But Burke could only counsel restraint until the outcome of such liberation was known: 'The effect of liberty to individuals is, that they may do what they please: We ought to see what it will please them to do, before we risk congratulations.'[14] Burke's warning was prescient, and with the descent into the violence of the Reign of Terror, the climate in England changed significantly: political theorists who had supported revolutionary principles in England were at risk of being charged with treason or sedition. As John Barrell has shown, after the execution of Louis XVI in 1793, any attempt to reform the unwritten English constitution in democratic directions was taken to assume a willingness to 'imagine the king's death' – and this *mens rea*, which aligns imagining reform with intending regicide, ensured that several members of the London Corresponding Society (who campaigned for constitutional change) were charged with constructive treason in 1794.[15] The work of 'imagination' so crucial to art was now considered criminally suspect. Paine in turn was charged with sedition and fled to America, leaving lawyers and writers behind in the old country to ponder the effects of state oppression and surveillance: the press was monitored closely, plays for the stage were directly censored by the Lord Chamberlain, and authors took to fiction and poetry to explore their responses to the Revolution in an attempt to avoid such prosecution themselves. There was some protection in the deployment of strategic ambiguity – but as William Godwin observed in the 'Preface' to his most famous novel *Caleb Williams*, penned in 1794 at precisely the time of the treason trials, when 'terror' was 'the order of the day', 'even the humble novelist might be shown to be constructively a traitor'.[16]

Radical and conservative forces were struggling to understand and communicate the precondition for any meaningful reform – could facts ever speak for themselves, or were representation and interpretation always required to make sense of events in the legal and political spheres? By the mid-eighteenth century, a confluence of factors ensured that the national English imagination was strongly forensic in character – the by now well-established institution of the trial jury depended on the assumption that the average lay-person was capable of determining questions of fact, the birth of the Royal Society committed natural scientists to the study of experiment, evidence and proof, and English theology became preoccupied with the truth of the 'evidences' of the Gospels as a record of historical events.[17] To gain assent from its readers, every text had to make claims for its own evidentiary realism, and the adversarial pull of prosecution and defence increasingly featured as an organizational principle of argument. For every case, there was an accuser and a respondent, and each had its own rhetorical style. The claim to sincerity and the language of plain fact was increasingly valorized in Protestant legal culture. As Sergeant William Hawkins insisted in his *Pleas of the Crown* (1721), men accused of crime required no assistance from lawyers in court, because

> generally every one of Common Understanding may as properly speak to a Matter of Fact, as if he were the best Lawyer; … it requires no manner of Skill to make a plain and honest Defence, which in cases of this Kind is always the best, the Simplicity and Innocence, artless and ingenuous Behaviour of one whose Conscience acquits him, having something in it more moving and convincing than the highest Eloquence of Persons speaking in a Cause not their own.[18]

This description of the ideal defendant places honest, artless narrative (which seemingly maintains a close relationship with the 'reality' it purports to describe) in competition with inventive rhetoric that may distort the relationship between fact and representation. In this highly influential model, the increasing professionalization of the criminal trial over the course of the next century brought the ethics as well as the efficacy of representation to the fore – what tactics were too low, too suspect, too emotional, to be trusted in this effort to test the limits of narrative representational efficacy? Was eloquence always untrustworthy, and sincerity always 'truthful'? Was it more or less impartial to speak in a cause not your own?

In Barrell's analysis, '[t]he path of reason is straight, direct; imagination leads us into error because it has a propensity to err, to wander':[19] Paine and Protestantism were seen to occupy the moral high ground here as imaginative error was positioned as the weakness of Catholics, the Irish and, when barristers were first allowed to work at the Old Bailey, criminal defence lawyers. The redoubtable Old Bailey pleader Charles Phillips – a great adversary of Charles Dickens in the 1830s and 1840s – was often dismissed by the writer as trebly unreliable on account of his nationality, his religion and his profession.[20] After 1836, when the passage of the Prisoners' Counsel Act finally extended full legal representation to those accused of felony, defence counsel were even more widely described as masters of fiction, as story-tellers whose fantastic tales of innocence bore no relation to the facts that spoke for themselves of the defendant's guilt.[21] These were the rhetorical co-ordinates that determined the production and reception of Bentham's own contribution to the agenda of Enlightenment reform.

Bentham's style

Bentham's place in this rhetorical arena was hard for his contemporaries to assess. According to John Stuart Mill, Bentham had played a foundational role in stimulating late eighteenth-century agendas of reform: 'to Bentham more than to any other source might be traced the questioning spirit, the disposition to demand the why of everything, which had gained so much ground and was producing such important consequences in these times … Bentham broke the spell'.[22] In this way, the prose style of his earliest works was seen to share many points of contact with Paine's profession of simplicity, forthrightness and clarity in speech, and Bentham, too, seems to have contributed to critiques of conservative elegance and ornament in rhetorical style if they were achieved at the expense of intellectual substance. For example, in *A Fragment on Government* (1776), Bentham registered the gulf between the admirable style and the ignominious content of William Blackstone's *Commentaries on the Law of England*, the chosen antagonist whose blind adherence to authority and tradition enabled Bentham to articulate his own rationale for reform (much as Burke's *Reflections* was to do for Paine a decade later). Bentham accuses Blackstone of intellectual servility and mendacity, but he concludes by noting his merits of elegance and propriety:

> [Blackstone] it is, in short, who first of all institutional writers, has taught Jurisprudence to speak the language of the Scholar and the Gentleman: put a polish upon that rugged science: cleansed her from the dust and cobwebs of the office: and if he has not enriched her with that precision that is drawn only from the sterling treasury of the sciences, has decked her out, however, to advantage, from the toilette of classic erudition: enlivened her with metaphors and allusions: and sent her abroad in some measure to instruct, and in still greater measure to entertain, the most miscellaneous and even the most fastidious societies.
>
> The merit to which, as much perhaps as to any, the work stands indebted for its reputation, is the enchanting harmony of its numbers [and numbers here means its conformity to a certain regular beat, its seductive rhythm]: a kind of merit that of itself is sufficient to give a certain degree of celebrity to a work devoid of every other. So much is man governed by the ear.[23]

Accepting the controversial division between style and content, Bentham proceeds to critique Blackstone's style as a charming encrustation that belies or even conceals the intellectual speciousness and vacuity of his substantive arguments. Yet overall, Bentham's treatment of the *Commentaries* is profound in its interrogation, suggesting the superficial appeal of style: Bentham rejects Blackstone's portrait of the law as necessarily labyrinthine and gothic in its architecture, with all the functional utility of an old inherited stately home; he repudiates any appeal to authorities outside the text for the creation of meaning (notably a Supreme Being); he is sceptical of any recourse to Law Latin, which he sees as communicating little and disguising much; and above all, he proposes the technique of paraphrasis to translate figurative or metaphysical sentences into ever more literal or 'real' units of meaning.

Bentham then sets out the formal essentials of utilitarian style. Taking as his unit of meaning the sentence, Bentham maintained that the closest correspondence between linguistic representation and the real could be achieved by the techniques of phraseoplerosis and paraphrasis. These require that firstly, the sentence should be expanded to reveal and fill out any encryption in its meaning, and then it should be stripped back to its most austere form, shedding any figurative or metaphysical terms that may tend to 'complicate' the conveyance of its essential message:

> A word may be said to be expounded by paraphrasis, when not that word alone is translated into other words, but some whole sentence of which it forms a part is translated into another sentence, the words of which latter are expressive of such ideas as are simple, or are more immediately resolvable into simple ones than those of the former. … This, in short, is the only method in which any abstract terms can, at the long run, be expounded to any instructive purpose: that is in terms calculated to raise images either of substances perceived, or of emotions; sources, one or other of which every idea must be drawn from, to be a clear one.[24]

In Dryden's influential schema, 'Paraphrase' was defined as 'Translation with Latitude', which allows for 'amplification' as well as 'reduction' in the words used to describe the 'original' idea. Fiction could thus be understood as an elaborate 'paraphrase' of a Biblical parable for example – retaining the Scriptural message but 'amplifying' the narrative thickness with which the moral transaction is recounted: this is particularly true of the episodes of the Good Samaritan and the Prodigal Son, which undergird so many examples of imaginative literature in the early- to mid-nineteenth century.[25] Fiction, especially, thrived on this crucial formula of paraphrase as amplification and on the mental work a reader might be required to perform in response to any narrative expansion that generated a productive or fruitful ambiguity. But for Bentham, all 'translation' of ideas must thus move from the complex to the simple, from the poetic to the prosaic, from the spiritual to the emphatically rational and empirical – which seemed to result in the impoverishment of the lexicons, emotions and tonal registers available to those who worked with the competing public discourses of literature and theology.

Bentham's attacks on the liturgy of the Church, on the use of legal fictions to maintain an impression of continuity between the past and present, and the declaratory language of inalienable rights and obligations, were thus expressed as questions of form and style as well as of intellectual substance. In *Church-of-Englandism and its Catechism Examined* (1818), Bentham argued that the Church was a repository of restrictive trade-practices and empty ceremonial repetition: its survival depended on fraud and consequently it should be 'euthanazed'.[26] In his essay 'Nonsense upon Stilts', he famously asserted that foreclosing any argument with reference to 'rights' as some kind of metaphysical trump card is the equivalent of 'raising [your] voice to the people', a type of 'bawling upon paper: it proceeds from the same temper and the same sort of distress as produces bawling with the voice' – an exaggeration caused by yielding to passion and over-confidence rather than reason. He describes rights-talk as a form of 'Terrorist language'.[27] For Bentham, the only appeals should be to reason and utility, and this has stylistic causes and effects. Change the language, he counsels his readers – the choice to deploy 'ought not' instead of 'can not' will bring us back to utility.[28]

Bentham's unpopularity with Victorian authors arose from the ways in which his theory of phraseoplerosis and paraphrasis worked against the richnesses of metaphysical and liturgical language (which delighted in suggestive ambiguity and the possibility of multiple interpretations) to insist instead on a bare and unadorned instrumentalism. The assumption that a unit of meaning was formally substitutable in this way without any loss of value put Bentham at odds with the literary critics and historians from the late eighteenth century onwards who insisted on the essential inextricability of ideas, content and form in any written work – an organic synthesis that resisted systematic and reductive exposition. From the work of Romantic writers who venerated individual expressiveness as a mark of distinctive and singular genius, through to the writings of public moralists like Matthew Arnold who saw style as an essential feature of the national literary culture, the discipline of literary criticism evolved in association with the practice of close reading, underpinned by the belief that, as form changes, so too did the message it seeks to communicate. As Daniel Tyler has noted, while it might be assumed that 'style is an aspect of writing that is superadded to the plain sense of a passage … it is far from clear that these two things can ever be separated': instead, creativity 'does not exist apart from the style that renders it'.[29] Certainly the aesthetic and religious controversies that dominated the mid-Victorian period were to turn on the crucial role played by form in the creation of meaning – the belief that *technê* and praxis were the very means by which art contributed to the stock of human knowledge. And this placed thickness of narrative texture, rather than paraphrasis, at the heart of the Victorian ethical enterprise. If the law was positioned by its critics as concerned with the many rather than the one, with the general rather than the particular, with the maxim rather than any hard case that did not easily fit the rules, then this allowed literature to claim some space for itself as a tool of moral instruction infused with the spirit of equitable correction. According to Mill, Bentham felt 'all poetry was misrepresentation':[30] this overlooked the different sorts of effect that different art forms sought to generate in those who gave them sustained attention.

Criticisms of Bentham's style

Even as Bentham expressed a dual commitment to utility as the measure of reasonable conduct and instrumentalism in language as the gold standard of communication, this rhetorical clarity was something he failed to achieve over time. The perceptive review of Bentham's *Papers Relative to Codification* in the *Edinburgh Review* of 1817 acclaimed his genius, yet acknowledged his circumscribed effect on the practical world to date. Despite his generosity and his fifty years of patient labour, 'the beneficial effects which might have been expected from these masterly compositions, have not ... as yet been produced'. After a sustained celebration of his clear-sighted criticisms of the common law, the reviewer concluded with an acknowledgement of Bentham's defects:

> We are fully sensible of [his defects]; and we have observed them with deep regret; for we can regard in no other light than that of a public misfortune whatever prevents his writings from being known, and their utility and importance from being universally acknowledged. What principally obstructs their circulation, is the style in which they are composed. Unlike most authors, Mr Bentham's first publications are, in point of writing, the most perfect; and long habit and frequent exercise, instead of improving his language, seem only to have rendered it perplexed, obscure and uncouth. English literature hardly affords any specimens of a more correct, concise and perspicuous style than that of the *Fragment on Government* which was the first of Mr Bentham's works, or the *Protest against Law Taxes*, and a great part of the *Defence of Usury*, which were early productions of his mind. Since those publications, he seems, by great effort and study, to have rendered his style intricate, and his language obscure. His frequent inversions, his long parentheses, the novelty and harshness of many of the terms which he has so often, and, we must say, on many occasions, so unnecessarily invented, and the length and complication of his periods, have rendered some of his compositions illegible to all who will not, in spite of their repulsive forms, persevere in the difficult task of studying rather than reading them.[31]

William Hazlitt expressed this concern in even stronger terms a few years later in his essay on Bentham for *The Spirit of the Age* (1825):

> There is a technicality of manner, which renders his writings of more value to the professional inquirer than to the general reader. Again, [Bentham's] style is unpopular, not to say unintelligible. He writes a language of his own that darkens knowledge. His works have been translated into French – they ought to be translated into English. People wonder that Mr. Bentham has not been prosecuted for the boldness and severity of some of his invectives. He might wrap up high treason in one of his inextricable periods, and it would never find its way into Westminster Hall. He is a kind of Manuscript author – he writes a cypher-hand, which the vulgar have no key to. The construction of his sentences is a curious frame-work with pegs and hooks to hang his thoughts upon, for his own use and guidance, but almost out of the reach of everybody else. It is a barbarous philosophical jargon, with all the repetitions, parentheses, formalities, uncouth nomenclature and verbiage of law-Latin; and what makes it worse, it is not mere verbiage but has a great deal of acuteness and meaning in it, which you would be glad to pick out if you could.[32]

Hazlitt's jocular observation – that, having been made so widely available in French, Bentham's work would now benefit from translation into English – stimulates more than a cheap laugh: it takes readers to the heart of Bentham's stylistic paradox – that his clear-sighted and far-ranging attacks on legal obfuscation and shams could only be expressed in prose so tortured that it required a double translation into French and then back into English in order to gain access to a wider audience. The *Edinburgh Review* article also acknowledges this curious phenomenon:

> It is indeed when [Bentham] speaks by another's lips, that he appears to most advantage; and it is to the graces of style which Mr Dumont has given him that he owes the reputation which he has acquired, and which is, from that cause, much greater in foreign countries than his own.[33]

What does it mean to speak by another's lips? What ethical constraints are imposed on the choice of replacement words and phrases? What sorts of fidelity to the original are demanded? These are important questions in the context of Bentham's own insistence that language, particularly legislative language, should be self-interpreting, perfectly unambiguous and transparent. In his model, all glosses should be unnecessary, hermeneutic art would be redundant and meaning would reside at face value in the statute, the ur-text, the words printed on the page. Yet the *Edinburgh Review* suggests that Bentham, rather like Socrates of the ancient world or the Christ of the New Testament, can only be approached through the more accessible words of his chroniclers:

> As the merits of the greatest philosopher of antiquity would have been little known to posterity, but for the sublime writings of his eloquent disciple, so it is possible that, but for Dumont, Bentham's reputation might never have emerged from obscurity.[34]

For A.V. Dicey, assessing Bentham's achievements in his *Lectures on Law and Public Opinion in England during the Nineteenth Century* (1905), between 1800 and 1830 Bentham's work began to exert a marked influence in public life, but the decade of the Reform Bill belonged to Bentham alone.[35] Yet what textual sources were Victorians reading when they sought to digest or implement Bentham's ideas? As J.M. Robson has noted, this was a complicated matter – there were many options available, including Bowring's posthumous edition which appeared from 1838–43 – but Robson concludes that Mill's Bentham was primarily that of Dumont, and through Mill, Dumont shaped Bentham's reception in the mid- and late-nineteenth-century.[36]

Dumont's translations of Bentham's work

In *The French Revolution and the Creation of Benthamism*, Cyprian Blamires explores the complicated route by which Bentham's work was received in the wider Anglophone sphere. He quotes a contemporary source who observed in 1815:

> The history of these works is perhaps unique in the annals of Literature. Mr Bentham either too fastidious to be satisfied with his own performances, or too impatient to submit to the labour of giving his works that degree of order and arrangement requisite for publication, confided his Manuscript to his friend M. Dumont. ... Thus have these profound reflections on the Philosophy of Jurisprudence been rescued from that oblivion to which the carelessness of the author had probably doomed them; and the works of a man of whom England may well be proud, are known to his countrymen principally through the medium of a foreign language.[37]

Blamires notes that the occasion of this outburst was an inability to locate Bentham's work on the panopticon in English, with readers compelled to rely on Dumont's abstracts of them in *Traités* and in *Théorie des peines et des récompenses*, published in 1811. In David Leiberman's reading, this is 'a sobering reminder of just how absent Bentham was from the process by which Benthamism came to be invented'.[38]

As Blamires notes, it was the re-translation of one of Dumont's *Traités* back into English that enabled Bentham's thought to reach a wider audience, primarily in *The Theory of Legislation*, published initially in the United States in 1840 (and subsequently in London in 1864). The (re)translator of this work, Richard Hildreth, noted in his 'Preface' to the volume:

> [Bentham] published many treatises in English, but for the generality of readers they have very few attractions. He was not skilful in the art of composition; he did not possess the gift of eloquence. Though endowed with a great genius for investigation, he lacked the talent of communicating his ideas. During a long life, devoted solely and assiduously to the study of jurisprudence, besides his occasional publications, he produced an immense mass of manuscripts, containing a fund of most valuable ideas, but unshaped, unarranged, and in a state quite unfit for publication. Fortunately for the cause of science, these materials were not left to perish; an interpreter, a compiler, a spokesman was found, every way worthy of the task he assumed.[39]

In his capacity as a fellow translator, Hildreth considered Dumont's contribution to the dissemination of Benthamite thought. He quoted Dumont's disavowal that he in any way co-wrote Bentham's works: 'amid all the diversity of these writings, [they bear] the impress of one mind – a unity of plan, an original genius, as analytic and profound in the general design as in the execution of the parts'. Hildreth's inclusion of Dumont's lengthy account of the nature of his intellectual partnership with Bentham affords compelling insights into the project. Dumont noted:

> My labor, subaltern in its kind, has been limited to details. It was necessary to make a choice among various observations upon the same subject; to suppress repetitions; to throw light upon obscurities; to bring together all that appertained to the same subject; and to fill up those gaps which in the hurry of composition the author had left. I have had more to retrench than to add; more

to abridge than to expand. The mass of manuscripts, put into my hands, was considerable. I have had much to do in attaining correctness, and preserving uniformity of style; little or nothing as respects the fundamental ideas. A profusion of riches left me only the care of economy. As manager of this great fortune, I have spared no pains to realize it, and put it into circulation.

The changes I have made, have varied with the manuscripts. When I have found many treatises relevant to the same subject, but composed at different times and with different views, it has been necessary to reconcile them, and to incorporate them together, so as to form a perfect whole. The author perhaps had thrown aside some occasional composition, which now would not be interesting, nor even intelligible. Unwilling that the whole should perish, I have stripped it, like an abandoned house, of everything worth preserving. When he has delivered himself up to abstractions too profound, to metaphysics, I do not say too subtle, but too dry, I have endeavored to give more development to his ideas, to illustrate them by application, by facts, by examples; and I have allowed myself to scatter, with discretion, some ornaments. I have been obliged to write out some entire chapters, but always after hints and notes of the author.[40]

Dumont's list of the qualities that rendered Bentham's own prose virtually inaccessible to the general reader runs parallel to the devastating stylistic critique offered up by Hazlitt – a tendency towards 'dryness', abstraction and austerity. Hildreth concurred (1840, vi), offering his own very similar explanation for Bentham's failure to find his own audience in England before his death:

The author's Introduction to the *Principles of Morals and Legislation*, regarded by a small number of enlightened judges as one of those original productions which form an epoch and a revolution in science, in spite of its philosophical merit, and perhaps on account of that merit, produced no sensation, and remained almost unknown to the public – though in England, more than elsewhere, a useful book may come into notice, though it does not happen to be easy and agreeable. In using many chapters of that work to form the *General Principles of Legislation*, I have endeavored to avoid what prevented its success – terms too scientific, sub-divisions too much multiplied, analysis too abstract. I have translated not the words, but the ideas; I have sometimes made an abridgement, and

> at others a commentary, I have been guided by the advice and the hints of the author, contained in a preface, written many years after the work itself; and I have found among his papers all the additions of any consequence.

The same criticism recurs here – 'subdivisions too much multiplied, analysis too abstract'. But again Hildreth insisted on the controversial assertion that one can 'translate ... not the words but the ideas', as if the two are somehow easily separable. Can his prose really be 'stripped' of everything worth preserving 'like an abandoned house' without losing the qualities that make it, irreducibly, Bentham's work? In Dryden's terms, has Bentham's writing benefited from the 'lopping of superfluous branches', or once 'retrenched', is his work no longer his own? Unsurprisingly, Hildreth insisted on the integrity of his own edition and its authenticity in relation to the English and French 'originals', but his assessment of Bentham's achievements ended on a note of caution. He concluded that Bentham's 'preparatory labour ... is immense. No one can form an idea of it except by seeing the manuscripts, the catalogues, the synoptical tables in which it is contained.' But

> [i]t must be confessed that the care of arrangement and correction has few attractions for the genius of Bentham. While pushed on by a creative force, he feels only the pleasure of composition; when it becomes necessary to shape, to put in order, to finish, he experiences nothing but fatigue. If a work is interrupted, the evil becomes irreparable; the charm vanishes; disgust succeeds; and passion once quenched, can only be rekindled by a new object.[41]

Bentham's contemporaries – even those dedicated to the transmission of his work – concluded that his theories required paraphrase, translation and re-translation for successful reception, insisting on the substitution of elegance, ornament and principles of structural organization in place of Bentham's own austerity and metaphysical abstraction. In the final section of this chapter, I want to consider the ethical implications of the work of substitution, and what it means for one thing to stand for another in an age when 'representation' – whether aesthetic, legal or political – occupied centre stage of the national imagination.

Bentham, Coleridge and the ethics of imaginative writing

If the great intellectual contestation of the 1790s had been that of Burke and Paine, according to Mill, by the 1830s and onwards into the Victorian period it was that of Bentham and Samuel Taylor Coleridge, each a necessary foil to the other in terms of their linguistic and theological beliefs. In Mill's famous essays, 'On Bentham' and 'On Coleridge', published in the *Westminster Review* in 1838, he deployed each figure to serve as representatives of very different approaches to ethical deliberation and political reform. And yet, before probing such differences, it is also important to acknowledge that Bentham was admired as well as critiqued by Victorian poets and novelists who preferred Coleridge's defence of the value of literary and theological discourse. The magisterial parody of utilitarian language undertaken by Charles Dickens in *Hard Times* (1854) is well known, and I will return to it in a moment, but the novel published immediately prior to *Hard Times*, *Bleak House* (1852–3) – arguably Dickens's masterpiece – owes a vast debt to Bentham's programme of reform. In *Bleak House*, Dickens's attack on the labyrinthine, Gothic complexity of Chancery, the sinister self-interest of legal practitioners, and the rejection of children's testimony when these potential witnesses were not of an age to swear an oath, all testify to Bentham's influence on Dickens's work, and Dickens proposes public solutions very much in line with Bentham's own: improved literacy, better sanitation and a rejection of empty religious ceremonial in favour of wider school provision. As Kathleen Blake has explored at length in her study *The Pleasures of Benthamism*, the Dickens of *Bleak House* is as much a disciple of Bentham as Mill was.[42] The fault-lines exposed by *Hard Times* turn on Bentham's and Dickens's mutual commitments to the equal value of all in society alongside their total disagreement as to the best means by which existing inequality should be eliminated. In an age of democratization, are the individual and society to be treated as units of equal ethical value? And, if yes, what are the implications of one individual always being substitutable with another, that is, seemingly of no special value in and of themselves?

In John Bowen's analysis, 'there is a close relationship between what is called modernity and enumeration'.[43] As he worried away at the implications of this new preoccupation with counting citizens in his essays *On Liberty* and *Utilitarianism*, Mill observed:

> [Bentham's Greatest Happiness Principle] is a mere form of words without rational signification, unless one person's happiness, supposed equal in degree (with the proper allowance made for kind), is counted for exactly as much as another's. Those conditions being supplied, Bentham's dictum, 'everybody to count for one, nobody for more than one', might be written under the principle of utility as an explanatory commentary.[44]

According to this model, subjectivity is substitutable: one unit of life is as valuable as (but no more valuable than) any other. The philosopher Jacques Derrida defines this anxiety as what he calls the 'wound' of democracy: 'democracy counts, it counts votes and subjects, but it does not count, should not count ordinary singularities', and hence:

> [t]here is no democracy without respect for individual singularity or alterity, but there is no democracy without the community of friends, without the calculation of majorities, without identifiable, stabilizable, representable subjects, all equal. These two laws are irreducible to one another.[45]

Various strategies were designed to address this problem of incommensurability: religious communities formulated different theologies of substitutionary sacrifice, which might in some way justify the subjection of individual interest to the greater good, while law and politics both developed sophisticated theories of representation, in which one person 'stood for' another, in the court room or in the reformed House of Commons, thus allowing for an aggregation of individual interests, hopefully without too great a reliance on the rhetoric of sacrifice. Mill, on the other hand, uses the logic of induction to serve as what Nathan Hensley identifies as a 'mediating step between low and high': '[t]hus we see the tendency of general conceptions, as soon as formed, to substitute themselves as types, for whatever individual objects previously answered that purpose in our comparisons'.[46] Hensley concludes that the idea of the type performs the function of what Marx called exchange:

> On the level of logical process, the mode of departicularization Mill charts in the *Logic*, and that Marx critiques in *Capital*, subordinates particularity and makes alterity fungible ... [M]onetary logic transforms difference into sameness, flattening qualitative distinctions in order to produce repeatable, exchangeable units – equal parts that work, like money or citizens, as the chits

of a political-economic system now operating according to a metaphysics of counting.[47]

Mass democracy thus 'promise[s] impartiality' but depends on anonymity: as Marco Guidi has noted, the necessary value of impartiality implies in turn 'impersonality', for 'in evaluating the happiness of different individuals, it is not morally significant whose this happiness is: in other words, if it belongs to this individual, or that individual'.[48] In the utilitarian economy, subjectivity is homogenous, substitutable: one unit of life is as valuable as (but no more valuable than) any other. This was anathema to all the critics of industrialized capitalism, from Thomas Carlyle's anxiety that history no longer afforded a theatre for the education and leadership of 'great men' of character to John Ruskin's and William Morris's attacks on labour that depended on dehumanizing levels of mechanical repetition.[49]

Dickens's attack on utilitarian thought in *Hard Times* (1854) was given force by its compelling fusion of form and content – as the great critic F.R. Leavis recognized when he described it as Dickens's only wholly successful literary work, the novel enacts the very message it is seeking to communicate. *Hard Times* depends on richly metaphorical language to savage the scientific education of 'facts, and facts alone' that had reduced Mill himself to despair in his late adolescence, and it also alludes throughout to parables and scriptural teaching in order to counter utilitarianism's dependence on actuarial calculations. To give but one example, conflict in the community is resolved by the vicarious sacrifice of the virtuous working-man Stephen (the proto-martyr) in the Old Hell Shaft Mine, who sees the Christmas star and preaches forgiveness for all before his death. Christianity may have depended on its own scheme of vicarious punishment (professing that Christ in his innocence died to save mankind), but it provided a rich vocabulary for the recognition of the value of each individual sinner, unique in God's sight (see, for example, the parable of the lost sheep in the gospel of Luke). While Dickens's own faith wavered, he well knew its role in his popular commercial success, and he consequently positioned utilitarianism as the enemy he would otherwise have had to invent in order to promote the ethical importance of literary production.[50]

Dickens, like so many of his Victorian contemporaries, insisted that readerly sympathy was a crucial ingredient of any ethical education: according to Adam Smith in his highly influential *Theory of Moral Sentiments* (1757), an individual learnt to 'change places in fancy' with others as he/she read, thus extending the human capacity for compassion.[51] In this model, imaginative identification reveals to readers the extent of their ethical interdependence, a process reliant on the mental work of substitution. While Mill praised the precision of Bentham's logic, which could break units of meaning into ever more prescriptive formulas, he was equally sure as to the sorts of substitution that were imaginatively beyond him:

> In many of the most natural and strongest feelings of human nature [Bentham] had no sympathy; from many of its graver experiences he was altogether cut off; and the faculty by which one mind understands a mind different from itself, and throws itself into the feelings of that other mind, was denied him by his deficiency of Imagination.
>
> With Imagination in the popular sense, command of imagery and metaphorical expression, Bentham was to a certain degree endowed. For want, indeed, of poetical culture, the images with which his fancy supplied him were seldom beautiful, but they were quaint and humorous, or bold, forcible, and intense: passages might be quoted from him both of playful irony, and of declamatory eloquence, seldom surpassed in the writings of philosophers. The Imagination which he had not, was that to which the name is generally appropriated by the best writers of the present day; that which enables us, by a voluntary effort, to conceive the absent as if it were present, the imaginary as if it were real, and to clothe it in the feelings which, if it were indeed real, it would bring along with it. This is the power by which one human being enters into the mind and circumstances of another. … Without it nobody even knows his own nature, further than circumstances have actually tried it and called it out; nor the nature of his fellow-creatures, beyond such generalizations as he may have been enabled to make from his observation of their outward conduct.[52]

Dickens, on the other hand, made his name as the prophet of sympathy in an age of democracy – as the advocate or representative of the outcast who might be offered up as a sacrifice or scapegoat to bring about the reconciliation of the one and the many in a polity modelled on Malthusian lines. His teaching was designed to stimulate the emotions, to move a reader to action, through affective examples and case studies that used sentimental personification to tug at the heart strings. For example, when his heroine, Sissy the circus girl, is urged by her utilitarian schoolmaster to repeat that twenty-five deaths per year from starvation is acceptable, she reports:

> This schoolroom is an immense town, and in it there are millions of inhabitants, and only five-and-twenty are starved to death in the streets, in the course of a year. What is your remark on that proportion? And my remark was – for I couldn't think of a better one – that I thought it must be just as hard upon those who were starved, whether the others were a million, or a million million.[53]

Both Bentham and Dickens looked forward to the day when no one starved in the streets, but the strategies that both men hoped would enable society to reach that outcome were very different. For Dickens, the individual remained the responsible agent of action, and *Hard Times* famously concluded with his invocation to an implied singular 'one' of his actual mass readership: 'Dear reader, it rests with you and me whether such things shall be or not be.'[54]

Sympathy has subsequently fallen out of favour as a rather paternalistic mechanism for ethical education, which works at best slowly and with considerable partiality towards fairer opportunities for all, and at worst achieves nothing for any one.[55] Bentham's insistence on impartiality and on the reform of institutions to implement just outcomes among strangers as well as friends has better stood the test of time. Yet the questions posed by the definition of individuality as that which cannot easily be substituted, paraphrased or translated, remain important to us in our quest for the reconciliation of fairness for all and personal fulfilment for each uniquely valuable human being.

Notes

1 See for example, Clark, 1994; Clark, 2018; Livesey, 2001.
2 See Dzelzainis and Livesey eds. 2013.
3 Cited in Lamb, 2015, 156–7.
4 De Champs, 2015, 1–2.
5 Dryden, ed. Hooker and Swedenberg, 1961, 114–15.
6 Dryden, ed. Hooker and Swedenberg, 1961, 118–19.
7 Drury, 2015, 21.
8 Tytler, 1797, 12–14.
9 Tytler, 1797, 221.
10 Tytler, 1797, 224.
11 Warren, 1895, 324–53 at 328.
12 Dart, 1999, 38.
13 Wordsworth, *The Prelude* (1805), Book X, lines 692–3, in Wordwsorth, ed. J. Wordsworth, 1995.

14 Burke, 1993, 9.
15 Barrell, 2000.
16 Godwin, 1995, p. vi.
17 See McKeon, 1987; Shapiro, 2000; Schramm, 2000.
18 Hawkins, 1724, Book II, 400.
19 Barrell, 2000, 11.
20 See Schramm, 2000, 112–44.
21 See Langbein, 2003; Cairns, 1999; Schramm, 2000, 112–44.
22 Mill, ed. Leavis, 1980, 41–2.
23 Bentham, ed. Burns and Hart, 1977, 413–14.
24 Bentham, ed. Burns and Hart, 1977, 495 n.
25 On the relationship between fiction and parables see Colón, 2012, and Schramm, 2012. On the relationship between law and parables see Twining, 2006.
26 Bentham, 2011, 306–7.
27 Bentham, ed. Schofield *et al.*, 2002, 330.
28 Bentham, ed. Schofield *et al.*, 2002, 188–9.
29 Tyler ed., 2013, 11.
30 Mill, ed. Leavis, 1980, 64.
31 Samuel Romilly was the anonymous author of the review of 'Papers relative to Codification, and Public Instruction, including Correspondences with the Russian Emperor, and divers Constituted Authorities in the American United States', 1817, 217–37.
32 Hazlitt, 2000, 265–9, at 265.
33 Romilly, 1817, 236–7.
34 Romilly, 1817, 235.
35 Dicey, 1926.
36 Robson, ed. Parekh, 1993, 195–208.
37 Miss Morgan, letter 1815, cited in Blamires, 2008, 46.
38 Lieberman, 1985, at 201.
39 Hildreth, 1840, iii–iv.
40 Dumont, cited in Hildreth, 1840, v–vi.
41 Hildreth, 1840, vii–viii.
42 Blake, 2009.
43 Bowen, ed. Jones *et al.*, 2009, at 104.
44 Mill, ed. Robson *et al.*, 1969, 257.
45 Derrida, trans. Wills, 1995, 11.
46 Hensley, 2016, 94–5.
47 Hensley, 2016, 97.
48 Guidi, 2008, 42.
49 See for example, Carlyle, 1841; Morris, 2004; Ruskin, 2004.
50 See discussion in Schramm, 2012, Chapter 3.
51 Smith, 2002, 11.
52 Mill, ed. Leavis, 1980, 86–7.
53 Dickens, 1995, 33.
54 Dickens, 1995, 268.
55 See for example, Rawls, 1971, and Ricoeur, trans. Pellauer, 2000.

References

Barrell, J. *Imagining the King's Death: Figurative Treason, Fantasies of Regicide, 1793–1796*. Oxford: Oxford University Press, 2000.

Bentham, J. 'Nonsense upon Stilts', in *Rights, Representation, and Reform* (*CW*), eds. P. Schofield, C. Pease-Watkin, and C. Blamires. Oxford: Clarendon Press, 2002.

Bentham, J. *A Comment on the Commentaries and A Fragment on Government* (*CW*), eds. J.H. Burns and H.L.A. Hart. London, Athlone Press, 1977.

Bentham, J. *Church-of-Englandism and its Catechism Examined* [1817]. Oxford: Clarendon Press, 2011.

Blake, K. *Pleasures of Benthamism: Victorian Literature, Utility, Political Economy*. Oxford: Oxford University Press, 2009.
Blamires, C. *The French Revolution and the Creation of Benthamism*. Basingstoke: Palgrave Macmillan, 2008.
Bowen, J. 'Counting On: *A Tale of Two Cities*', in *Charles Dickens, A Tale of Two Cities, and the French Revolution*, eds. C. Jones, J. McDonagh, and J. Mee, 104–25. Basingstoke: Palgrave Macmillan, 2009.
Burke, E. *Reflections on the Revolution in France* [1790]. Oxford: Oxford University Press, 1993.
Cairns, D. *Advocacy and the Making of the Adversarial Criminal Trial, 1800–1865*. Oxford: Oxford University Press, 1999.
Carlyle, T. *Heroes and Hero-Worship*. London: Fraser, 1841.
Clark, J.C.D. *The Language of Liberty 1660–1832: Political Discourse and Social Dynamics in the Anglo-American World*. Cambridge and New York: Cambridge University Press, 1994.
Clark, J.C.D. *Thomas Paine: Britain, America, and France in the Age of Enlightenment and Revolution*. Oxford: Oxford University Press, 2018.
Colón, S. *Victorian Parables*. London: Bloomsbury Continuum, 2012.
Dart, G. *Rousseau, Robespierre, and English Romanticism*. Cambridge: Cambridge University Press, 1999.
De Champs, E. *Enlightenment and Utility: Bentham in French, Bentham in France*. Cambridge: Cambridge University Press, 2015.
Derrida, J. *The Gift of Death*, trans. David Wills. Chicago: University of Chicago Press, 1995.
Dicey, A.V. *Lectures on the Relation between Law and Public Opinion in England during the Nineteenth Century* [1905]. London: Macmillan, 1926.
Dickens, C. *Hard Times* [1854]. Harmondsworth: Penguin, 1995.
Drury, A. *Translation as Transformation in Victorian Poetry*. Cambridge: Cambridge University Press, 2015.
Dryden, J. 'Preface' to *Ovid's Epistles, Translated by Several Hands* [1680], in *The Works of John Dryden*, Volume I: *Poems 1649–1680*, eds. E.N. Hooker and H.T. Swedenberg. Berkeley: University of California Press, 1961.
Dzelzainis, E. and Livesey, R. eds. *The American Experiment and the Idea of Democracy in British Culture, 1776–1914*. London and New York: Routledge, 2013.
Godwin, W. 'Preface' to the first edition of *Caleb Williams* [1794]. Oxford: Oxford University Press, 1995.
Guidi, M. '"Everybody to Count for One, Nobody for More than One": The Principle of Equal Consideration of Interests from Bentham to Pigou', *Revue d'Études Benthamiennes* 4 (2008): 40–69.
Hawkins, W. *A Treatise of the Pleas of the Crown* [1721]. 2nd ed. London: Walthoe, 1724.
Hazlitt, W. 'Jeremy Bentham', in *The Spirit of the Age* [1825], reproduced in *The Fight and Other Writings*, 265–9. Harmondsworth: Penguin, 2000.
Hensley, N. *Forms of Empire: The Poetics of Victorian Sovereignty*. Oxford: Oxford University Press, 2016.
Hildreth, R. 'Translator's Preface', Jeremy Bentham, *The Theory of Legislation*. Boston: Weeks, Jordan and Co., 1840.
Lamb, R. *Thomas Paine and the Idea of Human Rights*. Cambridge: Cambridge University Press, 2015.
Langbein, J. *The Origins of Adversary Criminal Trial*. Oxford: Oxford University Press, 2003.
Lieberman, D. 'From Bentham to Benthamism', *The Historical Journal* 28:1 (1985): 199–224.
Livesey, J. *Making Democracy in the French Revolution*. Cambridge, MA: Harvard University Press, 2001.
McKeon, M. *The Origins of the English Novel, 1600–1740*. Baltimore, MD: Johns Hopkins University Press, 1987.
Mill, J.S. 'Utilitarianism', in *Essays on Ethics, Religion and Society*, eds. J.M. Robson, F.E.L. Priestley, and D.P. Dryer, *The Collected Works of John Stuart Mill: Volume X*. Toronto: University of Toronto Press; London: Routledge, 1969.
Mill, J.S. 'On Bentham' [1838], in *Mill on Bentham and Coleridge*, ed. F.R. Leavis. Cambridge: Cambridge University Press, 1980.
Morris, W. *News from Nowhere and Other Writings*. Harmondsworth: Penguin, 2004.
Rawls, J. *A Theory of Justice*. Cambridge, MA: Harvard University Press, 1971.
Ricoeur, P. *The Just*, trans. D. Pellauer. Chicago: University of Chicago Press, 2000.

Robson, J.M. 'Which Bentham was Mill's Bentham?' [1983], reprinted in *Jeremy Bentham: Critical Assessments, Vol. I.* ed. B. Parekh. London: Routledge, 1993, 195–208.
Romilly, S. 'Papers relative to Codification, and Public Instruction, including Correspondences with the Russian Emperor, and divers Constituted Authorities in the American United States', *Edinburgh Review* 29:1 (1817): 217–37.
Ruskin, J. *Selected Writings*. Harmondsworth: Penguin, 2004.
Schramm, J.-M. *Testimony and Advocacy in Victorian Law, Literature, and Theology*. Cambridge: Cambridge University Press, 2000.
Schramm, J.-M. *Atonement and Self-Sacrifice in Nineteenth-Century Narrative*. Cambridge: Cambridge University Press, 2012.
Shapiro, B. *A Culture of Fact: England 1550–1720*. Ithaca, NY: Cornell University Press, 2000.
Smith, A. *The Theory of Moral Sentiments* [1757], ed. K. Haakonssen. Cambridge: Cambridge University Press, 2002.
Twining, W. 'The *Ratio Decidendi* of the Parable of the Prodigal Son' [1990], reprinted in *Rethinking Evidence: Exploratory Essays*, 397–416. 2nd ed. Cambridge: Cambridge University Press, 2006.
Tyler, D. ed. *Dickens's Style*. Cambridge: Cambridge University Press, 2013.
Tytler, A.F. *Essay on the Principles of Translation* [1795]. 2nd ed. London: Cadell and Davies, 1797.
Warren, T. 'The Art of Translation', *Quarterly Review* 182·(1895): 324–53.
Wordsworth, W. *The Prelude* [1805], in *The Prelude: The Four Texts (1798, 1799, 1805, 1850)*, ed. J. Wordsworth. Harmondsworth: Penguin, 1995.

Chapter 6
'Is it true? ... what is the meaning of it?': Bentham, Romanticism and the fictions of reason

Tim Milnes

Introduction

The founding document for any understanding of Bentham's relation to British Romanticism is John Stuart Mill's essay on Coleridge, published in *The London and Westminster Review* in March 1840. Mill draws what would become an influential distinction between the ways in which the two thinkers approached human belief:

> By Bentham, beyond all others, men have been led to ask themselves, in regard to any ancient or received opinion, Is it true? and by Coleridge, What is the meaning of it? ... Bentham judged a proposition true or false as it accorded or not with the result of his own inquiries. ... With Coleridge, on the contrary, the very fact that any doctrine had been believed by thoughtful men, and received by whole nations or generations of mankind, was ... one of the phenomena to be accounted for.[1]

Mill's remarks are framed by his concerns about the relationship between Church and social progress, or more broadly, between tradition and custom on the one hand and social justice and reason on the other. England, he claims, had reached an impasse, a point at which the middle ground between radical reform and conservative consolidation could no longer hold. By neither embracing new, radical ideas nor quite managing to shut them out, by muddling along:

> England had neither the benefits, such as they were, of the new ideas nor of the old. We were just sufficiently under the influences of each, to render the other powerless. … This was not a state of things which could recommend itself to any earnest mind. It was sure in no great length of time to call forth two sorts of men … the one pressing the new doctrines to their utmost consequences; the other reasserting the best meaning and purposes of the old. The first type attained its greatest height in Bentham; the last in Coleridge.[2]

As Mill sees it, Bentham collects the torch of radicalism from his eighteenth-century Enlightenment precursors and shines it upon present-day institutions and the language that underpins them. The test he applies to such institutions is one of correspondence to *fact*: does our current polity, he asks, have a basis in truth? Coleridge, in contrast, resists this impulse. Where the fundamental imperative in Bentham's thought is epistemological and empirical, according to Mill, in Coleridge it is hermeneutic and aesthetic. Instead of testing the empirical validity of the traditions, customs and attachments of the people, Coleridge interprets them as expressions of the spirit of the age. For Coleridge, interpreting this expression, discovering its meaning, precedes the act of understanding itself. Mill, of course, has little time for Coleridge's more fundamental claim that the empirical understanding itself was inadequate for the purpose of comprehending historical change. Unlike Coleridge's followers (Carlyle, Emerson and the American Transcendentalists, most notably), Mill sides firmly with Locke and Bentham on questions of metaphysical principle. 'We see no ground for believing that anything can be the object of our knowledge except our experience,' he insists: 'We are therefore at issue with Coleridge on the central idea of his philosophy.'[3] Nonetheless, Mill's essay attempts to mediate between the polarized Benthamites and Coleridgeans by suggesting that, despite its flawed metaphysics, Coleridge's conservative, hermeneutic approach to history and politics was not without its merits.

In dividing early nineteenth-century thought into a reformist, fact-obsessed utilitarianism on the one hand, and a conservative, aestheticized Romanticism on the other, Mill introduces a binary into modern intellectual history that has remained surprisingly durable. What, after all, could be more contrary than Benthamite utility and Romantic feeling? I want to complicate this picture of Bentham's relation to his Romantic contemporaries. Indeed, even before it is brought under scrutiny, it is apparent that the great intellectual stand-off Mill describes between hard-nosed, forward-looking utilitarians and tender-hearted, homesick Romantics does not run on all fours, not least because Romantic writers do not always line up in ways one might expect. For example, although the poet Percy Bysshe Shelley sides with Coleridge by basing his defence of the autonomy of poetry upon a transcendent language of imagination, unlike Coleridge he explicitly *endorses* Bentham in redirecting this imaginative energy towards the goal of radical political change. The essayist William Hazlitt, meanwhile, attacks both Bentham *and* Coleridge: the first for his misbegotten attempt to achieve a perfect transparency in language by purging it of feeling and metaphor; the second for developing a poetics of metaphysical obscurity that was by instinct (and here Hazlitt would have agreed with Mill) politically reactionary. I will return to Hazlitt in the final section of this chapter.

I am not just arguing that Mill's binary is too simple adequately to describe the complicated philosophical and political alignments of many of the writers we think of as Romantic; nor do I want to turn it into a straw man by assuming that Mill would have pressed it too far. What I am interested in is the way in which questions of 'truth' and 'meaning' become entangled in a period in which the reform of language and the language of reform are incandescent topics. To understand how this happens, we need to examine the way in which the scepticism of David Hume ultimately lays the foundations for Bentham's theory of real and fictitious entities by destabilizing the relationship between truth and meaning. My argument is that the influence upon Bentham of Hume's account of the 'fictions' of reason leads the former to abandon the kind of positivist empiricism Mill defends and instead prioritize matters of meaning over matters of 'fact'. Conversely, the aestheticization of language in Romantic writers signifies not the abandonment of an Enlightenment model of 'truth', but its elegiac idealization.

Hume's conventionalism

The polarization Mill perceived in contemporary thought between those who prioritize questions of 'truth' and those who emphasize issues of 'meaning' has its roots in Hume's conventionalist treatment of language. Although Hume did not produce a fully developed theory of language, he made a number of remarks and observations on the subject, and his interest in the way that customs shape human nature drew him towards an account of language as social and conventional. One of the more celebrated of his comments arrives at the end of Section 2 of *An Enquiry Concerning Human Understanding* (1748). Here, Hume notes that one of the reasons why people are often hoodwinked by philosophical jargon is that they too readily assume that well-established and familiar terms have definite meanings attached to them in the form of determinate ideas. However, since all ideas are, by their very nature, faint and languid, and impressions and sensations are strong and vivid, Hume proposes that '[w]hen we entertain … any suspicion that a philosophical term is employed without any meaning or idea (as is but too frequent), we need but enquire, *from what impression is that supposed idea derived?* And if it be impossible to assign any, this will serve to confirm our suspicion.'[4] The semantic thesis implied by this statement is what M.A. Box, borrowing a term from Jonathan Bennett, classes as 'meaning-empiricism', that is, the thesis 'that meaning can be determined by demanding the birth certification in experience of an idea'.[5] Hume's suggestion that the meanings of terms must be cashed out into the currency of sense-experience, and that by 'bringing ideas into so clear a light we may reasonably hope to remove all dispute', would have far-reaching repercussions. It would ultimately inspire attempts by logical positivists in the early twentieth century to establish sensation (through various forms of verification principle) as the semantic index of scientific and philosophical discourse, an ambition crystallized in A.J. Ayer's declaration that '[i]t is the philosopher's business to give a correct definition of material things in terms of sensations.'[6] Despite this legacy, Hume himself remained doubtful about the possibility of providing 'correct' definitions of things purely in terms of sense-experience. Indeed, he finally denies that meaning must ultimately rest upon non-linguistic entities, regardless of whether these entities are understood to be intellectual essences or the raw data of sensation. For Hume, language is best understood as a set of conventions determined by and within social contexts.

To support this claim, Hume appeals to Berkeley's argument regarding the formation of abstract ideas. One of the paradoxes thrown up by Locke's corpuscularian epistemology was the notion of an idea that was simultaneously particular and general, encompassing the qualities of the members of the class it represented while being, in Locke's words, 'all and none of these at once'. Since general ideas lack corresponding particular objects, they remain 'Fictions and Contrivances of the Mind', and, therefore, Locke acknowledges, 'marks of our Imperfection'.[7]

Berkeley had attempted to overcome the empirical problem of how a single abstract idea could contain within itself all possible variants and instances of the thing conceived. For Berkeley, Locke's paradox exposes the fact that *all* knowledge is of particulars alone. The error that leads Locke to view general ideas as epistemologically suspect is that of supposing that the world can be divided into 'primary' (inherent) and 'secondary' (mind-dependent) qualities. This dualism can be seen to be both unnecessary and unhelpful, Berkeley maintains, once one grasps the full implications of the principle that to conceive of something is to have a sensation of that thing. If the *esse* of objects is *percepi*, then there is no *fundamental* difference, epistemologically, between ideas of general things and ideas of particular things.[8] Particular ideas become general ideas simply through a process of nomination; in other words, 'an idea, which considered in itself is particular, becomes general, by being made to represent or stand for all other particular ideas of the same sort'.[9]

Hume considers this claim, as he puts it, 'that all general ideas are nothing but particular ones, annexed to a certain term' to be 'one of the greatest and most valuable discoveries that has been made of late years in the republic of letters'.[10] Less palatable, however, was Berkeley's idealism, underpinned as it was by the assumption that all human perception is providentially supported by a '*spirit infinitely wise, good and powerful*'.[11] Uncoupling Berkeley's theory of abstraction from theology, Hume argues instead that abstract ideas are constructed through communicative contexts. By being attached to a word, individual ideas acquire a new signification, whereby a 'particular idea becomes general by being annex'd to a general term; that is, to a term, which from a customary conjunction has a relation to many other particular ideas, and readily recalls them in the imagination'.[12] By forging a close connection between reference and custom, Hume offers a naturalistic account of the meaning of general terms that extends the nascent pragmatism of Berkeley's nominalism: now it is habit and convention, rather than raw sensation, that determines the meaningfulness or otherwise of general terms. Linguistic customs become for Hume what Annette Baier describes as the 'social roots of reason, roots from which it draws its nourishment and its powers'.[13] In this way, Hume effectively recalibrates the basic relationship between language, thought and reality, abandoning the Lockean view of language as a system of signs arbitrarily assigned to individual ideas in favour of one in which the conventions of language constitute part of the fabric of social contexts that determine rational thought.

Viewing language as a convention can easily provoke doubt over the assumption that language represents thought. Accordingly, following the linguistic turn instigated by Locke and extended by Condillac, eighteenth-century empiricism undergoes a further, pragmatic turn, which itself draws upon insights from classical rhetorical theory as well as more recent philosophy. Of these, the most pertinent for the present purpose is an emerging awareness of the 'non-correspondence between form and function or language and thought'.[14] As Brigitte Nerlich and David D. Clarke have documented, these developments were in turn 'fed by a slow trickle-down of novel ideas', suggesting that language had functions other than the representation of thought; for example, the expression of emotion and the persuasion of other people.[15] Such ideas would eventually culminate in 'the rejection of a reductionist notion of the sentence as statement, affirmation, judgement, representation of thought or proposition' by Thomas Reid and others.[16] Indeed, this shift in paradigms becomes one of the main currents of 'protopragmatics' that would eventually lead to the emergence of pragmatics itself as a clearly defined sub-discipline of linguistics in the twentieth century.[17]

The importance of Hume to this development lies not just in his linguistic conventionalism, but also in the way in which he highlights the referential poverty of certain sentences, a move that enables later thinkers such as Reid to construct a more comprehensively performative theory of language. The *locus classicus* for this shift in outlook is Hume's analysis of the obligation of promises in the *Treatise*, in which he argues that only the necessity of custom and convention can explain the moral authority of something that is itself ontologically and epistemologically 'unintelligible', namely, an obligation that is created by a verbal utterance.[18] By treating promises as the issuing of 'a *certain form of* words … by which we bind ourselves to the performance of any action', Hume identifies the promise with a communicative act that, while philosophically dubious, is nonetheless 'requisite to beget mutual trust and confidence in the common offices of life'.[19] He repeats this claim in the second *Enquiry* by arguing that linguistic customs and the conventions of language are entangled with human customs and habits. Tellingly, this issue arises for Hume not in the context of discussing language *per se*, but amid his considerations concerning 'the social virtue of benevolence' in the Appendix. What Hume seeks to underline here is the *tacitly intersubjective* basis of moral norms, which, he notes, 'may be compared to the building of a vault, where each individual stone would, of itself, fall to the ground; nor is the whole fabric supported but by the mutual assistance and combination of its corresponding parts'.[20] Using the analogy of rowing, Hume maintains that not all conventions depend upon the explicit performance upon which promises are based. The sense of justice, Hume explains, is a convention that 'each man feels in his own breast, which he remarks in his fellows, and which carries him, in concurrence with others, into a general plan or system of actions, which tends to public utility'. In the same way that pace and rhythm are essential to the functioning of oarsmen in a boat, he continues, 'speech and words are fixed by human convention and agreement'.[21]

The virtues that keep morality afloat, then, depend upon the very same implicit conventions that make human communication possible. Above all, Hume emphasizes that it is the *performance* of these virtues that sustains both benevolence and meaning in the absence of an objective moral law and determining referents for words or sentences. Here, Hume's position on language is broadly in line with his epistemology and his moral theory, insofar as he claims that the inadequacy of our sensory input for the purposes of validating our cognitive, ethical and communicative lives indicates the constitutive nature of human habits, customs and behaviour in each of these spheres. What his Appendix to the *Enquiry Concerning the Principles of Morals* makes clear is that human conventions do not form the *foundation* of these spheres, but exist in a circular relation of mutual dependence with them: only 'if all perform their part' do they persist. Nicholas Phillipson expresses the virtuously circular relationship envisaged by Hume in the following way: 'the more stable a system of language was, the more reliable our understanding of the world would be and the better would be our power of judgement. But linguistic stability presupposed social stability.'[22] Essential to maintaining the balance of this delicate ecosystem, once again, is trust. As Baier notes, for Hume '[s]peech is our co-operative and trust-facilitated activity *par excellence*'.[23] From this standpoint, the interdependent relationships that exist between implicit conventions, the performance of social roles, and the maintenance of mutual trust form the conditions of possibility for human language and reason.

Hume's account of the finely balanced economy maintained by trust, language and custom in sustaining the fictions of belief necessary for civilized human life would have powerful repercussions for late eighteenth-century empiricism. In different ways, Thomas Reid and Jeremy Bentham would be led by its implications towards theories of language that prioritized social action rather than representations or mental states as their leading terms. Common sense thinkers such as Reid and Dugald Stewart would seek to cement Hume's pragmatic linking of truth and the (social) conventions behind language into apodictic philosophical first principles, while linguistic materialists such as John Horne Tooke and utilitarians such as Bentham seized on the opportunity that Hume's account appeared to offer to detach meaning from mental contents and to understand the fictions of human belief as linguistically and socially constructed. This involved taking seriously the proposition, as Leslie Stephen put it, that 'if reason is fiction, then fiction is reason'.[24] It's this idea that Bentham's theory of real and fictitious entities eventually internalizes.

Bentham: What is the meaning of it?

Bentham turns to address some of the problems of knowledge and language relatively late in his career, and he approaches them with some reluctance. His impatience with metaphysical questions, however, is not simply a manifestation of the intolerance of the legal reformer for 'theory'. Instead, it is rooted in the conviction that any attempt to separate the 'theory' and 'practice' of human life is an error. Bentham assessed philosophical questions in relation to utility. This in turn means that, for Bentham, the epistemologist's mission to abolish error from the grounds of knowledge must ultimately be subordinated to *eudæmonics*, or an understanding of proper human functioning and the good life. Accordingly, as he indicates in the Appendix to his 1815 work, *Chrestomathia*: '*Eudæmonics* … may be said to be the *object* of every branch of *art*, and the *subject* of every branch of *science*.'[25]

While Bentham's tone sounds confident here, by the time he wrote *Chrestomathia* he had already spent several decades attempting to overcome the philosophical problems that he had recognized early in his career and which are apparent in his great work on jurisprudence, *An Introduction to the Principles of Morals and Legislation*.[26] In the *Introduction*'s important chapter 'Of Motives', Bentham's discussion of the notion of 'motivation' swiftly encounters difficulties due to his realization that the word 'motive' has two meanings: one literal and legitimate, the other figurative and fictitious. The first denotes 'any of those really existing incidents from whence the act in question is supposed to take its rise'; the second, 'a certain fictitious entity, a passion, an affectation of the mind, an ideal being'.[27] Bentham realizes that the *Introduction* is not the best place to work through these problems. Indeed, it is not until the early 1810s that he finally turns to address the issues in which he had become entangled. He does so in a series of essays, which include 'A Fragment on Ontology', the 'Essay on Logic', the 'Essay on Language' and 'Fragments on Universal Grammar'.[28] Logical fictions such as 'motive' differ importantly from poetical fictions like centaurs in that they cannot be extirpated from thought. As Bentham observes in 'Fragment on Ontology', '[i]n the mind of all, fiction, in the logical sense, has been the coin of necessity; – in that of poets of amusement – in that of the priest and the lawyer of mischievous immorality'.[29] Nonetheless, he ultimately perceives that fictitious entities in law are linked to a web of figuration that stretches much further into human thought and language than he had previously imagined. The language of reform and the reform of language could not, in the end, be separated:

> Confining himself to the language most in use, a man can scarce avoid running, in appearance, into perpetual contradictions. … To obviate this inconvenience, completely, he has but this one unpleasant remedy; to lay aside the old phraseology and invent a new one.[30]

To Bentham, it appeared that utilitarianism, could not, after all, simply muddle through without a thoroughly worked-out ontology, an epistemology and a theory of logic or language. The first two of these would jointly distinguish between real entities like physical bodies and 'individual perceptions' on the one hand and fictitious entities such as '[f]aculties, powers of the mind, dispositions' on the other.[31] The task of the theory of logic and language, meanwhile, was to 'give direction and assistance' to human thought by converting the discourse of fictitious entities (as far as possible) into that of real entities. For Bentham, this in turn meant translating *highly* figurative language into a *less* figurative language that was based in sensations of pleasure and pain. By doing this, Bentham reinforced his eudæmonics with the epistemological argument, as stated in *A Table of the Springs of Action* (1817), that '[p]*leasures and pains* [are] *the basis of all other entities*'. Furthermore, the same utilitarian principle leads Bentham to deny that any psychological phenomenon is epistemically privileged: all human awareness, he maintains, regardless of immediacy, is mediated via the '*receptacles*' of pleasure and pain.[32] This denial that sensation is 'pure' or value-neutral in turn supports Bentham's pragmatic insistence in the 'Essay on Logic' that 'in no place is anything to *be known*, but in the same place there is something to be *done*'.[33] It also forms the immediate context for his development of a new 'phraseology', which, based upon the translation of abstract statements into a lexicon of pleasure and pain, was indifferent to the Cartesian problem of whether, and to what extent, the 'mind' corresponded to the 'world'.

At this point, however, another problem confronted Bentham: that of the method of analysis by which such a translation could take place. In a footnote to *A Fragment on Government* (1776), he had already dismissed the traditional method of definition *per genus et differentiam* favoured by D'Alembert and the *encyclopédistes*. Fictitious entities or abstractions, he argues, cannot have examples or instances, and so cannot be defined in terms of a superior genus. Accordingly, when Bentham asks, rhetorically, 'what is a *disposition*?' He imagines the reply: '"A *disposition* is a … :" and there we stop. The fact is, a *disposition* has no *superior genus*: a *disposition* is not a … , any thing'.[34] Conventional analysis is inadequate for interpreting fictitious entities because the meaning of fictitious entities is *always* over-determined. As Bentham puts it in the 'Essay on Logic,' unlike physical aggregates, such as a bushel of apples, logical aggregates are *indeterminate*, in that they remain open to 'the unlimited powers, of decomposition and recomposition possessed by the human mind'. For Bentham, the standard view of analysis and synthesis as 'counterpart' processes is a myth: it is not possible to 'unpack' an abstract idea in the same way that one would unpack a suitcase.[35]

Similarly, the Lockean method of explicating individual terms by tracing such units back to simple ideas or primitive perceptions assumes the presence of an accessible field of neutral data (ideas or impressions), the existence of which Bentham does not accept. Instead, his theory of real and fictitious entities, which pragmatically presupposes the always-already evaluative status of sensation, allows that language itself endows ideas with a kind of 'verbal reality, so to speak, … without which the matter of language could never have been formed'.[36] By accepting that linguistic figuration descends even to the referent, Bentham draws the sting from the claim that reason and metaphor cannot be distinguished. As Esterhammer observes, in this way 'Bentham's theory … embraces the principle … that language does in fact succeed in creating immaterial objects and endowing them with at least a form of reality'.[37] By conceiving meaning as holistic and relational rather than psychological and causal, Bentham is able to allow that it is possible for a word to be used correctly and successfully by individuals who might associate it with different ideas (or even with no ideas). The meaning of a term is ultimately determined not by its causation, but by its context.

For Bentham, this position has two significant consequences. First, the fundamental basic units of meaning are now seen not as single terms, but as whole statements, speech acts or propositions. As he argues in the 'Essay on Language': 'Every man who speaks, speaks in propositions, the rudest savage, not less than the most polished orator, – terms taken by themselves are the work of abstraction, the produce of a refined analysis: – ages after ages must have elapsed before any such analysis was ever made.'[38] Second, in order to create his 'new phraseology', Bentham now develops a method of contextual definition, which he terms 'paraphrasis'. He gave many different accounts of this method, but one of the clearest can be found in the 'Essay on Logic': 'By the word paraphrasis may be designated that sort of exposition which may be afforded by transmuting into a proposition, having for its subject some real entity, a proposition which has not for its subject any other than a fictitious entity.'[39] Crucially, paraphrasis exhausts the metaphysical field of enquiry. As the non-foundational search for meaning, it is to be distinguished from 'Archetypation', or the tracing of an idea to its psychological origin.[40] For Bentham, this new method obviates the ontological embarrassment encountered by empiricists such as Locke and even John Horne Tooke: the very point of paraphrasis is that what counts as a 'real entity' is ultimately a matter of coherence within a linguistic community, not one of correspondence between word and object. As W.V. Quine notes of Bentham; '[h]e recognized that to explain a term we do not need to specify an object for it to refer to'. Paraphrasis enables one 'to explain talk of bodies in terms of talk of impressions by translating one's whole sentences about bodies into whole sentences about impressions, without equating the bodies themselves to anything at all'.[41] Viewed from this perspective, Bentham's theory of fictitious entities signals a reorientation in language theory and epistemology towards recasting the 'problem' of truth as a sub-category of the question of meaning.

Hume's conventionalist account of the primacy of the social function of language in the formation of general ideas had granted constitutive status to logical fictions or metaphors – in other words, to customary and habitual figures of speech that could not be distinguished in principle from the supposedly more 'literal' words and statements through which common-sense principles and the elements of reason were articulated. Even those who accepted Hume's conventionalist linguistics were troubled by this apparent outcome. Nonetheless, Bentham's refusal to put epistemology before ethics, and his thoroughly utilitarian approach to the contextual definition of logical fictions, enables him to adopt a more pragmatic view of the constitutive role played by figurative language in human speech acts. Ultimately, he does so by subordinating the question 'is it true?' to the question 'what does it mean?'

Hazlitt: Is it true?

This essentially pragmatic approach of Bentham to questions of truth can be contrasted with that of one of his antagonists, the quarrelsome Romantic essayist, William Hazlitt. Hazlitt was Bentham's tenant at 19 York Street, Westminster, between 1813 and 1819. During this time Hazlitt never encountered his famous landlord, who lived close by. For his part, Bentham seems to have been aware of the essayist only as a source of rent, for the non-payment of which Hazlitt was duly evicted in the winter of 1819. However, in his biting pen portrait of Bentham five years later, Hazlitt recounts Bentham's original plan to pull down number 19, which had once been the home of John Milton, to make 'a thoroughfare, like a three-stalled stable, for the idle rabble of Westminster'.[42] In Hazlitt's profile, later the leading essay in his collection of portraits *The Spirit of the Age* (1825), Bentham's indifference to the fate of the 'cradle of Paradise Lost' is presented as symptomatic of an age dominated by abstraction, which, by seeking to ground all human life in factual truth, loses sight of the non-rational powers of the human mind:[43]

> [Bentham has] reduced the theory and practice of human life to a *caput mortuum* of reason, and dull, plodding, technical calculation. … If the mind of man were competent to comprehend the whole of truth and good, and act upon it at once, and independently of all other considerations, Mr. Bentham's plan would be a feasible one, and *the truth, the whole truth, and nothing but the truth*, would be the best possible ground to place morality upon. But it is not so.[44]

The great irony of Bentham's work, Hazlitt suggests, is that its obsession with acquiring clear-sighted and comprehensive knowledge of life is the very thing that blinds it to truth. Abstracted, 'like an anchoret in his cell', Bentham's eye 'glances not from object to object, but from thought to thought'.[45] Nowhere is this more evident than in his use of language, which, in insisting on neutrality, betrays its own rationalistic bias; by striving for transparency, it achieves only technocratic opacity:

> Mr. Bentham's method of reasoning, though comprehensive and exact … is rather like an inventory, than a valuation of different arguments. … The construction of his sentences is a curious framework with pegs and hooks to hang his thoughts upon, for his own use and guidance, but almost out of the reach of every body else.

> It is a barbarous philosophical jargon, with all the repetitions, parentheses, formalities, uncouth nomenclature and verbiage of law-Latin … . In short, Mr. Bentham writes as if he was allowed but a single sentence to express his whole view of a subject in … .[46]

For Hazlitt, Bentham's thinking reflects some of the great philosophical blights of the age: empiricism in epistemology, materialism in ontology and egoism and utilitarianism in moral theory. That the last of these ills stemmed from the first two (which he saw as mutually sustaining) he spells out clearly in his *Prospectus of a History of English Philosophy* (1809). According to the ruling philosophy in Britain, he complains, 'the mind itself is nothing, and external impressions everything. All thought is to be resolved into *sensation*, all morality into the *love of pleasure*, and all action into *mechanical impulse*.'[47] In opposition to this tradition, Hazlitt makes it a cornerstone of his philosophy that '[t]he mind has laws, powers, and principles of its own, and is not the mere puppet of matter'.[48]

Hazlitt maintains that the error of 'people of sense', such as Bentham and Shelley, is that by mistaking the abstract, rational forms that quantify experience for the 'pith and marrow' of the thing itself, they come to know only 'the form, not the power of truth'.[49] Against this perspective, Hazlitt pits his moral idealism, his belief that the mind forms experience, and hence its own moral objectives (self-interested and disinterested alike). He accepts Hume's conclusion that the exhaustive determination of belief by sense-experience (the perfect correspondence of idea and world) is not a viable model for knowledge. But while for Hume this meant jettisoning the language of representation and deflating individual consciousness into an epistemology based upon custom and the social sentiments, Hazlitt responds to the same crisis of representation by *inflating* the cognitive function of consciousness still further. Consequently, knowledge for Hazlitt comes to consist in the *projection* of concepts or ideas upon the world by a powerful mind. For instance, in the *Plain Speaker* essay 'On Reason and Imagination', he defends 'natural feeling' against Benthamite considerations of the '*pros* and *cons* … of utility and inutility'. He also introduces a range of quasi-epistemic concepts, including 'sympathy', '*moral sense*' and 'instinctive perception', all of which are deployed to mediate between the estranged realms of bloodless calculation and passionate feeling.[50] Expressing a hatred for 'people who have no notion of any thing but generalities', Hazlitt argues that 'Logic should enrich and invigorate its decisions by the use of imagination.'[51] He insists that mental powers like common sense and genius, by operating at the border between abstract comprehension and an incommensurable world of infinitely plural truths, have the capacity to transcend abstraction through feeling and intuition. Accordingly, Hazlitt introduces a quasi-cognitive level of 'experience' that functions at the bounds of the knowable. In the 'Preface' to his *Abridgement of the Light of Nature Pursued* (1807) by Abraham Tucker, he mocks 'the grave professors of abstract reasoning' for 'attending only to one aspect of things' and 'leaving out always those minute differences and perplexing irregularities which disturb the sluggish uniformity of our ideas, and give life and motion to our being'. Fundamentally, he avers, abstraction is a mental adaptation to environment, 'a trick to supply the defect of comprehension', since the 'moulds of the understanding may be said not to be large enough to contain the gross concrete objects of nature'. Given this condition, anyone 'who disdains the use of common sense … is like a person who should deprive himself of the use of his eye-sight, in order that he might be able to grope his way better in the dark!'[52] This analogy forms, in turn, the basis for Hazlitt's distinction between:

> two sorts of philosophy; that of those who believe what they feel, and endeavour to account for it, and that of those who only believe what they understand, and have already accounted for. The one is the philosophy of consciousness, the other that of experiment; the one may be called the intellectual, the other the material philosophy … . The first of these is the only philosophy that is fit for men of sense, the other should be left to chymists and logicians.[53]

And yet, Hazlitt also attacks the tendency to romanticize nature and humanity. He worries that the Romantic aestheticization of the epistemological might produce an intellectual culture in which the boundary between reason and imagination, fact and fiction, blur into a form of indifference. Indeed, it is this very elision of poetic imagination and prosaic fact that he decries in Samuel Taylor Coleridge, who has, 'by an ambition to be every thing, become nothing. His metaphysics have been a dead weight on the wings of his imagination – while his imagination has run away with his reason and common sense.' Thus, he muses, although '[r]eason and imagination are both excellent things … perhaps their provinces ought to be kept more distinct than they have lately been'.[54]

This determination not to collapse the boundary between imagination and reason, fiction and truth, highlights the parallels between Hazlitt's epistemology, with its concern for twilight knowledge, and his aesthetics of the sublime. In the essay, 'Why Distant Objects

Please', for instance, the gap between the two drives of human nature is invoked to explain the enchanting effects of spatial and temporal distance. Thus, as Hazlitt notes:

> [i]t is not the little, glimmering, almost annihilated speck in the distance that rivets our attention and 'hangs upon the beatings of our hearts': it is the interval that separates us from it, and of which it is the trembling boundary. … Into that great gap in our being 'come thronging soft desires' and infinite regrets.[55]

Indeed, sublimity has a more general function in Hazlitt's thought. By arguing that knowledge rests upon *mind-formed* fictions of abstraction and imagination, Hazlitt metaphysically inflates the status of Hume's fictions by relocating them from the sphere of tacit social conventions to that of mental constructions. In Hazlitt's hands, empirical intuition is privatized and sublimed into the noumenal, indeterminate territory of a hypostatized 'common sense'.[56] Thus, the aesthetics of the 'trembling boundary' are not merely the product of his philosophy of knowledge and identity, but are also an integral part of his metaphysics.

Many will recognize this aestheticization of knowledge, whereby the para-epistemological agencies of creative imagination and ineffable common sense are established as the moderators of reason, as a characteristically Romantic response to the epistemological challenge of Hume. Accordingly, Uttara Natarajan observes that '[f]ollowing Hume, Hazlitt recognizes the sensory constraint upon imaginative capacity. But this theory, unlike Hume's, allows for such constraints to be altogether surpassed by the cultivation of the imagination.'[57] Natarajan is right to contrast Hume's deflationary account of the 'faint and languid' perceptions of imagination (as thought recedes from sensation and memory) with the dynamic faculty, which, in Hazlitt's *Essay*, '*creates* the object' of perception and 'pushes … ideas beyond the bounds of … memory and sense'.[58] Seen this way, Hazlitt's argument follows a familiar pattern of Romantic logic, whereby, as imagination is elevated and reason subordinated, philosophy's loss becomes art's gain. While Hume had sought merely to counterbalance the philosophical perspective of the anatomist with the civilizing, aesthetic skills of the painter, Hazlitt elevates the latter to a new level of precedence. Accordingly, 'the poet and painter of imagination are superior to the mere philosopher or man of science, because they exercise the powers of reason and intellect combined with nature and passion'.[59]

And yet, what is lost from Hume's picture in Hazlitt's new arrangement of philosophy and art is a constitutive role for intersubjectivity in human intellectual life. The 'internal principle' of Hazlitt's immanent idealism secures for the imagination a projective power that is won at the cost of sociability.[60] As Hazlitt describes it in his *Examiner* article 'Coriolanus' (1816), the poetic imagination, by reversing the process of abstraction, 'presents no immediate or distinct images to the mind'. Instead, insofar as it 'puts the individual for the species, the one above the infinite many, might before right', the 'language of poetry naturally falls in with the language of power'.[61] At the same time, the indeterminacy of experience, which for Hume is the result of the social intellect's dependence upon dialogue and conversation, is reinterpreted by Hazlitt as the sublime horizon of knowledge produced by the power of abstraction, a 'trembling boundary', navigable only by the quasi-cognitive faculty of common sense. This exchange of the pragmatics of conversation for aesthetic enchantment reflects a fundamental shift from communication to power, and from 'meaning' to 'truth', as the precondition of thought.

Conclusion

Behind the efforts of Bentham and the Romantics to address the relationship between meaning and truth lies what Ian Duncan has described as the Humean drama of a life doubled between 'a sceptical disillusionment from reality and a sentimental attachment to reality as illusion'.[62] Recognizing the constitutive role played by fictions of reason in thought and life leads, in turn, to the acceptance that '[t]ruth arises neither in alienated reflection nor in forgetful habituation, nor in some cognitive synthesis of the two, but in the temporal oscillation between them'.[63] The boundary between 'cognitive synthesis' and 'temporal oscillation' identified by Duncan is often subtle and difficult to determine, but it remains crucial. To distinguish between the two is to differentiate between the endeavour to lay new foundations for thought and the pragmatic acknowledgement of dividedness as a condition of human life. For this reason, as Duncan observes, it is important to distinguish between the pragmatic imagination of Hume's empiricism, which maintains an ironic oscillation between belief and the consciousness of necessary fictions, and 'the Kantian-Coleridgean "lyric" model ... which casts the imagination as trace of an alienated transcendental cognition'.[64]

Bentham's theory of logical fictions takes its cue from Hume by reducing epistemological problems to hedonic considerations of human well-being: on this analysis, those fictions that are least likely to promote happiness are those that we are under the strongest moral obligation to discard. Similarly, Hazlitt's 'trembling boundary' reflects the complexity of his response to a growing awareness, post-Hume, of the constitutive role played by epistemological fictions in thought. And yet, while Bentham's management of fictitious entities was progressive in the way that it anticipated the removal of residual fictions from social life through the systematic proliferation of information, Hazlitt's Romantic imagination explores the liminal ground between truth and fiction, evoking the shadows of lost certainties. In their different ways, both thinkers acknowledge that there is no way of answering Hume's scepticism on its own epistemological terms. Bentham's strategy is inherently pragmatic, subordinating final verification to paraphrasis. Hazlitt's response, in contrast, is to idealize truth by subliming it into an indeterminate ground between reason and imaginative fiction. Like the transcendental metaphysics of his youthful mentor Coleridge, Hazlitt's philosophy insists upon the overriding importance of truth by memorializing its absence.

In this essay I have tried to outline some ways in which the relationships between utilitarianism and Romanticism need to be rethought. Mill's 'truth/meaning' binary, though intuitively appealing, is less convincing once one begins to read Bentham as a proto-pragmatist and the Romantics as thwarted objectivists. What W.V. Quine, among others, has demonstrated is that Bentham always treats the question, 'is it true?' as subordinate to the question, 'what does it mean?' – that is, 'how does it translate in paraphrase?' For Bentham, the literal and the figurative, the factual and the fictional, shade into each other. As he writes in the 'Essay on Language': 'The discourse that … is *not* figurative is the discourse in which … no other fictions, – no other figures are employed than are *absolutely necessary*.'[65] The final words in this statement are crucial: they suggest that Bentham sees his task as ameliorating the effects of logical fictions in discourse, not removing them. Indeed, as Angela Esterhammer observes, Bentham's acknowledgement of the priority of the figurative over the psychological means that he embraces the performativity of language, with all its contingencies and breakdowns, precisely because he sees fiction as inescapable.[66] Conversely, for Hazlitt and many other Romantic writers, the fictions of reason are hypostatized as an ineffable territory that only art and feeling can access. In Hazlitt, the sublime 'power of truth' comes to reside at the 'trembling boundary' between reason and imagination. In the final analysis, then, Mill's characterization is only half right: Bentham's vision of truth is certainly progressive and reforming, while that of Hazlitt and his fellow Romantics is, more often than not, fundamentally nostalgic; and yet, it is the latter who asks, 'is it true?' and Bentham who demands, 'what is the meaning of it?'

Notes

1 Mill, 1840, 139–40.
2 Mill, 1840, 153.
3 Mill, 1840, 144–5.
4 Hume, ed. Selby-Bigge, 1975, 22.
5 Box, 1991, 67.
6 Ayer, 1990, 36.
7 Locke, ed. Nidditch, 1975, 596.
8 See Berkeley, ed. Luce and Jessop, 1949, 42. Berkeley declares of objects that '[t]heir *esse* is *percepi*, nor is it possible they should have any existence, out of the minds of thinking beings which perceive them'.
9 Berkeley, 1949, 32.
10 Hume, ed. Selby-Bigge, rev. Nidditch, 1978, 17.
11 Hume, ed. Selby-Bigge, rev. Nidditch, 1978, 72.
12 Hume, ed. Selby-Bigge, rev. Nidditch, 1978, 22.
13 Baier, 1991, 282.
14 Nerlich and Clarke eds. 1996, 11. Nerlich and Clarke identify the three other main sources of 'pragmatic insight' as: (1) classical categories of mood; (2) a theory of deixis, particularly in Humboldt, 'accounting for the linguistic anchoring of speech in the situation of discourse'; (3) rhetorical theories, particularly those of Aristotle, which focus upon an essentially 'pragmatic model of communication' (9–10).
15 Nerlich and Clarke eds. 1996, 374.
16 Nerlich and Clarke eds. 1996, 11.
17 Nerlich and Clarke eds. 1996, 13.
18 Hume, ed. Selby-Bigge, rev. Nidditch, 1978, 517.
19 Hume, ed. Selby-Bigge, rev. Nidditch, 1978, 543.
20 Hume, ed. Selby-Bigge, 1975, 305.
21 Hume, ed. Selby-Bigge, 1975, 306–7.
22 Phillipson, ed. Mason, 1987, 238.
23 Baier, 1994, 175.
24 Stephen, 1902, 49. See also Clingham, 1998, 14. Clingham argues that the eighteenth century is the crucible of postmodernism's insight into 'the place of the fictive in the production of the real'.
25 Bentham, ed. Smith and Burston, 1983, 179.
26 Bentham, ed. Burns and Hart, 1970.
27 Bentham, ed. Burns and Hart, 1970, 97.
28 These four essays appear to have been intended as parts of a general study of logic and language but, as with much of his later writing, Bentham made little effort to prepare the material for the press. There is no authoritative modern edition of these works, though C.K. Ogden attempted to synthesize the manuscript sources in *Bentham's Theory of Fictions* (Ogden, 1932). Consequently, all references to the above essays are based on John Bowring's flawed but workable *The Works of Jeremy Bentham*, 11 vols (Bowring, 1843).
29 Bowring, 1843, viii. 199.
30 Bentham, Bentham, ed. Burns and Hart, 1970, 102.
31 Bowring, 1843, viii. 196.
32 Bentham, ed. Goldworth, 1983, 98.
33 Bowring, 1843, viii. 218.

34 Bentham, ed. Burns and Hart, 1977, 495.
35 Bowring, 1843, viii. 256–7.
36 Bentham, ed. Smith and Burston, 1983, 271.
37 Esterhammer, 2000, 72.
38 Bowring, 1843, viii. 321.
39 Bowring, 1843, viii. 246.
40 Bowring, 1843, viii. 246. For further discussion of the relation between paraphrasis and archetypation in Bentham see Harrison, 1983, 61–3 and Skorupski, 1993, 27.
41 Quine, 1969, 72. This is in marked to contrast to Elie Halévy, who dismissed the technique as vague and inferior to 'genetic definition': Halévy, trans. Morris, 1972, 459. Halévy's reading was in turn criticized by C.K. Ogden: Odgen, 1932, p. xxx.
42 Hazlitt, ed. Howe, 1934, xi. 6. For further background on Hazlitt's tenancy see Grayling, 2000, 157–8, 252.
43 For the background to this issue see Park, 1971.
44 Hazlitt, ed. Howe, 1934, xi. 8–9.
45 Hazlitt, ed. Howe, 1934, xi. 6.
46 Hazlitt, ed. Howe, 1934, xi. 14–15.
47 Hazlitt, ed. Howe, 1934, ii. 113–14.
48 Hazlitt, ed. Howe, 1934, ii. 116.
49 'On People of Sense', Hazlitt, ed. Howe, 1934, xii. 248.
50 Hazlitt, ed. Howe, 1934, xii. 45, 49, 51.
51 Hazlitt, ed. Howe, 1934, xii. 44–5.
52 Hazlitt, ed. Howe, 1934, i. 124–5.
53 Hazlitt, ed. Howe, 1934, i. 127.
54 Hazlitt, ed. Howe, 1934, xvi. 137.
55 Hazlitt, ed. Howe, 1934, viii. 257.
56 See Tomalin, 2009, 90–1, arguing that Hazlitt's account of 'a feeling, an inarticulable non-rational hunch' presents 'a creakingly precarious account of common sense'.
57 Natarajan, 2005, 118.
58 Hume, ed. Selby-Bigge, rev. Nidditch, 1978, 7; Hazlitt, ed. Howe, 1934, i. 26–7.
59 Hazlitt, ed. Howe, 1934, iv. 76.
60 Hazlitt, ed. Howe, 1934, ii. 147.
61 Hazlitt, ed. Howe, 1934, v. 347–8.
62 Duncan, 2007, p. xiv.
63 Duncan, 2007, 122.
64 Duncan, 2007, 124.
65 Bowring, 1843, viii. 331 (my emphasis).
66 See Esterhammer, 2000, 71: 'Like Derrida ... Bentham recognizes that the ever-present possibility of failure or abuse is part of what constitutes even the successful speech act.'

References

Ayer, A.J. *Language, Truth and Logic*. 2nd ed. London: Penguin, 1990.

Baier, A. *A Progress of Sentiments: Reflections on Hume's Treatise*. Cambridge, MA: Harvard University Press, 1991.

Baier, A. *Moral Prejudices: Essays on Ethics*. Cambridge, MA: Harvard University Press, 1994.

Bentham, J. *A Comment on the Commentaries and A Fragment on Government* (*CW*), eds. J.H. Burns and H.L.A. Hart. London: Athlone Press, 1977.

Bentham, J. *An Introduction to the Principles of Morals and Legislation* (*CW*), eds. J.H. Burns and H.L.A. Hart. London: Athlone Press, 1970.

Bentham, J. *Chrestomathia* (*CW*), eds. M.J. Smith and W.H. Burston. Oxford: Clarendon Press, 1983.

Bentham, J. *Deontology: Together with A Table of the Springs of Action and Article on Utilitarianism* (*CW*), ed. A. Goldworth. Oxford: Clarendon Press, 1983.

Bentham, J. *The Works of Jeremy Bentham*, ed. John Bowring. 11 vols. Edinburgh: William Tait, 1838–43.

Berkeley, G. *A Treatise Concerning the Principles of Human Knowledge*, eds. A.A. Luce and T.E. Jessop. London: Nelson, 1949.
Box, M.A. *The Suasive Art of David Hume*. Princeton, NJ: Princeton University Press, 1991.
Clingham, G. 'Introduction: The Question of History in Eighteenth-Century Studies', in *Questioning History: The Postmodern Turn to the Eighteenth Century*, ed. G. Clingham. Lewisburg, PA: Bucknell University Press, and London: Associated University Presses, 1998.
Duncan, I. *Scott's Shadow: The Novel in Romantic Edinburgh*. Princeton: Princeton University Press, 2007.
Esterhammer, A. 'Of Promises, Contracts and Constitutions: Thomas Reid and Jeremy Bentham on Language as Social Action', *Romanticism* 6:1 (2000): 55–77.
Grayling, A.C. *The Quarrel of the Age: The Life and Times of William Hazlitt*. London: Weidenfeld and Nicolson, 2000.
Halévy, E. *The Growth of Philosophic Radicalism*, trans. M. Morris. 3rd ed. London: Faber, 1972.
Harrison, R. *Bentham*. London: Routledge, 1983.
Hazlitt, W. *The Complete Works of William Hazlitt*, ed. P.P. Howe. London: J.M. Dent, 1930–4.
Hume, D. *Enquiries Concerning Human Understanding and Concerning the Principles of Morals*, ed. L.A. Selby-Bigge. Oxford: Clarendon Press, 1975.
Hume, D. *A Treatise of Human Nature*, ed. L.A. Selby-Bigge. 2nd ed., rev. P.H. Nidditch. Oxford: Oxford University Press, 1978.
Locke, J. *An Essay Concerning Human Understanding*, ed. P.H. Nidditch. Oxford: Oxford University Press, 1975.
Mill, J.S. 'Coleridge', *The London and Westminster Review* 65 (1840): 139–63.
Natarajan, U. 'Circle of Sympathy: Shelley's Hazlitt', in *Metaphysical Hazlitt: Bicentenary Essays*, eds. U. Natarajan, T. Paulin, and D. Wu. London: Routledge, 2005.
Nerlich, B. and Clarke, D.D., eds. *Language, Action, and Context: The Early History of Pragmatics in Europe and America, 1780–1930*. Amsterdam: John Benjamins, 1996.
Ogden, C.K. *Bentham's Theory of Fictions*. London: Kegan Paul, Trench, Trubner, 1932.
Park, R. *Hazlitt and The Spirit of the Age: Abstraction and Critical Theory*. Oxford: Clarendon Press, 1971.
Phillipson, N. 'Polites, Politeness and the Anglicisation of Early Eighteenth-Century Scottish Culture', in *Scotland and England, 1286–1815*, ed. R.A. Mason. Edinburgh: J. Donald, 1987.
Quine, W.V. 'Epistemology Naturalised', in *Ontological Relativity and Other Essays*. New York: Columbia University Press, 1969.
Skorupski, J. *English-Language Philosophy 1750 to 1945*. Oxford: Oxford University Press, 1993.
Stephen, L. *History of English Thought in the Eighteenth Century*. 3rd ed. London: Smith Elder, 1902.
Tomalin, M. *Romanticism and Linguistic Theory: William Hazlitt, Language and Literature*. Basingstoke: Palgrave Macmillan, 2009.

Chapter 7
More Bentham, less Mill

Anthony Julius

Preliminary

Literature and the visual arts, the focus of so much censoring energy these days, have been somewhat neglected in liberal thinking about free speech. Though this neglect is hardly the fault of one liberal thinker alone, Mill bears the greatest responsibility, in part because of the terms of his defence of free speech, in part because of the immense influence of that defence and in part because of his deprecations regarding Jeremy Bentham. If liberals are to develop better defences of free speech, giving literature and the visual arts an honoured place in the family of protected discourses, they need to distance themselves from Mill, and get closer to Bentham. This essay is a first attempt in trying to do that. If it has a polemical edge, it is because I have the sense that I am pushing against a consensus regarding Bentham. But no inference should be drawn of anything other than respect for Mill – still less, any doubt that it is only within the liberal tradition that a decent theory of free speech is possible.

Mill

1. In the matter of literary free speech, Mill has a high reputation

Mill's reputation stands on two pillars: first, in his various acknowledgments of poetry's immense value, a position that finds theoretical expression in his essays written between 1833–40, and its most complete personal expression in his *Autobiography*, published in 1873, the year of his death; second, the arguments made for free speech in the second chapter of *On Liberty* (1859). It is a reputation strong among creative writers and literary critics.

Let me take, among Mill's writings, the essays on Bentham (1838) and Coleridge (1840),[1] and let me take, among literary critics, F.R. Leavis, the most significant figure in English literary studies between the 1930s and 1970s. His introduction to *Mill on Bentham and Coleridge* was published in 1950. Mill's two essays, Leavis writes, 'deserve to be called classical for their intrinsic quality'. Mill's *Autobiography* is also 'a classic'. He is to be admired for 'his development out of pure Benthamism'. Leavis confesses to a 'propagandist' intention. Mill's essays must become 'current classics for the literary student', part of a 'liberal education' in which 'the critical study of literature' must play a 'central part'. The justice of Mill's assessments of Bentham and Coleridge is not questioned.[2] The essays are instead assimilated to Leavis's own cultural politics, in which literature, esteemed as the supreme discovery-invention of a supreme kind of thinking,[3] must be defended against the forces of 'technologico-Benthamism'.[4]

Major literary personalities welcomed *On Liberty*.[5] Walt Whitman commended Mill's 'profound essay' as setting out the conditions for 'a truly great nationality'.[6] Thomas Hardy was a devoted reader of *On Liberty*; his copy is more heavily annotated, underlined and underscored than any other surviving book in his library. It was the volume, he wrote, 'we students of that date knew almost by heart'.[7] In the late 1870s, his teachings were held responsible for a new art that exhibited 'the languor of exhausted animalism'.[8] Over a century later, *On Liberty*, and the values it endorsed, was blamed for what were regarded as the public art excesses of the 1960s, including masturbation on a public stage.[9]

2. Mill does not merit his high reputation

Mill was in fact rather feeble in his aesthetic positions and *On Liberty* is hostile to literary free speech.

2.1. Feeble aesthetic positions

In sum: Mill's literary sensibility was unadventurous, and conditioned disablingly by his personal crisis; he had modern literature-disqualifying views; he denied all originality to women's literary writing, in the face of compelling contrary evidence.

In his first adult years, Mill was a Benthamite tyro. He and his fellow Benthamites sought to persuade the public of the superior excellence of unselfish benevolence. The members of the Utilitarian Society did not expect the regeneration of mankind from any 'direct action' on 'selfish feelings'. The strategy was instead to get people to alter their opinions according to evidence. The utilitarians, Mill relates, took no account of the 'cultivation of feeling', and this led to a broader undervaluing of poetry and of imagination in general. He himself was, he tells us in the *Autobiography*, speculatively indifferent to poetry, though not hostile to it. He disliked any sentiments in poetry that he would have disliked in prose. He was blind to its place in human culture as a means of educating the feelings.

Perhaps Mill had in mind his essay 'Periodical Literature: Edinburgh Review', published in the *Westminster Review* in April 1824. Mill quotes Johnson: 'Shakespeare is so much more careful to please than to instruct, that he seems to write without any moral purpose. … This fault the barbarity of his age cannot extenuate; for it is always a writer's duty to make the world better, and justice is a virtue independent on time and place.' Mill comments:

> We should be sorry to be suspected of affecting prudery. It is one thing to be a moralist, another thing to be a poet; and a high degree of excellence in the one capacity is not incompatible with great deficiency in the other. But we assert that in a species of writing [i.e. literature] which admits so easily of being made subservient to morality, to be without a moral object is one of the greatest of defects.

He then turns to Scott:

> If to write without a moral purpose be a fault which the barbarity even of Shakespeare's age cannot extenuate, we presume it will be held to be still less excusable in Sir Walter Scott. He too shows no decided leaning between virtue and vice. There is no one of his productions from which, unless it be by chance, any one useful lesson can be derived. It is impossible to peruse them without being convinced that amusement, and amusement only, is there studied.[10]

Or perhaps he had in mind his essay in October of the same year, 'Brodie's History of the British Empire'. Literature, Mill finds, can mislead and corrupt even the most distinguished minds. 'Hume possessed powers of a very high order; but regard for truth formed no part of his character. He reasoned with surprising acuteness; but the object of his reasonings was, not to attain truth, but to shew that it is unattainable.' Mill then identifies the cause. 'His mind ... was completely enslaved by a taste for literature; not those kinds of literature which teach mankind to know the causes of their happiness and misery, that they may seek the one and avoid the other; but that literature which without regard for truth or utility, seeks only to excite emotion.' Not just any literature, however. It is 'pernicious' 'Romance', that 'infallibly allies itself with the sinister interests of the few'. They encourage the contemplation of events 'as they bear upon the pleasures and pains of an individual' rather than 'as they affect the great interests of mankind'. If damaging to Hume, how much more so to the generality of mankind?

> The pleasures and pains most interesting to an ill-cultivated mind are those of the one and of the few; of the men in exalted stations, whose lot is most conspicuous, whose felicity, to the ignorant, appears something almost divine, and whose misfortunes, from their previous elevation, most powerfully affect the imagination. The sufferings of the many, though multiplied almost beyond calculation from their indefinite extent, are thought nothing of: they seem born to suffer; their fall is from a less height; their miseries lie hidden, and do not meet the eye.[11]

We reach the crisis of 1827–8. Mill asked himself: would joy come to me in the realization of all my plans for reform of institutions and opinions? No, it would not, he answered. And his heart sank within him, and the foundations of his life fell down. We may identify two moments in the resolution of this crisis: the Marmontel moment, when the reading of some memoirs moved him to tears (a father dies, a son replaces him); and the Wordsworth moment, when he came under the influence of Wordsworth's poetry, a 'medicine' for his 'state of mind'. This second moment was the more important of the two. In Wordsworth, Mill found a source of inward joy, of sympathetic and imaginative pleasure, which could be shared in by all human beings. Though he considered himself cured, the cure had unhappy consequences, disabling him from thinking about poetry in any of its non-therapeutic aspects and reading sympathetically post-Romantic poetry (or fiction).

We find this dislike of contemporary literature expressed in several places in the 1830s. 'The time was, when it was thought that the best and most appropriate office of fictitious narrative was to awaken high aspirations, by the representation, in interesting circumstances, of characters ... whose actions and sentiments were of a more generous and loftier cast than are ... met with ... in every-day life.' But, Mill continues, 'now-a-days, nature and probability are thought to be violated, if there be shown to the reader ... characters on a larger scale than himself'. Mill despairs: 'The chivalrous spirit has almost disappeared from books of education; the popular novels of the day teach nothing but ... lessons of worldliness, with at most the huckstering virtues which conduce to getting on in the world; and, for the first time perhaps in history, the youth of both sexes of the educated classes are universally growing up unromantic.'[12] The tone is the same in the essay 'Civilisation', published three years earlier: 'literature is becoming more and more ephemeral: books, of any solidity, are almost gone by'.[13] Mill passed from deprecation to perplexity when confronted by Browning's poem 'Pauline', which he read as autobiographical: 'this writer seems to me possessed with a more intense and morbid self-consciousness than I ever knew in any sane human being. I should think it a sincere confession, though of a most unlovable state, if the "Pauline" were not evidently a mere phantom.'[14]

In the late essay 'Theism', published posthumously, Mill asks: 'To what purpose should we feed our imagination with the unlovely aspect of persons and things?' To little purpose, is his answer. All *unnecessary* dwelling upon 'the evils of life' is 'at best a useless expenditure of nervous force'. It is worse than useless to dwell upon life's 'meannesses and basenesses'. We should be aware of them; but we must not live in their contemplation. If we do, then we will be unable to maintain 'a high tone of mind'; our 'imagination and feelings' become 'tuned to a lower pitch'; 'degrading instead of elevating associations become connected with the daily objects and incidents of life, and give their colour to the thoughts'; 'associations of sensuality' become habitual for those 'who indulge freely' in the contemplation of the mean and the base. Mill concludes: 'the poetry is taken out of the things fullest of it, by mean associations'. And then, the final step, the question of 'regulation': 'in the regulation of the imagination literal truth of facts is not the only thing to be considered'. He elaborates, somewhat obscurely:

> Truth is the province of reason, and it is by the cultivation of the rational faculty that provision is made for its being known always, and thought of as often as is required by duty and the circumstances

> of human life. But when the reason is strongly cultivated, the imagination may safely follow its own end, and do its best to make life pleasant and lovely inside the castle, in reliance on the fortifications raised and maintained by Reason round the outward bounds.[15]

The Novel did not represent an aesthetic *project* to Mill. It was a feeble thing: 'the infinite distance, as to power of influencing the mind, between the best contrived and most probable fiction, and the smallest fact'.[16] F. Parvin Sharpless writes of 'Mill's rejection of the novel, since, in an age which reads novels for information rather than amusement, the novel comes to usurp a proper function of the analytic faculties'.[17] This is disastrous, because it offers ignominious pleasures only: 'The minds and hearts of greatest depth and elevation are commonly those which take greatest delight in poetry; the shallowest and emptiest, on the contrary, are, at all events, not those least addicted to novel-reading. … The most idle and frivolous persons take a natural delight in fictitious narrative.'[18] Mill could not take the novel seriously. In an October 1859 review of his friend Alexander Bain's *The Emotions and the Will*, he noted with approval Bain's absurd judgment that the pleasure in novel-reading is akin to the pleasure in watching horse-racing.[19] 'This grouping together of the emotions of hunting, of games, of intrigue of all sorts, and of novel-reading, with those of an active career in life, seems to us … original and philosophical.'[20]

Though poetry was typically the foil for his disparagements of the novel, it did not prompt him to write anything of any interest on the form. His praise was no more illuminating than his censure. Mill's two-part essay, 'Thoughts on Poetry and Its Varieties' (1833), splits and lumps to no valuable effect. The splitting is relentless. He distinguishes, for example, between the poet of culture and the poet of nature. In Wordsworth, the poetry is almost always the mere setting of a thought. He is essentially unlyrical – which is regrettable, because 'lyric poetry [is] more eminently and peculiarly poetry than any other: it is the poetry most natural to a really poetic temperament'. Shelley had this temperament 'to the greatest extent'. In Shelley, 'systematic intellectual culture … was wanting'. The splitting coexists with an egregious lumping. Mill is unable to grasp the critical distinction of form. One may write genuine poetry, and not be a poet, writes Mill. For whosoever writes out truly any human feeling, writes poetry. Whom, then, shall we call poets? 'Those who are so constituted, that emotions are the links of association by which their ideas, both sensuous and spiritual, are connected together.' 'Poetry' becomes a term to characterize writing oriented towards 'emotion'. The effect is to render invisible to Mill's argument poetry's structural complexities and distinct internal history.[21]

Last (though greater space would allow a more comprehensively adverse account), let me turn to Mill's *The Subjection of Women* (1869), and his account of literature written by women: 'If we turn from pure speculation to literature in the narrow sense of the term, and the fine arts, there is a very obvious reason why women's literature is, in its general conception and in its main features, an imitation of men's.'[22] The reasons he offers in support of this judgment are of no interest, because the judgment itself is so embarrassingly wrong. There *was* a women's literature – a 'literary feminism'[23] – well established by the mid-nineteenth century.[24] To G.H. Lewes, the 'subject' was 'momentous' and demanded considerable attention: 'The advent of female literature promises woman's view of life … . Hitherto … the literature of women … has been too much a literature of imitation.'[25] Note the 'hitherto'. Even if true in 1852 (which is questionable),[26] when Lewes made this claim (in the essay 'The Lady Novelists'), it was plainly false in 1869, when Mill repeated it. Among novelists, think of the three Brontë sisters, of Elizabeth Gaskell and of George Eliot. Among poets, think of Elizabeth Barrett Browning's *Aurora Leigh*, which precisely addresses the question of women's writing, and was praised by George Eliot for 'exhibit[ing] all the peculiar powers, without the negation, of [EBB's] sex'.[27] The considerable fact of a woman's literature was widely acknowledged, its features and likely trajectory widely discussed. In a review of Elizabeth Gaskell's *Life of Charlotte Brontë* (1857), the literary critic E.S. Dallas acknowledged it as 'the most singular literary phenomenon of the day – the feminine aspect of our fictitious literature'.[28]

2.2. Dangerous *On Liberty*

On Liberty is muddled, illiberal and anti-literature. It is the third objection that concerns me here. *On Liberty* is culpably silent on major literary censorship events in 1857; literature is extruded from the ambit of protected speech; censorship possibilities are admitted.

On Liberty was conceived in 1854. Mill finished the essay across the year in which, in London, the Obscene Publications Act was passed, and, in Paris, Flaubert was prosecuted for his novel *Madame Bovary* and Baudelaire was prosecuted for his poems *Les Fleurs du Mal*. Yet *On Liberty* contains no reflection on the threat to liberty posed by an obscenity law or any statement of solidarity with the prosecuted writers across the Channel. Indeed, Mill has practically nothing to say *expressly* about restrictions on literary or artistic expression, with the exception of the theatre (and then only historically, in connection with the Puritans, and not to the oppressive theatre censorship of his own time). What Mill says by *implication*, however, is somewhat endorsing of restrictions. When Mill champions 'absolute freedom of opinion and sentiment on all subjects, practical or speculative, scientific, moral or theological', we wonder, what of literature? Bertrand Russell thought that Mill's silence on the question was because it was not a current topic of concern.[29] But Russell was wrong about this. Literary free speech needed defending in 1857.

Mill finds no creative writers or artists among 'the multitude of promising intellects combined with timid characters, who dare not follow out any bold, vigorous, independent train of thought, lest it should land them in something which would admit of being considered irreligious or immoral'. It did not seem to have occurred to him that 'fear' might silence novelists, even though he had sufficient evidence before him to draw that conclusion. He gives us no reason to suppose that literary works could be the products of minds engaged in 'free and daring speculation', 'bold, vigorous, independent trains of thought', in 'Socratic dialectics' – the search for truth, as Mill understands it. Creative writers, we may concede, are not engaged in 'contradicting and disproving', or 'correcting and completing'; they are not typically 'on the alert either to defend themselves against the world, or to bring the world over to them'. They are not aligned with the hero of the chapter, Socrates, 'the head and prototype of all subsequent teachers of virtue, the source equally of the lofty inspiration of Plato and the judicious utilitarianism of Aristotle'. On the contrary – he was their adversary. But does that mean that creative writers should not be defended?

In Chapter IV, 'Of the Limits to the Authority of Society over the Individual', Mill explains that, '[i]t would be a great misunderstanding' of *On Liberty* to suppose that it promotes a 'selfish indifference' to 'the well-doing or well-being of others'. Quite the contrary: it is to be read as promoting 'a great increase of disinterested exertion' of effort for the good of others. Though such 'disinterested benevolence' is not typically best undertaken with 'whips and scourges', certain behaviours may properly be met with something akin to such instruments: 'There is a degree of folly, and a degree of … *lowness or depravation of taste*, which, though it cannot justify doing harm to the person who manifests it, renders him necessarily and properly a subject of distaste, or, in extreme cases, even of contempt.' Those who feel contempt may display it, in expression of their own finer individuality. 'Those who pursue animal pleasures', Mill explains, may quite properly be shunned, and discriminated against, by people of 'feeling and intellect'. Who could object to being exposed as 'a fool or being of an inferior order', especially if also warned of the further disagreeable consequences that might follow? The gratification of low, depraved tastes is to be deplored; those who indulge them have 'no right to complain' if steps are taken by others against them.

Mill returned in *Utilitarianism* (1863) to this distinction (in his view, a qualitative one) between beings of an inferior order and people of feeling and intellect: 'Men lose their high aspirations as they lose their intellectual tastes. ... It may be questioned whether anyone who has remained equally susceptible to both classes of pleasures, ever knowingly and calmly preferred the lower; though many ... have broken down in an ineffectual attempt to combine both.'[30] The sentiment implicit in 'combine' goes deep in the culture. It explains the puzzled delight that greets reports that some profound thinker favoured ostensibly trivial pastimes – say, Wittgenstein with detective novels and Hollywood musicals.[31] But I sense a more specific discomfort in this passage of Mill's, one with the creative literature of his own time – among many possible texts, we may instance Baudelaire's 'Femmes damnées' and 'Lesbos' among the poems condemned by the Paris court, and *Madame Bovary*, a novel populated with characters whose 'actions and sentiments' are neither 'generous' nor 'lofty', and who are altogether lacking in 'genuine unforced nobleness'.[32]

Mill anticipates an objection:

> If I am asked, what I mean by difference of *quality* in pleasures, or what makes one pleasure more valuable than another ... except its being greater in amount, there is but one possible answer. ... if there be one to which *all or almost all who have experience of both* give a decided preference, irrespective of any feeling of moral obligation to prefer it, that is the more desirable pleasure. If one of the two is, by *those who are competently acquainted with both*, placed so far above the other that they prefer it, even though knowing it to be attended with a greater amount of discontent, and would not resign it for any quantity of the other pleasure which their nature is capable of, we are justified in ascribing to the preferred enjoyment a superiority in quality, so far outweighing quantity as to render it, in comparison, of small account. Now it is an unquestionable fact that *those who are equally acquainted with, and equally capable of appreciating and enjoying, both*, do give a most marked preference

> to the manner of existence which employs their higher faculties. … From [the] verdict of the only competent judges … there can be no appeal. … the judgments of those who are qualified by knowledge of both, or if they differ, that of the majority, must be admitted as final.[33]

There are many difficulties here, but let us allow Mill his argument. I take it, in the intensity of its moral charge and the practicality of its terms (majority decision, no appeal), as laying the theoretical groundwork for a censorship board. I do not think this reading is fanciful. The jurisprudential criteria designed to separate art works from works of pornography – that is, works that appeal, respectively, to 'the intellect, the feelings, the imagination', and works that appeal to 'mere sensation'[34] – fit Mill's reasoning, which has a judicial tone.[35] Certainly, experts in obscenity cases tend to speak in Millian terms.[36]

Mill describes the path of the ascetic. This way of imagining human nature is conducive to censorship and self-censorship. Perhaps surprisingly, it ties in with the progressivism of the mid-nineteenth century. That a progressive person would be hostile to forms of sexual expression, and especially literary sexual expression, is something we would not now anticipate. But in that time, such a position would have been taken for granted. The disparaged sexual moralism of the Victorian years grows directly from the boldest, most progressive and refreshing features of late-eighteenth and early-nineteenth century culture, Michael Mason has explained.[37] A connection was made between sexual continence and human improvement. Anti-sensualism was the creed of the forward-looking. That literature might draw from such sexual material, that this material might serve a literary or more broadly aesthetic end, seems never to have been entertained by Mill. Sex and sensual pleasures generally were to be ranked among the lower pleasures. Mill's qualitative utilitarianism is the gateway to literary censorship.

To return to *On Liberty* – consider Chapter V, 'Applications'. Mill writes:

> There are many acts which, being directly injurious only to the agents themselves, ought not to be legally interdicted, but which, if done publicly, *are a violation of good manners*, and coming thus within the category of offences against others, may rightfully be prohibited. Of this kind are *offences against decency*; on which it is unnecessary to dwell, the rather as they are *only connected indirectly* with our subject, the objection to publicity being equally

> strong in the case of many actions not in themselves condemnable, nor supposed to be so. [Italics added.]

Mill is uncomfortable here, this is clear. He is keen to move on. But we surely wonder: what *are* these acts that, if done in private, are injurious only to the agents themselves, but if done in public, are a violation of good manners and come within the category of offences against others? Jonathan Wolff offers the example of public masturbation. Masturbation would have been taken, he writes, precisely to be in that class of acts 'directly harmful only to the agents themselves'. But what about the pedagogic implications of such an act? By masturbating in public, the philosopher Diogenes taught certain truths: the naturalness of sexual instincts; masturbation's utility in relieving sexual tension; the irrelevance in any rational morality of the private/public distinction; and the indefensibility of 'shame' as a moral category.[38] This cannot be dismissed as mere exhibitionism. And, to maintain the focus on the arts, we should also note the artist Vito Acconci's 1972 performance piece, *Seedbed*, in which he masturbated in a confined space under a ramp in an art gallery, stimulated by the sound of the gallery visitors walking overhead, his auto-erotic fantasising about them broadcast through the gallery space.[39] The piece could be retitled, to make explicit the terms of its aesthetic intervention, *The Art Work's Revenge*.

Many general objections can be made to Mill's exception. It is over-broad: much can be dragged into the category of 'violations of good manners'; and much of that, into the sub-category of 'offences against decency'. It is implicated in a whole system of social and political (and indeed, imperial) domination. It supposes a category distinction both between the civilized and the brutish, and between civilized nations and barbarians. It objects to the ill-bred, the vulgar, the boorish, the 'common'; it contributes justifications for their rule. It has its place in a whole vocabulary of class deprecation and condescension.[40] In its most socially coercive forms, it is associated with repressive forces. It is implicitly gendered, the phrase 'good manners', intimating an objectionable gallantry: 'There are ladies present!' Moreover, it collides with *On Liberty*'s largest argument against the stifling effects of social norms, including those enforced by tacit rules of politeness. The 'formidable evil' in 'collisions of opinions' is not 'violent conflict' but the 'quiet suppression' of the truth or part of it.[41]

In addition, it has adverse implications for literary free speech. First, because, since Aristophanes, it has been among literature's purposes precisely to insist upon those gross things from which the fastidious inhabitants of Mill's 'thinking world' recoil. Literature addresses the body; it concerns passion; it has erotic properties. Second, because an aesthetic of *unsettling* received social practices and understandings, including good manners, came to define literary writing in the mid-nineteenth century (Realism) and beyond (Modernism). Third, because it was precisely in decency's name that morality leagues and other agents of moral repression, animated by the spirit of Puritanism, moved against literature. They attacked it as 'indecent' – just as 'decent' was the word that that same literature ironized.

Bentham

3. In the matter of literary free speech, Bentham has a low reputation

Bentham has a low reputation, in a general sort of way. The reputation is of an *exemplary* philistinism, one that conceptually *annihilates* literature, or 'cuts the throats of the Graces'.[42] People of a literary disposition take their cue from Dickens. Marxists take their cue from Marx. Liberals take their cue from Mill. Dickens's objections are contained in a novel, and are thus elusive; Marx's objections are abusive, made in passing, confined to a few sentences, and contingent to his argument;[43] Mill's objections, in their judicious finality, constitute directions to future generations of liberals. He develops his objections most fully in the essay 'Bentham', written 'during a period of relative antipathy'.[44] Among these objections, two have special, self-incriminating force. In a brief discussion of 'Bentham's peculiar opinions on poetry', Mill writes:

> towards poetry in the narrower sense, that which employs the language of words, he entertained no favour. Words, he thought, were perverted from their proper office when they were employed in uttering anything but precise logical truth. He says, somewhere in his works, that, "quantity of pleasure being equal, push-pin is as good as poetry" ['*the First Aphorism*']: but this is only a paradoxical way of stating what he would equally have said of the things which he most valued and admired. Another aphorism is attributed to him, which is much more characteristic of his view of this subject: "All poetry is misrepresentation" ['*the Second Aphorism*']. Poetry, he thought, consisted essentially in exaggeration for effect: in

proclaiming some one view of a thing very emphatically, and suppressing all the limitations and qualifications.[45]

In this one devastating paragraph, Mill ensured that in the liberal imagination Bentham would thereafter be a figure of Mill's own devising. It is the 'false stock picture' that 'most people copy', wrote Mary Mack. 'Yet', she adds, 'few were in a better position to give a true one.'[46]

4. Bentham merits a higher reputation

We might make this case by reference to the use to that Bentham was put in literary criticism. We could instance the early nineteenth-century Benthamite review criticism – Isobel Armstrong has considered this material at length in her *Victorian Poetry: Poetry, Poetics and Politics* (1993).[47] We could also instance mid-twentieth-century Cambridge literary criticism. Empson's provocation to twentieth-century literary critics was as great as, and in the same spirit as, Bentham's provocations to eighteenth-century aestheticians. Critics, as barking dogs, are of two sorts: 'those who merely relieve themselves against the flower of beauty, and those, less continent, who afterwards scratch it up'. Empson then elaborates: he is of the second class. Unexplained beauty arouses an itch in him, a sense that this would be a good place to scratch.[48]

But I want to consider Bentham, *not* his disciples.

4.1. Interpretive modes

Let us distinguish three interpretive modes: the accusatory, the apologetic and the charitable.

In one version of the accusatory mode, the text or texts under review stand as if in a posture of defence before the interpreter's indictment. In another, even tougher version, the texts are barely to be seen; the interpreter proceeds on the *assumption* of their demerit. Mill's essay on Bentham is an exercise in the accusatory mode – a disguised exercise. F.R. Leavis was taken in (better: *wanted* to be taken in). Mill spent his life in a strenuous endeavour, pursued with magnificent integrity, to justify his contention that the Benthams and the Coleridges, 'these two sorts of men, who seem to be, and believe themselves to be, enemies, are in reality allies'. No attack, then. But Leavis was wrong. While it may be true that nowhere can more *malicious* commentaries on utilitarianism be found than in Marx and Engels,[49] it is certainly the case that nowhere can more *destructive* commentaries on Bentham be found than in Mill. He dresses up in a rhetoric of balance and judiciousness a repudiation, made all the more decisive by the note of personal witness that sounds in his prose.

One version of the apologetic mode is to offer the defence, 'He had other, more significant things on his mind.' Iris Murdoch's remarks comprise a generous (perhaps, the most generous possible) instance of this version:

> There is also, and has been, only now it is stronger than ever, a decent and comprehensible kind of utilitarian reaction against art. Philistines, of course, we have always with us, but I am thinking here not of Mr Gradgrind but of sincere people who feel that in a world reeling with misery it is frivolous to enjoy art, which is after all a kind of play. There is a familiar puritanical and Protestant ancestry to this thinking, which expresses itself in the philosophy of Jeremy Bentham, who refused to allow poetry a dignity which was higher than that of pushpin.[50]

Another version of the apologetic mode is to attack Mill by exposing the gap between his account of what Bentham said, and what Bentham actually said, about poetry. The relevant texts are *Rationale of Reward* and 'Nonsense upon Stilts'. *Rationale* was written in French in the 1780s, edited by Étienne Dumont and published in France in 1811, and then translated into English by Richard Smith and published in 1825. 'Nonsense' was written in English, translated into French by Dumont and published in 1816, under a different name. An English version, prepared by Richard Smith from Bentham's manuscripts, did not appear until the publication of the Bowring edition of Bentham's *Works*.

In Book III, Chapter I of *Rationale*, Bentham is concerned with 'Reward Applied to Art and Science'. By 'art', Bentham means 'practice;' by 'science', he means 'knowledge'. By 'the arts and sciences of amusement' Bentham means 'those which are ordinarily called the *fine arts*'. Within 'fine arts' he includes 'music, poetry, painting, sculpture, architecture, ornamental gardening, etc.' He declines a more complete enumeration; such 'metaphysical discussions' would lead him too far from his present subject. And then:

> The utility of all these arts and sciences … the value which they possess, is exactly in proportion to the pleasure they yield. Every other species of pre-eminence which may be attempted to be

established among them is altogether fanciful. Prejudice apart, the game of push-pin is of equal value with the arts and sciences of music and poetry. If the game of push-pin furnish more pleasure, it is more valuable than either. Everybody can play at push-pin: poetry and music are relished only by a few. The game of push-pin is always innocent: it were well could the same be always asserted of poetry. Indeed, between poetry and truth there is a natural opposition: false morals, fictitious nature: the poet always stands in need of something false. When he pretends to leave his foundations in truth, the ornaments of his superstructure are fictions; his business consists in stimulating our passions, and exciting our prejudices. The poet must see everything through coloured media, and strive to make everyone else to do the same. It is true, there have been noble spirits, to whom poetry and philosophy have been equally indebted, but these exceptions do not remove the mischiefs which have resulted from this magic art. If poetry and music deserve to be preferred before a game of push-pin, it must be because they are calculated to gratify those individuals who are most difficult to be pleased.

All the arts and sciences, without exception, inasmuch as they constitute innocent employments, at least of time, possess a species of moral utility, neither the less real or important, because it is frequently unobserved. They compete with, and occupy the place of those mischievous and dangerous passions and employments, to which want of occupation and ennui give birth. They are excellent substitutes for drunkenness, slander, and the love of gaming. …

It is to the cultivation of the arts and sciences that we must … ascribe the existence of that party which is now opposed to war: it has received its birth amid the occupations and pleasures furnished by the fine arts. These arts … have enrolled under their peaceful banners that army of idlers which would have otherwise possessed no amusement but in the hazardous and the bloody game of war.[51]

In 'Nonsense', Bentham writes of the 'Declaration of pretended Rights':

The logic of it is of a piece with the morality of it: a perpetual vein of nonsense flowing from a perpetual abuse of words. Words having a variety of meanings where words with single meanings were equally at hand: the same word used in a variety of meanings in the same page: words used in meanings not their own where proper words were equally at hand: words and propositions of the most unbounded signification turned loose without any of those exceptions or modifications which are so necessary on every occasion to reduce their import within the compass not only of right reason, but even of the design in hand, of whatever nature it may be. The same inaccuracy, the same inattention, in the penning of this cluster of oracles on which the fate of nations was to hang, as if it had been an oriental tale or an allegory for a magazine: stale conceits instead of necessary distinctions: figurative language preferred to simple: sentimental conceits as trite as they are unmeaning preferred to apt and precise expressions: frippery ornament preferred to the majestic simplicity of sound sense: the acts of the senate loaded and disfigured by the tinsel of the play-house.

> In a play or a novel, an improper word is but a word: and the impropriety, whether noticed or not, is attended with no consequences. In a body of laws an improper word may be a national calamity.

Bentham concludes with his own flourish: 'Out of one foolish word may start a thousand daggers.'[52] In *Rationale,* he passes from Aphorism One to Aphorism Two at 'The game of push-pin is always innocent', and then returns to Aphorism One at 'If poetry and music deserve to be preferred'. 'Nonsense' somewhat cools the heat of the Aphorism Two passage in *Rationale*.

Mill has not done justice to these passages. The works from which they are taken are not instances of the same form. The one is a treatise, classificatory in its essential drive, while the other is a polemic, the language driven by a strong wish to attack. What is more, in each work, the instantiated literary text (in *Rationale*, a poem, in 'Nonsense', a play or a novel) is paired with another text or activity in order to make quite distinct points. In *Rationale*, the point of the pairing is to open the possibility of an identity; in 'Nonsense', it is the reverse – to point out an essential difference. There is more to say here. But let us break off instead to return to Mill's treatment.

We might complain: Mill misquotes the first aphorism; he invents the second. But that does not take us very far. One can imagine Bentham saying both – as a provocation, or in rejoinder to some high-flown claim for poetry made in his presence. The objections to Mill's account lie elsewhere – in an argument about his intentions (of which he was perhaps not wholly aware). They are the product, in major part, of a certain denial on his part of a predicament he shared with Bentham as a fellow utilitarian, but from which he wished to extricate himself. They are also a product – which one intuits from that note of false insouciance in his prose – of his desire to separate himself from his father-proxy, and perhaps from his actual father too.

The predicament in respect of the first aphorism is the worry that by refusing to grant poetry's superiority to a child's game the utilitarians make themselves vulnerable to attack by their enemies, who object that they reduce all values to the single lowest common denominator of pleasure – call it the 'Pig Philosophy predicament' (to borrow Carlyle's colourful formulation).[53] The worry is so mind-flooding that Mill ignores the passages in *Rationale* that provide the resources for an effective rejoinder:

(a) The conditional language point: Bentham invites us to put prejudice to one side when considering the value of the arts and sciences of amusement and curiosity. We should assess each by reference to the common standard of the pleasure they yield. This in turn opens out onto the question of what needs to be done to access the pleasure. With push-pin, one must learn the rules, get the pins, acquire competence in the game by assiduous practice, earn the money for the wager, find a person to play with (and beat), etc. A question arises: for how long will the game give pleasure? With poetry, access raises different questions. It is to Bentham's merit that he raises these questions; it is to Mill's discredit that he shuts them down.

(b) The music point: Mill omits Bentham's reference to music: 'the game of push-pin is of equal value with the arts and sciences *of music* and poetry'. The suppression of the words 'of music' makes a stronger case against Bentham in respect of poetry than Bentham's own words mandate. That is to say: contrary to Mill, Bentham does *not* single out poetry for special disparagement in the first aphorism.

(c) The gambling point: In his condemnation of that 'mischievous and dangerous passion', 'the love of gaming', Bentham decisively sides with poetry against push-pin, played for economic advantage, the winnings comprising the pins themselves, which thereafter could be sold.[54]

These are not the only arguments that can be made.[55]

The predicament in respect of the second aphorism is the worry that a shared understanding of language leaves no space for poetry – call it 'the positivist predicament'. In brief, it is to the effect that both Bentham and Mill were caught up in the toils of a positivist account of language, which relegates literature to a miscellaneous, despised second category of statement, in which the condemnation of the especially despised instance, the 'metaphysical', catches other instances, including works of literature. Bentham is thus no more to be condemned than any other philosopher in this position – essentially, all those who stand in that line that runs from Hume through to the Vienna Circle. Leszek Kołakowski identifies the key tenets: positivism maintains the essential unity of the scientific method; it endeavours to eliminate all metaphysical assumptions; metaphysics should be treated like poetry: purely expressive or lyrical utterances; language must be analysed and, where necessary, reformed.[56]

M.H. Abrams connects this general position to Bentham and Mill in *The Mirror and the Lamp* (1953). In eighteenth-century discussions, poetry is taken to be truth, ornamented by fiction and figures in order to delight and move the reader. In Romantic discussions, poetry is the overflow or expression of feeling in an integral and naturally figurative language. In eighteenth-century discussions, the non-poetic discourse most frequently set up as the logical opposite of poetry is history. In Romantic discussions, the non-poetic discourse set up as the logical opposite of poetry is science. Wordsworth, for example, proposed an opposition between 'Poetry and matter-of-fact, or science'. These statements were intended only as logical devices for isolating and defining the nature of poetic discourse. However, in the Romantic period and thereafter, the prevalence of philosophic positivism, which held that the methods of the natural sciences constituted the sole access to truth, tended to convert this logical opposition into a competition of one. Poetry and science were not only antithetical, they were incompatible. If science is true, poetry must be false, or at any rate trivial. Abrams was dismissive of Bentham and generous to Mill. In later writings on the topic, he treated Mill as continuing Bentham's argument, not breaking with it – attempting to find a more honoured position for poetry, but still in the same second term of the same positivist binarism. Abrams concludes that Mill merely succeeded in demonstrating 'the gross unaptness of a positivistic theory of language, with its simple criterion of "either true or false"'. Unapt, among other reasons, because of its 'odd assumption that all discourse that is not science must be of a single kind'.[57] In summary:

Mill shares Bentham's philosophical position, but is troubled by it. Rather than confronting it, he searches for critical differences amid the details of mere biography.

In respect of both aphorisms there is this same note on Mill's part of false insouciance. He writes, 'somewhere in his works' and 'attributed to him'. Our first impression is of a puzzling indifference to getting the quotations exactly right – not for Mill, the dutiful, assiduous citation of volume and page, the careful writing out of the exact passage. Approximations are good enough. The question arises, of such a judicious, careful writer, *why* this descent into insouciance? It is indicative of a deliberate, even strained, distancing from Bentham, a disciple's repudiation of his master, a godson of his godfather, and thereby also a son of his father, the precursor disciple. It is a *false* insouciance, then. It indicates anxiety, not freedom from care. To argue for the inadequacy of Bentham's philosophy was to argue for the inadequacy of his father's parenting. How could we possibly deny the complicating pressure in Mill's prose as he works out, while disavowing, his divided feelings about his own origins and allegiances?

I do not reject this reasoning – it is certainly an improvement on those received accounts, which conceive of the precipitating crisis as having the finality, and elevation, of a 'conversion',[58] with everything written thereafter reflecting a settled, equilibriate position – supposedly confirmed in the 'Bentham' essay itself.[59] But defending Bentham by such a route takes us away from him – in the end, it is a diversion. And so we turn to the charitable mode. I take my understanding of this mode from Donald Davidson. The purpose of an act of interpretation is to maximize the rationality of what is being interpreted. There are several versions of Davidson's principle – including several offered by Davidson himself.[60] The version I adopt reconstructs a combined 'philosophical' and 'historical' Bentham.[61]

Here is an example of a *charitable* interpretation. Dinwiddy offers in confirmation of Bentham's reputation as an 'arch-philistine' these remarks (from a letter of Bentham's to Lord Holland): 'Everything that in the shape of poetry has ever issued from any press in Mexico … shall be faithfully collected and transmitted to Holland House … But Sir? … Oh yes, my Lord, I know the difference. *Prose* is where all the lines but the last go on to the margin: – *Poetry* is where some of them fall short of it.'[62] There is a teasing quality to this – Bentham is no doubt parodying himself. Stephen, missing the point, mocks him for it.[63] But consider Christopher Ricks: poetry creates and transmits information through line-endings; prose does not. In poetry, a line-ending is a word-processor's hard return; in prose, it is a soft return. We have to be educated into principled ignoring, which is sometimes an ignoring of what might look like information but is not.[64] The distinction Bentham makes *matters*, and continues to receive attention.[65] This is a small example. My next one takes up the rest of this essay. It proposes a charitable reconstruction of Bentham's aesthetics in his several engagements with Romanticism.

4.2. Romanticism

Bentham had an aesthetic.[66] We have to find it in work published in his lifetime, and work published almost two centuries later. It is to be understood principally by references to Bentham's various engagements with Romanticism. Bart Schulz says that Bentham cannot be *disentangled* from the Romantic movement.[67] But disentangling is needed, if we are to find the aesthetic potential in his thinking. I name these engagements: Fellow-Romantic, Anti-Romantic, Radical Romantic and Post-Romantic. I use the term 'Romanticism' as an 'expository convenience' to 'specify some striking parallels';[68] I am ready to regard it as a European cultural movement, or set of kindred movements.[69] I elide, as I must here, critical differences between German and English Romanticism.

4.3. Fellow-Romantic

Bentham is as much a creature of Romanticism as of the Enlightenment (we do not need to choose).[70] The easiest, quickest way to make the case for Bentham as a 'Fellow Romantic' is by pointing to certain concurrences or distinct points of correspondence between his positions and received Romantic positions. Take, first, the matter of 'fragments', a well-established *topos* in discussions of both Romanticism[71] and Bentham – where (typically) the sense of parts, fragments, uncompleted projects, visible in the early Bentham, is taken to comprise a constant in his life.[72] We find more consequential themes in a common sense of political disappointment and a common commitment to language-reform (poetic diction for the Romantics, legal language for Bentham).

The 'fellowship' can be developed further by reference to a common intensity and extent of ambition; a certain conviction of destiny (place Shelley's 'Poets are the unacknowledged legislators of the world'[73] alongside José del Valle's encomium to Bentham, 'Your works give you the glorious title of legislator of the world');[74] a common indifference to received ideas (place Stendhal's '*Il faut du courage pour être romantique, car il faut hazarder*'[75] alongside Bentham's unyielding refusal to accept the authority of customary practice); a common 'againstness' (place the Romantic rejection of neo-classical aesthetics[76] alongside Bentham's rejection of Blackstonian legal hermeneutics).

And then there is the question of Shelley, where we can contend for something like an inner affinity. There is their political radicalism, their anti-clericalism, their regard for Jesus as against 'the superstition that has disguised itself' under his name,[77] their common engagement with homosexuality as a topic for sympathetic investigation (though here, as elsewhere, Bentham proved himself the greater radical),[78] their stalwart defence of political and religious free speech, their contempt for the given state of the law and their demands for law reform,[79] the quantity of unpublishable work they wrote, and so on. And consider Shelley's unpublished, fragmentary *A Treatise on Morals*: 'A virtuous or moral action is that action which, when considered in all its accessories and consequences, is fitted to produce the highest pleasure to the greatest number of sensitive beings.'[80]

4.4. The Anti-Romantic

Distinguish, in respect of a discourse or movement, between the antagonistic and the oppositional or adversarial. The antagonistic situates itself outside the discourse or movement, to attack it. It constitutes the discourse or movement as a target; it is external to it. The oppositional, or adversarial, remains inside the discourse or movement, and develops, out of its positive or affirmative positions, countering positions. This is Bentham. We can be quick here – there are only a few surprises. Bentham mostly took positions *against* the standard Romantic ones on poetry's elevatedness; on the poet's elevatedness; on the centrality of the aesthetic; on poetry's cognitive value; on 'unbounded' meaning in language. Here, Bentham is working as something akin to a 'counter-spirit'[81] – though even this term somewhat simplifies the complexity of these adversarial engagements.

Against the Romantic celebration of genius, and of works of genius, we may place the deflationary language of *Rationale of Reward*. Against Coleridge's '[Poetry] is the language of heaven, and in the exquisite delight we derive from [it], we have … a type, a foretaste, and a prophecy of the joys of heaven',[82] we may place Bentham's ironic reference to legal obfuscations as 'poetry' in *Rationale of Judicial Evidence*.[83]

There is the greatest distance between pre-Romantic and Romantic understandings of the character of the poet. In the former, the poet is to be judged rhetorically, by his skill in ornamenting or embellishing a certain kind of content. The poem is an instrument in the moral education of the reader. In the latter, the poet is *altogether* a different kind of person – self-interrogating, adversarial, autonomous, a creator, a *vates* or prophet-priest.[84] There are also *collective* aspects of this new poetic identity, in a number of registers. There is, for example, an elevated notion of a *succession* of artists and writers – Ingres's notion of the apostolic succession of great artists, the '*apostolates*'.[85]

This new normative in turn generated a counter-normative. One finds both normative and counter-normative in Keats. Here is the normative: 'I have asked myself so often why I should be a Poet more than other Men – seeing how great a thing it is – how great things are to be gained by it' (10 May 1817); 'I find that I cannot exist without poetry' (18 May 1817); 'I am ambitious of doing the world some good' (27 October 1818); 'I could not live without the love of my friends' (9 April 1818); 'fellowship divine', 'the crown … of love and friendship' (*Endymion*, ll. 777, 800–1). And here is the *counter*-normative: 'I am quite disgusted with literary men and will never know another except Wordsworth' (8 October 1817); 'I am sometimes so very sceptical as to think Poetry itself a mere Jack-a-lantern to amuse whoever may be struck with its brilliance' (13 March 1818).[86]

Bentham's counter-normative, which was ferocious,[87] sits in his conception of the artist as a member of the 'fine arts aristocracy'. We find this in 'Codification Proposal, Addressed by Jeremy Bentham to All Nations Professing Liberal Opinions' (1822). His challenge is to the totality of the normative collective aspects, against which he posits 'the Literary Aristocracy' and 'the Fine-Arts Aristocracy'.[88] Dinwiddy summarizes:

> Bentham saw Britain as governed by a partnership or confederation of 'all the members of the government together with the opulent members of the different classes of the community in the character of persons unduly favoured by the laws and habits of government.' He sometimes referred to this elite as … the 'aristocracy,' using that term in an extended sense to include not only the peerage and landowners but also various sub-groups. … These confederated groups had a common interest in the protection of abuses and privileges. These comprised 'sinister interests,' and Bentham conceived of society in terms of a struggle between the ruling few and the subject many.[89]

This is Bentham at his most deflationary, of course. But his formulation also opens out onto a whole sociology of art. It also echoes Hazlitt's remarks in his 1816 essay on *Coriolanus* (published in the *Examiner*, and sure to have been read by Bentham): 'The language of poetry naturally falls in with the language of power. The imagination is an exaggerating and exclusive faculty; the understanding is a dividing and measuring faculty. The one is an aristocratical, the other a republican faculty.'[90]

Regarding the centrality of the aesthetic, let me take this statement of Friedrich Schlegel's to stand for the Romantic position: I consider art to be the heart of humanity.[91] Against this, surely we can put a Benthamite counter-conception of poetry as marginal, at best? Perhaps. Yet Bentham surprises us, even here. He writes in *Rationale of Reward* of the 'arts of amusement', which include the literary arts:

> It is not ... proper to regard [them] as destitute of utility: *on the contrary, there is nothing, the utility of which is more incontestable.* To what shall the character of utility be ascribed, if not to that which is a source of pleasure? All that can be alleged in diminution of their utility is, that it is limited to the excitement of pleasure: they cannot disperse the clouds of grief or of misfortune. They are useless to those who are not pleased with them: they are useful only to those who take pleasure in them, and only in proportion as they are pleased.[92] [Italics added.]

That is to say: if you are a hedonist, the arts will have a rather special value for you, since their very reason for existence is to give pleasure. The anti-Romantic stance here is less an affair of contradiction, more one of the alternative conceptualizing of a comparable esteem.

And poetry as cognitively valuable? This is an argument *within* Romantic aesthetics (for example, between Kant's *Critique of Judgment* (1790) and Hegel's *Aesthetics: Lectures on Fine Arts* (1835)) about whether art is cognitive. There is a related argument (for example, between the Schelling of the *System of Transcendental Idealism* (1800) and the Schelling of the *Philosophy of Art* (1802–3)) about art's priority over philosophy.[93] Keats makes his own wonderful intervention on this question in a letter (19 March 1819):

> Though a quarrel in the Streets is a thing to be hated, the energies displayed in it are fine; the commonest Man shows a grace in his quarrel. By a superior Being our reasonings may take the same tone – though erroneous they may be fine. This is the very thing in

> which consists Poetry, and if so it is not so fine a thing as philosophy – For the same reason that an eagle is not so fine a thing as a truth.[94]

The point here is that there is no determinate Romantic position; there is instead a field of argument, with many positions being taken. Bentham's own position seems to land him somewhere between the non-cognitive and the anti-cognitive – in *Rationale of Reward*, at least.[95]

Last, as to 'unbounded' meaning in language – here, roughly, is the Romantic position. The art work does not engage us in argument; it expands and deepens our understanding beyond the power of words to express. We recognize this in the doctrine that literary works cannot be paraphrased. They cannot be reduced to propositions; literary language does not submit to concepts. It is never possible for us to say in some final, dispositive way what a work of art is about.

Again, there are many variations on this position. Anita Brookner finds in the Romantics a refusal of the principle of finitude – an 'infinite longing'; a passing-up of lucid exposition in favour of language freighted with intimation.[96] She might have had Coleridge's remark in mind: 'Poetry gives most pleasure when only generally and not perfectly understood.'[97] Kant's notion of the 'aesthetic idea' is a very developed version of this remark. In the *Critique of Judgment*, he praises the artist of genius for his ability to express 'aesthetic ideas' in his work. These are 'representations of the imagination which induce much thought, yet without the possibility of any definite thought whatever, i.e. *concept*, being adequate to it, and which language, consequently, can never quite get on level terms with or render completely intelligible'. When a concept – for example, 'justice' – is 'attached' to a representation of the imagination – let us say, Shakespeare's *Measure for Measure* – the concept submits to 'an unbounded expansion'. The artist's creative imagination provokes in his readers thought that, 'while germane, no doubt, to the concept, exceeds what can be laid hold of in that representation or clearly expressed'.[98]

Bentham stands at the furthest possible distance, of course, from all this – the proof text here being 'Nonsense upon Stilts'. But before we leave it at that, with the sense that we have at last found a simple opposition between a Romantic position and a Benthamic position, consider the following from *Rationale of Punishment*: for 'the legislators of ancient days, men who spoke the significant and enchanting language of Ancient Greece, poetry was invited to the aid of law. No man had ever yet thought of addressing the people in the barbarous language that disgraces our statute-book, where the will of the legislator is drowned in a sea of words.'[99]

4.5. Radical Romantic

In a study of somewhat greater length than the present, this character of Bentham as a radical or avant-garde Romantic would need to be studied in four aspects: as democrat, as provocateur, as hedonist and as advocate of literary free speech. I must put to one side the first. As for the second, I merely cite the Auto-Icon project,[100] and acknowledge Kathleen Blake's reading of *Rationale of Reward*: 'Push-pin – what a figure! And what could sound sillier to praise? Except to give the reader a "push" to "set prejudice apart". I say, think again about the passage, and enjoy it.'[101] I want instead to return to the Romantic aesthetic implications of Bentham's hedonism, and then relate his free speech position to Romantic values. Essentially, the point in respect of each is the same: Bentham found common ground with his fellow Romantics, but then pushed *beyond* them.

4.5.1. Hedonism

Bentham extends and develops a central principle of Romanticism, its 'hedonism of the imagination',[102] wherever he writes by reference to these principles: (a) *for* Pleasure, *therefore* Utility; (b) *for* Pleasure, *against* Taste (c) *for* Pleasure, *therefore* Literature. We might designate these formulations as the slogans of Bentham's aesthetics.

For Pleasure, therefore Utility. – There is a received sense that the Romantic is hostile to the demand that art be useful. When asked, 'What's the *use* of art?' the Romantic will reply, defensively, exasperatedly, 'All art is quite useless.'[103] But if we step back from Wilde to Coleridge, we read this, in a letter he wrote to John Thelwall, expressing a preference for Schiller and Shakespeare over Collins, because they 'give *more general* pleasure, and I judge of all things by their utility'.[104] The Romantics were quite alive to the aesthetic possibilities in a generously conceived hedonism.

For Pleasure, against Taste. – To Bentham the criterion of taste is pernicious, though championed in the realm of the arts by critics, philosophers and satirists. It is an affair of prejudice, promoted by sinister interests, destructive of the pleasures of the many.[105] I defer to Malcolm Quinn's investigation of this aspect of Bentham's aesthetics.[106] He formulates the question of principle between Hume and Bentham thus: both Bentham and Hume espoused a view of taste as a social practice, but Bentham was concerned with the socially divisive effects of 'taste speech', while Hume was keen to promote the beneficial socializing force of specialized habits and practices of taste.[107] I only add to Quinn by making a connection with Romantic aesthetics. The Romantics did not defend 'taste' – not in any tepid, conformist sense, anyway. Hegel commented: 'What is called good taste takes fright at all the more profound effects of art. When great passions are unveiled, we are no longer concerned with the finer distinctions of taste and its pettifogging particularities. Genius strides contemptuously over such ground.'[108] Hegel, on genius's behalf, demands an encounter between spectator and work unhampered by received taste; Bentham, on pleasure's behalf, makes the same demand. It is a *stronger* demand.

For Pleasure, therefore Literature. – Here is Coleridge: '[Poetry] is the art of communicating whatever we wish to communicate, so as both to express and produce excitement, but for the purpose of immediate pleasure; and each part is fitted to afford as much pleasure, as is compatible with the largest sum in the whole.' He continues: 'In Poetry, the general good is to be given through the Pleasure, and if the Poet does not do that he ceases to be a Poet.' And then, to drive the point home: 'Pleasurable excitement is [poetry's] origin and object; pleasure is the magic circle out of which the Poet must not dare to tread.'[109] Bentham's pleasure principle is an especially appropriate criterion in relation to the fine arts, then (as he acknowledges). Their very purpose is to give pleasure.

But at this point Kant intervenes. Not *any* kind of pleasure will do. *Aesthetic* pleasure has specific properties. The 'pure judgment of taste', he explains in the *Critique of Judgment*, is 'independent of charm or emotion'. Indeed, 'taste that requires an added element of either for its delight has not yet emerged from barbarism'.[110] This attracted Nietzsche's mockery:

> We get from our philosophers … definitions in which the absence of more personal experience squats like a fat worm of crass error, as it does in Kant's famous definition of the beautiful. "Something is beautiful," says Kant, "if it gives pleasure *without interest*." Without interest! Our æstheticians never tire of weighing in on Kant's side, saying that under the magic of beauty men can look at even naked female statues "without interest". We can certainly laugh at their expense – the experiences of artists are more "interesting", with regard to this tricky point and Pygmalion, at any rate, was not necessarily an "unæsthetic man". Let us think all the better of the innocence of our æstheticians, reflected as it is in such arguments;

> let us pay tribute to Kant for expounding the ... sense of touch with the naïveté of a country-parson![111]

Mill's account in his 'Inaugural Address Delivered to the University of St. Andrews' (1867) of aesthetic experience had this same quality of the parsonical:

> We learn to respect ourselves only so far as we feel capable of nobler objects. ... Now, of this elevated tone of mind the great source of inspiration is poetry, and all literature so far as it is poetical and artistic. ... Nor is it only loftiness, only the heroic feelings, that are bred by poetic cultivation. Its power is as great in calming the soul as in elevating it in fostering the milder emotions, as the more exalted. It brings home to us all those aspects of life which take hold of our nature on its unselfish side, and lead us to identify our joy and grief with the good or ill of the system of which we form a part. ... Even apart from any specific emotional expression, the mere contemplation of beauty of a high order produces in no small degree this elevating effect on the character.[112]

This high-flown waffle was in keeping with the times.[113]

Bentham is to be situated in a line of dissenters from even the best instances of such reasoning[114] – a line of which Nietzsche is merely the most distinguished representative. In his unpublished writings on 'sexual irregularities', the unparsonical Bentham treated the pleasures of the sexual appetite as 'more conducive to happiness than any other'.[115] It is a special provocation to the ascetic, who makes war on it in the name of refinement. 'Of all pleasures, the most exquisite were the pleasures of the sexual appetite. Of all objects of sacrifice, these were best adapted to the nature of a God of the most refined class – of a God taken at the highest pitch of refinement and civilisation. The pleasure would indeed have been sensual: but the sacrifice of it was the reverse of sensual ... nothing imaginable could be more refined.'[116] The Benthamite, anti-Millian William Empson, the finest literary critic of the twentieth century, with an extraordinary intuitiveness, uses the same language as Bentham in his own thrust against the ascetic: 'The most refined desires are inherent in the plainest, and would be false if they weren't.'[117]

This refusal to separate the corporeal from the spiritual, the lower from the higher, which was characteristic of the Romantics, Bentham just took a bit further than most – but by no means all. Here is Blake: 'Energy is the only life, and is from the body; and reason is the bound or outward circumference of energy' (*Marriage of Heaven and Hell*). Here is Wordsworth, in the Preface to *Lyrical Ballads*:

> If I had undertaken a systematic defence of the theory upon which these poems are written, it would have been my duty to develop the various causes upon which the pleasure received from metrical language depends. Among the chief of these causes is ... the pleasure which the mind derives from the perception of similitude in dissimilitude. This principle is the great spring of the activity of our minds, and the chief feeder. From this principle the direction of the sexual appetite, and all the passions connected with it take their origin.[118]

And on posing the question, in *Endymion*, 'Wherein lies happiness', Keats explains, in his letter to John Taylor (30 January 1818): 'My having written that argument will perhaps be of the greatest service to me of anything I ever did. It set before me *the gradations of happiness*, even like a kind of pleasure thermometer.' [Italics added.][119]

4.5.2. Literary free speech

We may take for granted here the commitment of the Romantics to free speech. It was a particular concern of Shelley's, of course: 'Persecution for opinion is unjust. Persecution is the only name applicable to punishment inflicted on an individual in consequence of his opinions.'[120] Bentham at each point, at the very least, matched this commitment: 'Under a government of Laws, what is the motto of a good citizen? *To obey punctually; to censure freely*.'[121]

Bentham was alive to the damage that literature can do:

> As the amusement of a minister of state it must be confessed that a more suitable one might be found than a game at solitaire. [Yet it is] a pure and simple amusement, stripped of everything injurious, free from passion, avarice, loss, and regret. How much better was this minister occupied, than if, with the Iliad in his hand, he had stirred up within his heart the seeds of those ferocious passions which can only be gratified with tears and blood.[122]

In 'Sextus', and then in *Not Paul, but Jesus,* Bentham censures the many 'novels, and other works having amusement for their object' that introduce the topic of homosexuality in order to condemn homosexual practices. In doing so, they give 'vent and increase' to the 'popular antipathy' towards those practices (as well as stimulating the curiosity of the young among their readers). Bentham cites Smollett's *Roderick Random* and Fielding's *Joseph Andrews*. Such works do much damage, Bentham writes, by 'inflaming' this antipathy – though newspapers are even worse offenders in this regard, Bentham adds.[123]

Where does this leave the question of literary free speech? In good shape, I think. We can find in Bentham a defence of literary speech made up of these propositions: liberty of literary representation is to be implied from liberty of taste; literature is a unique resource, containing valuable truths of experience; state support of the arts should be encouraged; an aesthetics of mass art cannot be proscriptive; literary censors are among the 'sinister interests'; the acquisition of knowledge must not be hindered; censorship is both corrupting and ineffectual. Bentham was not, *pace* M.H. Abrams (see below), a Platonist. Again, I can only address in any detail one or two of these propositions.

We can begin with an implication. The long title of a proposed work reads: 'General Idea of a Work, Having For One of Its Objects the Defence of the Principle of Utility, so far as concerns the Liberty of Taste, against the Conjunct Hostility of the Principle of Asceticism and the Principle of Antipathy: and for its Proposed Title, proposed on the Ground of Expected Popularity, or at least Protection against Popular Rage – Not Paul, but Jesus.'[124] The work is a defence of liberty of sexual preference, and celebrates the 'pleasure of scratching where it itches'. It anticipates the opposition of 'religionists' and expressions of 'popular anger'. It rejects all prohibitions or acts of censorship on grounds of religion or superstitious attachment to notions of 'moral purity'. It speculates that censors are often motivated by envy, wishing themselves to perform the acts of the censored that they punish, or by fear, hoping themselves to avoid a like charge ('precautionary self-defence', Bentham calls it).[125] It contains an express defence of homosexuality. And it deplores the driving out of office and into exile of an admired politician, Sir William Meredith, on the grounds of his alleged homosexuality, and the driving into exile of an admired novelist, William Beckford, on the same grounds. The implication? That liberty of literary representation must follow from liberty of taste – what may be *practised* may also be *written about*.

Bentham finds resources in literature not found elsewhere. In 'Of Sexual Irregularities', he touches on the topic of homosexuality in the classical world. He relates a story from Virgil's *Aeneid*, in which two young men, who are plainly lovers, show conspicuous courage in an attack on the enemy's camp. Virgil's account, he notes, is full of admiration for them. He goes on to mention other instances of well-regarded homosexual 'heroes of classical lore'. And then he observes that 'fiction in its nature affords more conclusive evidence than any particular realities: it shews the conclusion drawn by opinion from universal and continual experience'.[126]

We can formulate Bentham's position (in contrast to Mill's) thus: literary speech should be free. This is not the common view. I refer to M.H. Abrams's assessment: 'So, after many centuries we find Jeremy Bentham following Plato's lead by banishing the lying poets from his society, which, like that of Plato, was to be planned and administered by philosophers. Bentham even recalls Plato's indictment of Homer for degrading the gods.'[127] This is absurd – though it prompts the thought that there is perhaps one respect in which Bentham might fairly be termed a Platonist – that is, in the *provisionality* of judgments about, *inter alia*, push-pin and poetry. Judgments need to be made 'prejudice apart'. Reasons must be adduced; conclusions must be open to revision. Recall Book X of *The Republic*. Socrates, in conversation with Glaucon, defending his notional banishing of the poets, then says the following:

> Shall I propose, then, that [poetry] be allowed to return from exile, but upon this condition only – that she make a defence of herself in lyrical or some other metre? Certainly. And we may further grant to those of her defenders who are lovers of poetry and yet not poets the permission to speak in prose on her behalf: let them show not only that she is pleasant but also useful to States and to human life, and we will listen in a kindly spirit; for if this can be proved we shall surely be the gainers – I mean, if there is a use in poetry as well as a delight? Certainly, he said, we shall be the gainers.

Bentham would have been open to that challenge, and could have made those arguments.

4.6. Post-Romantic

We can also praise Bentham for his intimations of an alternative aesthetics. His thinking casts an *aesthetic shadow*. There is an anticipation of Duchamp: 'Taste is an experience that I try not to let come into my life.'[128] There is an anticipation of Susan Sontag's 'Camp': 'The man who insists on high and serious pleasures is depriving himself of pleasure; he continually restricts what he can enjoy; in the constant exercise of his good taste he will eventually price himself out of the market, so to speak.

Here Camp taste supervenes upon good taste as a daring and witty hedonism.'[129]

There is also a congruence with Modernism – to be worked out. But just consider Ezra Pound. The 'swindling classes' use a 'fogged language', he wrote, like an exemplary Benthamite. 'Good writers are those who keep the language efficient. That is to say, keep it accurate, keep it clear.' 'A people that grows accustomed to sloppy writing is a people in process of losing grip on its empire and on itself.' 'The statesman cannot govern and men cannot agree on wise action without language, and all their deeds and conditions are affected by the defects or virtues of idiom.' Pound proposed the following exercise in a comparison of Milton and Swinburne: 'See how many useless words each uses, how many which contribute nothing, how many which contribute nothing very definite.'[130]

4.7. Low Romantic?

Fellow Romantic, Anti-Romantic, Radical Romantic, Post-Romantic … Is there *one* kind of Romantic that might capture all four of these characters? Perhaps, '*Low* Romantic'. The thought is prompted by the example of the French writer Georges Bataille. We might think of Bentham's position in relation to Romanticism as comparable to Bataille's relation to Surrealism.[131] Each was an internal subversive. Each went 'low' in response to the other's 'high'. Can we say then, Bentham was the Bataille of the Romantic movement? This might go slightly too far, though – because the 'low' version requires the exploitation of resources *within* Romanticism to reach contrary conclusions; and the declaration of a certain allegiance to Romanticism. We cannot sensibly maintain that Bentham met either of these conditions – certainly not the second one. For further examination.

5. Towards an art-friendly liberalism

From time to time, events occur that raise the question: is liberalism equal to the challenge of its times? Among the challenges of the present times: to redefine freedom of speech to give an honoured, and not a marginal, place to aesthetic expression. This requires liberals to take literature and the arts seriously – which in turn requires them to distance themselves from Mill, and get closer to Bentham. I agree with Schultz: we (especially we liberals) need to shake ourselves free of Mill's reading of Bentham.[132] Mill's attack on Bentham has blinded liberals to what is valuable in

Bentham, in the matter of a liberal aesthetics, and in reasoned defences of literary free speech. We can work with Bentham. We have to work *around* Mill.

Notes

1 Mill, ed. Robson and Stillinger, 1981, 75–116, 117–64.
2 Mill, ed. Leavis, 1950, 1–2, 9.
3 Ricks, 2003, 147.
4 Storer, 2009, 87.
5 Mill, ed. Robson, 1977, 213–310.
6 Whitman, 1982, 929.
7 Hardy, 1994, Vol. 2, 118–19.
8 Mallock, 1878, 289–302, 294–5.
9 'Mill ... made it possible, and plausible, for others to take that view, to think that smog and insecticides are perilous enough to call for restrictions on liberty, but that pornography and obscenity are not ... it is now permissible for a performer to masturbate on the stage, but only if he or she is paid the minimum wage.' G. Himmelfarb, 1993, 545.
10 Mill, ed. Robson and Stillinger, 1981, 319.
11 Mill, ed. Robson, 1996, 48.
12 Mill, ed. Robson and Stillinger, 1981, 459–60.
13 Mill, ed. Robson, 1977, 135.
14 Mill, ed. Robson and Stillinger, 1981, 596.
15 Mill, ed. Robson, 1986, 485.
16 Mill, ed. Robson and Stallinger, 1981, 489.
17 Sharpless, 1967, 100–1.
18 Mill, ed. Robson and Stallinger, 1981, 345.
19 Bain, 1859, 196–7.
20 Mill, ed. Robson, 1978, 363.
21 Mill, ed. Robson and Stallinger, 1981, 341–66.
22 Mill, ed. Robson, 1984, 259.
23 Moers, 1976, 122.
24 Showalter, 1977; Gilbert and Gubar, 2009.
25 Ashton, 2000, 104, 129, 183.
26 From a review of a novel, author's name withheld: 'We fancy we detect abundant evidence of female authorship. These are the usual characteristics of the best novels of our day, which are the mintage of the noble hearts and the well-informed heads of gifted women.' Anon, 1842, 49–65, 50.
27 Browning, ed. Reynolds, 1996, 407.
28 See ed. Skilton, 1993, 167.
29 Russell, ed. Schneewind, 1968, 16–17.
30 Mill, ed. Robson, 1986, 213.
31 Monk, 1991, 355, 422–3 (watching a movie was 'like a shower bath', 'washing away his thoughts of the lecture'), 443, 521, 577.
32 Mill, ed. Robson and Stillinger, 1981, 459.
33 Mill, ed. Robson and Stillinger, 1985, 211–13.
34 Mill, ed. Robson and Stillinger, 1985, 211.
35 M.S. McPherson follows this tone when he writes of 'judges' and 'verdicts': 'Mill's Moral Theory and the Problem of Preference Change'. McPherson, ed. Smith, 1998, Vol. I, Pt. 2, 174–6.
36 In the London *Chatterley* trial, the defence experts praised the novel: it 'condemns promiscuity;' it is a 'study in compassion;' it has 'a moral purpose'; it is 'highly virtuous.' And they praised the novelist: a 'literary moralist;' 'part of the great Puritan stream of writers'. They challenged the prosecutor's loathing account of the novel's 'sensuality' and its violation

of 'standards', of 'restraint', of 'mental and moral discipline'. Bedford, 2016, 46, 48, 12–13, 61, 64, 72.

37 Mason, 1994, *passim*.

38 Wolff, 1998, 1–16, 11–12.

39 See eds. Warr and Jones, 2000, 117.

40 'The first step towards civilisation is the correcting of instinct by reason; the second, the deliberate rejection of immediate satisfactions with a view to obtaining subtler ... From these primary qualities ... may spring a host of secondaries: a taste for truth and beauty ... good manners ... a contempt for utilitarianism and philistinism.' Bell, 1932, 162–4. See also Nicholson, 1955, Ch. I, 'The Necessity of Manners'.

41 Mill, ed. Robson, 1977, 257. See Mort, 2010, 60.

42 Dickens, 2003, 124.

43 Marx, *Capital*, 1976, Vol. I, 758–9 and fn. 51.

44 Harrison, 1983, 5.

45 Mill, ed. Robson and Stillinger, 1981, 113.

46 Mack, 1962, 2–3.

47 Compare Andrew Hemingway: 'Many of those who accepted the Benthamite critique of aesthetic culture were not prepared to subject the Fine Arts to the same reductive and philistine measure as the philosopher himself.' Hemingway, 2018, 150.

48 Empson, 1966a, 9.

49 Welzbacher, 2018, 152.

50 Murdoch, 1999, 237.

51 Bowring, 1843, ii. 253–4.

52 Bentham, ed. Schofield *et al.*, 2002, 321–2.

53 Carlyle, 1898, 319.

54 Gomme, 1898, Vol. II, 64, 86; Watson, 1856, Vol. II, 608.

55 See Mack, 1962, 247; Schofield, ed. Zhai and Quinn, 2016, 94–5. 'Russell is a consistent utilitarian in that he draws no ethical distinction between the qualities of different forms of satisfaction. One is as good as another if the quantity of satisfaction is the same. ... This is less paradoxical than it sounds, because he is using the word "satisfaction" very widely to cover the fulfilment of any end. ... He does not fall into the common utilitarian error of assuming that all desire is for pleasure.' Ayer, *Russell*, 1972, 125. Cf. Frederick Rosen on Bentham generally: 'We should note that Mill ignored those aspects of Bentham's philosophy which might have formed a reply.' Rosen, 2013, 53.

56 Kołakowski, 1972.

57 Abrams, 1989, 221, 90.

58 Warren, 1950, 67.

59 'Mill had finally settled his intellectual accounts with Bentham, and thus partly with his father.' Mazlish, 1975, 267.

60 Glüer, 'The Status of Charity I: Conceptual Truth or A Posteriori Necessity?' and Pagin, 'The Status of Charity II: Charity, Probability, and Simplicity', in ed. Baghramian, 2013, 144–66.

61 Schofield, ed. Engelmann, 2011, 427–8, 453.

62 Dinwiddy, 1989, 114; Bentham, ed. Dinwiddy, 1988, 570.

63 Stephen, 1900, Vol. I, 231.

64 Ricks, 1988, 95.

65 See Farley and Symmons Roberts, 2018, 290; Culler, 1975, 188; Culler, 2011, 25.

66 '[Bentham's and Diderot's] aesthetic theories were ... alike', writes Mack. Yes, agreed. In this essay, however, I contend for the Romantic aspects of his aesthetic. See Mack, 1962, 112.

67 Schultz, 2017, 55.

68 Abrams, 1989, 117.

69 See Ferber, 2010, 10.

70 Canuel, ed. Engelmann, 2011, 501.

71 McGann, 1983, 47; Eldridge, 1998, Vol. 4, 176.

72 Harrison, 1983, 16.

73 Shelley, ed. Clark, 1988a, 297.

74 Schofield, 1998, 115–47, 115.

75 The Romantic must take risks; he must test every received idea to destruction. Brookner, 2000, 4–5.

76 Lovejoy, 1960, 237.

77 Shelley, ed. Clark, 1988b, 232.
78 Bieri, 2008, 410.
79 Brinton, 1966, 170.
80 Shelley, ed. Clark, 1988c, 182.
81 McCalman, 2001, 3.
82 Ed. Roberts, 2016, 8.
83 Bowring, 1843, vi. 308.
84 Frye, 1968, 21–2; McGann, 1983, 70; Abrams, 1984, 56.
85 Brookner, 2000, 103, 183.
86 Keats, ed. Gittings, 1987, 11, 27, 59, 73, 157.
87 Mill's version of this counter-normative was mildness itself, by comparison. To his diary (12 February 1854): '[Carlyle's] exaltation of the literary character ... the new priesthood, and so on' makes 'that very feeble and poor minded set of people, the writers of this country, so conceited ... that it has inflated their vanity and lowered their ambition. They would like to be indeed a priesthood, an aristocracy of scribblers, dividing social importance with the other aristocracies.' Mill concludes: 'Starve them that they may work! Refuse them honour that they may be honest!' Elliot, 1910, Vol. II, 370–1.
88 Bentham, ed. Schofield and Harris, 1998, 285, fn. a.
89 Dinwiddy, 1989, 87.
90 Hazlitt, 1998, 345–6. I have omitted ellipses.
91 Schlegel, 2003, 300.
92 Bowring, 1843, ii. 253.
93 Hammermeister, ed. Mininger and Peck, 2016, 174–80; Schelling, 1978, 231–3.
94 Keats, ed. Gittings, 1987, 230. On a certain passage from the Neo-Classical to the Romantic, from Dr Johnson to Coleridge, from conceiving of poetry as 'the art of uniting pleasure with truth' to conceiving of poetry as 'proposing for its *immediate* object pleasure, not truth', see Abrams, 1984, 5, 13.
95 Bowring, 1843, ii. 213, 253, 254.
96 Brookner, 2000, 3, 11.
97 Coleridge, ed. Richards, 1961, 304.
98 Kant, 2007, 143–4.
99 Bowring, 1843, i. 465.
100 Ed. Crimmins, 2002.
101 Blake, 2009, 71.
102 McGann, 1983, 129.
103 Wilde, 2008, 4.
104 Coleridge, ed. Coleridge, 1895, Vol. I, 197.
105 Bowring, 1843, ii. 254.
106 Quinn, 2015.
107 Quinn, 2015, 59.
108 Hegel, 2004, 39.
109 Ed. Roberts, 2016, 16–18. See also: '[Dickens] would have accepted happiness or pleasure as an absolute criterion, as against the emphases of most other contemporary religious and philosophic systems.' Williams, ed. Slater, 1970, quoted in Blake, 2009, 4.
110 Kant, 2007, 54.
111 Nietzsche, 2017, 75.
112 Mill, ed. Robson, 1984, 254.
113 '"A great work of art," [the artist G.F.] Watts wrote [in 1879], "is a noble theme treated in a noble manner, awakening our best and reverential feelings, touching our generosity, our tenderness, or disposing us generally to seriousness."' Girouard, 1981, 154.
114 Though inexplicably omitted from Faas, 2002, which is a study of precisely this line of dissent.
115 Bentham, ed. Schofield *et al.*, 2014, 147–9.
116 Bentham, ed. Schofield *et al.*, 2014, 73.
117 Empson, 1966b, 114.
118 Wordsworth, ed. Stafford, 2013, 111.
119 Keats, ed. Gittings, 1987, 59–60.
120 Shelley, ed. Clarke, 1988, 77.
121 Bentham, ed. Burns and Hart, 1977, 399.

122 Bowring, 1843, ii. 254–5.
123 Bentham, ed. Schofield *et al.*, 2014, 85, 142.
124 Bentham, ed. Schofield *et al.*, 2014, 117.
125 Bentham, ed. Schofield *et al.*, 2014, 136.
126 Bentham, ed. Schofield *et al.*, 2014, 32–3.
127 Abrams, 1971, 301.
128 Tomkins, 2013, 29.
129 Sontag, 2009, 291.
130 Pound, 1951; Menand, 2008.
131 Stoekl, ed. Hollier, 1989, 930, and ed. Kritzman, 2006, 413; Surya, 2002, 129–30.
132 Schultz, 2017, 57.

References

Abrams, M.H. *The Mirror and the Lamp: Romantic Theory and the Critical Tradition*. Oxford: Oxford University Press, 1971.

Abrams, M.H. *The Correspondent Breeze: Essays on English Romanticism*. New York: Norton, 1984.

Abrams, M.H. 'Positivism and the Newer Criticism' and 'Belief and the Suspension of Disbelief', in *Doing Things With Texts: Essays in Criticism and Critical Theory*. New York: Norton, 1989.

Anon. 'Article II', *The British and Foreign Review* 13 (1842): 49–65.

Ashton, R. *G.H. Lewes: An Unconventional Victorian*. London: Pimlico, 2000.

Ayer, A.J. *Russell*. London: Collins, 1972.

Bain, A. *The Emotions and the Will*. London: John W. Parker and Son, 1859.

Bedford, S. *The Trial of Lady Chatterley's Lover*. London: Daunt Books, 2016.

Bell, C. *Civilisation*. London: Chatto and Windus, 1932.

Bentham, J. *'Legislator of the World:' Writings on Codification, Law, and Education* (*CW*), eds. P. Schofield and J. Harris. Oxford: Clarendon Press, 1998.

Bentham, J. *A Comment on the Commentaries and A Fragment on Government* (*CW*), eds. J.H. Burns and H.L.A Hart. London: Athlone Press, 1977.

Bentham, J. *Of Sexual Irregularities, and Other Writings on Sexual Morality* (*CW*), eds. P. Schofield, C. Pease-Watkin, and M. Quinn. Oxford: Clarendon Press, 2014.

Bentham, J. *Rights, Representation and Reform* (*CW*), eds. P. Schofield, C. Pease-Watkin, and C. Blamires. Oxford: Clarendon Press, 2002.

Bentham, J. *The Correspondence of Jeremy Bentham: Vol. 7* (*CW*), ed. J.R. Dinwiddy. Oxford: Clarendon Press, 1988.

Bentham, J. *The Works of Jeremy Bentham*, ed. John Bowring. 11 vols. Edinburgh: William Tait, 1838–43.

Bieri, J. *Percy Bysshe Shelley*. Baltimore, MD: Johns Hopkins University Press, 2008.

Blake, K. *Pleasures of Benthamism: Victorian Literature, Utility, Political Economy*. Oxford: Oxford University Press, 2009.

Brinton, C. *The Political Ideas of the English Romanticists*. Ann Arbor: University of Michigan Press, 1966.

Brookner, A. *Romanticism and Its Discontents*. New York: Farrar, Straus and Giroux, 2000.

Browning, E.B. 'From Westminster Review (January 1857)', *Aurora Leigh*, ed. Margaret Reynolds. New York: Norton, 1996.

Canuel, M. 'Bentham, Utility, and the Romantic Imagination', in *Selected Writings of Jeremy Bentham*, ed. S.G. Engelmann. New Haven, CT: Yale University Press, 2011.

Carlyle, T. *Latter-Day Pamphlets* [1850]. London: Chapman and Hall, 1898.

Coleridge, S.T. 'Selections from *Anima Poetae*', in *The Portable Coleridge*, ed. I.A. Richards. New York: Viking Press, 1961.

Coleridge, S.T. *Letters of Samuel Taylor Coleridge*, ed. Ernest Hartley Coleridge. London: Heinemann, 1895.

Crimmins, J.E. ed. *Bentham's Auto-Icon and Related Writings*. Bristol: Thoemmes Press, 2002.

Culler, J. *Structuralist Poetics*. London: Routledge, 1975.

Culler, J. *Literary Theory: A Very Short Introduction*. Oxford: Oxford University Press, 2011.

Dickens, C. *Hard Times*. London: Penguin, 2003.

Dinwiddy, J.R. *Bentham*. Oxford: Oxford University Press, 1989.
Eldridge, R. 'Romanticism – Philosophy and Literature', in *Encyclopedia of Aesthetics*, ed. M. Kelly. Oxford: Oxford University Press, 1998.
Elliot, H.S.R. *The Letters of John Stuart Mill*. London: Longmans, 1910.
Empson, W. *Seven Types of Ambiguity*. New York: New Directions, 1966a.
Empson, W. *Some Versions of Pastoral*. London: Penguin, 1966b.
Faas, E. *The Genealogy of Aesthetics*. Cambridge: Cambridge University Press, 2002.
Farley, P. and Roberts, M. Symmons. *Deaths of the Poets*. London: Jonathan Cape, 2018.
Ferber, M. *Romanticism: A Very Short Introduction*. Oxford: Oxford University Press, 2010.
Frye, N. *A Study of English Romanticism*. New York: Random House, 1968.
Gilbert, S.M. and Gubar, S. *The Madwoman in the Attic*. London: Yale Nota Bene, 2009.
Girouard, M. *The Return to Camelot: Chivalry and the English Gentleman*. New Haven, CT: Yale University Press, 1981.
Glüer, K. 'The Status of Charity I: Conceptual Truth or A Posteriori Necessity?', in *Donald Davidson: Life and Words*, ed. Maria Baghramian. London: Routledge, 2013.
Gomme, A.B. *The Traditional Games of England, Scotland and Ireland*. London: Nutt, 1898.
Hammermeister, K. 'Truth', in *German Aesthetics: Fundamental Concepts from Baumgarten to Adorno*, eds. J.D. Mininger and J. Michael Peck. London: Bloomsbury, 2016.
Hardy, F. *The Life of Thomas Hardy*. London: Studio Editions, 1994.
Harrison, R. *Bentham*. London: Routledge, 1983.
Hazlitt, W. 'Coriolanus', in *Selected Writings*. London: Pickering and Chatto, 1998.
Hegel, G.W.F. *Introductory Lectures on Aesthetics*. London: Penguin, 2004.
Hemingway, A. 'Genius, Gender, and Progress: Benthamism and the Arts in the 1820s', in his *Landscape between Ideology and the Aesthetic: Marxist Essays on British Art and Art Theory, 1750–1850*. Chicago: Haymarket Books, 2018.
Himmelfarb, G. 'Liberty: "One Very Simple Principle"?', *The American Scholar* 62:4 (1993): 531–50.
Kant, I. *Critique of Judgment*. Oxford: Oxford University Press, 2007.
Keats, J. *Letters of John Keats*, ed. R. Gittings. Oxford: Oxford University Press, 1987.
Kołakowski, L. *Positivist Philosophy: From Hume to the Vienna Circle*. Harmondsworth: Penguin, 1972.
Lovejoy, A.O. 'On the Discrimination of Romanticisms', in *Essays in the History of Ideas*. New York: Putnam, 1960.
Mack, M. *Jeremy Bentham: An Odyssey of Ideas 1748–1792*. London: Heinemann, 1962.
Mallock, W.H. 'A Familiar Colloquy', *Nineteenth Century* 4 (1878): 289–302.
Marx, K. *Capital*. London: Penguin, 1976.
Mason, M. *The Making of Victorian Sexuality*. Oxford: Oxford University Press, 1994.
Mazlish, B. *James and John Stuart Mill: Father and Son in the Nineteenth Century*. New York: Basic Books, 1975.
McCalman, I. 'Introduction', in *An Oxford Companion to the Romantic Age: British Culture 1776–1832*. Oxford: Oxford University Press, 2001.
McGann, J.J. *The Romantic Ideology: A Critical Investigation*. Chicago: University of Chicago Press, 1983.
McPherson, M.S. 'Mill's Moral Theory and the Problem of Preference Change', in *John Stuart Mill's Social and Political Thought*, ed. G.W. Smith. London: Routledge, 1998.
Menand, L. 'The Pound Error', *New Yorker*, 9 June 2008.
Mill, J.S. 'Brodie's History of the British Empire' [1824], in *Essays on England, Ireland, and the British Empire*, ed. J.M. Robson. Toronto: University of Toronto Press; London: Routledge, 1996.
Mill, J.S. *Autobiography and Literary Essays*, eds. J.M. Robson and J. Stillinger. Toronto: University of Toronto Press; London: Routledge, 1981.
Mill, J.S. *Essays on Equality, Law and Education*, ed. J.M. Robson. Toronto: University of Toronto Press; London: Routledge, 1984.
Mill, J.S. *Essays on Ethics, Religion and Society*, ed. J.M. Robson. Toronto: University of Toronto Press; London: Routledge, 1986.
Mill, J.S. *Essays on Philosophy and the Classics*, ed. J.M. Robson. Toronto: University of Toronto Press; London: Routledge, 1978.
Mill, J.S. *Essays on Politics and Society: I*, ed. J.M. Robson. Toronto: University of Toronto Press; London: Routledge, 1977.
Mill, J.S. *Mill on Bentham and Coleridge*, ed. F.R. Leavis. London: Chatto and Windus, 1950.

Mill, J.S. *Utilitarianism* [1863], eds. J.M. Robson and J. Stillinger, *Essays on Ethics, Religion and Society*. Toronto: University of Toronto Press; London: Routledge, 1985.
Moers, E. *Literary Women*. New York: Doubleday, 1976.
Monk, R. *Ludwig Wittgenstein: The Duty of a Genius*. London: Vintage, 1991.
Mort, F. *Capital Affairs: London and the Making of the Permissive Society*. New Haven, CT: Yale University Press, 2010.
Murdoch, I. 'Salvation by Words', in *Existentialists and Mystics*. London: Penguin, 1999.
Nicholson, H. *Good Behaviour*. London: Constable, 1955.
Nietzsche, F. *On the Genealogy of Morality*. Cambridge: Cambridge University Press, 2017.
Pagin, P. 'The Status of Charity II: Charity, Probability, and Simplicity', in *Donald Davidson: Life and Words*, ed. Maria Baghramian. London: Routledge, 2013.
Pound, E. *ABC of Reading*. Norfolk, CT: New Directions, 1951.
Quinn, M. *Utilitarianism and the Art School in Nineteenth-Century Britain*. London: Routledge, 2015.
Ricks, C. 'F.R. Leavis', in *Reviewery*. London: Penguin, 2003.
Ricks, C. *T.S. Eliot and Prejudice*. London: Faber, 1988.
Roberts, A. ed. *Coleridge: Lectures on Shakespeare 1811–1819*. Edinburgh: Edinburgh University Press, 2016.
Rosen, F. *Mill*. Oxford: Oxford University Press, 2013
Russell, B. 'John Stuart Mill', in *Mill: A Collection of Critical Essays*, ed. J.B. Schneewind. London: Macmillan, 1968.
Schelling, F.W.J. *System of Transcendental Idealism*. Charlottesville: University of Virginia Press, 1978.
Schlegel, F. 'On Incomprehensibility', in *Classic and Romantic German Aesthetics*, ed. J.M. Bernstein. Cambridge: Cambridge University Press, 2003.
Schofield, P. 'Jeremy Bentham: Legislator of the World', *Current Legal Problems* 51:1 (1998): 115–47.
Schofield, P. 'Bentham and the Principle of Utility', in *Selected Writings of Jeremy Bentham*, ed. S.G. Engelmann. New Haven, CT: Yale University Press, 2011.
Schofield, P. 'Jeremy Bentham on Taste, Sex, and Religion', in *Bentham's Theory of Law and Public Opinion*, eds. X. Zhai and M. Quinn. Cambridge: Cambridge University Press, 2014.
Schultz, B. *The Happiness Philosophers: The Lives and Works of the Great Utilitarians*. Princeton, NJ: Princeton University Press, 2017.
Sharpless, F.P. *The Literary Criticism of John Stuart Mill*. Paris and The Hague: Mouton, 1967.
Shelley, Percy Bysshe. 'A Defence of Poetry', in *Shelley's Prose*, ed. D.L. Clark. London: Fourth Estate, 1988a.
Shelley, Percy Bysshe. 'A Philosophical View of Reform', in *Shelley's Prose*, ed. D.L. Clark. London: Fourth Estate, 1988b.
Shelley, Percy Bysshe. 'A Treatise on Morals', in *Shelley's Prose*, ed. D.L. Clark. London: Fourth Estate, 1988c.
Showalter, E. *A Literature of Their Own: British Women Novelists from Brontë to Lessing*. Princeton, NJ: Princeton University Press, 1977.
Skilton, D. ed. *The Early & Mid-Victorian Novel*. London: Routledge, 1993.
Sontag, S. 'Notes on Camp', in *Against Interpretation and Other Essays*. London: Penguin, 2009.
Stephen, L. *The English Utilitarians*. London: Duckworth, 1900.
Stoekl, A. 'The Avant-Garde Embraces Science', in *A New History of French Literature*, ed. D. Hollier. Cambridge, MA: Harvard University Press, 1989.
Stoekl, A. 'Georges Bataille', in *The Columbia History of Twentieth-Century French Thought*, ed. L.D. Kritzman. New York: Colombia University Press, 2006.
Storer, R. *F.R. Leavis*. London: Routledge, 2009.
Surya, M. *Georges Bataille: An Intellectual Biography*, trans. K. Fijalkowski and M. Richardson. London: Verso, 2002.
Tomkins, C. *Marcel Duchamp: The Afternoon Interviews*. Brooklyn, NY: Badlands Unlimited, 2013.
Warr, T. and Jones, A. eds. *The Artist's Body*. London: Phaidon, 2000.
Warren, Jr., A.H. *English Poetic Theory*. Princeton, NJ: Princeton University Press, 1950.
Watson, J.F. *Annals of Philadelphia and Pennsylvania in the Olden Time*. Philadelphia: J.B. Lippincott, 1856.
Welzbacher, C. *The Radical Fool of Capitalism: On Jeremy Bentham, the Panopticon, and the Auto-Icon*, trans. E. Lauffer. Cambridge, MA: MIT Press, 2018.

Whitman, W. 'Democratic Vistas', in *Complete Poetry and Collected Prose*. New York: Literary Classics of the United States, 1982.
Wilde, O. *The Picture of Dorian Gray*. Oxford: Oxford University Press, 2008.
Williams, R. 'Dickens and Social Ideas', in *Dickens 1970*, ed. M. Slater. London: Chapman and Hall, 1970.
Wolff, J. 'Mill, Indecency and the Liberty Principle', *Utilitas* 10:1 (1998): 1–16.
Wordsworth, W. *Lyrical Ballads*, ed. Fiona Stafford. Oxford: Oxford University Press, 2013.

Part III.
AESTHETICS, TASTE AND ART

Chapter 8
Enlightenment unrefined: Bentham's realism and the analysis of beauty

Malcolm Quinn

Introduction

Jeremy Bentham was born at a time when civil discourse on aesthetics and taste in Britain had begun to shift from the idea of beauty as a harmonious order that is perceived by an 'inner sense' of taste towards a more practical aesthetics appropriate to commercial society. This practical aesthetics exchanged fixed rules of art and taste for an analytical power that was attributed to the 'verdicts of sentiment' of critics of taste. Definitions of beauty began to focus on the possibility of achieving an unbiased and objective analysis of pleasurable sentiments.[1] Bentham's challenge to aesthetics, which was aligned with his utilitarian ethics, was to reject both rules of taste and the powers of judgment accorded to the person of taste, and replace them with a predilection or disposition towards pleasure. For Bentham, pleasure is what explains human behaviour, not what needs to be explained. This approach took no account of critical judgments on what was ugly and what was beautiful, of the kind that could be used to construct general 'agreements on the agreeable'. This makes Bentham difficult to include in narratives of British aesthetics – in Timothy M. Costelloe's survey of British aesthetics 'from Shaftesbury to Wittgenstein', Bentham only rates a couple of mentions as the background to a discussion of the aesthetics of John Stuart Mill.[2] We are more familiar, however, with attacks on Bentham's hedonic utilitarianism as a form of cultural barbarism, ranging from criticism by Thomas

Macaulay,[3] Karl Marx and Matthew Arnold[4] in the nineteenth century, to Roger Scruton[5] in more recent times. In this chapter, I will argue that we should not rest content with Marx's assertion that 'the arch-philistine, Jeremy Bentham' was the 'heavy-footed oracle of the "common sense" of the nineteenth-century bourgeoisie'.[6] Instead, I will define Bentham as someone who saw that a typically bourgeois, practical, empirical and experimental approach to the analysis of beauty would become mired in contradictions if it attempted to impose social norms that could separate the beautiful from the ugly.

In Bentham's view, there was no reason whatsoever why a predilection towards pleasure would be guided by distinctions between the ugly and the beautiful. Moreover, he also favoured a social order that could make use of socially beneficial predilections and proclivities, which had always been regarded as inimical to impartial judgments of taste. Bentham took up the cudgels for empiricism by defining the social norms imposed by taste as a form of harmful blindness. As I have argued elsewhere,[7] Bentham's theory of language indicates that the turn towards the refined judgments of the critic of taste was not an embrace of empiricism but a rejection of it. In this chapter, I will show how Bentham's *The Rationale of Reward* offers a counter-strategy that returns us to the empirical by allowing us to choose between refinement and utility, while also offering the chance for an enlightened exit from aristocratic modes of social life.

In what follows, I will begin by defining what my title refers to as 'Bentham's Realism' as a means to establish his contribution to debates on aesthetics. I will show how Bentham's criticisms of Claude Adrien Helvétius, Joseph Addison and David Hume, along with the analysis of taste and predilection in his manuscripts on sexuality, offer a thorough critique of those forms of practical aesthetics that advocated realism about the connections between beauty and human desire and emphasized the cultural power of the ordinary observer. I will then discuss Bentham's own definition of cultural barbarism, through an analysis of his comments on what I define as the 'centrally managed' practical aesthetics of Helvétius. This is followed by an account of Bentham's attack on Joseph Addison's proposals for 'self-management' through the practice of taste. I will then turn to the question of how the emphasis on cultural observation in practical aesthetics placed the artist in a subordinate position to the spectator and the critic. In this regard, I will suggest that Bentham's praise for William Hogarth opens up the possibility for a distinction between the 'Addisonian' Hogarth that is presented in his treatise on *The Analysis of Beauty* (1753) and the 'Benthamite' Hogarth of the prints *Beer Street* and *Gin Lane* (1751) (Figures 8.1, 8.2).

Figure 8.1: William Hogarth (1697–1764), *Beer Street*, 1751.
Wiki/Commons.

Figure 8.2: William Hogarth (1697–1764), *Gin Lane*, 1751.
Wiki/Commons.

In these two prints, Hogarth anticipates Bentham's position on aesthetics by 'doubling down' on realism, presenting a practical ethics that takes account of taste as inclination and predilection rather than self-management. In conclusion, I will comment on the display of Bentham's auto-icon in the exhibition 'Like Life' at the Met Breuer Museum in New York in 2018, in order to suggest some lessons that the unrefined enlightenment of Bentham might have to offer for contemporary practices of cultural management and self-management.

Bentham's realism

An otherwise favourable review of Jeremy Bentham's book *The Rationale of Reward* in the *Political Examiner* of 30 May 1825 noted that the book had caused 'a havock ... in our predilections' with its assertion that 'Prejudice apart, the game of push-pin is of equal value with the arts and sciences of music and poetry.'[8] In that same year, the journalist John Neal referred to the received opinion that Bentham's followers were 'a body of youthful conspirators against government, order and morality, the fine arts, and all the charities and sympathies and elegancies of life.'[9] *The Rationale of Reward* is the text most often cited by those who have accused Bentham of cultural barbarism, philistinism and a rejection of the finer things in life. It is, therefore, worth noting that *The Rationale of Reward* contains its own criticisms of utilitarian cultural barbarism. Bentham directs this criticism at Claude Adrien Helvétius's assumptions concerning a form of utilitarian legislation in which beauty is offered as a reward for service to the state and through which the legislator is given power over the social distribution of pleasure. Bentham's criticism of Helvétius is entirely consistent with his comments on push-pin and poetry in *The Rationale of Reward*, as well as his criticisms elsewhere in this text of the promotion of refinement of taste by Joseph Addison and David Hume. Bentham's answer to Helvétius, Addison and Hume does not advocate a return to fixed rules of taste, but instead emphasizes a greater degree of realism, specifically the kind of realism about sexuality that Bentham sets out in detail in his manuscripts on 'Sexual Irregularities' of 1814–17.[10] In these manuscripts, Bentham rejects any natural or assumed link between sexual pleasure and reproductive activity. Refusing to define sexuality by referring to a normal set of behaviours, aims and objects, means that Bentham at once includes sexual behaviour within a variety of human tastes and propensities and rejects the association of taste with refinement, claiming that 'Taste for any object is an aptitude or disposition to derive pleasure [from] that object.'[11] In a note added to this sentence in the manuscripts, Bentham added: 'Here give illustrations from other objects of taste – ex. gr. subjects of the fine arts.'[12]

The 'havock … in our predilections' brought about by Bentham's rejection of favoured objects of culture in his comments on push-pin and poetry should, therefore, be understood in relation to the realism about sexuality that is offered in 'Of Sexual Irregularities'. In addition, Bentham's views on sexuality and culture must be seen in relation to his condemnation of the potential for cultural barbarism in aesthetic realism. In *The Rationale of Reward*, this potential for barbarism is located in socially normative definitions of beauty, which are 'centrally managed' by Helvétius's utilitarian legislator and 'self-managed' in the cultural choices of the refined spectator favoured by Addison and Hume. For Bentham, the central management of beauty described by Helvétius would be barbaric because it assumes that there can be state control over the allocation and social distribution of individual pleasure. The self-management of beauty advocated by Addison was also barbaric, because it asserted the authority of the person of refined taste to dismiss what was extravagant or absurd in the arts and to crush a variety of propensities and inclinations towards pleasure 'under the strokes of his club'.[13]

The connection that Bentham makes in 'Of Sexual Irregularities' between sexuality and taste also indicates why the need for the management of beauty arises within aesthetic realism. Once fixed rules of taste are abandoned in favour of the position of the ordinary observer, it is hubristic to assume that this observer will be the ideal conduit for a socially normative definition of beauty and the general 'agreements on the agreeable' that can provide the basis of a legislative science of taste. The potential for cultural barbarism that is inherent in the idea of the favoured observer of a socially normative idea of beauty finds its opposition in the idea of sexuality as a 'sixth sense' in 'Of Sexual Irregularities', where Bentham notes that, 'Till of late years, the number of senses had by usage been fixt at *five*: of late years, a sense corresponding to and put in exercise by the act of sexuality[14] has been added to the number.'[15] Bentham's assertion that there is 'a sense corresponding to and put in exercise by the act of sexuality' implies that the gratification of sexual desire relies for its fulfilment on a specific type of observation that receives and responds to information about possible sources of sexual pleasure. The sociologist Niklas Luhmann has reminded us that we have forgotten the importance of sexuality as a form of social observation, through which the body 'makes its own distinctions and decides whether or not to be sexually attracted. Observing this observer leads us to ask whether or not it dutifully follows cultural imperatives, or whether there is unavoidable *akrasia* (lack of self-control), as the Greeks would have said, a lack of *potestas in se ipsum* (self-control) in humans and social systems.'[16] The argument that Luhmann makes here about sexual desire as an unruly observer of cultural imperatives was anticipated by Bentham's inclusion of both 'subjects of the fine arts' and sexual acts under the general heading of taste as disposition and inclination. Bentham went further and argued that this 'unruly' observer of culture could, nonetheless, counteract the blindness of prejudices of taste and provide insights into social problems. An example of this is provided in 'Of Sexual Irregularities', when Bentham suggests that a suppressed aspect of Thomas Robert Malthus's reasoning proves the propriety and ethical value of homosexuality as a check on over-population, 'though his situation, in the double character of a Clergyman of the Established Church and an instructor of youth, does not admitt of his proposing it, or directly advocating it'.[17] When read together, *The Rationale of Reward* and 'Of Sexual Irregularities' disclose the fallibility of the idea that the analysis of pleasurable sentiments can be used to propose socially normative definitions of beauty. Rather than imposing a practical aesthetics based on reproductive sexuality, *The Rationale of Reward* and 'Of Sexual Irregularities' advocate utilitarian social practices that embrace a multitude of dispositions to derive pleasure.

Bentham on Helvétius

The Rationale of Reward emerged from manuscripts written between 1786 and 1787 when Bentham was staying with his brother Samuel in Russia. Bentham described it in a letter to George Wilson in 1787 as a work that 'touches upon all the possible applications of the matter of reward, ordinary and extraordinary'.[18] These manuscripts were later edited and published in French by Étienne Dumont in 1811 and translated into English by Richard Smith in 1825. Nonetheless, as Ross Harrison has pointed out, the long genesis of *The Rationale of Reward* gives it the character of a message from the eighteenth-century enlightenment that is received in the Britain of the Industrial Revolution.[19] Part of this message is about barbarism, and is directed at Helvétius's assumptions about the possibilities for utilitarian legislation. Bentham's statement is worth quoting at length:

> One word on the last article of reward – *Pleasures*. Punishment may be applied in all shapes to all persons. Pleasure, however, in the hands of the legislator, is not equally manageable: pleasure can be given only by giving the means by which it is purchased: that is to say, the matter of wealth which every one may employ in his own way. Among certain barbarous or half civilized nations, the services of their warriors have been rewarded by the favours of women. Helvetius appears to smile with approbation at this mode of exciting bravery. It was perhaps Montesquieù that led him into this error. In speaking of the Samnites, among whom the young man declared the most worthy selected whomsoever he pleased for his wife, he adds that this custom was calculated to produce most beneficial effects. Philosophers distinguished for their humanity; both of them good husbands and good fathers, both of them eloquent against slavery, how could they speak in praise of a law which supposes the slavery of the best half of the human species? How could they have forgotten that favours not preceded by an uncontrolled choice, and which the heart perhaps repelled with disgust, afforded the spectacle rather of the degradation of woman than the rewarding a hero? The warrior surrounded by palms of honour, could he descend to act the part of a ravisher? And if he disdained this barbarous right, was not his generosity a satire on the law?[20]

Miriam Williford has argued that this passage shows that 'Bentham in his enthusiasm for women's rights even goes so far as to reprimand his mentor, Helvetius, and the customs Helvetius supported.'[21] While Bentham's support for equality between the sexes is beyond doubt, what should be emphasized is that Bentham is also arguing against Helvétius's idea of a utilitarian state, in which, for example, there could be a science of public taste that could be used to discover 'the particular knowledge of what pleases the public in a certain nation'.[22] The passage in Helvétius's *De l'esprit* to which Bentham refers claims that, in general, virtues attended by the promise of sensual pleasure are those that are the most sought after. Helvétius offers martial virtue rewarded by female beauty as an example of this, using Montesquieu's reference, in his *De l'esprit des lois*, to the 'excellent' custom of the Samnites, who begin by choosing a young man who embodies the fine qualities and services rendered to his country. This young man 'took for his wife the daughter he desired … Love, beauty, chastity, virtue, birth, even wealth, all this was, so to speak, the dowry of virtue.'[23] There is debate as to whether Helvétius agreed with Montesquieu in this instance,[24] but what is certain is that Helvétius's version of a practical aesthetics of state-managed taste depends on a social science of beauty. This science of beauty is not based on the rules of art, or even on the powers of the critic of taste, but on the efficacy of a manager/observer whose power is never revealed, but who can define what will be sought after in a particular cultural situation.[25] What Helvétius's utilitarianism cannot relinquish is the possibility of gaining access to knowledge concerning a normative definition of the beautiful. Bentham's interest, in contrast, is in why the possibility of defining social standards of beauty vanishes when we examine our predilections. His response to Helvétius is to argue that pleasure, in the hands of the legislator, is not manageable and depends on an 'uncontrolled choice' in which what is desired is not determined by social identities and cultural mores but instead by stubborn dispositions and propensities to derive pleasure from a variety of objects and activities. In Bentham's view, the assumption that reproductive sexuality can underpin cultural definitions of beauty and social mechanisms of reward is not tenable. The practical aesthetics of Helvétius gives power to a manager/observer who can discern the ways in which social standards of beauty determine norms of behaviour. As I have said, Bentham rejects the idea of such a privileged observer and puts a predilection or disposition in its place. Accordingly, Bentham's idea of social observation, as it is expressed in the panopticon, links human predilections to an architectural mechanism, one in which power over others can only be established by using an apparatus for monitoring empirical differences. In his manuscripts on the panopticon, Bentham contrasts his inspection house with the Sicilian prison of 'The Ear of Dionysus', a cave whose structure, it was said, allowed the warder to hear what the prisoners were saying to each other and 'pry into the secret recesses of the heart'.[26] The structure of the panopticon prison, on the other hand, is designed solely for the monitoring of overt acts, a task that can be performed by anyone who has a predilection for it. Bentham asserts that the panopticon 'will supply … the place of that great and constant fund of entertainment to the sedentary and vacant in towns – the looking out of the window'.[27] Putting curiosity to use within the social apparatus of the panopticon is a very different matter from assuming that a normative idea of beauty can be used as a mechanism of social coercion. In fact, Bentham opposed a utilitarian ethics of social observation to normative ideas of beauty. In a discussion of the personal taste of legislators in his manuscripts on 'On the Influence of Time and Place in Matters of Legislation', Bentham introduces the anecdote of a surgeon who cuts off the one remaining healthy finger on a patient's damaged hand for aesthetic reasons, 'because it would have looked ridiculous'.[28] In this example, aesthetics is used as the means to exert power over others but proves to be a very poor guide to ethical action. The utilitarian alternative is to be found in the panopticon hospital, where the surgeons 'might with the least trouble possible watch as much as they chose to watch, the progress of the disease, and the influence of the remedy'.[29] The apparatus of the panopticon hospital locates social power within the activity of inspection, but only insofar as this contributes to utility. This is why Michel Foucault's description of the panopticon as a disciplinary mechanism is tendentious: it makes Bentham's hedonic utilitarianism identical with the disciplining of bodies,[30] an assumption that is contradicted by Bentham's comments on warriors rewarded by the favours of women. The panopticon is not built around the power of an individual subject to classify what it observes, as Foucault suggests.[31] Instead, the structure of this 'simple idea in Architecture'[32] means that the actions of both the observing subject and the subject who is being observed are subsumed within a particular social task of inspection (penal, medical, pedagogic, etc.) that can contribute to general utility. A present-day equivalent of the actual distribution of social power in the structure of the panopticon hospital can be found in the detection of eye diseases, where monitoring by artificial intelligence is now superior to the scrutiny of human specialists.[33] If we can understand how, in principle, the apparatus of the panopticon hospital might correct the point of view of the surgeon who cut off the healthy finger and thus alter his conception of 'the good', we can also understand why Bentham used a demand for utility to raise the stakes to the point where the possibility of cultural barbarism is revealed.

Bentham on Addison

In his manuscripts on the panopticon, Bentham recommends his inspection house to Joseph Addison as a means for monitoring the virginity of young ladies and to Claude Adrien Helvétius as a means of testing his theory that 'anybody may be taught anything, one person as well as another'.[34] Bentham's intention is partly satirical and partly serious. It is satirical because these offers to Addison and Helvétius are among several suggested applications of the panopticon apparatus that also include a solution to a fictional situation that is encountered in Cervantes' *Don Quixote*. His intention is also serious, because the purpose of Bentham's satire is to point out the precision and 'sharpness' of the panopticon as an apparatus for monitoring overt behaviour.

Bentham's offer of his inspection-house to 'the grave and moral Addison' relates to Bentham's half-remembered reference to 'a contrivance for trying *virginity* by means of *lions*' that was discussed by Addison in *The Spectator*.[35] The important distinction here is between Addison's idea of morality and Bentham's. As I have mentioned, where Helvétius offers a utilitarian, 'centrally managed' practical aesthetics, Addison proposes a means for 'self-management' through the practice of taste. In Bentham's view, both Helvétius and Addison are at fault for promoting socially normative definitions of the beautiful that cause harm to others. This was not how Addison saw it; for him, the power of being able to discover one's own reasons for finding something pleasing or beautiful carried moral force, because it meant that the subjects of commercial society became the guarantors of their own happiness, rather than locating this happiness within the seductions of the external world. In Addison's writing on taste in *The Spectator* between 1711 and 1714, we can see the articulation of a specific ethical problem – how is a person with weak social connections to make their way in the world without losing their integrity by doing so? Addison's practical aesthetic solution was to exchange the contingent and therefore dangerous pleasures of the world for the structured and controlled pleasures of good taste and good judgment. What is distinctive about this solution is that, on the one hand, it unites all mankind on the ground of ordinary perception and, on the other, it divides mankind into those who can learn to rely on the pleasures of taste and those who are content with the pleasures of the world. It also gives a very specific social role to the arts. For Addison, his new conception of taste could be used to oppose sectarian rules of art; in his words, 'A man of an ordinary Ear is a judge whether a Passion is express'd in Proper sounds, and whether the Melody of those Sounds be more or less pleasing.'[36] This sets up an opposition between the true social standard of judgment offered by a 'man of an ordinary Ear' and the false social standard offered by the public appetite for certain kinds of music. It also offered a means to distinguish bad taste from good taste. Bad taste was demonstrated in the cultural choices of those who, for example, were not actively developing their 'ordinary Ear' to judge 'whether a Passion is express'd in Proper sounds' and who were therefore passively content with all that was extravagant, childish and absurd in the performing arts. In this way, the connoisseur who trains himself to recognize the particular qualities of an object of art is challenged by the Addisonian person of taste who uses objects of art to train his own perception. Good taste would triumph, Addison thought, if public taste stopped bowing to the arbitrary rules of art and art started accommodating itself to the rationale provided by 'the general Sense and Taste of Mankind':

> Musick, Architecture, and Painting, as well as Poetry, and Oratory, are to deduce their Laws and Rules from the general Sense and Taste of Mankind, and not from the Principles of those Arts themselves; or, in other Words, the Taste is not to conform to the Art, but the Art to the Taste.[37]

In opposing Addison, Bentham's focus was on the social consequences that followed from the employment of an evaluation of pleasurable sentiments as the preferred means to distinguish good taste from bad taste. For Bentham, this way of establishing standards of taste meant that something that was previously an object of amusement and enjoyment for oneself or someone else could become an object of ridicule and contempt. While Addison's version of enlightenment seems to open up a new horizon of liberty that places the sensibility of the ordinary spectator at the centre of events within the chaos of commercial society, Bentham shows how this reproduces the arbitrary violence of aristocratic privilege in new ways. Bentham's alternative, which proceeds through utility, offers an unrefined enlightenment through which the social violence of refinement can be overcome. In *The Rationale of Reward,* Bentham first isolates the problems of Addison's refined enlightenment in a discussion of the relationship of the fine arts to refined taste. He then frames the alternative of an unrefined enlightenment, by separating Addison's aesthetic solution from his ethical problem and offering the possibility of a choice between Addisonian refinement and Benthamite utility. Bentham's unrefined enlightenment does not follow Addison's logic of rejecting the rules of art and replacing them with a refined sensibility. Instead, it seeks a point of refuge from that same refined sensibility, a position from which we can examine how the cultural value of refinement determines the social role of the arts. The problem is, to use Bentham's words, how can we choose 'A pure and simple amusement'? When 'to be hard to please, and to have our happiness dependant on what is costly and complicated, shall be found to be advantageous'?[38] The difficulty that Bentham faces in his endeavour to establish the terms of a utilitarian choice for a simple amusement, is that Addison's elevation of a refined sensibility as the basis of the standard of taste claims to annex the very possibility of choice and judgment to itself. This 'checkmate' on alternatives to refinement is re-affirmed in Mill's criticisms of Bentham's apparent blindness to the opportunities of reading moral character through judgments of taste, and Mill's famous remarks on Socrates and the satisfied fool in his essay on 'Utilitarianism' of 1861, in which Socrates is given the power to evaluate whatever it is that the fool is satisfied with, while the fool is not accorded the same privilege.[39]

Bentham's solution to the 'checkmate' of good taste in *The Rationale of Reward* begins with his analysis of the relationship of the practice of art to the practice of taste. Bentham begins by describing an inseparable connection between 'science' which is defined as the knowledge of how to achieve certain goals within a field of human endeavour and 'art' which is defined as the process of acquiring this knowledge. Utility, then, enters the picture as the basis on which to divide the arts and sciences according to how they contribute to the happiness of society. One half of the divide is occupied by the arts and sciences of utility, such as medicine and legislation, and the other half by the arts and sciences of amusement and curiosity. Here we need to focus on the manner in which an initial alignment of theory with practice is followed by a division of the arts and sciences according to how they contribute to the happiness of society. Bentham assembles the fine arts under a single category of 'arts and sciences of amusement' in which he includes music, poetry, painting, sculpture, architecture and ornamental gardening. He also draws attention to a paradox by pointing out that the fine arts are sources of amusement which also have the potential to deprive others of the sources of their amusement. He argues that on the terms set by critics of taste such as Joseph Addison and David Hume, the fine arts please only those refined individuals who are difficult to please and who can only obtain their pleasure through cultivating antipathy towards the pleasures of others, thus effecting a social separation between the pleasures of taste and the pleasures of the world.

Bentham then shows us an exit from the horizon of judgment set by Addison's 'general Sense and Taste of mankind'. To do this, Bentham has to demonstrate that we can make an enlightened, empirical choice between refinement and utility that steers clear of social and cultural norms, in the face of Addison's claim that 'the general Sense and Taste of Mankind' is the best foundation for a valid judgment. Addison's view is that good taste can protect us from bad choices, but Bentham argues instead that what may look like a 'bad choice' can protect us from social mischief. To achieve this goal, Bentham alters the relationship between ethics and aesthetics within an Addisonian idea of cultural value. He begins by isolating a social problem of choice, by observing that, insofar as the fine arts have become the vehicles of a refined sensibility, they please those that are hard to please. Bentham then shows us how we can mark out the route to an enlightened choice between refinement and utility, in the face of the claim that refinement is the only route to a valid judgment. He achieves this by reframing a choice between a 'high status' pleasure (*The Iliad*) and a 'low status' pleasure (solitaire) as a choice between refinement and utility. Bentham begins by outlining a utilitarian position on whether a statesman should play solitaire or play cards in company. He notes that while the statesman can play cards in company all night, playing solitaire is frowned upon, even though, as Bentham says, 'how incomparably superior is this solitary game to many social games, so often anti-social in their consequences!'[40] Having identified an immediate problem of social isolation that accompanies the choice of a pure and simple amusement, he then introduces a further difficulty by saying, 'How much better was this minister occupied, [at solitaire] than if, with the Iliad in his hand, he had stirred up within his heart the seeds of those ferocious passions which can only be gratified with tears and blood.'[41] What makes the choice of a pure or simple amusement so difficult to make is not just the stigma of social isolation, but the gratification afforded by the use of culture as a means of self-aggrandizement and self-justification. To surmount this difficulty, Bentham supplements this aesthetically determined choice between 'high' and 'low' culture (the *Iliad* or solitaire), with the third option of playing cards in company, which transforms it into a decision about utility versus refinement. When this third element is in place, it becomes clear that for the statesman to choose solitaire is simultaneously to choose the best option from the point of view of utility and the worst option from the point of view of a refined sensibility. For him to choose the *Iliad* is to occupy the opposite position; here we might refer to David Hume's explanation, in his essay 'Of the Standard of Taste' of 1757, of how the *Iliad* can be used to demonstrate the niceties of a refined sensibility. It is one thing to claim, as Bentham frequently did, that we should accept that no form of gratification is placed higher than any other; it is quite another to dismantle the Addisonian distinction between the pleasures of taste and the pleasures of the world, which is what Bentham sets out to do in *The Rationale of Reward*. To achieve this goal, Bentham's task is not to tell us to prefer push-pin to poetry, because that would simply replace one person's privilege with another's. Instead, he must first show us why choosing poetry over push-pin gives us access to the social power conferred by distinctions between good taste and bad taste, and then show us why employing these distinctions, within which gratification is present but disguised as refinement, is likely to be contrary to public utility. To challenge aesthetics, the very form of criticism had to change, as is evident in Bentham's comment that David Hume, despite 'his proud and independent philosophy',[42] yielded to literary prejudice on the grounds of taste when he praised the Duke of Buckingham for satirizing the popular theatrical entertainments of his day. Bentham's new utilitarian form of criticism would have to disturb the privileges of the observer on which practical aesthetics depended. It would be able to identify Addisonian aesthetics as a means of self-gratification that was not justified by its claims on analytical power or moral autonomy, but rather should be condemned for the manner in which it negated the simple pleasures of others.

The concept of an unrefined enlightenment relates to a key question that emerges in *The Rationale of Reward*, namely, how 'without violence or injustice, hereditary nobility … [could be] … deprived of the greater part of its injurious prerogatives'.[43] This sentence is part of a discussion of Catherine the Great's use of meritocracy as a way to reform the Russian Civil Service. It is not a reference to the possibility of a violent overthrow of the nobility, but rather to the possibility of creating a meritocracy that does not reproduce the injurious prerogative of claiming to have been born to rule. The nearly forty-year gap between the origins of the text in Bentham's visit to Russia and its English publication meant that Bentham had learnt something in the interim, as is demonstrated in his self-enlightening 'Remarks by Mr Bentham' in the preface to the 1825 edition, in which he qualifies his earlier favourable comments on Catherine the Great in the light of his new commitment to representative democracy. Nonetheless, the key question at stake is not the question of nobility itself but how to think about social value in an enlightened way. The opposition between refinement and utility in *The Rationale of Reward* describes an enlightenment project whose exit from aristocratic prerogatives could be accomplished either by the refined enlightenment of Addison, with its emphasis on culture and taste, or the unrefined enlightenment of Bentham, with its emphasis on utility as a means to identify a variety of routes to pleasure. From Addison's point of view, on the other hand, there is only one exit – good taste is what allows us to separate the esteem we give someone because of their refined sensibility from the deference that might be due to a hereditary title.

Bentham on Hogarth

Bentham's direct attack on Addison in *The Rationale of Reward* takes place on the terms set by an Addisonian worldview, in which the arts have been co-opted to a project of refinement; however, I have also suggested that the manner in which Bentham frames a choice between refinement and utility showed that it was possible to develop a counter-strategy. In this part of the chapter, I will suggest what this counter-strategy implied for artists, by referring to Bentham's praise for William Hogarth, whose illustrations to Samuel Butler's *Hudibras* were displayed on the walls of Bentham's home.[44] Michael Quinn has noted that Bentham identifies Hogarth as someone who could promote healthy alternatives to socially mischievous desires that might otherwise warrant prohibition and punishment.[45] Bentham wrote that, in Hogarth's print *Beer Street* of 1751, everything has the aspect of health and jollity, while its companion print *Gin Lane* showed misery and disease, concluding, 'That admirable artist was one of the best of moralists.'[46] Bentham's suggestion that Hogarth was on a par with the best of moralists suggests a very different social role for the arts than the one he outlines in *The Rationale of Reward*. It is worth noting, however, that David Bindman has argued that, 'It seems beyond argument that Hogarth's enterprise was Addisonian, in that his moral series implicitly advocate a middle way between vice and excessive virtue.'[47] Other Hogarth scholars such as Ronald Paulson and David Solkin have given support to this idea of Hogarth as an Addisonian artist. Addison's *Spectator* actually makes an appearance at the centre of one of Hogarth's paintings, *The Edwards Hamilton Family* of 1734 (Figure 8.3).

Figure 8.3: William Hogarth (1697–1764), *The Edwards Hamilton Family on a Terrace*, 1734.

Private collection, printed by kind permission of Patrick Goetelen.

At the request of his patron Mary Edwards, Hogarth painted her holding *The Spectator*, no. 580 of 13 August 1714, in which Addison discusses the omnipresence of the deity. *The Spectator*, no. 22 of 26 March 1711, which condemns 'the false Taste of the Town', may also have been one of the sources for Hogarth's early print *The Bad Taste of the Town* of 1723 (Figure 8.4).

Figure 8.4: William Hogarth (1697–1764), *The Bad Taste of the Town*, 1723–4.

Wiki/Commons

This print features an imaginary 'Accademy of Art' which is modelled on Burlington House, Piccadilly, the home of Richard Boyle, third earl of Burlington. This fantasy academy, whose doors are firmly shut, is shown to be failing to stem the general decay of public taste that is illustrated in the foreground, in the form of crowds being led towards the facile and shallow amusements of masquerades and Italian operas. In the middle of the image, plays written by Addison and other English dramatists such as Shakespeare, Congreve and Dryden, are being carted off in a wheelbarrow to be sold as wastepaper. Here Hogarth stays true to Addison's injunction that 'Taste is not to conform to the Art, but the Art to the Taste' and the viewpoint of 'Mr Spectator' that separates the true pleasures of refined taste from the false pleasures of popular entertainment. Hogarth's Addisonianism is carried to its furthest extent in his treatise *The Analysis of Beauty*,[48] published in 1753, where Hogarth attempts a rational, impartial analysis of the truth of beauty, in order to assist the ordinary observer and defeat the artificial rules of art promoted by connoisseurs of art. In this text, Hogarth followed Addison's emphasis on the power of being able to discover one's own reasons for finding something pleasing, as well as a concomitant rejection of arbitrary rules of art and a subsequent embrace of 'the general Sense and Taste of mankind'. Hogarth's wish to lend the privileges of the Addisonian critic of taste to anyone who would like to have them founders because his 'Analysis of Beauty' does not establish a universal definition of beauty so much as rehearse the social and cultural privileges associated with reproductive sexuality that British men already enjoyed. Hogarth tells us that, 'if I have acquired anything in my way it has been wholy obtain'd by Observation',[49] which counteracts a 'perversion of the sight' in which 'the eye may be subdued and forced into forming and disposing of objects even quite contrary to what it would naturally see them'.[50] This allows him to declare that the elegant curved lines in the body of a living woman are more beautiful than a statue of Venus,[51] and that the form of a woman's body surpasses that of a man. The art historian Ronald Paulson saw Hogarth as pursuing a radical project in *The Analysis of Beauty*:

> Hogarth is attempting to create an aesthetics that acknowledges that if we place a beautiful woman on a pedestal we will inevitably and appropriately desire her and may discover, moreover, that she is not strictly virtuous. This is an anti-aesthetics, or a practical aesthetics, in relation to the theoretically pure aesthetics of Shaftesbury, where the human body can only be beautiful if divorced from function, fitness and utility.[52]

It can also be argued, however, that Hogarth's attempt to 'fix the fluctuating ideas of Taste' by means of direct observation works against his own ambition for a rational and formal analysis. This is because it installs a preferred definition of beauty based on reproductive sexuality at the heart of that analysis. The effect of this is coercive – as Jenny Uglow has argued, Hogarth's 'real mistake ... was to defy the tyranny of rules by inventing a new rule himself, and insisting that it was an absolute truth'.[53] It can also be argued that Hogarth's mistake in this instance is actually Addison's mistake, insofar as the persuasive and liberal notion of the general sense and taste of mankind leads Hogarth to adopt not so much an anti-aesthetic but rather an anti-artistic position in *Analysis of Beauty*, which begins, somewhat paradoxically, by arguing vehemently against the notion that 'painters and connoisseurs are the only competent judges'.[54] Adam Komisaruk has argued that 'Hogarth replaces one fetish (the classical simulacrum) with another (the living woman)' while emphasizing 'how risky a strategy this inflated masculinism can be'.[55] We can go further, and say how risky a strategy empiricism can be – the ambition for clear and unprejudiced vision leads from the classical statue to the living woman, but, in Bentham's terms, a definition of beauty based on reproductive sexuality was not tenable, because sexuality was an inclination without a fixed object that ignored the distinction between the beautiful and the ugly.

In *Beer Street* and *Gin Lane*, on the other hand, we see Hogarth approaching empiricism in a different way, by outlining the harms that result from a predilection for gin, and the benefits that derive from substituting this predilection for the consumption of beer. The knowledge that is made available by comparing these two images does not require an analysis of beauty.[56] The distinction between *Gin Lane* and *Beer Street* is not guided by a difference between the ugly and the beautiful, but rather by the difference between the pleasure of a predilection and the social harm it causes. Bentham also reminds us that a fixation on a specific object of desire is a work of the imagination, which must be understood in its particularity as an inclination towards pleasure, rather than reasoned out through an analysis of beauty:

> A value of affection is rarely appreciated by third persons; it requires highly enlightened benevolence, a philosophy quite out of the common, to sympathize with tastes that we do not share. The Dutch florist, who exchanges a tulip bulb for its weight in gold, scoffs at the antiquary who gives a great price for a rusty lamp.[57]

In his writing 'Of Sexual Irregularities', Bentham also makes the following observation:

> In the case of the fine arts, when the object is of a complex nature, by being made to observe this or that circumstance that he had not observed before – this or that feature of defect or excellence which till now had passed unobserved – a man may now and then be made to change his taste. But in the field of appetite – of physical appetite – so simple is the object, no place can be found for any such discovery. The man to whom habit has rendered the use of tobacco a source of gratification, whether in the way of snuffing, smoking or mastication, by nothing that any one can say to him will he be convinced that that taste of his is a bad taste. Let him see that by taking it he inflicts annoyance on those in whose presence he is taking it, you may make him abstain from it, but never can you make him in his own mind acknowledge it to be a bad taste.[58]

Hogarth's *The Analysis of Beauty* asserts that it is the artificial rules of art and the verbiage of the connoisseur that prevents the ordinary spectator from seeing something 'he had not observed before', namely that the living woman is more beautiful than the statue. Bentham argues that this way of seeing things as they really are is self-defeating, because it narrows the field of vision to what we are 'made to observe' by the person of taste. The field of vision described by a search for things as they actually are can instead be occupied by any object that is a source of gratification, whether that is a tulip bulb, a rusty lamp or a tobacco pouch. In *Gin Lane* and *Beer Street*, Hogarth made these kinds of objects the subject of his art. The distinction between the Addisonian and the Benthamite Hogarth that I have made in this chapter also shows us how we can begin to map out a conceptual distance between the role of art in affirming the social power of normative judgments on the beautiful, and a contrasting aim to define the social power of art by marking out its position in the world. Bentham does the latter when he defines Hogarth as an admirable artist who was also 'one of the best of moralists'.

Conclusion: An unrefined enlightenment

If enlightenment, broadly speaking, means freedom from tutelage, from being told what to think or how to behave by someone else and gaining freedom from prejudice and superstition, what is an 'unrefined' enlightenment? It is enlightenment won in a battle against refinement, a battle that Jeremy Bentham conducted throughout his life. In this chapter, I have argued that, taken together, *The Rationale of Reward* and 'Of Sexual Irregularities' show us that, once we have embraced an empirical attitude to aesthetics, the agreements on the agreeable that are required by refined taste are unstable. We have to name what is actually barbaric, such as rewarding warriors with women, rather than concerning ourselves with a dubious bid for civilization by naming what is in 'bad taste'. I have also given an account of the enlightened exit from aristocratic forms of social life that Bentham describes in *The Rationale of Reward*, and contrasted Bentham's approach with the practical aesthetics of Addison and Hume, who see the esteem we give someone because of their refined sensibility as the enlightened alternative to the deference that might be due to a hereditary title. The time that has elapsed from the end of the 'long eighteenth century' to the beginning of the twenty-first century has sidelined Bentham's challenge to aesthetics, while retaining an Addisonian emphasis on the privileges accorded to the ordinary observer of culture, as well as versions of Helvétius's ambition to obtain a controlling interest in socially normative definitions of the beautiful. When the award of the Nobel Prize in Literature to Bob Dylan in 2016 challenged elitist cultural distinctions of the kind that would separate Bob Dylan from John Keats, it thereby affirmed the cultural status of the ordinary observer within judgements of taste, over and above the interests of literary cliques. However, as was the case with Hogarth's *The Analysis of Beauty*, the cultural status accorded to the ordinary observer could be more precisely defined as the restatement of existing privileges accorded to a particular social group. As one journalist put it, giving the Nobel Prize to Bob Dylan was actually an indication of 'prevailing educated taste among Swedish Baby Boomers'.[59] It is also worth noting that when cultural institutions do question the logic of taste, they do this on the ground Joseph Addison chose for his new conception of the social role of the arts, namely the importance of everyday experience to the definition of cultural value. To give an example, Alistair Hudson, during his tenure as director of Middlesbrough Institute of Modern Art (2014–17), declared it his intention to make the museum the sum of the activity of all of its users.[60] However, this attempt to substitute community values and civic value for aesthetic value is not what Jeremy Bentham was concerned with. He was not interested in the question of what counts as cultural value, but rather in the more fundamental question of whether culture has any value at all to a project of enlightenment. For Bentham, the answer to this question turned on the issue of a change in the social meaning of taste from enjoyment to refinement. He opposed this turn from enjoyment to refinement by showing that the ambition to obtain knowledge about the beautiful becomes irrelevant when we examine our predilections.

An opportunity to observe a contrast between Bentham's unrefined enlightenment and current relationships between the 'central management' and 'self-management' of culture was provided by the display of Bentham's auto-icon in a major art exhibition *Like Life: Sculpture, Color and the Body (1300–Now)*, curated by Luke Syson and Sheena Wagstaff, which ran from 21 March to 22 July 2018 at the Met Breuer museum in New York. While Bentham's auto-icon has been the subject of artworks by Marcel Broodthaers and Luc Tuymans, in this exhibition it was being used as part of an exercise in practical aesthetics that defined realism in sculpture, using objects from different eras that were more or less 'Like Life', ranging from Duane Hanson's sculpture 'Housepainter I' (1984) that might easily be mistaken for a living person, to Charles Ray's 'Aluminum Girl' (2003), an all-white three-quarters sized female nude that juxtaposes extreme representational detail with classical conventions of sculpture. Comments on the auto-icon in the exhibition catalogue placed it in the cross-hairs of a debate on the relationship between art and verisimilitude, noting that the wax head of Bentham (by Jacques Talrich, a French military surgeon, later anatomical wax modeller for the Faculté de Médecine in Paris) 'combines the conventions of portraiture and the acute realism available through wax modelling'.[61]

In her essay in the catalogue for 'Like Life', the exhibition's co-curator Sheena Wagstaff referred to the 'aesthetic shock' that was brought about by the discovery of the polychrome characteristics of classical sculpture, which signalled the literal presence of the body in the realm of art. If the intention of the curators of 'Like Life' had been to challenge our understanding of sculpture by including Bentham's auto-icon alongside Duane Hanson, Charles Ray and a copy of Philippe Curtius's mechanical waxwork *Sleeping Beauty* (1765, remade 1989) loaned from Madame Tussauds, it seems to have worked. In *The New York Review of Books*, James Fenton argued that the exhibition had succeeded in drawing our attention to 'a kind of perceptual trick played on us by the history of taste'[62] in which any sculpture that is coloured is perceived to have lower cultural value. This did not, however, make everyone entirely comfortable with what was on display – in a review for *The New Yorker*, Peter Schjeldahl said that he was 'torn between praising it [the exhibition] as visionary … and reporting it as a mugging to the taste police'.[63] Another review by Ben Davis on *Artnet* went so far as to suggest that the exhibition was courting a new kind of taste based on a much older model of the 'Wunderkammer' or cabinet of curiosities: 'The sensibility proposed by "Like Life" is a taste for the Curious – or whatever you call the thrill you get from seeing philosopher Jeremy Bentham's preserved corpse, propped up in a glass box.'[64] This last comment on the 'Like Life' exhibition indicates the necessity of more clearly identifying Bentham's challenge to aesthetics, the nature of his commitment to realism and his opposition to distinctions of taste. This challenge is not about broadening our cultural outlook, so that the thrill of seeing Bentham propped up in a glass box can bring us from the specialized aesthetic realms of the terror of the sublime or the refined sensibility of taste to arrive at mere goggle-eyed curiosity. We have to go one step further and put curiosity in the service of utility. Within the panopticon, as Bentham remarks, curiosity can be put to good use, because the structure of the apparatus means that an inclination towards looking out of the window is necessarily transformed into the business of inspection. Outside the panopticon, however, if you are feeling curious about Bentham's preserved corpse in an exhibition, what you are seeing is Bentham as he appears within your personal cultural itinerary. Within this self-managed cultural itinerary, your commitment to the value of seeing things in your own way is very clear, and, moreover, is supported by the central management and the curatorial agency of an exhibition such as 'Like Life'.[65] Your relationship to utility, however, is obscure. Staring at Bentham's auto-icon in an exhibition would tell you very little about Bentham's challenge to the arts. On the other hand, noticing how, in *Gin Lane* and *Beer Street*, Hogarth makes predilection both the subject of his art and an anchor for the social role of art in general tells you what this challenge is all about.

Notes

1 One place from which to chart this shift of emphasis in British aesthetics is through the influence of the Abbé Dubos, whose 'Réflexions critiques sur la poésie et sur la peinture', first published in 1719, was acknowledged by David Hume. See Jones, 1982, 97, where Jones argues for the debt Hume's essays on taste owe to Dubos: '[for Dubos] the role of reason is to justify the verdict of sentiment by determining the causes of our pleasure; tasks that are properly undertaken by critics who engage in discussion and analysis'.

2 Costelloe, 2013, 220, 227.

3 See Thomas Babington Macaulay's comments on the dangers of cultural 'levelling' from Benthamism in his article 'Mill's Essay on Government: Utilitarian Logic and Politics', (Macaulay, 1829, 159–89, 183) 'The civilized part of the world has now nothing to fear from the hostility of savage nations. … But is it possible that institutions may be established which, without the help of earthquake, of famine, of pestilence, or of the foreign sword, may undo the work of so many ages of wisdom and glory, and gradually sweep away taste, literature, science, commerce, manufactures, everything but the rude arts necessary to the support of animal life?'

4 See Arnold, 1869, 28–9: 'So, after hearing Bentham cried loudly up as the renovator of modern society, and Bentham's mind and ideas proposed as the rulers of our future, I open the *Deontology*. There I read: "While Xenophon was writing his history and Euclid teaching geometry, Socrates and Plato were talking nonsense under pretence of talking wisdom and morality. This morality of theirs consisted in words; this wisdom of theirs was the denial of matters known to every man's experience." From the moment of reading that, I am delivered from the bondage of Bentham! the fanaticism of his adherents can touch me no longer; I feel the inadequacy of his mind and ideas for being the rule of human society, for perfection.'

5 Scruton, 1987, 604.

6 Marx, trans. Fowkes, 1976, 758.

7 Malcolm Quinn, 2017.

8 Anon, 1825, 335–6, 336.

9 John Neal, 1830, 44. For an assessment of Neal as a fellow traveller of the Benthamites, see King, 1966, 47–65.

10 Bentham, ed. Schofield *et al.*, 2014.

11 Bentham, ed. Schofield *et al.*, 2014, 4.

12 Bentham, ed. Schofield *et al.*, 2014, 4n.

13 Bentham, 1825, 209.

14 Defined as 'an immediate gratification to the sexual appetite'. Bentham, ed. Schofield *et al.*, 2014, 51.

15 Ibid. See also n. 1, 51, where it is suggested that the idea of sexual attraction as a sixth sense may have arisen with the Comte de Buffon's description of sexuality as a sense that, although intermittent, commands the others senses when it acts.

16 Luhmann, 1993, 763–82, 764.

17 Bentham, ed. Schofield *et al.*, 2014, 142.

18 Bentham, ed. Christie, 2017, 524.

19 Harrison, 1983, 5.

20 Bentham, 1825, 17–18.

21 Williford, 1975, 167–76, 168. Willford's interpretation of this passage in *The Rationale of Reward* is later echoed by Campos Boralevi (1984, 9).

22 Helvétius, 1825, 413.

23 Montesquieu, 1771, 141.

24 See Montesquieu, 1795, Vol. 2, Book 7, Chapter 16, 167–8: 'Les *Samnites* avoient une coutume, qui, dans une petite république, et sur-tout dans la situation où étoit la leur, devoit produire d'admirables effets. On assembloit tous les jeunes gens, et on les jugeoit. Celui qui étoit déclaré le meilleur de tous, prenoit pour sa femme la fille qu'il vouloit ; celui qui avoit les suffrages après lui choisissoit encore ; et ainsi de suite. Il étoit admirable de ne regarder entre les biens des garçons que les belles qualités & les services rendus à la patrie. Celui qui étoit le plus riche de ces sortes de biens choisissoit une fille dans toute la nation. L'amour, la beauté, la chasteté, la vertu, la naissance, les richesses même, tout cela étoit, pour ainsi dire, la dot de la vertu. Il seroit difficile d'imaginer une récompense plus noble, plus grande, moins à charge à un petit état, plus capable d'agir sur l'un & l'autre sexe.' Helvétius's ostensible note on this passage (n. 1, 167) is 'Are women a flock without liberty and inclination?' which has led David Wooton to argue that 'If this is indeed Helvetius, then D. W. Smith (the doyen of Helvetius scholarship) is mistaken to follow Diderot in thinking Helvetius's 'sexual ethics were advocated entirely from the male point of view', although De l'esprit and De l'homme are open to this interpretation.' Wootton, 2000, 307–36, 314.

25 Helvétius argues that, while taste can be defined as what merits the esteem of mankind, there is no universal taste common to all ages and countries. He proposes that taste as 'the more particular knowledge of what pleases the public in a certain nation' can be understood in two ways – as an informal daily practice that enables anyone to judge the merits of a particular work such as a theatrical production, and as a rational taste, grounded in 'long study both of the public taste, and of the art or science in which a person pretends to the title of a man of taste'. Helvétius, 1825, 413.

26 Bentham, ed. Božovič, 1995, 94.

27 Bentham, ed. Božovič, 1995, 45.

28 Bowring, 1843, 181.

29 Bentham, ed. Božovič, 1995, 83.

30 See Foucault, trans. Sheridan, 1975, 199–200: 'All the mechanisms of power which, even today, are disposed around the abnormal individual, to brand him and to alter him, are composed of those two forms [the binary division of a population and the differential distribution of individuals] from which they distantly derive. Bentham's *Panopticon* is the architectural figure of this composition.'

31 Foucault, trans. Sheridan, 1975, 203. Foucault compares Bentham's panopticon with the centralized structure of Louis Le Vau's (1612–70) menagerie at Versailles, an octagonal central pavilion with a viewing balcony, surrounded by seven enclosures: 'one finds in the programme of the Panopticon a similar concern with individualizing observation, with characterisation and classification, with the analytical arrangement of space.'

32 Bentham, ed. Božovič, 1995, 31.

33 Today Online, 2018.

34 Bentham, ed. Božovič, 1995, 91.

35 Bentham, ed. Božovič, 1995, 90. Bentham notes that he has forgotten whether this reference occurs in *The Spectator* or the *Tatler*. The reference is to 'the received Opinion, that a Lion will not hurt a Virgin' in *The Spectator*, no. 13, 15 March 1711.

36 Addison, *The Spectator*, no. 29, 3 April 1711.

37 Addison, *The Spectator*, no. 29, 3 April 1711.

38 Bentham, 1825, 210.

39 Mill, 1863, 14.

40 Bentham, 1825, 210.

41 Bentham, 1825.
42 Bentham, 1825, 209.
43 Bentham, 1825, 9.
44 See Wheatley, ed. Grint, 2015, 10: 'My bed room is a small oblong chamber; the bed such a one as we used to call a crib, at school. One side of this my room is filled up with bundles of printed papers. On the walls are hung portraits of Shakespear, Milton, Dryden, Gower, Cowley, Ben Jonson, and Waller, also the plates of Hogarth's Hudibras.'
45 Michael Quinn, 2017, 1, 11–33, 28.
46 UC lxxxvii. 66.
47 Bindman, 1997.
48 Hogarth, ed. Paulson, 1997.
49 Hogarth, ed. Paulson, 1997, 122.
50 Hogarth, ed. Paulson, 1997, 83.
51 Hogarth, ed. Paulson, 1997, 58–9.
52 Hogarth, ed. Paulson, 1997, p. xxxiii.
53 Uglow, 1997, 525.
54 Hogarth, ed. Paulson, 1997, 18.
55 Komisaruk, 2004, 369–97, 390.
56 See Fry, 1934, 41–2: 'one cannot help wishing that he [Hogarth] had paid more attention to cultivating his own very genuine gifts as a painter and less to improving other people. For I think his influence on British art has been bad upon the whole. It has tended to sanction a disparagement of painting as a pure art – has tended to make artists think that they must justify themselves by conveying valuable, or important, or moral ideas. … It has obscured the truth that art has its own specific function, that it conveys experiences that are sui generis, not to be defined or valued by anything outside – experiences which have immense, but quite inexplicable, value to those who are sensitive to them.'
57 Bentham, trans. Dumont, 1914, 78.
58 Bentham, ed Schofield *et al.*, 2014, 77.
59 O'Sullivan, 2016.
60 See 'Building a user-generated museum: a conversation with Alistair Hudson': https://civilsocietyfutures.org/building-a-user-generated-museum-a-conversation-with-alistair-hudson/ [accessed 11 January 2019]. For an extensive discussion of Alistair Hudson's position on 'usership' in museums of art, see Gogarty, 2017, 117–32, 121.
61 Kumar, ed. Syson *et al.*, 2018, 100–7, 105.
62 Fenton, 2018.
63 Schjeldahl, 2018.
64 Davis, 2018.
65 In his foreword to the catalogue, D.H. Weiss, President and CEO of The Metropolitan Museum of Art says '*Like Life: Sculpture, Color, and The Body* focuses on sculptures from the fourteenth century to the present, juxtaposing objects from different eras to test our preconceptions about the human form, the canon of Western art, and our understanding of ourselves.' (Kumar, 2018, p. vi.)

References

Addison, J. *The Spectator*, no. 13, 15 March 1711.

Addison, J. *The Spectator*, no. 29, 3 April 1711.

Anon. 'The Rationale of Reward: By Jeremy Bentham', *Political Examiner*, 30 May 1825, 335–6.

Arnold, M. *Culture and Anarchy*. London: Smith, Elder and Co., 1869.

Bentham, J. 'On the Influence of Time and Place in Matters of Legislation', in *The Works of Jeremy Bentham,* ed. John Bowring, 11 vols., Vol. I. Edinburgh: William Tait, 1838–43.

Bentham, J. *Bentham's Theory of Legislation*, trans. Étienne Dumont. London: Humphrey Milford, 1914.

Bentham, J. *Of Sexual Irregularities, and Other Writings on Sexual Morality (CW)*, eds. P. Schofield, C. Pease-Watkin, and M. Quinn. Oxford: Clarendon Press, 2014.

Bentham, J. *The Correspondence of Jeremy Bentham, Volume 3, January 1781 to October 1788 (CW)*, ed. I.R. Christie. London: UCL Press, 2017.
Bentham, J. *The Panopticon Writings*, ed. M. Božovič. London and New York: Verso, 1995.
Bentham, J. *The Rationale of Reward*. London: John Hunt, 1825.
Bindman, D. *Hogarth and His Times: Serious Comedy*. London: British Museum Press, 1997.
Campos Boralevi, L. *Bentham and the Oppressed*. Berlin and New York: Walter de Gruyter, 1984.
Costelloe, T.M. *The British Aesthetic Tradition from Shaftesbury to Wittgenstein*. Cambridge: Cambridge University Press, 2013.
Davis, B. 'With 'Like Life', the Met Breuer Has Arrived at Something New, Paradoxical, and Strangely of Its Time', *Artnet*, 1 May 2018: https://news.artnet.com/exhibitions/like-life-met-breuer-1275932 [accessed 5 July 2018].
Fenton, J. 'A Spitting Image', *The New York Review of Books*, 19 July 2018: https://www.nybooks.com/articles/2018/07/19/sculpture-bodies-spitting-image/ [accessed 22 July 2018].
Foucault, Michel. *Discipline and Punish, The Birth of the Prison*, trans. A. Sheridan. London: Allen Lane, 1975.
Fry, R. *Reflections on British Painting*. London: Faber, 1934.
Gogarty, L.A. '"Usefulness" in Contemporary Art and Politics', *Third Text* 31:1 (2017): 117–32.
Harrison, R. *Bentham*. London and New York: Routledge, 1983.
Helvétius, C.A. *De L'Esprit, or Essays on the Mind and its Several Faculties*. London: Thomas Davison, 1825.
Hogarth, W. *The Analysis of Beauty*, ed. R. Paulson. New Haven, CT: Yale University Press, 1997.
Hudson, A. 'Building a user-generated museum: a conversation with Alistair Hudson', *Civil Society Futures*: https://civilsocietyfutures.org/building-a-user-generated-museum-a-conversation-with-alistair-hudson/ [accessed 11 January 2019].
Jones, P. *Hume's Sentiments: Their Ciceronian and French Context*. Edinburgh: Edinburgh University Press, 1982.
King, P.J. 'John Neal as a Benthamite', *The New England Quarterly* 39:1 (1966): 47–65.
Komisaruk, A. 'Pygmalion's "Wanton Kind of Chace": Hogarth, Rowlandson and the "Line of Beauty"', *Studies in Eighteenth-Century Culture* 33 (2004): 369–97.
Kumar, B. 'Likeness', in *Like Life: Sculpture, Color, and The Body*, eds. L. Syson, S. Wagstaff, E. Bowyer, and B. Kumar. New Haven, CT: Yale University Press, 2018.
Luhmann, N. 'Deconstruction as Second-Order Observing', *New Literary History* 24:4 (1993): 763–82.
Macaulay, T.B. 'Mill's Essay on Government: Utilitarian Logic and Politics', *Edinburgh Review* 49 (March 1829): 159–89.
Marx, K. *Capital*, trans. B. Fowkes, Volume I. London: Penguin 1976.
Mill, J.S. *Utilitarianism*. London: Parker, Son and Bourn, 1863.
Montesquieu, *The Complete Works of Montesquieu*, Volume I. London: T. Evans, 1771.
Montesquieu, *Oeuvres Complètes de Montesquieu, Nouvelle Édition, Avec les notes D'Helvétius sur l'ésprit de Lois*. Paris: Pierre Diderot l'aîne, II, 1795.
Neal, J., ed. *Principles of Legislation, from the MS. of Jeremy Bentham; Bencher of Lincoln's Inn. By M. Dumont*. Boston: Wells and Lily, 1830.
O'Sullivan, F. 'Bob Dylan's Nobel Prize Might Be the Most Swedish Thing Ever', *City Lab*, 13 October 2016: https://www.citylab.com/design/2016/10/dylans-nobel-prize-might-be-the-most-swedish-thing-ever/504017/ [accessed 13 January 2019].
Quinn, Malcolm. 'Jeremy Bentham on Liberty of Taste', *History of European Ideas* 43:6 (2017): 614–27.
Quinn, Michael. 'Jeremy Bentham, Choice Architect: Law, Indirect Legislation, and the Context of Choice', *History of European Ideas* 43:1 (2017): 11–33.
Schjeldahl, P. 'Living Color' a review of 'Like Life' at the Met Breuer, *The New Yorker*, 2 April 2018.
Scruton, R. 'Modern Philosophy and the Neglect of Aesthetics', *Times Literary Supplement*, 5 June 1987.
Today. 'Google's AI beats doctors at spotting eye disease', *Today Online*, 14 August 2018: https://www.todayonline.com/world/googles-ai-beats-doctors-spotting-eye-disease [accessed 4 January 2018].
Uglow, J. *Hogarth: A Life and a World*. London: Faber, 1997.
Wheatley, George. *A Visit (in 1831) to Jeremy Bentham*, ed. K. Grint. London: Bentham Project, UCL, 2015.

Williford, M. 'Bentham on the Rights of Women', *Journal of the History of Ideas* 36:1 (1975): 167–76.
Wootton, D. 'Helvétius: From Radical Enlightenment to Revolution', *Political Theory* 28:3 (2000): 307–36.

Chapter 9

Jeremy Bentham's principle of utility and taste: An alternative approach to aesthetics in two stages

Benjamin Bourcier

In the first part of this chapter, I explain how Bentham places the liberty of taste among the fundamental political liberties that all good government should guarantee. His argument relies upon an extensive critique of the principle of asceticism. In the second part, I explain that the political defence of the liberty of taste raises the question of its relation to private ethics. Since Bentham's principle of utility assumes a continuity between public and private ethics, how should we understand the place of the liberty of taste in Bentham's private ethics? Since private ethics aims to explain how an individual can contribute to the greatest happiness when not subjected to coercion, I demonstrate that liberty of taste is moderated by the educational role of the private deontologist.

1. Why taste matters to politics: The liberty of taste as a political liberty

Bentham is intimately associated with the principle of utility. All sentient beings are motivated by a desire for pleasure and an aversion to pain, and this fact is recognized by Bentham's principle of utility or the greatest happiness of the greatest number. In *An Introduction to the Principles of Morals and Legislation* (hereafter *IPML*), Bentham famously states:

> Nature has placed mankind under the governance of two sovereign masters, *pain* and *pleasure*. It is for them alone to point out what we ought to do, as well as to determine what we shall do. On the one hand the standard of right and wrong, on the other the chain of causes and effects, are fastened to their throne. They govern us in all we do, in all we say, in all we think: every effort we can make to throw off their subjection, will serve but to demonstrate and confirm it. In words a man may pretend to abjure their empire: but in reality he will remain subject to it all the while. The *principle of utility* recognizes this subjection, and assumes it for the foundation of that system, the object of which is to rear the fabric of felicity by the hands of reason and of law. Systems which attempt to question it, deal in sounds instead of sense, in caprice instead of reason, in darkness instead of light.[1]

For Bentham, the principle of utility is the only principle that grounds moral thinking on an objective assessment of pleasures and pains and at the same time provides guidance for reforming legal codes and public institutions for the sake of the greatest happiness of the greatest number.

In contrast, Bentham unifies in one phrase – 'making war upon pleasures'[2] – the opposite idea that characterizes misrule and bad government. 'Making war upon pleasures' means that some groups or governments prevent, forbid, punish and attempt to abolish common and innocent pleasures and, therefore, set aside the liberty of taste. 'Making war upon pleasures' can take different political forms, each of them implying different kinds and degrees of pains and negative experiences, from individual mischiefs to social domination, violence and fear for the preservation of one's life. Yet they all have in common a violation of a political liberty, that is of each individual's 'equal right to happiness'.[3] Hence, Bentham's approach to aesthetics and tastes initiates a radical political turn. Liberty of taste is an issue of entitlement and the government must ensure respect for, and equal treatment of, each individual's tastes, that is the 'aptitude or disposition to derive pleasure' from some state of affairs.[4] Liberty of taste is political; it means that the government should never impose one particular conception of happiness on all, and that the liberty of taste is necessary for achieving the greatest happiness of the greatest number. Bentham's alternative approach to aesthetics and taste is conceptualized as a political problem and rejects, therefore, the autonomy of aesthetics.

1.1. What is 'making war upon pleasures'?

In order to trace the origin of Bentham's opposition to the autonomy of aesthetics, it is necessary to start with his understanding of pleasure. He considers all pleasures to be good, whatever their source, nature, extent and social implications (even if they counteract social norms, traditions, religious beliefs or customs). Indeed, regarding moral evaluation, he argues that the quantity of pleasure is the only criterion that matters. This is evident from the fourth chapter of *IPML* where he explains that:

> To a person considered by *himself*, the value of a pleasure or pain considered *by itself*, will be greater or less, according to the four following circumstances:
>
> 1. Its *intensity*.
> 2. Its *duration*.
> 3. Its *certainty* or *uncertainty*.
> 4. Its *propinquity* or *remoteness*.[5]

These circumstances constitute the value of a pleasure or a pain. The degree of intensity in the experience, the quantity of time (duration), the epistemic quality (certainty or uncertainty), and the point in time (propinquity or remoteness) together indicate the value of a pleasure or a pain. They form the essential components through which one can evaluate the tendency of an act. Bentham's primary objective is to affirm that quantity is the only legitimate rational criteria by which to assess the moral value of pleasure. All that matters is the quantity of pleasure, which means that no other criterion carries any normative value. This is precisely the point that Bentham reaffirms in *Not Paul, but Jesus*:

> According to the principle of utility, taking in its entirety the whole mass of pleasure in question – presence or, in case of absence, propinquity and certainty, i.e. probability, being given or out of the question – quantity is the sole measure of value: considered in themselves all other circumstances and incidents, shape and source, for example are regarded as matters of indifference.[6]

Since the only legitimate moral criterion is the quantity of pleasure, there are no bad pleasures – all pleasures are good. Dismissing certain tastes as illegitimate has the effect of reducing the quantity of pleasure and hence is, by definition, wrong. In his writings on sexual morality and religious asceticism, Bentham criticizes limitations placed on the liberty of taste. He notes that sexual pleasures and the common pleasures of drinking and eating are the first pleasures to be banned by the religious ascetic: 'The pleasures against which the most unrelenting war has thus been kept up – the pleasures which have borne the principal marks of this hostility – have been the pleasures of the *table* and the pleasures of the *bed*.'[7] Bentham devotes many pages to analysing the different sorts of pleasures of eating, drinking and sex. For example, in his essay 'Sextus', he describes two modes of sexual conduct, terming one 'regular' in reference to what is normal under prevailing social conventions, and the other 'irregular' insofar as it violates these social rules. He then lists eight different cases of sexual irregularities.[8]

In describing these different types of pleasures, Bentham is saying that they all count in a positive way, and is highlighting the wrongness of discounting them, such as when some social groups or government in general forbids the exercise of them.[9] The immediate consequence of the prohibition of these pleasures is the creation of mischief through the loss of pleasure. To deprive people of pleasure is to act in an anti-utilitarian way because, at best, it is lowering the quantity of pleasure and, at worst, it is creating pain. Bentham connects 'mischief' to a loss of pleasure as much as to the actual creation of pain: 'Danger for losing Happiness arises: 1st. From events at large: or 2dly. From Actions. Unhappiness from events is stiled Calamity. Unhappiness from action is stiled Mischief.'[10] The epithet of 'mischief' describes the actions, policies and decisions of a government that forbids certain pleasures based on a particular moral, political and religious ideology. A government that creates mischief ruins the expectations of individuals, which often leads to pain and ends by 'making war upon pleasures'. A bad government systematically violates the equal consideration of each individual's right to happiness and the fundamental liberty of taste in the name of one particular idea of happiness. The wrongness of this 'war upon pleasures' is the trademark of tyrannical or despotic government.

1.2. The politics of taste: How and why?

Bentham's defence of the liberty of taste appears in its political dimension when he critically analyses discourses and theories (religions, philosophies, art critics and so on) that value pleasures on the basis of non-utilitarian criteria (such as purity/impurity; good taste/bad taste; fine arts/popular arts; intellectual pleasures/pleasures of the body and so on). Bentham's recently published texts on sexual morality and religious asceticism[11] show his proactive criticism of all ideologies that, for different political, moral or religious reasons, establish a politics of taste that forbids some tastes and pleasures, lowers the quantity of happiness in a society and imposes specific tastes on all. In these writings, the social function of the politics of taste is the central concern of Bentham's criticism.

Indeed, Bentham thinks that the ideological role of such politics of taste is to support the interests of the dominant class, in particular to strengthen their privileges and other social advantages. Behind the prohibition of pleasure imposed by the ruling few always lies some form of hypocrisy.[12] The first dimension of this hypocrisy is the pretence of acting virtuously, which is an essential component of the discourse of the ruling few. The hypocrite expresses his unconditional love and respect for the objective moral standard that guides his virtuous conduct. The claim of virtue plays an important function in justifying the prohibition of certain pleasures. The second dimension of this hypocrisy is that the 'love of virtue' benefits the political ambition of the ruling few, that is, the promotion of the interests of their own class based on the sacrifice of the interests of the subject many. The politics of taste always aims to serve the interests of the privileged class, and not the moral and political ends ostensibly declared. To address the liberty of taste as a political issue implies, for Bentham, the exposure of the hypocrisy of the privileged and its evil consequences.

Bentham identifies the principle of asceticism as the main source of the hypocrisy of the ruling few. Recent scholarship has demonstrated the key role played by advocates of the principle of asceticism in the prohibition of pleasure, that is, in prohibiting actions that others (and possibly themselves) find pleasurable and yet harm no one.[13] Bentham attacks the moral and political implications of the prohibition of pleasure based on the principle of asceticism. In *IPML*, he defines the principle of asceticism as follows:

> By the principle of asceticism I mean that principle, which, like the principle of utility, approves or disapproves of any action, according to the tendency which it appears to have to augment or diminish the happiness of the party whose interest is in question; but in an inverse manner: approving of actions in as far as they tend to diminish his happiness; disapproving of them in as far as they tend to augment it.[14]

Bentham describes two sorts of proponents of asceticism: the philosophical ascetics (the Stoics) and the religious ascetics.[15] Both praise virtue and have a strong commitment to the love of virtue. Ascetics make 'war upon pleasures' because they evaluate common pleasure according to anti-utilitarian criteria (purity/impurity, intellectual/physical, good taste/bad taste and so on). These criteria introduce confusion in the way people conceive of pleasure. More precisely, Bentham thinks that ascetics erect their personal tastes (disgusts, aversions and preferences) into an objective standard of taste. In this process, Bentham identifies the 'love of virtue' as a motive that plays a crucial role in building the standard of good taste and hence the pretended standard of morality. He explains that the 'love of virtue' is not a condition of real virtue; it is nothing less than an attachment to one particular motive and source of pleasure, namely the 'love of reputation'.[16] The attachment to the 'love of virtue' leads the ruling few to value what they conceive to be in their interest as intrinsically good and as the expression of the standard of right and wrong itself. In a discussion of the nature of antipathy, but just as relevant to the nature of asceticism, Bentham argues that, by displaying a hatred of what they consider to be vice, they demonstrate their love for the opposite and correspondent virtue'. Hence, the 'love of virtue' is a means by which the ruling few promote their particular interest.[17]

The motive of 'love of virtue' leads some privileged persons to implement the 'war upon pleasures'. Bentham looks more closely at the social status of these persons, namely members of the aristocratic or dominant class, religious authorities, poets, philosophers, and art critics. Their 'love of virtue' pushes them to develop criticisms against what they consider the crude pleasures of the poor. The authority of their social position combines with the ambition and particular interest of their own class and thereby produces a conflict with the interest of the subject many. They deploy aesthetical, metaphysical, religious and ethical considerations in their discourses in order to legitimate their vocabulary about taste ('pure', 'sublime', 'delicacy' and so on). Catholic authorities, for instance, consider that the love of God demands the rejection of the pleasures of the flesh, while art critics and poets claim that the 'purity' of 'higher' pleasures demands the avoidance of 'lower' pleasures. Ultimately, for Bentham, these forms of hypocrisy translate into an abuse of power, namely when rules and laws enforce the politics of taste.[18]

Bentham's alternative approach to taste and aesthetics moves in a different direction from most of the moral and political theorists of his time.[19] I will now explain how Bentham's opposition to Rousseau further demonstrates how the liberty of taste as a political liberty is a radical thesis that aims to avoid all temptation to moralize aesthetics, taste and art. Rousseau wrote a famously strong criticism of the theatre in his letter to D'Alembert,[20] commenting on the vices and political danger that are promoted by the pleasures of amusement. Rousseau condemns the establishment of a theatre in Geneva and expresses worries about the deleterious moral effects produced by the fine arts. For Rousseau, the theatre, like other fine arts, necessarily leads to the corruption of the moral sense and the hearts of the people. Following a theme largely developed in his *First Discourse* on the Arts and Sciences,[21] he argues that amusement will lead to the corruption of morals and will condemn Geneva to the same tragic destiny that Egypt, Greece and Rome had experienced in ancient history. The progress of the arts contributes to the loss of the authentic morality of human nature. Rousseau considers aesthetic pleasures to be a symptom of the civic and moral regress of the citizen and the people and, therefore, that amusement is not an innocent pleasure, but the symptom of a much more acute danger for the political community. Hence, he opposes the liberty of taste. In *Preparatory Principles*, Bentham criticizes Rousseau's view:

> Every amusement, says Mr Rousseau, that is useless is an evil to a being to whom life is so short and time so pretious.
>
> For the word Amusement, I suppose, we may, without imputing any signification to his words different from what he intended they should have, render into pleasure. By the word unprofitable, or, as it is in the original, useless, we may render unproductive of other pleasures. According to this interpretation, then, what Mr Rousseau wishes us to understand is that every pleasure that is not productive of other pleasures is an evil.
>
> If this be the meaning of the proposition, one may venture, I think, boldly to deny the truth of it. We may venture to say, on the contrary, that every pleasure, although unproductive of other pleasures, so as it be not productive of any pains that are more than equivalent to it, is good.
>
> That a sophism like this, a sophism that carries on it the point of austere virtue, should have passed upon Mr Rousseau is not very extraordinary. What surprizes one is that a philosopher of such cool discernment as Mr Marmontel, a critic who has taken it into consideration for the express purpose of combating the conclusions drawn from it, should not have ventured to contest

> it. Such is sometimes the power of popular prejudice over the strongest minds.
>
> Instead of denying the truth of the general proposition that an amusement that is useless is in itself an evil, he endeavours to elude the force of it. He alledges that, though the particular amusement in question, admitting it to be an evil, should be excluded from the place in question, another amusement equally an evil would fill its place. $2^{\text{dly.}}$ That the amusement in question is not useless. $3^{\text{dly.}}$ That if it were, it would be difficult to bring men to give it up. $4^{\text{thly.}}$ That allowing it to be an evil, that is to the community: yet if the community allows of it, there is no harm done.[22]

In this passage, Bentham not only explains the extent to which Rousseau is wrong to consider amusement as an evil, but also demonstrates how he perfectly illustrates the hypocrisy of the modern opponent to pleasure and the theorist who is 'making war upon pleasures'. Contrary to what Rousseau states, amusement is not an evil, but a good, which takes its source in a subjective preference for a particular taste (perhaps the theatre or music) and should be respected and considered as equal to any other taste producing the same quantity of pleasure. The love of amusement, like all pleasures related to the fine arts, are enjoyed by privileged people who are more difficult to satisfy than people from other classes. However, amusement is not a 'higher' and better taste. All tastes are equal insofar as they tend to produce the same quantity of pleasure. For Bentham, each individual should be left free to enjoy whatever taste gives him pleasure. If some individual's taste leads him to enjoy 'push-pin' while another prefers music by Handel (like Bentham himself), then so be it and government should not place any limitation on such a choice. The equal consideration of each person's taste is at the heart of Bentham's defence of liberty of taste as a political liberty. Governments, therefore, should not impose constraints on the tastes of the people.

The pleasures of sex should not form an object of consideration for government. All pleasures matter and should not be repressed except insofar as they produce greater pain. According to Bentham's defence of the liberty of taste, there is no pleasure derived from taste that, quantity aside, is right or good, while another is wrong or evil. Moreover, there is no other legitimate source of moral praise or blame than the balance of pleasure or pain produced. In this sense, each individual is free to pursue the sort of pleasure he likes. An implication of Bentham's defence of liberty of taste is that the state respects the tastes and pleasures of all individuals. The happiness of society consists in the aggregate happiness of each of its members. Consequently, the liberty of taste gives rise to an important political truth. There is no possible justification for a government enforcing or prescribing one particular conception of happiness on its members. Conceived as such, the liberty of taste is a key-stone in Bentham's political thought and is necessary to the promotion of the greatest happiness of the greatest number.

2. How Bentham treats aesthetics and taste in private ethics

Given that Bentham's principle of utility assumes a continuity between public and private ethics, his defence of liberty of taste in the political sphere must have implications for the individual acting privately. Bentham's defence of the liberty of taste, as I have shown, demands that a utilitarian government respect and secure each individual's choice in matters of taste where, to do so, does not result in preponderant harm.[23] What, then, is the role of the private deontologist – the moralist – in relation to such matters? Consideration of utilitarian private ethics raises the question of the relation between utility and taste from a different perspective. For Bentham, the best utilitarian outcome results from the perfect correspondence between an individual's interest and his duty. How, then, can the junction between interests and duty occur in relation to taste? The answer is that, while Bentham rejects any form of coercion on the grounds of aesthetics and taste as a means of promoting virtue, he gives the role of advising and educating individuals as to how they might reap the greatest pleasure from their own choices to the private deontologist.

2.1. Why private ethics is concerned with the liberty of taste

Bentham's 'private ethics' or 'private deontology' aims to show how an individual can reap the most happiness at the least cost. Before examining the relation between aesthetics and private deontology in Bentham's thought, it is worth recalling that by 'deontology' Bentham means ethics or morality, in other words the study of the manner by which happiness is promoted or maximized.[24] He then develops a distinction between 'public deontology' and 'private deontology' where 'private deontology' refers to individual ethics, that is the means by which an individual can, through his own judgment and knowledge, act and live as a utilitarian, in other words create a junction between his interest and his duty.[25]

Bentham scholars have debated the place of 'private deontology' in Bentham's philosophy. Scholars have unanimously condemned the version of *Deontology* produced by John Bowring shortly after Bentham's death. Mack thinks that the book is 'an oversimplified moralist textbook',[26] Baumgardt discards *Deontology* from his analysis of Bentham's ethics[27] and Burns judges it 'the worst book ever written on an important subject'.[28] The more recent *Collected Works* edition of *Deontology*, which attempts to be faithful to Bentham's manuscripts, has permitted a more accurate interpretation of Bentham's views on private ethics. Emmanuelle de Champs argues for a perfect match between private and public deontology,[29] and Ross Harrison and Philip Schofield agree that there is a compatibility between Bentham's general utilitarian thought and his private ethics, even if the latter is less developed.[30] I will follow this reading of Bentham's private ethics. While Bentham develops an original defence of liberty of taste as a political liberty, the aim of 'private ethics' is to address the issue of morality for the individual. Conceived as such, in his 'private deontology' Bentham addresses the relationship between aesthetics and ethics in a different way from that presented in his legislative theory.

2.2. Subjectivism and taste

Bentham's approach to 'private ethics' is grounded in the individual's judgment and the subjective tastes that determine his interests. I begin by explaining Bentham's commitment to subjectivism and its relativist implications. In doing so, I demonstrate how taste is related to 'private ethics'. Bentham recognizes that the individual is the best judge of his own interest: 'Every person is not only the most proper judge, but the only proper judge of what with reference to himself is pleasure: and so in regard to pain.'[31] The individual remains the best authority to judge his own pleasure, and it will be difficult to persuade anyone otherwise, even if experiencing some particular pleasure turns out to be obnoxious in some way.

> The man to whom habit has rendered the use of tobacco a source of gratification, whether in the way of snuffing, smoking or mastication, by nothing that any one can say to him will he be convinced that that taste of his is a bad taste. Let him see that by taking it he inflicts annoyance on those in whose presence he is

> taking it, you may make him abstain from it, but never can you make him in his own mind acknowledge it to be a bad taste.[32]

It is worth emphasizing the point that Bentham is making here. Each individual, according to Bentham, values his interest according to the subjective feelings of pleasure and pain he is experiencing at any given time. If he finds the use of tobacco pleasurable, it makes no sense to tell him that he does not. The individual may abstain, for the sake of not causing annoyance to others, but he will resent the sacrifice of what he considers to be a pleasure. Nevertheless, the possibility for the individual to promote successfully his own happiness relies on a choice of pleasures that will not, in the long run, create greater pain for himself. Bentham's approach to happiness is subjectivist in this sense: if an individual cares for something, then it is because he values positively this pleasure, no matter what others think or no matter what science (or any rational discourse) says about the mischievous consequences likely to ensue after the initial enjoyment of the pleasure. Subjective judgment is the highest authority for each individual's pleasures. This subjectivist approach to well-being and happiness allows Bentham to explain that an individual's taste may change, when he stops deriving pleasure from one source and begins to reap it from another. More precisely, Bentham explains that such changes appear in different situations and involve different aspects. An individual can change his taste, for example, in relation to the fine arts:

> In the case of fine arts, when the object is of a complex nature, by being made to observe this or that circumstance which he had not observed before – this or that feature of defect or excellence which till now had passed unobserved – a man may now and then be made to change his taste.[33]

His taste changes because he has been shown a new dimension that modifies the disposition from which an individual derives pleasure from the experience in question. Bentham describes a second situation. The individual changes his taste because the pleasure he once experienced from an object or act has evaporated and it now causes him pain. Bentham develops this idea in *Deontology* with the example of wine or food:

> At an early part of his life, for instance, a man had a taste for wine in general, or for a particular species of food. Finding it disagree

> with his constitution, little by little the uneasiness attendant on the gratification of the desire has become so frequent in experience, and so continually present in idea, that the idea of the future but near and certain pain has gained such strength as to overpower the impression of the present pleasure – or, what comes to the same thing, the idea of it at the moment preceding that at which, but for the idea of the attendant pain, it would have been reaped. *In fine*, the idea of the consequent and greater though more distant pain has operated as an extinguisher upon the idea of the lesser though immediate pleasure.[34]

In this example, the balance between a present pleasure and a distant pain provokes a change in the individual's taste. His 'aptitude or disposition to derive pleasure from an object' or taste changes.[35] His revised assessment of the likely balance of pain over pleasure, evaluated from the point of view of the distant future, has provided him with a reason to change his taste.

In both cases, we have an example of how an individual's taste can change over time. Given that individual tastes are contingent, Bentham's subjectivist account of value here encounters the problem of moral relativism. If individual tastes are not permanent and can be subject to change, even radical change, it may be objected, how can the very project of deontology – the development of a private morality based on the principle of utility – be possible? How can Bentham advocate the liberty of taste and at the same time avoid some sort of private moral anarchy, where the individual escapes all utilitarian moral duty bar that imposed by the legislature? As I will explain in response, Bentham adopts an educationalist strategy to solve the problem and to escape the relativist threat. Bentham's approach to individual ethics relies on the ability of the private 'deontologist' or moralist to guide and educate the individual in his efforts to live a happy life.

2.3. 'Private ethics' and the role of the deontologist

'Private deontology' is not concerned with the question about how an individual can maximize his own happiness through his own efforts alone. This is because his tastes are unstable, the social influences to which he is subjected so strong, and his ignorance of individual circumstances so great, that he can never on his own achieve his own greatest happiness. Doing so on one's own is illusory because an individual's interests cannot be separated from the wider interests prevalent in society. This insight requires the inclusion of considerations relative to taste, understood in Bentham's sense as the choice of pleasures, in the general conception of individual ethics itself. For Bentham, in 'private deontology', the advice of the moralist is necessary to support the individual in understanding how to join his interest with his duty. The moralist's role demonstrates that Bentham has an educationalist conception of individual ethics.

> Moralist – his function, proper and actual. In regard to ends: 1. So far as man's self-regarding interest alone is concerned, to strive to engage him to prefer greater remote to less present interest. 2. So far as the interest of the community is concerned, to engage each man in his pursuit of self-regarding interest, to pay as much regard as possible to the social interest.[36]

Hence, 'private deontology' requires an individual to consider his interest overall. An individual, however, is vulnerable to many influences that emanate from society. What does this mean for the deontologist's role if society is always, in some sense, participating in the formation of an individual's interest?

> What then is the business of the Deontologist? In every instance to bring out of their obscurity, out of the neglect in which they have hitherto in so large a proportion been buried, the points of coincidence to the extent of which extra-regarding interest is connected and has by the hands of nature been identified with self-regarding interest: and this in such sort and with such effect that by the alliance thus formed, by this conjunct kind of interest, the force of self-regarding in those shapes in which it is purely self-regarding is commonly already in use, to be outweighed and overpowered. In this way it will, it is believed, be found that for this species of artist there is no want of work. Nature has provided no inconsiderable quantity of useful work which as yet remains unattempted, and thus it will be his own fault if this office be a sinecure.[37]

The deontologist works by refocusing the individual's self-regarding interest so that it allies with his social situation and duty. The deontologist is not a despotic commander who obliges the individual to do his duty, but more an auxiliary or a companion that helps him refocus his conception of his own interest. Having a better understanding of his own interest matters for the individual because thinking more deeply about his pleasures and their conformity to his duty will lead him to revise his pleasures and hence his conduct. The moralist can only play his role as an educator by pointing out the relevant consequences in terms of pain and pleasure that will ensue to the individual from the various choices that he is in a position to make:

> Means the deontologist can have no other to work with but pleasures and pains. In so far as they are not of his creation, they will be suggested as likely of themselves to result from the supposed act in question: viz. applying to his self-regarding or social interest, as above.[38]

'Private ethics' aims to assist the individual to do what he ought to do, without anything else but advice from the moralist, who turns out to be any person who can influence the individual because of his authority or social position. The role of the deontologist and the possibility of 'private deontology' are related. Bentham, therefore, advocates a positive role for 'private deontology' in teaching and promoting the utilitarian virtues of probity and beneficence. The principle of utility is the source of the moral advice, guidance or instruction that the deontologist gives.

> The office and use of the extra-regarding branch of deontology – meaning private deontology – is to engage men in the practice of probity and beneficence by shewing, as far as this is the case, the coincidence of the dictates of probity and beneficence with those of self-regarding prudence.[39]

For Bentham, 'private ethics' is designed to educate the individual to calculate the value of different pleasures and pains.[40] Bentham considers three uses of 'private deontology':

> One is, among the several consequences, good or evil or both, with which human action or forbearance in the several situations in question is apt to be attended, the bringing to view, in a greater or lesser proportion, some which, if not thus brought to view, might have failed to present themselves to the mind: in this way, no new motives are created.
>
> Another is the giving birth, as it were, to an ordinance of the popular or moral sanction bearing upon the point in question, the Deontologist as such being, as it were, the member on whose motion the ordinance to the effect in question is established.

Third and last is the operating in [such a] way upon the minds of those in the country in question in whose hands reside the powers of legislation and other powers of government as to engage them to add to the force of the popular or moral sanction the [force] of the political including the legal sanction: the political sanction displaying its force on this occasion by giving birth and expression to such ordinances as afford a promise of giving practical effect to the ordinances supposed to be established by the popular or moral sanction as above.[41]

The role of the deontologist is to overcome the difficulties and tensions within individual ethics.[42] Indeed, the role of the deontologist and the point of 'private deontology' is to educate the individual to make the correct utilitarian choices and in that sense, where appropriate, to modify his tastes, in other words his choice of pleasures. What may be described as Bentham's paternalistic approach in this respect shows that he does not view the liberty of taste, in the sphere of individual ethics, as absolute. To this extent, neither a principle of aesthetics nor a free-for-all solves the problem of private ethics.

3. Conclusion

Bentham confronts the arguments in favour of aesthetics in an original, critical and powerful way. In the first part of this chapter I argued that, in the public sphere, Bentham defends the liberty of taste as a negative liberty. This radical commitment to the liberty of taste has political implications in that it secures government against the slippery slope arguments of a conservative politics of taste. In the second part, I explained that the liberty of taste does not play an unrestricted role in Bentham's conception of private ethics. Indeed, the purpose of private ethics is to reconcile interest and duty and this leads to a rejection of a radical, individualist liberty of taste.

Notes

1 Bentham, ed. Burns and Hart, 1970, 11 [hereafter *IPML*].
2 Bentham, 2013, 19 [hereafter *NPBJ*].
3 Bentham, ed. Schofield *et al.*, 2002, 68. Bentham's formulation appears in French as 'Chacun a un droit égal à tout le bonheur dont sa nature est susceptible.'

4 Bentham's definition of taste is founded on its relationship to pleasure: 'Taste for any object is an aptitude or disposition to derive pleasure [from] that object.' See Bentham, ed. Schofield *et al.*, 2014, 4.
5 *IPML*, 38.
6 *NPBJ*, 18.
7 *NPBJ*, 25.
8 Bentham, ed. Schofield *et al.*, 2014, 53–7.
9 In contrast to some proponents of present-day utilitarianism, Bentham's views on the liberty of taste led him to adopt a moderate position in relation to food ethics and the virtues of vegetarianism.
10 Bentham, ed. Schofield and Long, 2016, 117.
11 i.e. *Not Paul, But Jesus*, Vol. III, and 'Of Sexual Irregularities'.
12 See Bourcier, 2019.
13 Schofield, ed. Quinn and Zhai, 2014, 90–119; Quinn, 2017; T.Y. Koh, 2019.
14 *IPML*, 17–18.
15 Bentham, ed. Schofield *et al.*, 2014, 18–19; *NPBJ*, 66, 96.
16 *IPML*, 105–8.
17 Bentham, ed. Schofield *et al.*, 2014, 20.
18 Bentham, ed. Goldworth, 1983b, 230: 'One element upon which the magnitude of the mischief depends is consequently the quantity of power belonging to the situation of him by whom the notions thus disseminated are imbibed. For abuse of power, or to speak still more largely, abuse of influence, is the immediate source of the mischief which it is their tendency to produce.'
19 For Bentham's opposition to Hume see Quinn, 2016.
20 Rousseau, ed. Gagnebin and Raymond, 1995, 1–125, in answer to D'Alembert's article 'Genève', first published in 1757, *Encyclopédie*, Vol. VII, éd. Diderot et D'Alembert.
21 Rousseau's *First Discourse* begins: 'Has the restoration of the sciences and the arts contributed to the purification or to the corruption of morality?'
22 Bentham, ed. Schofield and Long, 2016, 351–2.
23 Bentham outlines the limits to legislative interference more generally in his chapter on 'Cases unmeet for Punishment' in *IPML (CW)*, 156–64.
24 Bentham, ed. Goldworth, 1983b, 124–5: 'Deontology, or Ethics (taken in the largest sense of the word), is that branch of art and science which has for its object the learning and shewing for the information of each individual, by what means the net amount of his happiness may be made as large as possible; of each in so far as it is dependent on his own conduct: the happiness of each individual separately being considered, and thereby that of every individual among those whose happiness is on this occasion object of regard.'
25 Bentham, ed. Goldworth, 1983b, 249: 'For distinction sake, in so far as it takes for its subject matter that part of the field to which Government applies itself, Public Deontology is the name that may be employed: in so far as the application of it is considered as confined to those parts of the field of thought and action which Government has left free, Private Deontology is the name that may be employed. … By Private Deontology considered as an art, understand the art of maximizing the net amount of happiness in that part of the field of thought and action which is left free by the power of law and government. To the words "proper" and "propriety", by this definition, the only end which is either intelligible or useful is assigned.'
26 Mack, 1962, 249.
27 Baumgardt, 1966.
28 Burns, 1978, 24.
29 De Champs, 2008, 92–3.
30 Harrison, 1983, 267; Schofield, 2006, 49.
31 Bentham, ed. Goldworth, 1983b, 150. See also 131, 175.
32 Bentham, ed. Schofield *et al.*, 2014, 77.
33 Bentham, ed. Schofield *et al.*, 2014, 77.
34 Bentham, ed. Goldworth, 1983b, 155–6.
35 Bentham, ed. Schofield *et al.*, 2014, 4.
36 Bentham, ed. Goldworth, 1983a, 67.
37 Bentham, ed. Goldworth, 1983b, 193.
38 Bentham, ed. Goldworth, 1983b, 69–70.
39 Bentham, ed. Goldworth, 1983b, 196–7.

40 Bentham, ed. Goldworth, 1983b, 199–200.
41 Bentham, ed. Goldworth, 1983b, 205.
42 Bentham, ed. Goldworth, 1983b, 151: 'it is incumbent on such censor to show and render it preponderantly probable – not only that in this or that determinate shape evil will be the result of it, but that the sum of that evil at the end of the account will be preponderant over the sum of the good produced by the same cause'.

References

Baumgardt, D. *Bentham and the Ethics of Today*. New York: Octagon Books, 1966.

Bentham, J. 'A Table of the Springs of Action: Marginals', in *Deontology: Together with A Table of the Springs of Action and Article on Utilitarianism* (*CW*), ed. A. Goldworth. Oxford: Clarendon Press, 1983a.

Bentham, J. 'Considérations d'un Anglois sur la composition des Etats-Généraux y compris réponses aux questions proposées aux Notables &c. 1788', in *Rights, Representation, and Reform: Nonsense upon Stilts and Other Writings on the French Revolution* (*CW*), eds. P. Schofield, C. Pease-Watkin, and C. Blamires. Oxford: Clarendon Press, 2002.

Bentham, J. 'Deontology', in *Deontology: Together with A Table of the Springs of Action and Article on Utilitarianism* (*CW*), ed. A. Goldworth. Oxford: Clarendon Press, 1983b.

Bentham, J. *An Introduction to the Principles of Morals and Legislation* (*CW*), eds. J.H. Burns and H.L.A. Hart. London: Athlone Press, 1970.

Bentham, J. *Not Paul, but Jesus*, Vol. III: *Doctrine*. London: Bentham Project, UCL, 2013 [http://discovery.ucl.ac.uk/1392179/3/npbj.pdf].

Bentham, J. *Of Sexual Irregularities, and Other Writings on Sexual Morality* (*CW*), eds. P. Schofield, C. Pease-Watkin, and M. Quinn. Oxford: Clarendon Press, 2014.

Bentham, J. *Preparatory Principles* (*CW*), eds. P. Schofield and D.G. Long. Oxford: Oxford University Press, 2016.

Bourcier, B. 'Rescuing Politics from Lying and Hypocrisy: Utility and Truth in Jeremy Bentham's Thought', in *Ethics, Politics, and Society* 2 (2019): 155–76.

Burns, J.H. 'Dreams and Destinations: Jeremy Bentham in 1828', in *The Bentham Newsletter* 1 (May 1978): 21–30.

De Champs, E. *La déontologie politique ou la pensée constitutionnelle de Jeremy Bentham*. Genève and Paris: Droz, 2008.

Harrison, R. *Bentham*. London: Routledge, 1983.

Koh, T.Y. 'Bentham on Asceticism and Tyranny', *History of European Ideas* 45:1 (2019): 1–14.

Mack, M.P. *Jeremy Bentham: An Odyssey of Ideas, 1748–1792*. Toronto and London: Heinemann, 1962.

Quinn, M. 'Jeremy Bentham on Liberty of Taste', *History of European Ideas* 43 (2016): 614–27.

Rousseau, J.-J. *Lettres à D'Alembert sur les spectacles* [1758], eds. B. Gagnebin and M. Raymond. Paris: Pléiade, Gallimard, 1995.

Schofield, P. *Utility and Democracy: The Political Thought of Jeremy Bentham*. Oxford: Oxford University Press, 2006.

Schofield, P. 'Jeremy Bentham on Taste, Sex, and Religion', in eds. M. Quinn and X. Zhai, *Bentham's Theory of Law and Public Opinion*. Cambridge: Cambridge University Press, 2014.

Chapter 10
From pain to pleasure: Panopticon dreams and Pentagon Petal

Fran Cottell and Marianne Mueller

Art, architecture and social space

As an artist and an architect, we are approaching 'Jeremy Bentham and the Arts' from the perspective of practice. We are presenting a narrative of our experience of practical research and developing work connected to Bentham's project for an inspection house and its proposed site in Millbank. As an interdisciplinary team we have been collaborating on projects where we have been using site-related architectural plans in order to subvert or open up the uses and interpretations of found spaces and to create socially active/alive/democratic spaces. These projects explore the relationship between architectural form and social behaviour – a dependency that Bentham built upon with his plans for the inspection house or panopticon. In contrast to his utilitarian ideas, our work aims at opening up a discursive and undetermined relationship between the articulation of a place and its potential social effects. The process of editing and reinterpreting architectural plans in this context is central to our ambition of redefining found spaces and reconditioning any normative behaviour to which they might be linked. This use of local plans has the added value of providing recognition of the memories and understanding of site-related communities.

One of the spaces we have been working with is the Rootstein Hopkins Parade Ground in Millbank, central London. This large open public square is situated at the heart of the Chelsea College of Arts and adjacent to Tate Britain. The site was part of the land originally purchased by Jeremy Bentham in 1799 to realize his visionary panopticon prison, a plan that would never materialize. It subsequently became the site of the infamous Millbank Prison, the largest prison in the UK of its time, and characterized by its isolation cells. After the demolition of the prison, the site accommodated a military hospital with a parade ground and is now home to the Chelsea College of Arts and Tate Britain (Figure 10.1).

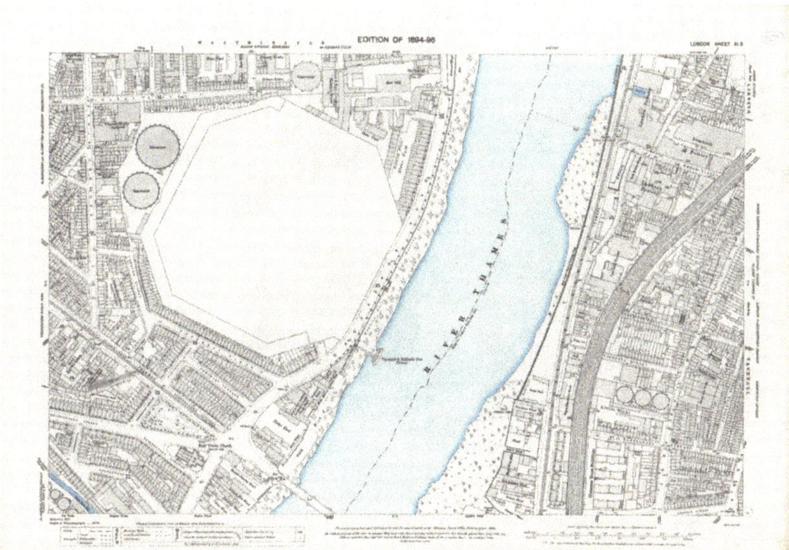

Figure 10.1: Ordnance Survey. London, Sheet XI. 3., 1895.

Reproduced with the permission of the National Library of Scotland.

Physically all four structures – panopticon, prison, parade ground and art school – occupied the site at different times and have left their traces. In an overlay (Figure 10.2, overleaf), we traced the vast expanse of Millbank Prison against the present urban layout of the Chelsea College of Arts, Tate Britain and the Millbank Estate, thereby demonstrating how the shape of the prison remains inscribed into the urban fabric of today.

The construction material of the prison never really left the site; it too remained and is very much still part of the physical make-up of the site. For instance, the ground floors of the Millbank Estate are constructed from the original bricks of the prison after its demolition, with part of its perimeter ditch presently used for drying clothes. Behind Tate Britain, which still houses some of the prison's underground structures, is a section of the original perimeter wall.

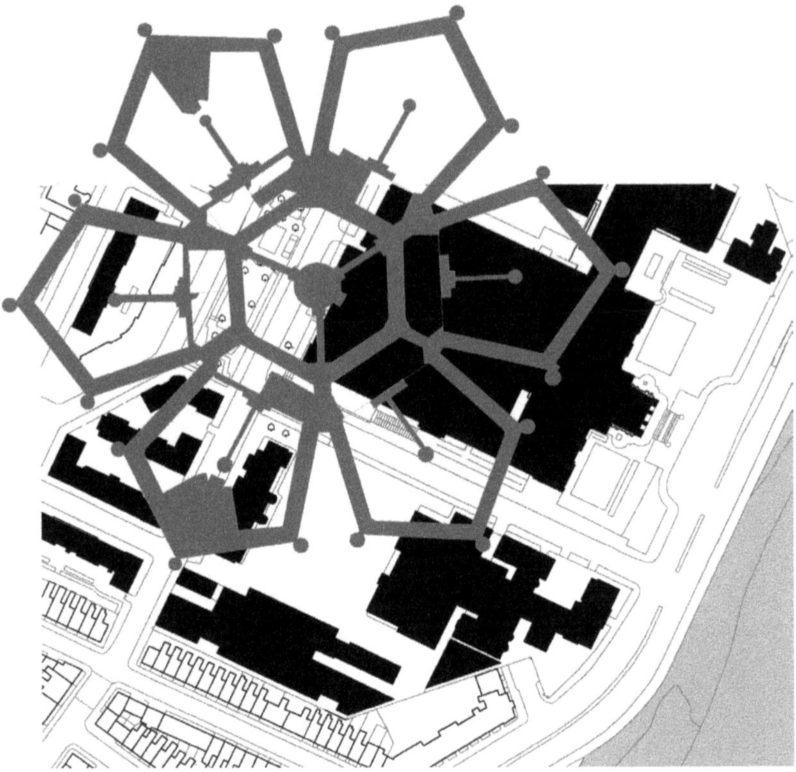

Figure 10.2: Overlay of Millbank Prison onto the present site.

The Rootstein Hopkins Parade Ground thus represents a cross-section through different social modes and architecture's power to orchestrate them: from the social confinement of the isolation cell of Bentham's earliest imagined panopticon (he later rejected solitary confinement in favour of cells holding two inmates) and the real Millbank Prison, to the military organization of a group as 'one' in a parade ground, to today's neo-liberal forms of socializing and gathering in the context of the arts. We decided to build on these different strata and the site's social history of controlling and (dis)empowering the individual and the crowd, focusing on the floor plan of Millbank Prison.

The two very different structures of the panopticon and Millbank Prison are widely conflated in the public mind. The panopticon was brought to the public's attention by Foucault, who added considerably to the interest in Bentham's plan for an inspection house/panopticon while underplaying the fact that it was never built.

The imagined panopticon: The physical structure

Although Jeremy Bentham's ideas for a panopticon would never be realized at Millbank, his plans for the penitentiary inspection-house remain an ongoing source of inspiration and point of reference. We begin by examining several aspects of this plan: first, the proposed physical structure; second, Bentham's influences and references; third, the legacy; and fourth, the dreams and utopias that were related to it.

Bentham's inspection-house was a circular building with a radial layout. The circular shape and radial organization is one of the key characteristics for Bentham, offering a number of important advantages. The accommodation for the prisoners, or the 'cells', are situated on the perimeter of the building with the apartment of the inspector, or the 'lodge', located at its centre. The empty space between the 'cells' and the 'lodge' is called the 'intermediate' or the 'annular area',[1] and separates the two realms – the realm of the prisoner from the realm of the inspector (Figure 10.3).

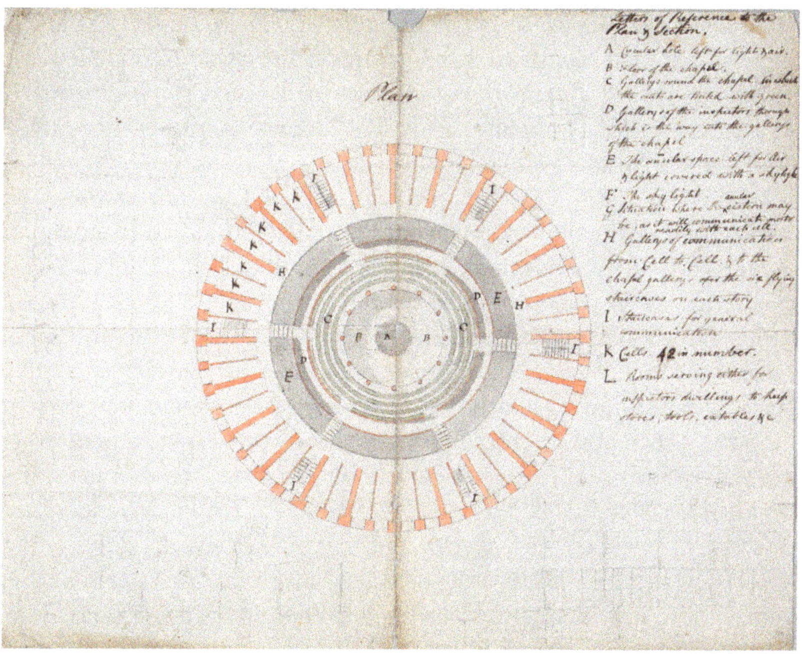

Figure 10.3: Willey Reveley (1760–99), Plan of the panopticon penitentiary, UC cxix. 120v (*c.* 1791).

University College London Special Collections.

It is this particular spatial arrangement, with the 'lodge' at the centre of the building and the 'cells' arranged in a circle at a distance around it, that formulates the key relationship Bentham seeks to organize with his plan: the relationship between the inspector and the prisoner, between the observer and the observed. All other moves that follow are set by this fundamental arrangement and articulate it further. Principles of perceptibility (conditions of light) and the detailed organization of the relationship based on visibility (spatial geometry) are at the core of this arrangement. Through the distribution of physical structures and light, the inspector surveys the prisoner while the prisoner is not able to see him. The inspector is 'seeing without being seen'[2] and he does that at a distance. This is a one-to-one relationship, inspector to prisoner, individual to individual, as everything is done to keep the prisoner in isolation and from being able to communicate with his fellow inmates. Spatially the 'cells' are divided from one another by the means of partitions, radial walls running from the circumference of the building towards its centre, extending beyond the cell's enclosure so that the prisoner cannot look around them, his visual field constrained. These 'protracted partitions',[3] as Bentham called them, were also extremely thin, a fact that Bentham liked to underline as it exemplified the superiority of his system of surveillance and visual containment. He writes: 'the thickest walls have been found occasionally unavailing: upon this plan, the thinnest would be sufficient'.[4]

Towards the lodge, the cells were enclosed by iron grating. The combination of the thin walls laid out in a radial fashion, the transparent iron grating, and the position of the inspector at the centre of the house, meant that the inspector would have the 'perfect view'.[5] This ideal view of seeing everything at once, this instant panoramic gaze over the entirety of the cell and indeed the whole house, would allow just one man to observe many by barely moving himself: an extremely efficient set up. The circular form plays an important role, offering an ideal shape in plan that no other geometry can rival. The circular layout also provides the shortest travel distance between 'lodge' and 'cell', meaning that the circle renders the relationship between the inspector and any prisoner equally close.

The extreme proximity between inspector and prisoner is important to note here. Bentham explains that, in his inspection house, prisoners would not need to be chained because their every move or facial expression could easily be seen. If we look at the actual distance between the lodge and the cells in Bentham's plans, this only measures 14 feet or 4.26 metres. This is a surprisingly short distance and means that the relationship between inspector and prisoner would indeed have been quite intimate. Bentham's inspection house as a whole was small, measuring only 100 feet or 30.48 metres in diameter.

The inspection house was also surprisingly transparent. Another efficiency that the circular building shape offered was the maximum penetration of light into and through the building, based on the principle of the shortest distance. Every cell contained a large window – as large as technically possible – to allow light to penetrate deep into it, fully illuminating it, and all the way into the lodge at the centre. The outer circumference wall in Bentham's plan shows more windows than wall sections, resulting in a perforated prison building. Later, Bentham considered using materials other than stone to make the inspection house even more transparent. At night, the idea of a see-through and well illuminated building was extended through the use of lamps with reflectors.

The section drawings of the panopticon clearly demonstrate the penetration of light and the idea of an illuminated building (Figure 10.4).

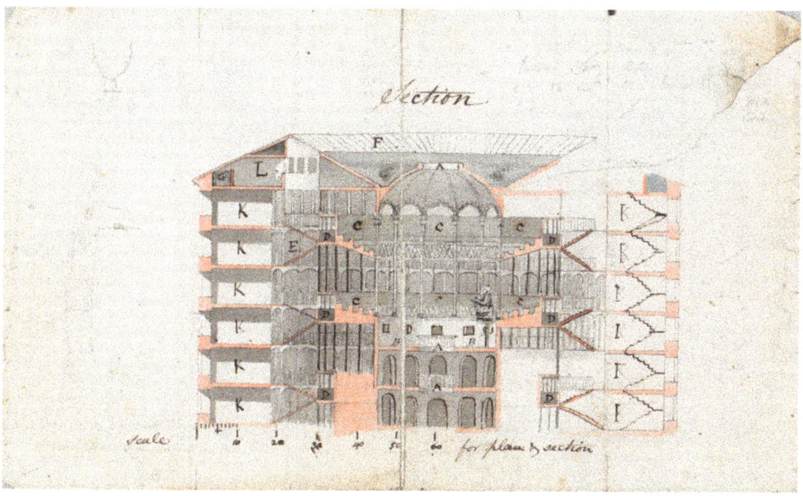

Figure 10.4: Willey Reveley (1760–99), Section of the panopticon penitentiary, UC cxix. 122v (*c.* 1791).

University College London Special Collections.

Bentham's inspection house was to be bright, light, healthy and clean; well heated and well ventilated; it had sanitation and there was running water to all the cells. Bentham's cells measured 6 feet in width and 13 feet in length, which equates to about 7 square metres of space for two prisoners. Contemporary American jail cells often provide only 4.4m^2 of space. The Red Cross currently recommends 5.4m^2 and the

European Committee for the Prevention of Torture and Inhuman or Degrading Treatment or Punishment recommends 6m^2 of living space for a single-occupancy cell, rendering Bentham's cells less than generous by today's standards. There were 48 cells on one floor. One lodge could serve two floors. This arrangement could then be repeated by vertical stacking or horizontal repetition. Bentham drew up different variations, including some inspection houses with a central lantern that would bring additional light to the centre of the building.

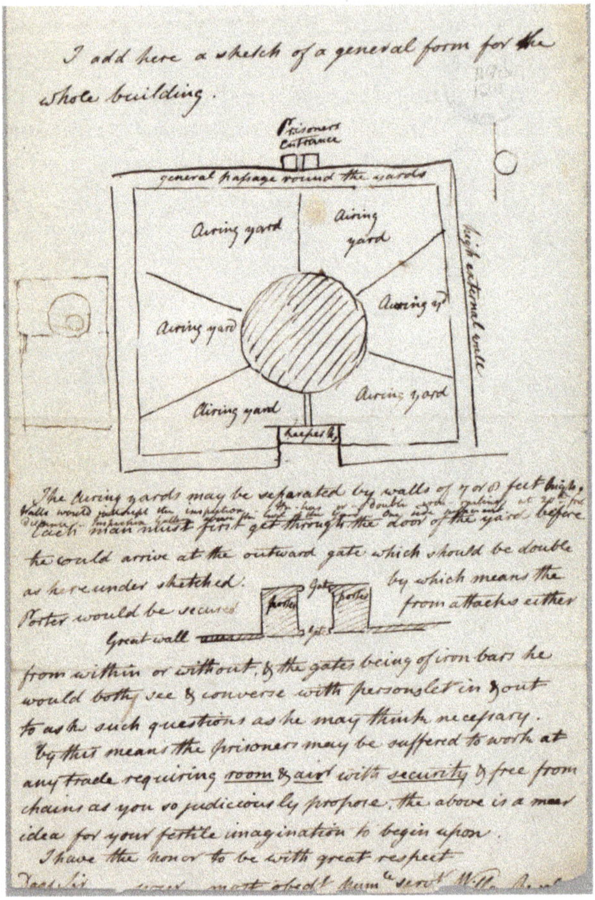

Figure 10.5: Willey Reveley (1760–99), Sketch of the panopticon penitentiary and its airing yards, UC cxix. 129 (c. 1791).

University College London Special Collections.

Bentham did not only consider the interior of the prison but also made plans for possible external spaces surrounding the inspection house. He sketched out plans for integrating airing yards, work yards and gardens. Some of these return to the idea of a circular layout for the surroundings but some work with a square plan around a circular building at its centre (Figure 10.5).

Bentham and Foucault

When we started working on the Rootstein Hopkins Parade Ground, we noticed that Millbank Prison was widely conflated with, and referred to as, Jeremy Bentham's panopticon. In common with many people, we first read about, and initially saw the panopticon, through the prism of Foucault's employment of it in *Discipline and Punish: The Birth of the Prison* (1977) as 'an emblem of modern power'.[6] We then reconsidered this in light of the work of the historian Janet Semple in her article 'A Defence of Panopticism' (1992) in which she considers the complexity of the relationship between Foucault and Bentham. She observes that Foucault brings his own 1960s Parisian historical perspective to his work, is ill-informed on the subject of eighteenth-century English penal history and has a negative interpretation of the aims and intentions of the Enlightenment reformer's motives. She concedes that Bentham made many problematic statements, which appear to support Foucault's thinking, but argues that Foucault, when talking about the panopticon, did not consider it in light of Bentham's later constitutional writings and tolerance of individual diversity. She concludes that 'Foucault extrapolates from the particular device of the panopticon inspection tower to generalize that "Bentham laid down the principle that power should be visible and unverifiable. … The Panopticon is a machine for dissociating the see/being seen dyad … in the central tower, one sees everything without being seen".'[7] However the 'panoptic qualities of [Bentham's] *Constitutional Code* were designed to allow the subject to observe the ruling few'[8] and this is what Foucault should have taken into account. Bentham insisted that his prison must be accessible, and this would control the power of the governor, or the inspector, in the centre of the prison. 'Bentham believed that democracy was essentially fragile', notes Semple, 'and could be upheld only by the light of freedom of information and discussion.'[9] Bentham wanted to create a humane prison. 'His three principles of management were lenity, severity and economy',[10] 'but the overriding principle was lenity that the prisoner should be deprived only of liberty not of health or life.' But, according to Semple, Foucault had a negative interpretation of reformers' motives. He believed that 'they were being deceived or rather were part of a process that masked their real intentions'.[11]

Bentham compared criminals to children. He considered that 'criminals were a work in progress and the problem was with drink and idleness', that 'criminals, like other men, were potentially rational beings responsible for their own actions. … Bentham's central belief was the rational mechanism of human morality could be refashioned, the criminal mind literally reformed' by sobriety and work.[12]

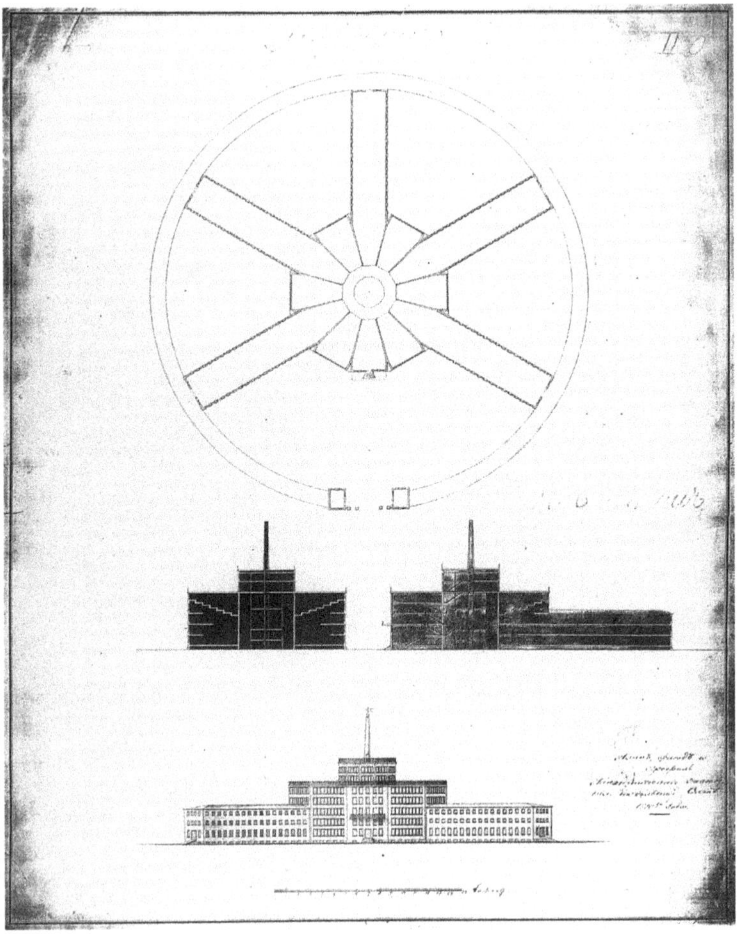

Figure 10.6: Samuel Bentham (1757–1831), Plan, elevation and two sections, 1807.

Reproduced by kind permission of the Rossiiskii Gosudarstvennyi Arkhiv Voenno-Morskogo Flota, St Petersburg, fond 326, opis' 1, delo 10043.

The reach of the panopticon

For Bentham, the panopticon was more than effective prison design. He believed that the panopticon principle could be beneficial in other contexts where surveillance was important. He therefore considered it for use in schools, hospitals and workhouses. His brother Samuel, with whom the idea of the panopticon originated,[13] adapted the panopticon principle for an art school project in St Petersburg as well as for a house of industry (Figure 10.6, opposite).

Other industrial estates of the time started to borrow Bentham's principles of efficient and well-surveyed buildings, such as the now demolished Round Mill at Belper, Derbyshire, constructed in 1811, following the plans of architect William Strutt.

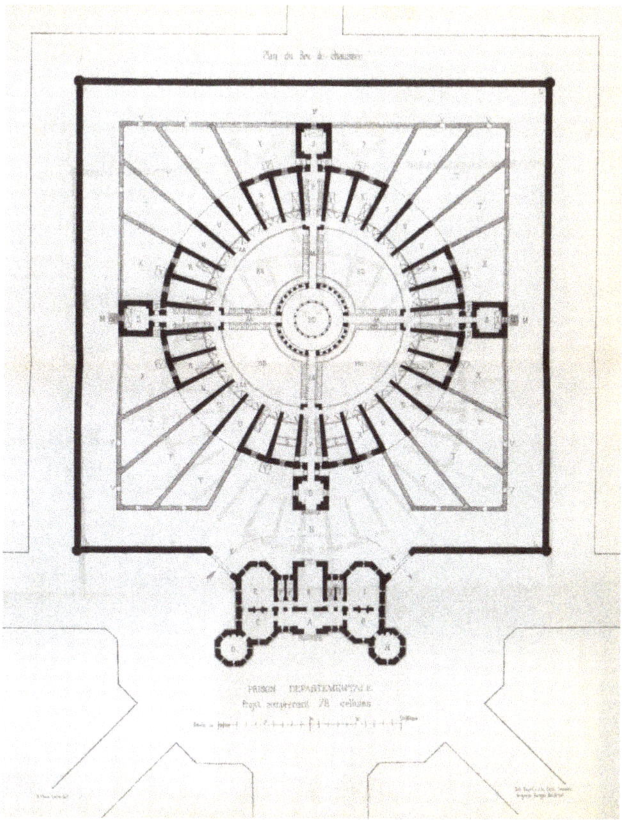

Figure 10.7: Guillaume-Abel Blouet (1795–1853), *Plan du Rez-de-chaussée Prison Départementale*, 1841.

Brown University.

Although Bentham's panopticon was never built, his plans were widely known and have remained highly influential for prison design until today. French architect Guillaume-Abel Blouet's design for a Department Prison in 1841, included in 'Instruction et programme pour la construction des maisons d'arrêt et de justice: atlas de plans de prisons cellulaires', bears a strong resemblance to Bentham's panopticon both in terms of internal layouts as well as its setting in the site (Figure 10.7, previous page).

Blouet saw himself as a reformer in his country, attempting to redefine prison design. Like Bentham, he believed in architecture as a tool for implementing social reform and understood the prison as a reformatory institution that acted through work and education.

In twentieth-century prison design, moreover, there are a number of built examples that make reference to Bentham's plans. The Presidio Modelo, a model prison on the Isla de la Juventud in Cuba built in 1926 and consisting of five circular buildings, displays many of the characteristics of Bentham's panopticon, such as the radial plan with the central watchtower topped by a lantern. Five floors of inmates were surveyed from one single tower. A photograph of the prison cells from 1926 demonstrates most dramatically the transparency of the building, with the prisoner's silhouettes lined up in rows and lit starkly from behind, as Bentham intended (Figure 10.8).

Figure 10.8: Presidio Modelo, *Cuba*, 1926.

Arnhem Penitentiary, designed in 1884 by architect Johan Frederik Metzlaar, is one of three panopticon-style prisons in the Netherlands that were built for solitary confinement and used a central watchtower. Similar in size to Bentham's inspection house, Arnhem measures 56 metres in diameter, and has the same number of cells per floor.

Interestingly, Arnhem prison became popular with inmates once prison rules were relaxed and inmates were allowed to wander around in the central area, which was used for playing football and other games. The watchtower was subsequently converted into the guard's canteen, thereby reversing the relationship of the observer and the observed. In 1980 the Office for Metropolitan Architecture proposed an architectural project for the adaptation of the by then iconic prison, which was already operating almost like a public space with work, recreation and meetings ongoing in its central yard. OMA took this idea further and proposed to cut two sunken streets into it. This would have taken away the eye of the panopticon and created communal and entertainment spaces for the prisoners out of sight, but was never implemented (Figure 10.9).

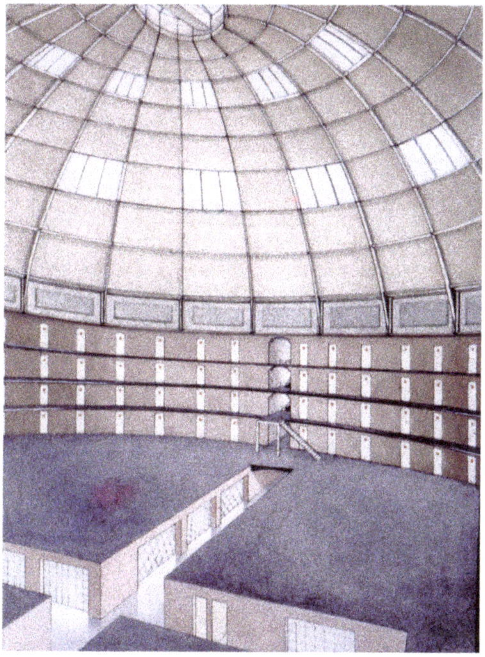

Figure 10.9: Koepel Panopticon Prison, Arnhem, 1980.

Image courtesy of the Office for Metropolitan Architecture (OMA).

Another prison influenced by Bentham's panopticon is the Stateville Penitentiary in Illinois designed by architect C. Harrick Hammond, built in 1919 and operating until 2016. This high security prison had an armed central watchtower and four storeys of cells, and is the only surviving panopticon-style prison building in the United States. It was famously photographed by Andreas Gursky in 2002.

Dreams and utopia

For Foucault, the panopticon 'presents a cruel, ingenious cage. The fact that it should have given rise, even in our own time, to so many variations, projected or realized, is evidence of the imaginary intensity that it has possessed for two hundred years. But the panopticon must not be understood as a dream building: it is a diagram of a mechanism of power.'[14] But Foucault acknowledges the lightness of the panopticon and how it would replace the old prisons with 'their fortress-like architecture'.[15] Bentham's wish was for the panopticon to be 'a lantern', a thing of beauty, 'a glass beehive'.[16] There were particular cultural influences on Bentham's panopticon plan. 'Bentham's vision was of a beautiful building', notes Semple, 'a stately pleasure dome … comparable he said to the Rotundas at Ranelagh and Dublin, or the circus at Bath'.[17] Ranelagh Gardens were a public pleasure garden in Chelsea, outside London. The Rotunda there was designed by William Jones and could indeed have served as an inspiration for Bentham. As the Rotunda was already complete in 1742, one could assume that Bentham might have visited this prominent venue, which Canaletto had famously painted in 1754 (Figure 10.10).

Figure 10.10: Canaletto (1697–1768), *Interior of the Rotunda at Ranelagh*, London, 1754.

National Gallery, Wiki/Commons.

Built entirely for the purpose of pleasure, the Rotunda displays surprising similarities to Bentham's later plan for the panopticon prison. It, too, was a circular building with a lodge and a lantern at its centre. The division of walls was radial. Even the diameter of the Rotunda at 120 feet (37 metres) was close to Bentham's projected building. Most strikingly, the Rotunda's façade and gallery design were of an unusual transparency for its time – one could almost see through its filigree structure (Figure 10.11).

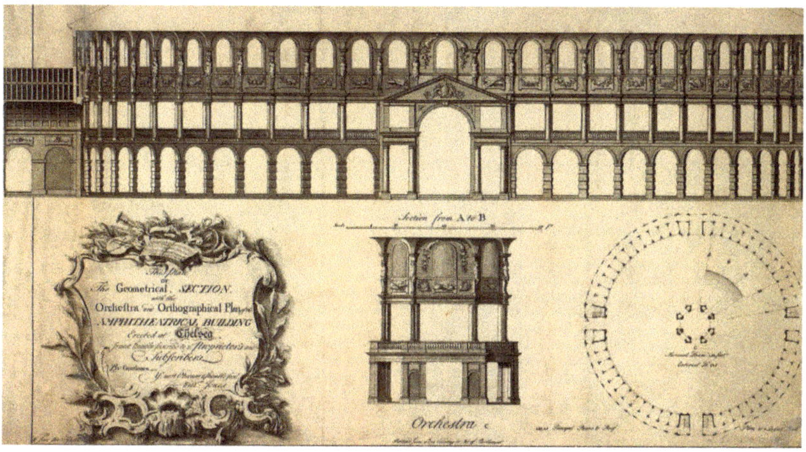

Figure 10.11: After William Jones (d. 1747), *Ranelagh*, 1742.
Royal Collection Trust, RCIN 702471.

As stated previously, Bentham was considering using the very latest materials and manufacturing innovations for his panopticon; for example cast iron for the pillars, the arches, staircases and galleries. The first iron bridge at Coalbrookdale had been built in 1779, only 12 years before Bentham printed 'Panopticon; or, The Inspection-House'. Techniques had recently been invented for manufacturing glass on a larger scale. Bentham wanted plaster floors instead of wood, because he thought they would be more hygienic and fire-proof. As Semple suggests, 'Architecturally, the panopticon foreshadows Paxton's Crystal Palace rather than Pentonville'.[18]

Bentham not only referenced architecture, but also found inspiration for the panopticon in novels. He acknowledged Bishop Fénelon's pastoral Arcadian novel *The Adventures of Telemachus* as the inspiration for utilitarianism. This was an instructive French novel originally published in 1699 that proved very popular, being republished many times in the course of the eighteenth century. Inventing a sub-plot to Homer's *Odyssey*, the story recounts the educational travels of Telemachus, son of Odysseus. The heroine in this story has a glass palace that Bentham considered to be the archetype for the panopticon.[19] This may explain why the panopticon looks so pink and pretty in the architectural section drawings.

Bentham made private notes and had secret visions for the panopticon. Semple describes him as 'a man with a vision, a vision that had its origins in the English utopian tradition and in the Arcadian romance of the pastoral idyll. The panopticon was an enclave of reason, isolated from the temptations and disorders of the ordinary world.'[20] She makes the argument that Bentham was influenced by utopian ideas; although he described Thomas More's *Utopia* as anti-rational, there are noticeable similarities between More's ideas and Bentham's. More's fictitious capital Amaurot was to be built on a gentle slope of a tidal river, not unlike the Thames, and similar to Bentham's detailed plans for the panopticon. It had piped water, spacious housing, gardens and music at meal times. In More's Utopia, there was a strong emphasis on labour, of which Bentham would have approved. As in the panopticon, idleness was the worst sin. Bentham also admired the work of seventeenth-century philosopher and statesman Francis Bacon, who harnessed scientific inventions for the benefit of his new society in his fictional utopia New Atlantis.[21] Reflecting Bentham's own wide-ranging interests, Bacon's plans for his new society included breeding silkworms, keeping bees, curing diseases, inventing flying machines and submarines, harnessing and reflecting light and inventing 'conversation tubes to convey sounds through pipes'. Conversation tubes, of course, were incorporated in the design of panopticon.

George Bentham, the son of Bentham's only surviving sibling Samuel and his wife Mary Sophia Fordyce, became a prominent botanist, inspired no doubt by his mother's interest in the subject. Mirroring Bentham's own early ambitions, George travelled the world and published books on the classification of plants, with several being named after him.[22] Jeremy Bentham maintained a keen interest in botany and in discovering new plants; in his private thoughts and ambitions for the panopticon he talks about it being a centre for collecting plants, even sending out explorer expeditions from the panopticon to collect seeds that would then be propagated in special panopticon nurseries. His planning went as far as drafting an advertisement for a panopticon physician in which he states that it would be useful if the applicant had an interest in plants.

Figure 10.12: Charles Fourier (1772–1837), *City with Guarantees (ville garantiste)*, 1820s: a panoptic utopia?.

Bentham had plans for creating an extensive infrastructure around the prison: he envisaged a complete panopticon town. Building houses into the walls of the prison, he proposed a tavern with a terrace where visitors could watch firework displays and promenade along a covered walkway to the river. He had fantastical structural ideas for how he would like his new town to be developed. There would, for example, be aerial garden walkways inter-connecting the balconies of his shops and buildings.

The real Millbank Prison

Bentham's panopticon on London's Millbank site remained a dream. The site was hugely problematic and after many obstacles the government abandoned the plans in 1803, much to Bentham's dismay. In 1812 a new competition was announced to find an architect for the National Penitentiary at Millbank. It was a troublesome project from the start and involved a succession of architects: William Williams, Thomas Hardwick, John Harvey and finally Robert Smirke, who completed the building. The task to build on swampy and unstable ground meant that design and construction processes were riddled with problems and excessively expensive. In 1816 the Millbank Penitentiary opened as the largest prison in Britain of its time (Figure 10.13, overleaf).

Figure 10.13: Aerial photograph of Millbank Prison taken from a balloon, *London from Aloft*, *Strand Magazine*, 9 May 1891.

Millbank Prison is often confused with a panopticon structure. William Williams's design, however, owes little to the idea of the panopticon except for some formal motifs, such as the placement of the chapel in the centre of the building, while isolation cells and watch towers are used entirely differently. As a whole, the structure did not function as a panopticon, since it lacked clarity of conception and layout. Semple describes it as 'a labyrinth of a building, full of dark corridors and passages, winding staircases and innumerable doors and gates. So confusing it was that wardens would blaze their trails with chalk marks on the walls.'[23] In many ways, this vast labyrinthine structure was the exact opposite of what Bentham had imagined.

The overall layout of Millbank Prison was configured as a series of hexagonal shapes, or petal shaped wings, each of them three storeys tall with a central watchtower. Each of these petals was further divided into five separate courtyards. It was a massive fortress-like structure with very small windows, little visibility and a significant distance between watchtower and cells. One wonders how the watchtower/inspector actually functioned without the immediate access that Bentham would have provided between the tower/inspector and the cell/prisoner. The intimate relationship he envisaged was not at all possible here. From the tower the guard could observe only parts of the cells at great distance, and gaining access was a difficult and time-consuming undertaking. Moreover, the access corridor to the cells was located on the outer wall of the building, so that it was not possible to observe wardens interacting with prisoners. For Bentham, the visibility of this interaction was an important part of his plan. The fact that the inspector was able to inspect the wardens and their contact with the inmates, just as he might inspect the prisoners themselves, was another layer of transparency within Bentham's well thought-out system.

Only when one compares the physical dimensions and numbers of cells in Millbank Prison to Bentham's panopticon does one really start to grasp the sheer excess of Millbank's slack structure opposed to the neat efficiency of Bentham's lean inspection house (Figure 10.14).

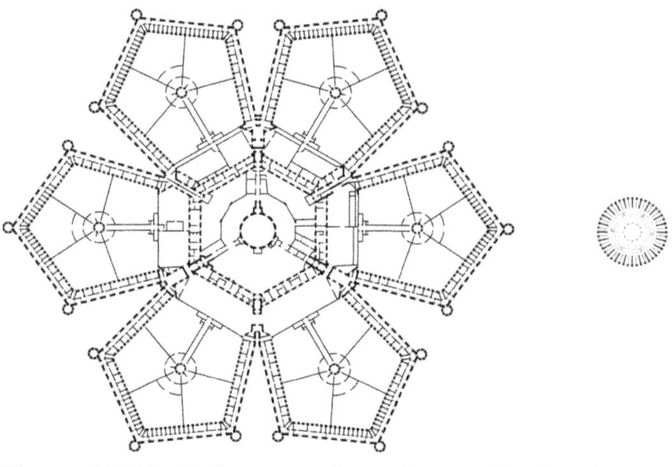

Figure 10.14: Scale comparison: Jeremy Bentham's panopticon and Millbank Prison.

While Bentham's inspection house was visually transparent and productively so, Millbank's transparency was acoustic and problematic: its ventilation system was so bad that it would carry sounds across the facility, allowing prisoners to communicate with each other, even though kept in isolation. Poor sanitation and lack of ventilation meant that the prison was soon riddled with disease. While Bentham's panopticon was heated, healthy and well lit, Millbank was dark and unhygienic. As one Victorian author noted:

> If the ground plan of the building at Millbank is a geometric puzzle, the interior is surely an eccentric maze, long dark and narrow corridors, twisting passages in which the visitor unaccustomed

> to the dubious twilight has to feel his way. Double locked doors, opening at all sorts of queer angles and leading sometimes into blind entries and frequently into stone staircases so steep and narrow, are not unlike the devious steps by which the traveller reaches the towers of Strasbourg or some other cathedrals except that they are even more gloomy.[24]

The prison's ultimate failure was due to a combination of facts, but particularly the unhealthy environment and the lax rules and regulations that led to mutiny. After a major epidemic, the prison had to be evacuated and became a depot for convicts awaiting transportation, before reverting back in 1853 to an ordinary prison. In 1892 the prison was closed down and the site started to be redeveloped into its present shape.

Pentagon Petal, architectural (un)determinism or pleasure: Bentham and Herzberger

In his work on the panopticon, Bentham uses architecture as a device to control and organize human behaviour and to promote social discipline. Architecture, or more specifically the physical structure of a building, is utilized to forge particular relationships and to formalize certain structures, hierarchies or orders. Architecture, in this context becomes an important tool in the process of establishing order and executing discipline and, with it, punishment. Pain in the context of Bentham's panopticon is not inflicted through maltreatment, hunger, cold or disease, as in the case of Millbank Prison, but through the means of architecture. The panopticon is well lit, has large windows, is heated and clean, but yet it is still a cruel place. It is through the architectural tools of layout, spatial arrangement and the configuration of light and material that Bentham establishes his idea of punishment and reform.

Moving from pain to pleasure, we would now like to consider pleasure in the context of architecture's power to organize human relationships and ensure social discipline. Beyond the panopticon, people are surprisingly resistant to architecture's power to control them and are often sceptical towards overtly functional set-ups or any form of social determinism, employing imaginative responses to subvert or re-appropriate. In fact, a lot of pleasure can be generated in daily life from misusing objects and spaces or using them for purposes that were not intended or uses that were not part of their original function. There is positive engagement in the creative and active moments of these acts of appropriation. Developing this context, in our work as an artist and an architect, we refer to Herman Hertzberger, a contemporary Dutch architect and educator who has spent most of his life collecting and designing architectural settings that allow for and stimulate the spontaneous interpretation of users in pursuit of pleasure and empowerment. He argues that architecture has to be conceived in an open-ended way and advocates making spaces more receptive to unexpected uses and forms of interpretation and appropriation. Hertzberger states:

> If something is geared very specifically to a certain aim it functions the way it has been programmed to function, i.e. as it was expected to function. This is the sort of functionalism that the functionalists talked about, but it is also the minimum of utility that can be expected of architecture. And in order to achieve more than the minimum in the diversity of situations as they arise I am pleading for form and space with a greater 'accommodating' potential, like a musical instrument that sounds the way the player wants it to sound. The point is to increase this 'accommodating potential' and thus to make space more receptive to different situations. Once you start looking for them it is easy to find even in the most unexpected corners examples of usage that the designer (if any) certainly never envisaged.[25]

When working on our proposals for the Rootstein Hopkins Parade Ground, Bentham's original panopticon site and the site of the failed Millbank Prison, we envisaged strategies that would oppose the idea of utilizing architectural means for the implementation of power/pain and were looking for structures that could be more open-ended and pleasurable, that could somehow be interpreted and appropriated, an intervention where use might not be predetermined, but an offering, something that could be imagined and would contain an active and creative act.

Pentagon Petal

Pentagon Petal was a temporary intervention in the summer of 2016 that reorganized the social environment of the Rootstein Hopkins Parade Ground. The intervention was based on the plan of Millbank Prison, editing and reinterpreting it into a more socially active figure: a flower-shaped bench. The intervention played with ideas of exclusion and segregation while offering a generous place within the larger barren square (Figure 10.15, overleaf).

Figure 10.15: Cottell/Mueller, Pentagon Petal, Terry Watts, 2016.

This process of editing and reinterpreting floor plans is key for us in redefining and reconditioning any normative or social behaviour linked to a particular space and recalibrating power structures. For Millbank, we went through a number of steps: we started by looking at the original plan of Millbank Prison and erased all structures that were related to control, oppression or surveillance. We removed the watchtowers, the guards' quarters and the prison administration from the plan, leaving only the prisoners' cells, accommodation and communal kitchens from the original floor plan. At the next step we radically scaled this figure down to a manageable size. By scaling it, we could reimagine its use. Figure 10.16 shows the vast plan of Millbank Prison drawn at 1:350 scale in comparison to our bench drawn at 1:40 scale. Both geometric objects seem similar, yet each of them has a very different potential in terms of use, sociability and scope for public interaction. At the final step, we brought this new figure back onto the site and calibrated it for the specific location and its communities.

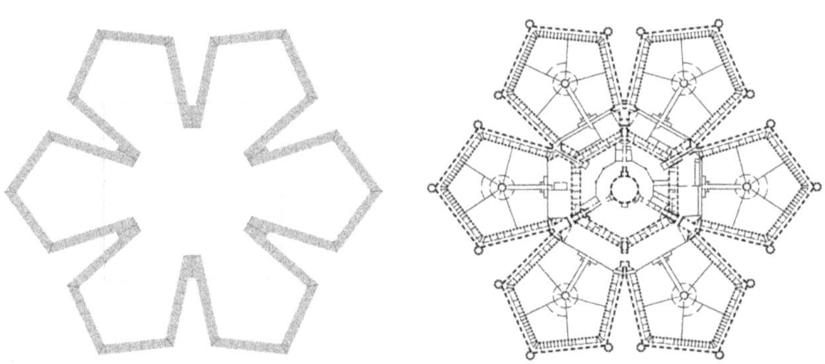

Figure 10.16: Millbank Prison and Panopticon Petal drawn at different scales.

When scaling and editing the plan, we were thinking about spatial dimensions and their impact on social uses and possible interpretations, very much like Bentham, but with the opposite motivation. We wanted the dimensions of this new object to be ambiguous and open, and yet relate to something familiar. We looked at the widths of a bed in the prison cell and we looked at the dimensions of a garden bench, and arrived at something that could be interpreted as either a bed or a bench. Our bench was an enormous 120 metres long and was able to accommodate up to 300 people, the same number as the first generation of prisoners in Millbank or the approximate number of prisoners in a Bentham-style six-storey panopticon.

What interested us in the bench was that it is a very unassuming object. It is one you usually share. On a bench, you accept that you may be sitting next to somebody you do not know. More profoundly, sitting is a way of taking hold of a site – of appropriating and occupying a public site. In the urban environment, benches can be seen as highly problematic since they can produce loitering, which is often not desired. Contemporary urban benches can specifically be designed so that they cannot be slept on or used to congregate. We wanted the bench for the Rootstein Hopkins Parade Ground to be as generous as possible. This unconditional generosity was a very important aspect for us (Figure 10.17).

Figure 10.17: Cottell/Mueller, Pentagon Petal, Terry Watts, 2016.

Figure 10.18: Cottell/Mueller, Pentagon Petal, Terry Watts, 2016.

To achieve this, the dimensions of the bench were kept deliberately ambiguous. You could see it as a platform or a pier, suggesting that you could walk on it. Or you could use it as a bench, and there were different opportunities for how to sit or lie on it: in a one-to-one in order to have a private conversation, or in a group around the pentagons, or you might lie down and enjoy the view. Each of the six pentagons or 'petals' – originally shaped to facilitate social control and designated for solitary confinement – was now reinterpreted by groups of students, staff or tourists for informal gatherings and for pleasure, in different configurations and were used almost like rooms. The corners became specifically productive: many people liked to sit there, where they could face each other, or they would sit on the edges surveying the scene. Others would have picnics on it, sitting next to each other or opposite each other (Figure 10.18).

By sitting together, the project brought the disparate communities loosely linked to the site together: the community of the college, the students, the staff, the tourists that were passing by on their way to the Tate, but also local communities living in the housing estates nearby. There was a group of local youngsters who used to congregate every night on one of the V-shapes around our bench, moving every night to a different section. When it was used for a staff party, the participants unilaterally adopted one of the pentagon shapes as the 'dancing room'. Local residents walked their dogs on the grass in the centre.

Through the intervention, there was suddenly an opportunity for people to gather in informal and unpredicted ways, in ways that were not forced and which brought together people who would usually not congregate. We were amazed at how many people came to us and said: 'I sat on your bench and still remember that as a special moment on the journey from one place to another.' The installation tried to make sense of the otherwise barren nature of this large urban square by shrinking it into a confined space with a clear definition. We deliberated over whether the bench should be open or not, and how, if it was closed, this large object would form a barrier within the site. But this barrier turned out to be productive in generating and disrupting social activities. By providing a physical back for the occupants, the bench turned this previously unappealing exposed central grass square into an enclosed social, almost private, space. From being negative, it became usable and interactive, providing a small arena within the larger open square.

This brings us back to Bentham and another scale comparison. Figure 10.19 shows an overlay of Bentham's prison and the Pentagon Petal installation. From our previous description, the relatively intimate size of the Benthamic panopticon should be clear. Pentagon Petal is of comparable size, slightly smaller, tracing out Bentham's building on the Rootstein Hopkins Parade Ground into which it would have easily fitted; the two structures of comparable size facilitate very different types of social observation and interaction.

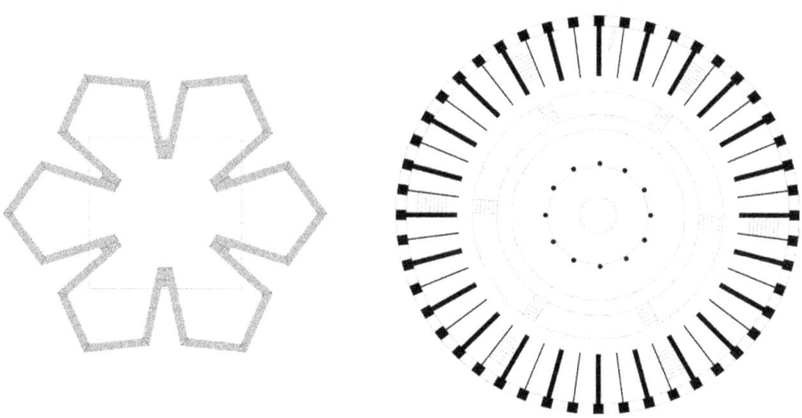

Figure 10.19: Scale comparison: Jeremy Bentham's panopticon and Panopticon Petal.

Pentagon Petal could be observed from three sides from the windows of Chelsea College of Arts, as seen here in Malcolm Quinn's photograph taken from his office window (Figure 10.20).

Figure 10.20: Cottell/Mueller, Pentagon Petal, Malcolm Quinn, 2016.

Unlike the panopticon, the viewing point is shifted from the centre to the periphery. As previously noted, for people who live and work in the area, including the staff and students at the college, the plan of Millbank Prison is often, albeit mistakenly, referred to as Jeremy Bentham's panopticon. It is an image that is part of the cultural memory of this site, a figure that everyone recognizes.

Our intention with this intervention, reflecting Bentham's spirit, was to bring some clarity and utility to this place, but in contrast to him, in a non-determined and open-ended way. We were not pursuing an architectural determinism, we were not attempting social levelling, but rather to challenge fixed hierarchies and to produce a dynamic and, perhaps, democratic type of space that preserves life or rather the breadth of aliveness – a place of leisure rather than oppression. This intervention, which temporarily re-configured this site, re-calibrated its social offering from one of pain to pleasure.

Notes

1 Bentham, ed. Božovič, 1995, 6.
2 Bentham, ed. Božovič, 1995, 12.
3 Bentham, ed. Božovič, 1995, 6.
4 Bentham, ed. Božovič, 1995, 16.
5 Bentham, ed. Božovič, 1995, 12.
6 Semple, 1992, 105–20, 108.
7 Semple, 1992, 117.
8 Semple, 1992, 116.
9 Semple, 1992, 116.
10 Semple, 1992, 115.
11 Semple, 1992, 113.
12 Semple, 1993, 155.
13 Semple, 1993, 99–100.
14 Foucault, 1991, 205.
15 Foucault, 1991, 202.
16 Semple, 1993, 116.
17 Semple, 1993, 114.
18 Semple, 1993, 117.
19 Semple, 1993, 304.
20 Semple, 1993, 301.
21 Semple, 1993, 286.
22 Semple, 1993, 304.
23 Semple, 1993, 309, quoting from Griffiths, 1875, 33.
24 'Convict Life at Millbank Penitentiary', *Penny Illustrated Paper*, 14 October 1865, 308–9, at 308. This article was apparently written by Thomas Archer and reprinted in his *The Pauper, The Thief, and The Convict; Sketches of Some of their Homes, Haunts, and Habits* (1865, 189–207).
25 Hertzberger, 1991, 176.

References

Archer, T. *The Pauper, The Thief, and The Convict; Sketches of Some of their Homes, Haunts, and Habits*. London: Groombridge and Sons, 1865.
Bentham, J. *The Panopticon Writings*, ed. Miran Božovič. London and New York: Verso, 1995.
Foucault, M. *Discipline and Punish*. 4th ed. London: Penguin, 1991.
Griffiths, A. *Memorials of Millbank, and Chapters in Prison History*. London: H.S. King, 1875.
Hertzberger, H. *Lessons for Students in Architecture*. Rotterdam: 101 Publishers, 1991.
Semple, J. 'Foucault and Bentham: A Defence of Panopticism', *Utilitas* 4:1 (1992): 105–120.
Semple, J. *Bentham's Prison: A Study of the Panopticon Penitentiary*. Oxford: Clarendon Press, 1993.

Chapter 11
Bentham's image: The corpo-reality check

Carolyn Shapiro

Among Jeremy Bentham's myriad manuscripts, the arduous reading, editing and transcribing of which contributes to the work of many a scholar in this volume and quite a few scholars before now, one particularly peculiar manuscript was withheld from circulation at the time of Bentham's death by his then editor John Bowring. This manuscript, written at some point close to his death in 1832, was entitled 'Auto-Icon; or, Farther Uses of the Dead to the Living'.[1] It argues for the benefits of preserving and displaying the heads of our dead bodies, a last act that would uphold Bentham's utilitarian principle of the greatest happiness of the greatest number. Bentham's amusing proposed models for Auto-Iconism ranged from New Zealanders 'in reference to the preservation of their friends',[2] to Persian edifices constructed by the skulls of men slain in battle,[3] to the performances of the 'Lecturer-Errant or Itinerant upon heads' George Alexander Stevens[4] (Figure 11.1).

The late Canadian scholar Robert Fenn's carefully annotated version of this essay attempts to correct what he deemed the damage done to Bentham's legacy by the prudish Bowring. Bentham's anti-religious writings and his manuscripts redeeming sexual irregularities were similarly considered inappropriate to be published. In this chapter, I would first like to discuss the Auto-Icon: the title of Bentham's preserved body itself, the essay by the same name, and Bentham's instructions annexed to his Last Will and Testament explaining the process by which he wanted his body to be 'Auto-Iconized'. For Bentham, his self-portrait is what he described as 'an auto-graph of a higher order':[5] autographic, in the sense that like a signed autograph, Bentham's image works as an indexical 'graph', or piece of writing, 'of' himself, bearing the physical trace – or more than a trace – of its subject. 'Auto-Icon will soon be understood,' Bentham proposes, 'for a man who is his own image. … Is not identity preferable to similitude?'[6] Despite a few infelicities-to-be about the robustness of the body itself (for example, the separated head being stolen by prankster King's College, London students), Bentham's Auto-Icon was arguably the fullest realization of his greatest happiness principle. Through the mingling of writing, image and corporeal body, Bentham's Auto-Icon is the corpo-realization of what underlies Bentham's theories of language, logic and legislation: the resolution to work language back to a tangible real entity. In many ways, as will be elaborated below, Bentham's theories of language can be said to be his primary vehicle for his overall proposition of the requisite corporeality underlying his greatest happiness principle.

Figure 11.1: Thomas Rowlandson (1757–1827), *A Lecture on Heads,* 1808.

Metropolitan Museum of Art, New York.

I propose that Bentham's notion of real entities is throughout his writings insistent, in particular, on a foregrounding of the human body. This foregrounding is evident through his applied metaphors of the body. But just as 'the image of Bentham' is not a figure but the 'real thing', so too in his writing Bentham works beyond metaphorical figure. For Bentham, the act of writing itself works to infuse his metaphorical figures of speech with the 'real substance' of the human body, realized not only through the hindsight of his Auto-Icon corpse, but through his construction of his vast body of writing as corpus. Ultimately, I want to consider Bentham's writing – he did a lot of it! – as performative act. Reading *Of Sexual*

Irregularities, and Other Writings on Sexual Morality, and *Not Paul, but Jesus* in conjunction with the Auto-Icon supports Bentham's aspiration for language to be grounded by physical substance. On some psychological level, conscious or unconscious, Bentham's writing is a physical, corporeal activity that I want to examine in relation to the physical pleasures afforded by the 'eccentric propensities' and 'equivalent pleasures' offered by not Paul, but Jesus. In this sense, 'Bentham's Image' encompasses the felicities and physical pleasures of the act of writing. Furthermore, 'Bentham's Image', being Bentham's own body, is also part of the negotiation of bequeathed 'property' that takes place upon one's death. In Bentham's world of greatest happiness, the physically closer an entity is to what it refers to, that is, the more an entity comes from an 'own-ness', the more successfully utilitarian it is. This tendency towards felicity happens because something *proper to* another thing is going to be more grounded in materiality and less prone to fictionalization. The Auto-Icon, Bentham says, would allow for 'every man [to be] his own broker' or 'every man [to be] his own lawyer'.[7] Bentham proudly announces that, 'A spick-and-span new subject-matter of property is brought for the first time into existence.'[8] The image of Bentham is, therefore, highly Utilitarian not only in its social contribution but also in its epitomizing of the proper that comes through in Bentham's overall philosophy: the image is Bentham's 'own'.

A brief foray into Bentham's contention with legal fiction lays the groundwork of Bentham's desire to ground everything in the physicality of the human body. He particularly decries the maintenance of the 'Fictions of Law', legal 'bodies' constituted solely through linguistic positing. These fictional bodies of law get reiterated so frequently that what the language merely *signifies* is taken for something 'real'. In a footnote to his discussion of motion, Bentham presents his allegory of the sitting automaton, a figure that *appears to be* real in that it is presented 'in the dress of a man … constructed by the ingenuity of the mechanist'[9] (Figure 11.2).

As such, the constructed automaton personifies the deceptive operation of fiction that forms the bedrock of bad legislation and morality. The fiction of the legal person is part of Bentham's overall critique of fiction. Charging from the earliest moment of his writing career onwards that the spread of Fiction is 'pestilential',[10] Bentham's immoderate solution of auto-iconization should not be surprising. The Auto-Icon as 'legal person' is not a function of language, but an annexation of real property, and, as such, it is the 'bodying forth', the propriation, of the legal person[11] (Figure 11.3).

Figure 11.2: Detail of automaton drawing reprinted from Brian Selznick, *The Invention of Hugo Cabret*.

Figure 11.3: The Auto-Icon.

University College London.

Bentham's *Last Will and Testament* bequeaths not only his manuscripts – his corpus – but, first of all, his corpse, to the University of London Medical School.[12] Revised on 30 May 1832, the Will opens with instructions for his dead body, as soon as ascertained dead, to be immediately delivered to his close friend Dr Southwood Smith, who was to preserve it in the manner expressed in the 'Annex' to the *Will*. But even preceding the explicit instructions in the 'Annex', Bentham tells his executors what is to be done with his skeleton: it is to be propped up in a chair 'in the attitude in which I am sitting when engaged in thought in the course of time employed in writing,' clad (and stuffed) in one of his typical black suits, his staff in hand.[13] Part B of the *Will*, also entitled 'Auto-Icon', is dated before the first part of the *Will* at 13 April 1830, and is written in a different hand from that of the *Will*: 'What follows in a hand different from mine was drawn up some little time ago at my desire by Dr. Southwood Smith M.D. witness my hand Jeremy Bentham. [Bentham signs].'[14] Bentham's amanuensis will also become Bentham's dissector. Three days after Bentham died, Southwood Smith carried out Bentham's request. The doctor delivered an oration over Bentham's corpse at the Webb Street School of Anatomy and Medicine and the dissection was performed shortly afterwards.[15]

Southwood Smith's hand, in both capacities of *amanuensis* and dissector, has a parallel in the editing hand. To say that Bentham wrote prolifically would be an understatement; he seemed to write obsessively, continuously, for over sixty years. He would have been writing with the presumption, and invitation, for the cutting, shaping hand of the editor. The sheer amount of handwritten pages in the manuscript boxes in UCL Library comprise a corpus: so many analogies can be drawn between Bentham's written corpus and his actual body, both of which required intervention by a fashioning hand in order to achieve a presentable finished product, for the greater good. He also frequently inserts his own 'hands' into his manuscripts where he wants to make additions (Figure 11.4).

Reading the editors' introduction to *Of Sexual Irregularities, and Other Writings on Sexual Morality*,[16] one gets a distinct sense of the physical materiality of the manuscripts. Bentham had an elaborate writing process by which he left himself, and his future editors, indications or suggestions about insertions, incorporations, earmarks, chapter headings and sub-headings, running headings, descriptive headings, titles, margins, footnotes, 'rudiments' and appendices to the text sheets composed of unruled composition paper.[17] Other notable markings include brackets and braces, numbering of various chapters and sections, deletions and emendations (Bentham's own and the editors' too). Bentham apparently was not consistent with punctuation,[18] and so relied upon his editors for this mode of clarification. In order to help his editors with such sprawling textual stuff, Bentham organized the manuscripts into what he called 'spencers', on which he wrote descriptive headings. These so-called spencers served as helpful indexes in the content.[19] He creatively re-deployed a word which, following the Oxford English Dictionary, otherwise refers to either a kind of wig, or a short double-breasted overcoat without tails, or to a kind of close-fitting jacket or bodice commonly worn by women and children.[20] But Bentham's usage of it also implies his writing is a body needing to be clothed, the spencers also helpfully giving that body its *organ*ization.[21] Approaching Bentham's work as a material writing scenario, the manuscripts are almost plastic in their readiness to be shaped, beckoning to be 'worked' by supplemental hands. We certainly get a sense of tangible substance. This substance is corporeal material, directly emanating from Bentham's hand, a parallel body to what would become his Auto-Iconized body.

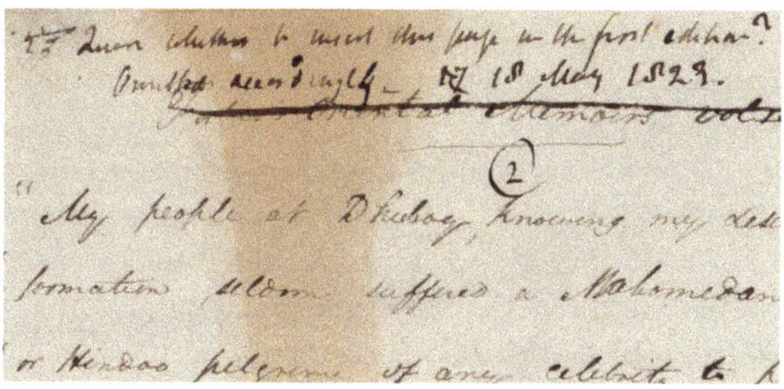

Figure 11.4: A manicule, in Bentham's hand (18 May 1823).

UC cxxxix. 330.

Throughout his writing, Bentham's greatest happiness principle is conveyed figuratively through a fundamentally bodily lexicon. In more recent philosophical applications, we have seen that a bodily lexicon gets conferred upon consciousness and subjectivity. Bentham's bodily approach was generally not about consciousness or subjectivity as much as it was about the way in which language, and the actions conferred by language, ought to be backed by the reality of a body. In this sense, the body worked as the material gateway to good principles of morals and legislation. For Bentham, ontology or being itself could only be based in substance that is perceived through the bodily senses. A real existing entity is real, for example, because it is 'tangible'.

Bentham's language is infused with signifiers of the body. Although his fundamental measuring units of pleasure and pain may signify beyond literal bodies, both those terms do bear immediate bodily denotations. Other terms also have bodily assumptions, although not so immediate. I am particularly interested in Bentham's fundamental notion of 'mischief'. 'Mischievousness' is the name given by Bentham to signify what is perhaps the launching point of his entire philosophical project: the infelicitous outcome of legislation based upon the fiction of natural and so-called unwritten law. 'Mischief' is Bentham's name for the 'the divergency from the common end of Happiness'.[22] Bentham loved his etymological footing and his choice of the word 'mischief' is felicitous in and of itself. From the Middle English and Anglo-French word *mes-chef*, for misfortune, and from Old French *meschever*, to come out badly, without a head, chief, or end, 'mischief' is the ideal discourse for infelicitous outcomes that would have been the result of having no proper head, and, by inference, no proper body. We know that the head for Bentham stands in, synechdocally, for the entire body, because of what will be proposed in his Auto-Icon final essay. Once aware of the body-language Bentham loves to use so much, we see that most parts of the body frequently find their way into his general lexicon. Another term worth mentioning, particularly in the context of his writings on sexual irregularities, is 'noxious'. In one of the main examples of the use of this term, Bentham condemns public opinion's severe condemnation of what he sees as the 'least noxious, or altogether *innoxious*' instances (such as irregular sexual acts) because these condemnations are little governed by utility, whereas acts which he deems 'most noxious' are indulged.[23] Bentham also gives us the example, in *Not Paul, but Jesus*, of the act of usury being 'innoxious', and therefore not justifiably punishable by law.[24] The Latin word *noxa* means 'harm'. But the etymologically astute Bentham, 'grecianized ear' always on the alert,[25] also knew that before the Latin *noxa* came the Greek word *nekros*, meaning 'dead body'. 'Noxious' refers to harm – deadly harm – done *to the body*.

But Bentham was not operating exclusively on the levels of figurative language and etymology. He also addressed the primacy of the body on a thematic level. A consideration of Bentham's anti-religious manuscripts debunking existence in the after-life reveals his proposition for the primacy of the body to be the foundation of existence. In his very helpful book *Bentham: A Guide for the Perplexed*,[26] Philip Schofield recounts Bentham's rebuttal of his contemporaries' religionist proposition that the soul would exist in the after-life without the body:

> Bentham noted that during life human beings experience sensation and thought, and that such sensation and thought was located in the brain and nervous system. At death, however, both brain and nervous system ceased to function. Bentham asked: 'A mind altogether without a body, in what sense, respect or degree is it to be identical with the same mind united with its body as in the present state?' Mind, a fictitious entity, consisted in nothing more than a combination of pleasures, pains, wants, desires and propensities. All the pleasures and pains of the mind had their source in pleasures and pains of the body. How are these wants to be supplied, desires gratified, and propensities given way to, by a mind without a body?[27]

Bentham's 'objections absolutely insuperable'[28] to the Christian proposition that a soul could 'exist' without a body as its indicator of pleasure and pain become manifest in his writing on sexual irregularities.

In *Of Sexual Irregularities, and Other Writings on Sexual Morality*, Bentham's exposition of 'that antipathy which springs up on the ground of taste … produced by difference of taste'[29] provides a more complex understanding of Bentham's contentions. 'Antipathy' also has bodily co-ordinates: the human breast, Bentham repeatedly writes, is the seat of antipathy. Bentham uses the word 'breast' in this context so frequently that it would prompt any close reader to try to figure out exactly how and why he employs it. The breast, for Bentham, is the ready seat of public odium, and he positions it as part of the artillery of injustice:

> The truth is that, by the epithet *unnatural*, when applied to any human act or thought, the only matter of which it affords any indication that can be depended upon is the existence of a sentiment of disapprobation, accompanied with passion, in the breast of the person by whom it is employed: a degree of dissocial passion by which without staying to enquire or to consider with himself whether the practice, and thence the conduct and character of him whose practice it is, be or be not in any way, and if in any way in what degree, noxious to society, he endeavors, by the use thus made of this inflammatory word, to kindle and point towards the object of his ill-will, that same dissocial passion in other breasts, for the purpose of inducing them to join with him in producing pain in some shape or other in the breast of him by whom the passion has been excited.[30]

Here, Bentham's uses words such as 'passion', 'inflammatory', 'kindle', 'join', and 'excited' to characterize what happens when the word 'unnatural' gets affixed to any given event or practice, public opinion thus spreading, like fire, to 'other breasts'. Bentham follows this with several more examples of breast-passion, including the rebellion of the Stuart claimants to the throne having been deemed 'unnatural', thus '[producing] ... in all breasts that are not already on his side, a disposition to join in whatsoever measures may be taken for causing him to suffer',[31] going on to set up antipathy, public opinion and judgmental taste as being unworthy foundations for morals and legislation, as they would most certainly fail the test of utility for the greater good.

Religion was the main culprit in Bentham's eyes for things antithetical to his greatest happiness principle. As we shall see in the essays on sexual irregularities as well as in *Not Paul, but Jesus*, the dominance of Mosaic law and of the Mosaic dispensation of justice constructs active barriers against the general reception of Bentham's radical revisioning of a non-metaphysical, non-moralizing foundation for legislation. He is up against the vengeful passion held and distributed across the 'breasts' of the people. Bentham proposes that Moses and the Old Testament laid the groundwork for religion itself and its 'theatre of rigours'.[32] This theatre of rigours was responsible, he writes, for the transposition of physical dirt and impurities into moral impurity. The belief in moral impurity took its strength in the lodging of fear of punishment into the adherents of Mosaic law. Much to Bentham's horror, what is deemed 'immoral', for example, sexual intercourse with someone of the same sex or with another species, cannot be 'washed away but with blood',[33] instigating a relentless justification for boundless cruelty and misery which has no 'real' grounding. Bentham shows that the introduction of religion justifies the consequent leap from physicality to morality by invoking the breast as the seat of the gratification of antipathy and fear:

> In the breast of Moses, the sentiment of antipathy found an object and an exciting cause in every sort of irregularity belonging to this class. Religion was at his command: in Religion, every caprice to which, in his fertile brain, imagination had ever given birth found a ready instrument, and that an irresistible one. In English the word impurity, in most other languages some other word or words that correspond to it, had been applied alike to objects unpleasant to sense, and offensive to imagination. In the head of tyranny, at the nod of caprice, physical impurities were converted into moral ones. Under Moses as under Bramah, the list of impurities thus created,

sometimes out of nothing, sometimes out of physical impurities, was a labyrinth without end. The more extensive and above all the more indefinite the system of penal law, the more transgressions on the part of the subject many: the more transgression, the more fear: the more fear in the breast of the subject many, the more power in the hand of the ruling few. *Wherever the people are in a shivering fit, the physician of their souls is absolute.* Observation was made of physical impurities, discovery was made of moral, and then converted into religious impurities: for the cleansing of physical impurities water might serve: moral impurities required blood.[34]

Here, the quick conversion from something physical to the register of the moral fed the fear, causing a 'shivering fit' and requiring an 'absolute' physician. For Bentham, operating in the abstract realm of antipathy and morality is dangerously ungrounded, paving the way for tyranny and absolutism. What gets lost in this transposition into antipathy is the requisite tangibility of the real body that ought to manage the springs of action.

The anti-utilitarian, ascetic conversion from physical impurity to moral impurity presented as the starting point of Bentham's critique on religion receives explicit parsing and exposition in a compelling subtext entitled 'Purity – impurity' that spans the bottom of three pages.[35] Implying the arbitrariness of names and signs in typical proto-semiotic fashion, Bentham homes in on the word 'impurity', from which so much misery has flowed. An 'impure' thing, he points out, can easily be brought back to its real state of purity because a real body, which is, for example, covered in dust, can be washed with water to become 'pure' again. An impure mind, on the other hand, would be characterized by sin, wickedness and guilt. Hence, an impure body can become pure when the body is cleansed, and by analogy, an impure, guilty mind can be purified by cleaning away the psychological impurities. However, when an impure body bypasses the literal bodily referent (dirt, sexual irregularities, etc.) to signify immediately psychological impurities, here the play of fiction instigates its inexorable take-over, as Bentham states: 'Filth is on the body, therefore guilt, sin, wickedness, impurity is in the mind: here comes the false logic – here comes the wandering of the imagination – here comes the pernicious error. … Error is now mounted upon error.'[36]

In order to check this error-mounted-upon-error, a problem that is specific to religionists and moralists but which also affects all other applications of language, Bentham devised a complicated 'filling up' operation he called 'phraseoplerosis', followed by what he called 'paraphrasis'. In these dual operations, language is worked towards the physical, supplied with and thus translated into 'real entities' in order to move away from fictional abstraction.[37] Philip Schofield clarifies this operation: '[P]araphrasis occurs when a sentence in which the name of the fictitious entity appears is translated into another sentence in which the words are either real entities, or are more nearly related to real entities. There is both a translation of the sentence, and a movement towards the physical.'[38] One particular pathway to the physical that Bentham himself practices is the anchoring of his own writing in the etymological origins of given words. Bentham's avowed possession of a 'grecian ear', which he is happy to impart 'to an ungrecian ear' in need of explanation,[39] affords him an immediacy with the material, real referent behind a word, and so we can assume that he chooses his words carefully, that is, *paraphrastically*. In one example discussed in *Chrestomathia*, the word *obligation* comes from the Latin root *ligo*, meaning, to bind. The root produces an image of a band that not only visualizes the word *obligation* (which names the practice of being bound or fastened to any other) but grounds it in a material real entity – the original root. '[T]he root of the *word*, employed as a sign for the designation of that idea … lies in a material image, employed as an *archetype* or *emblem*: viz., the image of a *cord*, or any other *tie* or *band*.'[40] The archetype that comes forth from the etymological origin acts as an index into what is real: 'In the case of every name of an *immaterial object*, the *archetype* is at once an *index* and a *holdfast* to the sense of it', Bentham writes, adding, 'In the case of every name of a *fictitious entity,* the only sure test of intellection is *paraphrasis*.'[41] But the reality of the etymological archetype behind a word seems, typically, to get repressed, yielding to an 'original import [that is] misexpressive'.[42] Thus import itself, also to be understood as signification, works against expression, as indexed by the archetype, that would emanate from the real entity. The work of paraphrasis is considerable![43]

In today's lingo, we might say that these linguistic manoeuvres encourage an ongoing 'reality check'. From his writings on sexual irregularities, we can see that Bentham sees this movement away from the physical body into metaphysical abstraction as a hostile take-over of reality that results in vengeful and religiously justified violence such as using fire and blood instead of water to purify a dirty body. In *Not Paul, but Jesus*, Bentham sets up a binary opposition between Paul and Jesus, creating an axis respectively dividing mischief from utility. In this engaging text, Bentham takes issue with the religiously inspired principle of asceticism. Instigated by Mosaic law and propagated by Paul, asceticism's denial of bodily pleasure and its replacement of pleasure with the bidding of pain lies at the heart of Bentham's contestation of Religion and Natural Law. Bentham's exegeses on the New Testament and on the relevant books of the Old Testament scrutinize what he declares to be the fundamental mischievousness of asceticism. The focus on asceticism allows Bentham, and us, to comprehend in a more complex way the relation between the body and mischief in all of Bentham's philosophical propositions. Bentham proposes that 'under the principle of asceticism [favoured by Paul but not by Jesus], condemnation is passed on the pleasures of the body without enquiry',[44] and that, furthermore, a disastrous sublation of physicality by morality, of the body by the mind, takes place. The Paul/Jesus axis serves to pinpoint the pivotal leap of logic underpinning the mischief perpetrated by asceticism. Jesus is put forward here as denouncing the leap into groundless pronouncements of immorality. Jesus, explains Bentham, condemned the Mosaic assumption that 'by a trifling physical impurity, a serious moral depravity might be produced'.[45]

Reading this pronouncement we cannot help but note that Bentham is not simply saying that religion and asceticism are *replacing* the body with the abstract mind. He is objecting to the heart being trafficked into the moral order:

> Here then may be seen a sentence of condemnation passed at any rate upon this part of the Mosaic Law: the assumption on which it had been grounded was the supposition that, by any thing taken in to a man's body in a *physical* sense, his *heart* (Mat. xv. 18; Mark vii. 19) in a *psychological* sense – his *heart* put as usual for his moral character – could be defiled.[46]

The asceticists are not discounting the body; they are taking up the body for their own 'erroneous' and 'disordered' purposes.

Bentham himself does not use the word 'misappropriation', but I think it is a useful term for characterizing the movement of mischief – which comprehends the linguistic move away from a word's immediate reference to the body, from being *proper to* that which it is referring, to a word *claiming* to be 'proper to' its referent but which drops its proper physical connection in a kind of trick, a sleight of hand. This chicanery is difficult to spot because of what happens when antipathy takes harbour in the breast: the breast houses the heart, through the heart blood courses. The prodigious momentum of *pathos* works to overtake the bodily grounding to which it vehemently lays claim. Bentham's abhorrence of legislated punishment through bloodletting (e.g. capital punishment) would be a good example of what he sees as a violent claiming of the body for mischievous and malign purposes.

The following passage from 'Of Sexual Irregularities' explains the persecution of homosexual irregularity as an example of the violent commandeering of the breast, by those for whom antipathy forms the basis of morality:

> Of the violence of that antipathy, whether real or affected, of which the propensities in question have, in the British isles, beyond all other countries, been the object – of the violence of that thirst which nothing less than the heart's blood of the intended victims marked out for slaughter by the dissocial appetite has hitherto been able to satisfy. The principal causes have now been brought to view: and in the view thus given of them it has been seen that, in the number of them, no such quality in it as that of a tendency to make in any shape a defalcation [deduction] from the aggregate sum of human happiness has place: and that, in this dissocial and misery-engendering affection, whatsoever fault there is has for its seat the breasts, not of those who are the objects of this antipathy, but of those who harbor it.[47]

Thus Bentham takes issue with the co-opting of the body by the ascetics who have laid claim to blood and breast, not to mention to pain itself. On the contrary, for Bentham, the 'sexual irregularity' of the homosexual, as a 'propensity', is the better utilitarian model in that the actions performed are proper to the body performing the action, unlike the misappropriated corpo-reality abused by moralizing religionists.

In this final section before I conclude, I would like to expand upon the character of the body that Bentham defends so rigorously. This body type that he puts forward is one that is epitomized by Jesus's teachings, by Jesus himself, and also by the homosexual body, defended examples of which abound both within the footnotes and body of Bentham's writings on sexual irregularities and on religion. I want to suggest, perhaps boldly, that for Bentham, the homosexual body, with its propensities eccentric and its social and sexual intercourses, is an open body, a body that invites others to be a part of it, to partake of it. It is also a propense body that fulfils the reality check required for acquiring greatest happiness. Like the 'socially effusive' Greek male homosexual relationships Bentham cites as examples that existed without the imposition of metaphysical 'spiritualization' of the lovers,[48] Jesus stands for a body felicitously open to the physicality of other bodies. Bentham argues that Jesus had intercourse with Mary Magdalene,[49] with St John, who, Bentham repeatedly tells us in italics, was 'lying on Jesus' breast'[50] (this would be an example of a 'good breast'), and with the young male 'stripling with loose attire' who remained Jesus' most faithful devotee.[51]

Jesus's intercourse, social and sexual, works here in opposition to the 'wall of separation' instituted by the Pharisees and their subsequent followers. For Bentham, 'the avowed design – of keeping up a wall – an everlasting wall – of separation between this and every other: the prevention of all convivial and thence of all social intercourse' is dissolved by Jesus when he says, in the books of Mark and Matthew: 'There is nothing from without a man, that entering into him can defile him: but the things which come out of him, those are they that defile the man.'[52] Bentham embraces this welcoming of entry into the human body, as we see throughout 'Of Sexual Irregularities' when he sets up an equivalence between the appetite for food and the appetite for sex. He is proposing an intercoursing body with 'inlets' to pleasure, which he characterizes in a footnote to the first chapter of *Not Paul, but Jesus*:

> Though not the seats nor the sources, the eye and the ear are, in the instance of every individual, the necessary *inlets* to a large proportion of such pleasures of the mind as it falls in his way to enjoy: viz. to all those derived from discourse, whether by signs audible or visible – whether from hearing or reading. So likewise in the case of all the rest of the fine arts – Music, painting, &c., &c., let the seat be in ever so large proportions of it in the mind, the necessary inlet to it is in the body.[53]

This body of inlets defies the multiple prohibitions of 'admixture' called for by Mosaic law.[54]

Conclusion

When Bentham wrote, and wrote, and wrote, he wrote with the assumption that other hands would be introduced into the corpus of his work; in particular the editorial hands of others, but also his own little drawn hands inserted into the manuscripts. One particular editor he desired to give his work shape, clarity, even some aesthetic guidance, the desire for whose editing hand was proposed in the concluding paragraphs of the chapter 'General Idea of *Not Paul, but Jesus*', was William Thomas Beckford, author of the *History of the Caliph Vathek*, published in 1786. Bentham invites Beckford to be his editor and collaborator in the *Not Paul, but Jesus* venture (Figure 11.5).

Figure 11.5: George Romney (1734–1802), *William Beckford MP*, 1781–2.

Beckford was a writer and collector known for his homosexual encounters, whose novel *Vathek* described the sensual activities that Bentham embraced at least philosophically. We might even call Beckford an aesthete. Bentham calls upon him to be a partner, with whom he might confide secrets, who might supplement the manuscript with his notable literary talent:

> the author is desirous of finding, in an appropriate social intercourse, an external support for his faculties under a burthen of such a magnitude: – a sort of partner, in whose honour, in point of secrecy and all other points, he could confide, and by whose sympathy he might be cheered and supported: a co-operator, in whose literary talents whatever deficiency there may be in his

> own might find a supply: who, in his own person, might find an amusement in giving form and order, and superior expression, and perhaps additional quantity, to the material which are in readiness to be supplied. ... For all this, the author's eye has turned itself of the author of the History of the Caliph Vathec.[55]

Bentham's proclivity towards social intercourse and his invitation for someone to supplement his manuscript are in character with the body type that he placed in the domain of Jesus and the homosexual: a body that happily admits entry, that does not erect boundaries of separation; a body that enjoys the pleasures of social and sexual intercourse, thereby providing material grounding for greatest pleasure and greatest happiness. Beckford's 'sympathy' and aesthetics are welcome because they are, in the figure of the homosexual Beckford, grounded in a real, propense body.

Is not Bentham's dear friend Southwood Smith, called upon to dissect Bentham's dead body, cutting into that body, a parallel figure to that of William Beckford, also called upon to give form and order, and expression, to the corpus in question, with his invited hand? We are back to Bentham's Image. Bentham's Image is Bentham's body, but it is also Bentham's writing, because Bentham's Auto-Icon is a form of writing – what he himself named, in his 'Auto-Icon' essay, '*auto-thanatography*'.[56] Working with the voluminous manuscripts and their editorial supplements, we have a sense that Bentham's relation to his own writing practice was one fully integrated with his radical philosophical departures from metaphysical foundations, namely, that the immediacy of the corporeal body is consistently present and that his written corpus is a body that invites the right of entry through various modes. Through this allowance of pleasure comes the greatest happiness of the greatest number. When the corpo-reality check is carried out, 'Bentham's Image' and his written corpus deliver a steady supply of tangible substance.

Notes

1 Bentham, ed. Fenn, 1992.
2 Bentham, ed. Fenn, 1992, 3.
3 Bentham, ed. Fenn, 1992, 5.
4 Bentham, ed. Fenn, 1992, 13.
5 Bentham, ed. Fenn, 1992, 5.
6 Bentham, ed. Fenn, 1992, 11.
7 Bentham, ed. Fenn, 1992, 1–2 & n. Fenn notes that Bentham here is citing Thomas Mortimer, 'Every Man His Own Broker; or, a Guide to the Stock Exchange, etc.', 1761ff, and Giles Jacob,

'Every Man His Own Lawyer: Or, a Summary of the Laws of England in New and Instructive Method, etc.', 1763ff.

8 In the Auto-Icon essay, Bentham offers two possibilities of classification for Auto-Icon as property. The first example, that of the Aerolite genus, refers to a meteorite, an object which is a part or fragment, an 'individual specimen of it which descended to us from above'. The object is a found-object, which, in its detachment from its original whole, always remains unable to be 'owned' in its entirety. On the other hand, this found-object fragment has given itself to be possessed, repossessed. The Auto-Icon could be read as a fragment of a whole – the whole, intentional subject. Bentham's proposal that it is the preserved heads of the deceased that primarily constitute auto-icons (with the exception of his own full-body Auto-Icon) reinforces the 'Aerolite' category of property as suitable for the Auto-Icon; the heads are parts that stand in for some larger whole: Bentham, ed. Fenn, 1992, 17.

9 'Beholding at a distance, in the dress of a man, sitting and playing upon an organ, an automaton figure, constructed … by the ingenuity of the mechanist, to take this creature of human art for a real man, is a sort of mistake which, at a certain distance, might happen for a time to be made by the most acute observer. In like manner, beholding a part of speech cast in the same mould with the name of a real entity, a really existing substance, no wonder if, on a variety of occasions, to the mental eye of a very acute observer, this fictitious entity thus accoutred should present itself in the character of, and be regarded and treated as if it were a real one. How should it be otherwise, when on every occasion on which, and by every person by whom it is spoken of at all, it is spoken of as if it were a real entity?' Bowring, 1843, viii. 129.

10 '[T]he pestilential breath of Fiction poisons the sense of every instrument it comes near.' 'Fragment' in Bentham, ed. Burns and Hart, 1977, 411 n.

11 It is Bentham's interest in this movement of the proper that the legal scholar Mary Sokol discusses in her essay 'Bentham and Blackstone on Incorporeal Hereditaments': (1994, 287–305). The essay gives us a fuller picture of Bentham's engagement in theoretical issues about the rapprochement between legal property and corporeality. Sokol concentrates on Bentham's legal reforms during the years of 1828 and 1832, the year of his death. These legal reforms responded to what he firmly believed to be yet another of Judge Blackstone's inadequacies as lawmaker: the inability of property law, in its current status, to account for intangible 'incorporeal hereditaments' such as company shares and copyright as personal property (287). Sokol notes that Bentham's contact with the Real Property Commission in 1828 spurred him on to propose reforms in property law that would rectify Blackstone's omissions on what constituted personal property. As Sokol elaborates, in 1830 Bentham was invited to draw up a list of incorporeal hereditaments with the conveyancer and Real Property Commissioner, John Tyrell. In his list, Tyrell reiterated what had already been established (primarily by Blackstone) as incorporeal hereditaments: (e.g. manors and signories, franchises, sporting rights, rents, commons, easements, advowsons, tithes and corodies). Bentham subverted the list, or, in his words, 'transposed' it, from being a list of 'incorporeal rights' of the owner, to being a list of 'corporeal subject matter operated upon … by the exercise of rights'. Sokol explains: the list of items would change under Bentham's reforms from being categorized as 'land' – a figment of legal fiction – to being categorized as accepted legal right, which would be able to include things like copyright and company shares (291). Sokol does not discuss Bentham's Auto-Icon at all, but her rigorous analysis of Bentham's attempted reforms in property law at the time of his preparation of the Auto-Icon provides a picture of the theoretical context engendered by the encounter between corporeality and property that so inspired Bentham.

12 The University of London, later named University College, was founded in 1826 and was known for its excellent medical school. See Marmoy, 1958, 1.

13 'Last Will and Testament' [1832], 37, reprinted in Bentham, ed. Fenn, 1992.

14 Bentham, ed. Fenn, 1992, 41.

15 Marmoy, 1958, 2. The primary inspiration for Auto-Iconism came from the conviction that dead bodies ought to be bequeathed towards the study of surgery and anatomy. This life-long advocacy of Bentham's and the Benthamite group represented by the *Westminster Review*, working against the popular conception of the sanctity of the corpse, finally came to fruition with the passing of Warburton's Anatomy Act of 1832, which provided legal means for obtaining the cadavers of unclaimed paupers for the purpose of dissection.

16 Bentham, ed. Schofield *et al.*, 2014.

17 Bentham, ed. Schofield *et al.*, 2014, p. xvi.

18 Bentham, ed. Schofield *et al.*, 2014, p. xxvii.
19 Bentham, ed. Schofield *et al.*, 2014, p. xxvii.
20 According to the OED, the term comes from the English family name *Spencer*. Bentham's use of the word is typical of his fun sense of play and humour. He may even be making a subtle reference to Earl Spencer, who objected to the panopticon being built at Battersea Rise.
21 An important contrast to this body that is clothed in a spencer which reinforces its 'real substance' is the fictional entity of legal *right*, which Bentham also explains using metaphors of clothing: 'The word *right* is the name of a fictitious entity ... spoken of as if it were a portion of matter such as a man may take into his hand, keep it for a time and let it go again. According to a phrase more common in law language than in ordinary language, a man is even spoken of as being *invested* with it. Vestment is clothing: invested with it makes it an article of clothing, and is as much as to say "is clothed with it."' Bowring, 1843, iii, 217–19.
22 Bentham writes: 'Now then, with respect to actions in general, there is no property in them that is calculated so readily to engage, and so firmly to fix the attention of an observer, as the *tendency* they may have *to*, or divergency (if one may so say) *from*, that which maybe styled the common *end* of all of them. The end I mean is *Happiness*: and this *tendency* in any act is what we style its *utility*: as this *divergency* is that to which we give the name of *mischievousness*. With respect then to such actions in particular as are among the objects of the Law, to point out to a man the *utility* of them or the mischievousness, is the only way to make him see *clearly* that property of them which every man is in search of; the only way, in short, to give him *satisfaction*.' 'Fragment' in Bentham, ed. Burns and Hart, 1977, 415–16.
23 Bentham, ed. Schofield *et al.*, 2014, 129.
24 Bentham, 2013, 54.
25 Bentham's attention to etymology is elaborated in, among other writings, Appendix IV, Bentham, ed. Smith and Burston, 1983 [1817]. Many thanks to Philip Schofield for his helpful compilation of passages throughout the Bentham corpus in which Bentham considers etymology in its various linguistic vicissitudes.
26 Schofield, 2009, 119–24.
27 Schofield, 2009, 122.
28 Schofield, 2009, 122.
29 Bentham, ed. Schofield *et al.*, 2014, 4.
30 Bentham, ed. Schofield *et al.*, 2014, 6.
31 Bentham, ed. Schofield *et al.*, 2014, 8.
32 Bentham, ed. Schofield *et al.*, 2014, 12.
33 Bentham, 2013, 13.
34 Bentham, ed. Schofield *et al.*, 2014, 12–13 (my emphasis).
35 Bentham, ed. Schofield *et al.*, 2014, 13–15.
36 Bentham, ed. Schofield *et al.*, 2014, 14.
37 Ultimately, what Bentham is aiming for in his linguistic operations of phraseoplerosis and paraphrasis is felicity, that is, when things come together or happen with the consequence of the greater good for as many people as possible. Felicitousness in language, which stands for felicitousness in legislation and other action, is most likely to occur when words work 'substantively', that is, 'expressively'.
38 Schofield, 2009, 52–3.
39 Bentham, ed. Smith and Burston, 1983, Appendix, Section XX, 274. Bentham's phrase, 'grecianized ear' is very telling about his own consistent engagement with returning to the physiological rather than the metaphysical: whereas most philosophers would embrace an etymological framework from the epistemological perspective of *knowing* one's Greek and Latin, Bentham's etymological framework is instantly of the body.
40 Bentham, ed. Smith and Burston, 1983, 265 n. Many thanks to Chris Riley for his helpful research into this query.
41 Bentham, ed. Smith and Burston, 1983, 274 n.
42 Bentham, ed. Smith and Burston, 1983, 274.
43 In Bentham's *Logic*, in a chapter entitled 'Of Clearness in discourse – where the seat of the unclearness, actual or apprehended, is considered as being in the words taken singly: – and hence, of exposition' (University College London Library, Bentham Papers, box 101, fos. 201–7, 214–16, 265–74 (16–18 August 1814)), we are treated to a long analysis about how sentences come to be unclear, despite being 'propositions'; these sentences being 'but too many'. Very broadly, exposition is the general action taken that attempts to clarify words,

with special attention given to the 'operation necessarily preliminary to that of definition': *disambiguation*. This forensic semiotic operation explicated by Bentham here points to what would later be observed to be the arbitrary nature of the sign (Saussure), and it works from the general assumption that language is fundamentally 'unclear', to use Bentham's term. A long exegesis on the example of the word *Church* and the progressive loss of its original etymological root meaning effectively illustrates the susceptibility of language to 'misexpressive import' – in other words, to the almost immediate transposition into the register of the sign (which is arbitrary). Bentham's word for this register of the sign is 'import' – and he is very canny about choosing the example of the word 'Church' to prove just how susceptible words are to successive 'diverse and multifarious imports', proving, through the exposition of its historical usage, that the word 'Church' is mightily 'capable of being subverted'. Thus, the work of exposition, of assiduous and dogged disambiguation, not unrelated to the work of *paraphrasis*, is *considerable*.

44 Bentham, ed. Schofield *et al.*, 2014, 21.
45 Bentham, 2013, 87.
46 Bentham, 2013, 86.
47 Bentham, 2013, 23–4.
48 Schofield, 2009, 134. Citing BL Add. MS 29, 808, fos. 13–17.
49 Bentham, 2013, 112–24.
50 Bentham, 2013, 183–5.
51 Bentham, 2013, 187–95.
52 Bentham, 2013, 90, 94.
53 Bentham, 2013, 23–4.
54 See Chapter 11 of *Not Paul, but Jesus*, entitled, 'Condemnation Passed on the Eccentric pleasures of the bed in the Mosaic Law – it had its source in an illusion of the Fancy', for Bentham's parsing of the prohibition of 'admixture' so central to the Old Testament, which included admixture within garments, within farming techniques, within food, within pleasures of the bed, 149–60.
55 Bentham, 2013, 122.
56 Bentham, ed. Fenn, 1992, 4.

References

Bentham, J. *Auto-Icon or, Farther Uses of the Dead to the Living* [1832], ed. Robert Fenn. Toronto: 1992.

Bentham, J. *Chrestomathia* (*CW*), eds. M.J. Smith and W.H. Burston. Oxford: Clarendon Press, 1983.

Bentham, J. *A Comment on the Commentaries and A Fragment on Government* (*CW*), eds. J.H. Burns and F. Rosen. London: Athlone Press, 1977.

Bentham, J. *Not Paul, but Jesus*, Vol. III: *Doctrine*. London: Bentham Project, UCL, 2013 [http://discovery.ucl.ac.uk/1392179/3/npbj.pdf].

Bentham, J. *Of Sexual Irregularities, and Other Writings on Sexual Morality* (*CW*), eds. P. Schofield, C. Pease-Watkin, and M. Quinn. Oxford: Clarendon Press, 2014.

Bentham, J. *The Works of Jeremy Bentham*, ed. John Bowring. 11 vols. Edinburgh: William Tait, 1838-43.

Marmoy, C.F.A. 'The "Auto-Icon" of Jeremy Bentham at University College London', *Medical History* 2:2 (1958): 77–86.

Schofield, P. *Bentham: A Guide for the Perplexed*. London and New York: Continuum, 2009.

Sokol, M. 'Bentham and Blackstone on Incorporeal Hereditaments', *Journal of Legal History* 15 (1994): 287–305.

Index

The following is a combined name and subject index. Under Bentham's name, only references to his works that appear in the text (and not in the footnotes) are included. The abbreviation (*CW*) indicates that the title in question is either a volume in the new authoritative edition of *The Collected Works of Jeremy Bentham* or is included in one of those volumes.

CPSIA information can be obtained
at www.ICGtesting.com
Printed in the USA
BVHW091152170920
589018BV00001B/2